Into the Jaws of Hell

Into the Jaws of Hell

Jefferson Hunt:
The Death Valley '49ers Wagon Train & His Adventures In California

1846-1857

Tom Sutak

Tom Sutak

Pine Park Publishing
Danville, CA

Into the Jaws of Hell
Jefferson Hunt: The Death Valley '49ers Wagon Train &
His Adventures In California 1846-1857
Pine Park Publishing
Danville, CA

Book design by Robin Simonds, Beagle Bay, Inc.

ISBN Hardcover: 9780983551065
ISBN Paperback: 9780983551034
ISBN EPub: 9780983551089
LCCN: 2012930901

First Edition

Printed in the USA
17 16 15 14 13 12   1 2 3 4 5 6 7 8 9 10

Dedication

In memory of my Parents

Mary & Andy Sutak

Without whose love and sacrifice this work would not have been
completed

Table of Contents

PART III

Settler and Politician

Table of Maps

Into The Jaws of Hell

Introduction

During the first week of November 1849, the Death Valley '49ers left a wagon train guided by Jefferson Hunt to follow an unknown route to the West. Most later returned to the known trail and followed in Hunt's steps, but nearly one hundred continued on and found themselves in the desolate desert they named Death Valley—the lowest spot in the Western Hemisphere. The definitive account of this trip was included in a book, published in 1894, entitled *Death Valley in '49* written by William Lewis Manly, one of the heroes of the expedition. The book you are reading now is intended to be an addition to that historical account.

Three questions no doubt arise in the reader's mind:

Who was Jefferson Hunt?
Why was he guiding that particular wagon train?
Why did such a large group break off into the unknown?

The answer to the first reveals that Hunt was heavily involved in California during the Mexican War, and following the Gold Rush, was intimately involved with the settlement of San Bernardino and with California politics. The answers to the second and third reveal more complex reasons than have been generally reported. Accordingly, this book deals with Jefferson Hunt's life and experiences for the eleven year period from 1846 through 1857.

In August 1849, hundreds of emigrants bound for the goldfields of California gathered in Salt Lake City. Those attending Mormon services on one Sunday may have heard Jefferson Hunt give a spirited talk encouraging all to have faith in God lest they find themselves going "into the jaws of hell." A little over two months later, some of them preparing to leave the Old Spanish Trail may have heard him warn that if they decided on trying the untested and unknown route they were about to take, they might find themselves going "into the jaws of hell." About two months after Hunt's warning, some of those same pioneers found themselves on the verge of death due to starvation and dehydration. On foot, they were struggling to survive and reach Los Angeles over two hundred miles away. Surely they thought they had arrived in hell.

When the Death Valley '49ers arrived in Death Valley about Christmas 1849, Jefferson Hunt had already been safely enjoying the safety and comforts of Isaac Williams' ranch in Chino for over a week. Those who followed him had endured some hardships, but nothing like those who had not.

Jefferson Hunt was an accomplished leader and mountaineer when he began to guide the wagon train south from Utah Valley. By the Fall of 1849, Hunt had traveled over 5,000 miles in the Western United States, been to California twice, and been over all three of the major overland migration routes to California, including what became known as the Gila River Route (sometimes referred to as the Southern Route), the western portion of the Old Spanish Trail route (also called the Mormon Road, or the Salt Lake City to Los Angeles Road, and also the Southern Route), and the Northern Route or Humboldt River Route across Nevada and the Great Basin. Very few men possessed the same experience as Hunt. This distinguished group included Kit Carson and mountain man Joseph Walker. Most of them are much better known to history than Jefferson Hunt.

Hunt's Western experience began with his service as the commander of Company A in the Mormon Battalion during the Mexican War. The Mormon Battalion was a volunteer outfit of 500 men organized into five companies that walked from Council Bluffs, Iowa, to San Diego, California, a distance of about 2,000 miles in a little over six months. Brigham Young, the president of the Mormon Church, had designated Hunt as "Senior Captain," or the highest ranking Mormon in the Battalion. During this march, Hunt acquired many of the mountaineering skills that would prove invaluable to him in the following years.

In November 1848, about a month following his arrival in Salt Lake City from California and Battalion duty, Hunt pioneered Mormon travel along the route that went southwestward about 750 miles to Chino and Los

Angeles, much of it along the Old Spanish Trail. There, he and his companions gathered cattle and cuttings and seeds for planting and returned the following Spring. While Hunt and his party were in Southern California, other Mormon Battalion veterans were directly involved in the discovery of gold 400 miles to the north.

A little over a year later, the Gold Rush began and over a thousand emigrants had gathered in Salt Lake City. Unable to adequately provide for them, and fearing the influence they might have on his religious community, Brigham Young encouraged them to take the relatively safe Southern Road to California that Hunt had traveled the year before. Probably at the behest of Young, or certainly with his cooperation, Hunt offered to guide 100 wagons through for ten dollars a wagon, or $1,000. This wagon train, eventually consisting of about 107 wagons, began its travel during the first week of October 1849. One month later, just north of the present border of Utah and Arizona, most of the wagon train (100 wagons and over 400 people) broke off to the west as the train disintegrated. Hunt continued on with seven wagons and a little over twenty people, mostly Mormons. Soon, most of those who broke off turned around and followed his trail. Some of those who continued west ventured into Death Valley about two months later.

Hunt spent the following year in California, probably mining and assisting two of the Church's apostles, Amasa Lyman and Charles Coulson Rich, in ministering to the California Saints. In January 1851, he returned to Utah along the same route and assisted another of the apostles, George A. Smith, in founding the site for the Iron Mission at Cedar City, Utah. With Hunt came the word that the Territory of Utah had been created and Brigham Young was the territorial governor.

Within a few short months, Hunt, now with his family, was again on his way to California to help establish the Mormon settlement of San Bernardino. Almost immediately following his arrival, Hunt entered the political arena, probably at the behest of Brigham Young and/or the Apostles Lyman and Rich. He first represented the new colony in a convention held in Santa Barbara to discuss a division of the State of California. He then served on the first Board of Supervisors of Los Angeles County, and was elected to the California Assembly as a representative of Los Angeles County. He served in the

Assembly from 1853 through 1857 and became the second most senior member of that body in his final year. At the same time, he was commissioned as a Brigadier General in the California Militia, responsible for the southernmost counties in the state, and served as the chair of the Assembly Military Affairs Committee. His first piece of legislation, which was adopted, was the creation of San Bernardino County in 1853. Jefferson Hunt has accurately been called the "Father of San Bernardino County." With the approach of federal troops to Utah in 1857, Hunt and most of his family joined those who were recalled by Brigham Young to Utah, ending his impact on California history.

Perhaps because he left the state in 1857, Hunt has been virtually ignored in the historical literature related to California's first years in the American Union. In this volume, it is this author's hope to reveal Jefferson Hunt as one of the important, but nevertheless ignored, figures in the history of California, the Gold Rush and the American West.

Chapter 1

The Early Years

Jefferson Hunt was born in Bracken County, Kentucky, on January 20, 1803, to John and Martha (Jenkins) Hunt. There is some disagreement within the Hunt family regarding his date of birth; both January 22, 1803 and January 4, 1804 are mentioned as birthdates. Jefferson Hunt's biographer and descendant, Pauline Udall Smith, accepted the January 20, 1803 date based on Nauvoo Temple records, Mormon Battalion rolls and the High Priests rolls (Smith 1958, 288; Smith papers, Utah State University).

There is also some disagreement about his given name. Several descendants believe that his given name was Charles Jefferson Hunt. Later, he named one child, who died in infancy, Jefferson. But four of his grandchildren were named "Charles Jefferson," four were named "Jefferson," and two were named "Thomas Jefferson." Pauline Udall Smith believed that Hunt's parents named one of their sons "Thomas" and a second son, "Jefferson" after President Thomas Jefferson. She dismissed the possibility that Jefferson was actually named "Charles Jefferson" (Smith 288). In the absence of conclusive evidence to the contrary, the author accepts Smith's analysis and believes that Jefferson Hunt was born on January 20, 1803.

The Hunt family sold their farm in Kentucky in late 1815 and moved to southeastern Illinois, near the present community of Albion. In December 1823, twenty-year-old Jefferson married eighteen-year-old Celia Mounts. Following their marriage, he remained at the Hunt family home where he continued to farm, following the death of his father. The Hunt's first child, Gilbert, was born in April 1825, and soon after, they moved to the Mounts farm nearby. In 1830, Hunt bought the Mounts' farm (Smith 1958).

Jefferson Hunt's life was soon inseparably tied to a new religion that began in upstate New York. In the Spring of 1830, Joseph Smith Jr. printed the Book of Mormon and organized the Church of Jesus Christ of Latter Day Saints (Mormons). Organized during a period of religious reformations that had captured much of the nation, the new church began attracting members. Not long after, the Saints, as they became known, began to gather in Kirtland, Ohio, at the instruction of Smith. Shortly afterwards, other Saints began to gather in Jackson County near Independence, Missouri, which they planned to be their City of Zion. But by early 1834, mobs forced the Missouri Saints to leave Jackson County and flee to Clay County to the north. One of the Missouri attorneys who represented and helped the Mormons during this difficult period was Alexander Doniphan, an attorney and state legislator, who would also assist the Mormons in a few short years and then again during the Mexican War more than a decade later.

Even this location was not far enough from those Missourians who continued to resent and harass the Mormons. By 1836, most Mormons moved further north to what is now Caldwell and Daviess counties. Doniphan sponsored legislation in the statehouse to create these new counties for his Mormon friends. Mormon leaders in Missouri purchased land in Caldwell County that became the site of the community of Far West, which was to be the new center of the LDS religion. Joseph Smith and most of the other Mormons left Kirtland, Ohio for Missouri. At the same time, many new converts to the religion also began moving to Caldwell County.

Among the new arrivals in Caldwell County in late 1836 or early 1837 were Jefferson Hunt and his family. In the Fall of 1834, the Hunts were introduced to the teachings of Joseph Smith by Solomon Hancock, one of the missionaries dispatched by Joseph Smith to find converts. Some of Hunt's biographers, including Pauline Udall Smith and Norma Elliot, have written that Levi Hancock was responsible for the Hunts' conversion. However, Solomon's son, Charles Brent Hancock, a Mormon Battalion member, clearly recalled that it was his father, Solomon, and not his uncle, Levi, who converted Jefferson and Celia (Charles Brent Hancock, n.d., 25). While this may seem like a minor detail, it is important to the Hunt story in light of the subsequent difficulties between Levi Hancock and Hunt on the march of the Mormon Battalion twelve years later.

On March 7, 1835, Celia and Jefferson Hunt were baptized in the LDS Church by Charles Patten. They continued to live in eastern Illinois, but eventually decided to join the other Mormons in Missouri. First, Hunt traveled to Caldwell County to locate property in advance of moving his family. On December 6, 1836, he filed papers for forty acres of land on Log Creek in Kingston Township, a little over four miles southeast of Far West (Caldwell County records). With property secured near the heart of the new Mormon headquarters, the Hunt family was able to gather with the rest of the Saints.

About two weeks later, on December 19, 1836, the Hunts sold their farm and prepared to move West (Smith 1958, 27.) Shortly after, Jefferson and Celia, who was expecting her sixth child in May, traveled across Illinois and Missouri to their Caldwell County home. They arrived by February 1837, and on February 2nd, Hunt filed on an additional forty acres of land in the Mirable Township near Tub Creek, about a mile-and-a-half northwest of his first property. Later that year, on October 11th, he filed on eighty acres in Kingston Township, about two miles west of the present community of Kingston (Caldwell County records). Approximately one month later, Hunt's future friend and future LDS apostle, Charles Coulson Rich, filed on a forty acre parcel less than a mile from his Log Creek property. Nearby neighbors included Orin Porter Rockwell, Hosea Stout and Amasa Lyman—a future apostle who would play a key role in Hunt's California experiences.

A common practice in the LDS community was for established settlers to host newly arrived converts for a short period while the new arrivals obtained land and familiarized themselves with the region of their new home.

Jefferson Hunt was no exception to this practice, and one of the new arrivals
he hosted was John Doyle Lee. A new convert, Lee arrived at Far West in early
June 1838. According to his autobiography, written nearly forty years later as
he waited to be executed for his role in the Mountain Meadows Massacre, Lee
stated:

> "We remained at the house of elder Joseph [Jefferson] Hunt, in
> Far West, several days. He was then a strong Mormon, and was
> afterwards first captain in the Mormon Battalion. He, as an el-
> der in the Church, was a preacher of the gospel; all of his family
> was firm in the faith. Elder Hunt preached to me the necessity
> of humility and a strict obedience to the gospel requirements
> through the servants of God. He informed me that the apostles
> and elders were our true teachers, and it was our duty to hear,
> learn and obey; that the spirit of God was very fine and delicate,
> and was easily grieved and driven from us; that the more hum-
> ble we were, the more of the Holy Spirit we would enjoy" (Lee
> 1877, 56-57).

Clearly, Lee meant to say Jefferson rather than Joseph, since Hunt's
son, Joseph, was only thirteen months old in June 1838. This may have been
an intentional or unintentional mistake, but most likely was either made by
an editor or his attorney who published the book following his death. Lee
came to know both Jefferson and Joseph very well in later years and could
not have been confused by their names. He refers to both by their correct
names later in his book. As we shall see, Lee used a future meeting with
Joseph Hunt to sling barbs at Jefferson and the Hunt family. Lee's actions
during the march of the Mormon Battalion probably created some animosity between the two men; Lee tried to coerce or intimidate Hunt, but Hunt
would have none of it. A week or so after his arrival, Lee settled near Gallatin in Daviess County.

In Kirtland, Ohio, the first Mormon temple was built and dedicated,
mills and stores were opened, and the Kirtland Safety Society Bank was es-

tablished by Joseph Smith and Sidney Rigdon. The state refused to charter the bank; however, it continued to operate and printed its own notes as was customary at the time. The reluctance of non-Mormons to accept the notes, combined with real estate speculation and a national financial crisis, caused the bank to fail. Some of the Mormons blamed Smith for the collapse and the loss of their money. The resulting dissention and apostasy led to a fracturing of the foundation of the LDS Church at that center. Many of those who remained loyal to Smith and the fundamental teachings of the Church began to head toward Missouri.

By the middle of March 1838, Smith had completed his withdrawal from Kirtland and arrived at Far West. Caldwell County, near America's Western frontier, had become the center of the LDS faith. But even this was not to last for long. Caldwell County soon became crowded with the arriving Mormons, and many began to settle in the surrounding counties—much to the dismay of the non-Mormons residing there. By the Summer of 1838, tensions were beginning to fester between the Mormons and their nearby neighbors.

The unease with the Missourians was coupled by strain within the LDS community in Far West. Dissent began to show up during 1837, and before Joseph Smith's arrival in early 1838, local authorities took action to quell it. On February 10th, the High Council, the presiding Bishop and his council removed several men from office, including Oliver Cowdery and John Whitmer, who had been close associates of Joseph Smith in the earliest days of the Church. Jefferson Hunt apparently impressed local leaders with his abilities, beliefs and commitment to the Church, because at a meeting on February 24th he is listed as one of those sitting "on the right of the president" of the High Council and Bishopric at Far West (Cannon and Cook 1983, 141). Hunt became increasingly visible in the documentary record, particularly in relation to militia activity.

In June of 1838, Sampson Avard and others organized a group of men to deal with dissenters and help protect the community. This group, which came to be known as the Danites, may or may not have been established with the knowledge of Joseph Smith. It may have lasted only a few months, or survived for decades. The group's secretive nature and the rumors and legends surrounding it have made its history very difficult to track. In any case, it did exist during the Summer of 1838.

As was the normal practice, a county militia had been created to respond to difficulties at the order of local or state leaders. Jefferson Hunt was a Major in this militia, and on July 4th was one of the assistant marshals for the parade and celebration. This is Hunt's first appearance as a military officer. Some historians believe that Hunt's participation in the parade indicates he was a Danite. However, Mormon scholar Alexander Baugh points out that the marshals that day included both militia and Danite officers, and that Hunt was a militia officer and not a member of the Danites (Baugh 1996, 87). Clearly, Hunt was well-regarded to be afforded the honor of being a marshal in this event. Hunt's service as a militia officer would soon prove to be more than ceremonial.

The ongoing conflict between the Mormon settlers and their non-Mormon neighbors erupted in violence on Election Day, August 6, 1838, at Gallatin, the county seat of Daviess County. The non-Mormons of Daviess County believed that Mormons could only settle in Caldwell County, and that those who settled in their county should be expelled. About eight Mormons showed up to vote, and were met by a mob of forty or fifty who denied them access to the polls. A general fight broke out, with both sides using clubs and sticks as weapons. In the end, the Mormons voted and then fled. A number on both sides were injured, but no one died.

During the next several months following the Election Day battle, numerous threats were made against the Mormons and several legal actions were taken against Joseph Smith and others. Once again, Alexander Doniphan, acting as an attorney, or in his capacity as a militia commander, was able to intercede and assist the Mormons in their conflict with the Missourians. During a trial involving Joseph Smith, Sterling Price, a state representative from Chariton County to the east of Carroll County, noted the Mormons' courtroom testimony and then traveled to Far West to observe the Mormons first-hand. Price returned home satisfied that the Mormons were peaceful and law-abiding (Baugh 1996, 122-123). Within a decade, the paths of the Mormons, Alexander Doniphan and Sterling Price would again cross. Unfortunately, the legal actions and the efforts of Doniphan and others did not resolve the problems; they only delayed the eventual armed confrontation.

In September 1838, non-Mormon residents of Carroll County, just south-east of Caldwell County, began a mob action to drive Mormon settlers from the town of De Witt. The Mormons sent an emissary to appeal to Governor Lilburn Boggs for assistance, which he refused to provide. After a siege and several attacks, the outnumbered Mormons fled to Far West on October 11th. Soon thereafter, Mormon militias retaliated against non-Mormons in Daviess County, looting a number of properties and burning some buildings. This set the stage for a major armed conflict between the Mormons and their adversaries.

Samuel Bogart of the Ray County militia assembled a unit of about thirty-five men, and on October 23rd began patrolling the border where northern Ray County met southern Caldwell County. He and his force made several intrusions into the Mormon county, where some families were threatened. During this escapade, he took three Mormons hostage. When word of this action got back to Far West on the evening of October 24th, Church leaders decided to begin a counter-action to rescue the hostages and disperse the mob along their southern border. David Patten, a militia officer and an apostle, was directed to lead the effort.

Patten was able to muster about forty men at Far West. Charles C. Rich, Jefferson Hunt's neighbor at the Log Creek settlement, set out to gather as many additional men as possible. Hunt, a member of the militia, was one of those who joined the force. The Mormon contingent, numbering about sixty men, rode south about six miles below Log Creek to confront Bogart and his men. At a point along a small stream called Crooked River, the Mormons located Bogart's men, who had taken a strong defensive position on the stream banks. About dawn on the morning of October 25th, Patten's men approached the Ray County militia's position. A picket set well in front of Bogart's lines detected the approaching Mormons and fired a shot which inflicted a fatal wound on eighteen-year-old Patrick Obanion, a non-Mormon who had been recruited to act as a guide for the Mormons (Baugh 1996, 232).

The picket guards fled back to their position as Patten's Mormons advanced. There was general firing on both sides. To counter the defensive advantage held by Bogart's men, Patten formed three companies and charged the enemy from the front and sides. Leading his men, David Patten was fatally wounded as the charge began. However, the action was successful and Bogart's men fled across Crooked River and headed south to the interior of Ray County.

Another Mormon, Gideon Carter, was killed during the battle, and nine other Mormons were wounded. The three hostages were rescued, although one of them, William Seeley, was wounded. The Ray County militia suffered one fatality and six wounded.

News of the battle at Crooked River spread throughout Missouri very quickly. Many of the reports were greatly exaggerated, claiming that the Mormons were solely responsible for the action and that the losses of the Missourians were much greater. On the day following the battle, the Clay County militia arrived and one of its members, Peter Burnett—who later became the first governor of California—observed the battlefield (Baugh 1996, 242).

Word of the battle reached Governor Lilburn Boggs two days later on October 27th. Boggs' reaction was immediate. He ordered: "The Mormons must be treated as enemies, and must be exterminated or driven from the state" (Baugh 1996, 251-252). Shortly thereafter, several thousand militia troops arrived near Far West to enforce the order. The imminent threat of physical violence caused the Mormons eventually to surrender to the Missourians and then flee their homes once again.

On October 30, 1838, even before the extermination order became known, a substantial force of armed men from nearby Livingston County and refugees from Daviess County attacked the Mormon settlement at Haun's Mill, in the southeastern corner of Caldwell County. Seventeen people were killed and another fourteen wounded. The victims included men, women and children (Baugh 1996, 253, 298). This violence and the immediate threat of further violence caused the Mormon leadership to begin preparations to flee Missouri entirely.

In early November, Joseph Smith and several other Church leaders were arrested. When militia Colonel Alexander Doniphan was ordered to execute them, he refused and informed his commander, Major General Samuel D. Lucas, that he would hold him responsible should the Mormons be executed (Baugh 1996, 337-338). Smith and the others were sent to several different jails, and at Richmond, Ray County, some were placed under the custody of militia officer Sterling Price. Doniphan, acting as a lawyer, subsequently represented Smith and the others in court actions, and the Mormons were essentially allowed to escape custody in the Spring of 1839 (Baugh 1996, 379).

Most of the Mormons fled Missouri to Illinois, and many of them stayed briefly in or near Quincy. In early May 1839, Joseph Smith purchased the settlement of Commerce, Illinois, as the new home for the Mormons. Within a short time, the name was changed to Nauvoo and a new city was laid out along the Mississippi River, about 175 miles northeast of Caldwell County, Missouri. In Illinois the attitude of the residents seemed much more sympathetic to the Mormons.

Nauvoo steadily grew and prospered. The Hunt family settled on a farm near Bear Creek, about twenty miles southeast of Nauvoo, and closer to the Hancock County seat of Carthage than to Nauvoo. For the rest of his life, Hunt tended to settle closer to the fringes of Mormon settlement rather than in the main Mormon community. This pattern reflected his entrepreneurial spirit and independence more than anything else. He was fortunate in all of his ventures and showed no tendency to deviate from the spirit or principles of his religion.

Joseph Smith was successful in getting a city charter from the legislature for the City of Nauvoo. One of the first things he did was to create the Nauvoo Legion, a substantial and strong militia group, for protection. By 1842, over 2,000 men were enrolled, and by 1844, over 5,000. One officer was Jefferson Hunt, who again held the rank of Major.

But military readiness wasn't the only activity occupying the time of the Mormon men. Also during 1842, the Masonic Lodge was instituted in Nauvoo and many of the prominent Mormons joined. It is not clear when Jefferson Hunt became a member, but later events indicate that he was a Mason and probably joined at this time.

By 1842, Lilburn Boggs was no longer governor of Missouri. He owned a store in Independence and was running for a seat in the state senate. On the evening of May 6th, he was sitting in his home when a single shot was fired through the window of his study. Boggs was hit in the head and neck by four bullets, two of which barely penetrated his skull. His wounds were serious and it was believed that he would die. Boggs spent months recuperating and eventually migrated to California in 1846.

A British-made pepperbox revolver was found in a rain puddle very near the shattered window. Unlike Colt revolvers which had a single barrel with a revolving cylinder carrying the cap, powder and ball for each charge, the pepperbox had several revolving barrels. It was found that only one barrel had been discharged and that the others were all loaded with an extra charge of gunpowder and four balls, rather than the one ball the weapon was designed to fire (Schindler 1993, 67-69).

The Author, a trained, certified and licensed defensive handgun instructor for nearly fifty years, has conducted an analysis of what likely occurred. That inquiry indicates that the assassination attempt failed because the shooter didn't fully understand the physics involved when loading the weapon. In attempting to maximize the impact of the shot with additional gunpowder and extra balls, the recoil was increased substantially. This caused the revolver to fly out of the shooter's hand and into the puddle where it was found. Boggs survived because the bullets had much less energy than one ball would have had. The balls did not have enough ballistic force to penetrate deeply enough to cause fatal injuries.

After some investigation, authorities discovered that Porter Rockwell had been in the city at the time and may have stolen the weapon at Boggs' own store. Following the shooting, Rockwell fled to Nauvoo and then Philadelphia, but was eventually caught in St. Louis and brought back to Independence for trial. The prosecution could not prove that Rockwell was responsible and he was found not guilty.

Most people then believed—and many historians now agree—that Rockwell was indeed the one who shot Boggs. His own subsequent behavior and statements seem to support that idea. Much less clear is whether or not he was acting at the behest of Joseph Smith. At the time, accusations were made that Smith had given money to Rockwell following the assassination attempt, or that he directed Rockwell to kill Boggs. Smith and Rockwell both went into hiding for some time. This incident helped inflame Illinois residents against Smith and the Mormons.

By 1844, there was once again dissention within the Mormon community, much of it caused by the revelation of polygamy, which was read to the High Council in August 1843. Some of the Saints began to leave the Church, and the Mormon's neighbors began to see the Nauvoo Legion as a threat. Many of the non-Mormons were envious of the general success of the Mormon economy and disliked what they saw as autocratic control by Joseph Smith and the other Mormon leaders. Attitudes toward the Mormons began to significantly deteriorate, and within the Church a number of dissenters were excommunicated.

Matters came to a head on June 7th, when a group of dissenters, including former Mormons and non-Mormons, published the *Nauvoo Expositor*, the first and only issue of a newspaper that criticized Joseph Smith, the principle of polygamy and Smith's political ambitions. The following day, the City Council found the paper guilty of libel and ordered the press be destroyed. On June 10th, members of the Nauvoo Legion demolished the press and type, setting in motion the events that would lead to the death of their leader and Prophet, Joseph Smith.

The outcry for retaliation against Smith and the Mormons was immediate. Militia units from around the region traveled to the county seat in Carthage, and Governor Thomas Ford arrived to calm the situation. Relying on assurances of protection from the governor and militia commanders, Joseph Smith and his brother, Hyrum, surrendered and were placed in the Carthage jail on June 24th. On June 27th, Governor Ford traveled to Nauvoo

to address the Mormons there. A number of the militia units had been discharged, and only a small portion of the local unit was present to protect the
Carthage jail and Smith. Some Mormons, including the apostle John Taylor,
visited the Smith brothers and remained at the jail to help protect them. Recognizing their vulnerability, the jailer allowed them to use his quarters on the
second floor.

Shortly after 5:00 p.m., a mob probably composed of militia members
from Warsaw, Illinois, led by Thomas Sharp, an anti-Mormon and editor of
the Warsaw paper, stormed the jail. Hyrum was killed almost immediately by
a shot fired through the door of the second floor room. The mob stormed the
jailor's quarters. Joseph was shot and killed as he attempted to escape through
a window. John Taylor was seriously wounded, but survived.

Joseph Smith was much more than the founder and leader of the LDS
religion. The faithful regarded him as the Prophet, Seer and Revelator. The
murder of Smith dealt a serious blow to the Mormons.

A crisis of succession immediately fell upon the Mormon Church.
Smith's brother, Hyrum, had been the logical successor to lead the Mormons,
but he, too, had been murdered, and Joseph had left no clear line of succession. Some felt that Joseph Smith III, Joseph's minor son, should become leader, while others believed that Sidney Rigdon, Smith's First Counselor, should
lead. Other pretenders, some notable within the LDS Church and others not
so well known, also surfaced as possible leaders. The Saints were confronted
with a decision that had the potential of either destroying or saving the young
Church.

The hierarchy of the Church had been divided into the First Presidency and the Quorum of the Twelve Apostles. Prior to his death, the First
Presidency consisted of Joseph Smith as president and his counselors, including Sidney Rigdon. Brigham Young was the president of the Quorum of the
Twelve Apostles. With no clear succession plan in place, there was contention
whether leadership should fall to those in the First Presidency, or the Quorum, or even to someone else, such as a descendant of Smith.

Most of the Twelve Apostles were not in Nauvoo at the time of Smith's murder. They had been summoned when problems broke out over the destruction of the press, and most arrived in Nauvoo by August 6th. Rigdon, who had disagreed with Joseph Smith and had left Nauvoo before the murder, returned to the town and called a meeting for the morning of August 8th. About 5,000 people gathered and heard Rigdon deliver a long, disjointed speech, which gave little confidence about his ability to lead.

Immediately following Rigdon, Brigham Young addressed the crowd, and in a short talk announced that there would be another meeting at two o'clock that afternoon. These brief remarks made an immediate and immense impression on everyone there. George Q. Cannon, the fifteen-year-old nephew of John Taylor, stated that:

> "it was the voice of Joseph himself; and not only was it the voice of Joseph which was heard, but it seemed in the eyes of the people as though it was the very person of Joseph which stood before them. They both saw and heard with their natural eyes and ears, and then the words which were uttered came, accompanied by the convincing power of God, to their hearts, and they were filled with the Spirit and with great joy" (Arrington 1985, 115).

Numerous other accounts reported the same. Everyone agreed that Brigham Young had spoken to them as if he were Joseph Smith. For a brief few minutes, Young had assumed the persona of the beloved Smith, and he gave the assembled Saints exactly what they wanted to hear—continuity. Over the next thirty years, Brigham Young would repeatedly use the reassuring technique of telling his listeners what they wanted to hear, whether they realized it or not. This effective communication tool helped him lead the Saints through some very difficult and controversial times ahead.

During the afternoon session, Young argued that the rightful succession of leadership fell to the Quorum of Twelve Apostles, of which he was president. He and Apostles Amasa Lyman and Parley Pratt argued that Joseph Smith had established the apostles as the foundation of the Church and they were responsible for providing leadership. As the meeting concluded, the assembled Church members voted to sustain the apostles as the successors to Joseph Smith. Reports indicate that there was unanimous, or very nearly unanimous, support for that proposition.

Brigham Young was not elected as the new leader of the Mormons that day. Leadership was vested with the Quorum of the Twelve Apostles, but Young was the president of that group, and as such, effectively became the new leader of the Church. Several years later, the First Presidency was reinstated and Young officially became the president of the Latter Day Saints.

Throughout the rest of 1844 and well into 1845, the Mormons of Nauvoo continued to build their community and various Church buildings, including the Temple. But by mid-1845, it became clear that Nauvoo would have to be abandoned because of regional opposition to the Mormons. Young and other leaders determined from the reports of John C. Fremont and others that the most logical destination for their next settlement was in the Rocky Mountains, most likely in the Valley of the Great Salt Lake. By late 1845, the decision had been made to move the following Spring. In addition, Brigham Young directed Sam Brannan, the president of the New York Saints, to lead a contingent by sea to San Francisco on the California Coast. Of note is the fact that, at that time, the Rocky Mountain destinations, including the Valley of the Great Salt Lake and the California Coast, were part of Mexico and not the United States.

Unfortunately, conditions between the Mormons and their neighbors did not improve; altercations continued between the Mormons and non-Mormons in the area, and statewide political support for Nauvoo declined. During the final weeks of 1845 and the first weeks of 1846, Brigham Young and other Church officials tried to meet the Saints' religious needs by performing ceremonies in the nearly completed Nauvoo Temple before the exodus began. On February 2, 1846, Church leaders announced that Nauvoo would be abandoned and the Mormons would move to the Rocky Mountains. Within a few days, the migration began to cross the Mississippi River. By May, over 10,000 people had left and were stretched across Iowa between the Mississippi and Missouri rivers. The decision was made to stop on the Missouri River at a place the Mormons called Kanesville, now Council Bluffs, and at Winter Quarters, now Florence, part of Omaha, Nebraska.

On July 12, 1845, Celia Hunt gave birth to twins, Mary and Parley, at their home on Bear Creek. The Hunt family now consisted of ten children, five of whom were ten or younger. And the family would soon increase further. The practice of plural marriage (polygamy) had been in place for some years but was still not officially acknowledged by Church leadership. It had been discussed with the High Council and many knew of the practice, but others within the Church considered polygamy to be only a rumor.

In early 1846, there were probably fewer than 150 Mormon men with more than one wife. Plural marriages could not be entered into without approval of Brigham Young or other leaders at the very top of the Church hierarchy (Daynes 2001, 35, 194). Permission was granted only to those who were close to the leadership and considered worthy of the celestial benefits. Jefferson Hunt was one of those men.

A family named Nease lived near the Hunts at Bear Creek. Both the father and mother died in late 1845, leaving one married daughter and four minor children. Rhoda Nease, fifteen, went to live with her married sister, Mary Ann. The other three, Matilda, seventeen, Peter, eleven, and Ellen, nine, were taken in by the Hunt family.

On January 2, 1846, the day after Matilda Nease's eighteenth birthday, she, Jefferson and Celia Hunt received their endowments in the Nauvoo Temple. On February 7th, Celia and Matilda were sealed to Jefferson in a second Temple ceremony (Smith 1958, 46). Hunt had joined the select few polygamists within the Church. His children, Gilbert and Nancy, were both older than Matilda, and Marshall was only a year younger. Matilda's siblings, Peter and Ellen, were adopted into the Hunt family. As they prepared to leave Illinois for the unknown West, the Hunt family consisted of fifteen men, women and children. In addition, it appears the Hunts had taken in an elderly couple, John and Jane Bosco, who were British converts unable to handle the trek West on their own.

The Hunts crossed the Mississippi on February 15ᵗʰ as part of the party that contained Brigham Young and the apostles Willard Richards and George A. Smith (Smith 1958, 48-49). The Saints crossed the present state of Iowa in groups of fifty families. Semi-permanent camps were set up at a number of locations including Garden Grove and Mount Pisgah, where farms were established to grow crops for the ensuing year. Young and others continued on toward the Missouri River at Council Bluffs where they decided to spend the following Winter before pushing on to the Rocky Mountains.

On June 13, 1846, Young and the advance party camped near Mosquito Creek, just east and south of Council Bluffs. The Hunt party may have been with them, since they also camped on Mosquito Creek. But their respite was short. Unbeknownst to them, within about a month they would again be on the move, this time toward California.

Part I

The Mormon Battalion

The story of the Mormon Battalion is a triumph of human endurance and spirit. The Battalion marched two thousand miles—nearly a thousand miles of it uncharted desert. They faced unexpected hardships and obstacles. Twice the Battalion nearly collapsed, yet its success far exceeded expectations. Its contributions forever changed the American West and the United States. This is the story of the leadership that saved the Battalion and carried it into legend; it is the story of Jefferson Hunt's introduction to the American West and the conversion of California from an obscure Mexican Territory to a powerful American state.

Chapter 2

The Mexican War

In 1844, the territory of the United States stopped at the Western boundary of the Louisiana Purchase. On the southwestern corner, the United States was bounded by the Republic of Texas. To the west and northwest of Texas was the Mexican province of New Mexico; beyond that to the west and northwest was the Mexican land called Alta California, which included most or all of the present states of California, Arizona, Nevada, Utah, and the western portions of Colorado and Wyoming. To the northwest, the land between the Continental Divide and the Pacific Ocean was called Oregon and was claimed by both the United States and Great Britain.

New Mexico had been under Spanish—and later, Mexican—rule for most of the previous 300 years. By the 1830s, the Mexican government was firmly in control. The few Americans in Santa Fe were either traders or former trappers who enjoyed the comforts of a pleasant climate. California, first colonized about seventy years earlier, was sparsely populated with little governmental control. A handful of Americans lived among the ranchos and in the few small villages such as Monterey, San Diego, Yerba Buena (later to become San Francisco) or Los Angeles. There was also a colony named New Helvetia created by the Swiss entrepreneur, John Sutter. A few missionaries and farmers had made it to Oregon from the United States and resided there along with the remnants of the Hudson's Bay Company.

When Texas gained its independence in 1836, Mexico refused to give up the claim to its former territory. For the next nine years, Texas remained an independent republic since there was no opportunity for annexation to the United States, although discussions were held between the administration of President John Tyler and President Sam Houston of the Lone Star Republic. James K. Polk ran for President of the United States in 1844 on a platform that included the annexation of Texas and Oregon.

During the first months of 1845, both the House of Representatives and the Senate voted for the annexation of Texas, and on March 1st, departing President Tyler signed the resolution. On March 4th, James K. Polk was sworn in as the President of the United States. Annexation set the course for war between the United States and Mexico.

On March 6th, Mexican Minister General Juan Amonte broke diplomatic relations with the United States and called the annexation "an act of aggression." During the next year, Mexico experienced a series of political upheavals. At the same time, the United States sought to resolve both the annexation and domestic issues that came with admitting Texas as a slave state. President Polk first chose to follow a course of negotiation with Mexico. He was prepared to offer up to $40 million for a settlement of the issue. Mexico, however, was not in a mood to enter negotiations, believing that their territory and national honor were at stake. When the Mexican government, gripped in a morass of domestic politics, refused to receive the United States' emissary, John Slidell, Polk ordered General Zachary Taylor to advance from Corpus Christi into the disputed territory to the west and on to the Rio Grande. By April 1846, Taylor's troops were digging in on the banks of the Rio Grande across from Matamoros. Taylor's command of nearly 4,000 men amounted to about one-half of the American Army; on the other side of the Rio Grande stood nearly 5,000 Mexican troops.

President Polk's strategy was brazen and complex. It called for the annexation of Texas, not at the Nueces River, the line informally recognized by Mexico, but farther to the west at the Rio Grande. The plan called for an overland army, Stephen Watts Kearny's Army of the West, to capture and occupy Santa Fe and New Mexico and then proceed to the Pacific Coast to control California. Other portions of this Army would march south to capture El Paso and enter the northern portions of Mexico. A small body of troops, under the command of John C. Fremont already exploring in California, would be joined by a naval force. Most of the Army would be transported by the Navy to various points along the Gulf Coast of Mexico and proceed inland to the very heart of Mexico itself. This plan required far more troops than existed in the American Army. It would depend on the extensive use of volunteer units from throughout the United States.

On the morning of April 25, 1846, two squads of American troops commanded by Captain Seth B. Thornton were ambushed on the east—or Texas side—of the Rio Grande, about twenty miles upriver from the main body of troops. Eleven men were killed and wounded; most of the rest were captured. The dispute with Mexico had become an armed conflict; the Mexican War had begun. When the war ended with the signing of the Treaty of Guadalupe Hidalgo thirty-two months later on February 2, 1848, the territory of the United States spanned the continent from the Atlantic to the Pacific and the new map of the contiguous United States became essentially as it is today. All or part of the territory located in eleven Western States became part of the United States.

The Mexican War was not greeted with unanimous support in the United States. Many Americans, particularly those in the Border States, saw it as an appropriate measure to increase the amount of land available for settlement. Others saw the vast new natural resources that were sure to be discovered as the entitlement of those who would work to recover them. Some saw glory and adventure in the first American war to be fought on foreign soil. Others saw the military as a way to escape the drab conditions of the Eastern cities. Some politicians, such as Democratic Senator Thomas Hart Benton of Missouri, saw the war as the inevitable result of Manifest Destiny—the belief that the United States was destined to span the continent. Other politicians, especially Whigs from the Northeastern and Mid-Atlantic states, saw the war as an effort to extend slavery to new territories, and thus to expand the political power of Southern slave-holding states.

Internally, both the Whig and Democratic parties were divided on their support for the war. It is hard today to imagine a United States with a western boundary that followed the Continental Divide through Colorado, Wyoming and Montana. Nevertheless, that was precisely what many politicians, newspaper editors, literati and Northeasterners were willing to accept. Stated objections included imperialism, aggression, fraud, religious persecution, excessive costs, loss of life, and little value in the territory to be gained. In reality, the main issue was slavery—or more precisely, whether or not slavery would be extended to the new territories. Abolitionists were very concerned that slavery would spread, and some members of both parties feared that new slave states would upset the delicate regional balance between North and South. And that is exactly what was about to happen.

When the first shots of the Mexican War were fired, the United States Army consisted of fewer than 5,600 officers and men. During the war, the number in the Regular Army rose to nearly 43,000, and another 73,500 troops joined the volunteer units formed in most states and territories (Bauer 1974, 397). Many recruits were immigrants who found it difficult to find work in Eastern cities. Others joined to gain free travel to new opportunities in the West. Many saw little problem in deserting to the Mexican side in hopes of finding better opportunities there. Some joined to experience the excitement of war, but most joined in response to a patriotic call for additional forces.

Of the 116,000 men who served during the Mexican War, 1.5% were killed in action or died of combat wounds. Nearly 10% more died from disease, accidents or other non-combat related causes. Nearly 8% more deserted before their enlistments were up (Bauer 1974, 397). The death of 11.5% of the soldiers is the highest fatality rate of any war in American history, including the Civil War.

The genesis of the Mormon Battalion was not in Washington or with the leaders of the military; rather it was the idea of Brigham Young. It can be argued that the original idea of Mormon troops performing service to the United States military was Joseph Smith's. Before his death in 1844, he proposed to Washington officials that Mormons be contracted to provide military protection along the Western trails and outposts. Smith's proposal was rejected by Washington, but was remembered by Young, who also made a futile bid to post troops along the Oregon Trail to help finance the Mormon's Westward Migration.

By the time the first shots were fired in the Mexican War, the Mormon Exodus from Nauvoo was well underway. The impoverished Mormons who had sold their land and most of their possessions for pennies on the dollar stretched from the Mississippi River to Council Bluffs, over 300 miles across the width of present-day Iowa. The Mormons originally named the location of their camp on the Missouri Millers Hollow after one of their own who was among the first to arrive. A short time later, the name was changed to Kanesville in honor of Thomas Kane. After the Mormon departure, the remaining inhabitants changed the name to Council Bluffs in recognition of a council held there by Lewis and Clark and the Otoes. For clarity, the name Council Bluffs will be used in this book.

Many of the Mormons had been instructed to establish temporary communities to raise crops for the following year's push to the West. They were also to build bridges and shelter for themselves and following emigrants. By the end of May 1846, the advance group had reached the Missouri River at present-day Council Bluffs. Many of the others were in the temporary settlements that had been set up at Garden Grove and Mount Pisgah and scattered elsewhere along the trail. Mount Pisgah was the name given to the camp the Mormons established near present-day Thayer, Iowa.

The thousands of Saints who had departed Nauvoo struggled mightily to advance westward. Many began their journey in the middle of Winter; nearly everyone fought the mud, swollen streams and rivers of the Spring. Every family faced sickness, and many died on the prairies of Iowa. Everyone was disheartened at having again been forced from their home, tired from the physical and emotional strains of the emigration, and the labor of creating temporary camps and farms.

It was clear to Brigham Young that the federal government could play a significant role in financing the Westward Migration. Any assistance to that end would be welcomed.

On February 4, 1846, the same day the first of the Saints crossed the Mississippi in flight from Nauvoo, the chartered ship *Brooklyn* left New York with roughly 230 Mormons bound for California. The leader of this enterprise was Sam Brannan, who had been in charge of Mormon affairs on the Eastern Seaboard. Brannan tried several schemes to obtain federal aid for the Westward Migration, but all had been unsuccessful. Instead, Brannan left behind several difficult situations where he used his power as Brigham Young's representative and his political connections to try to derive personal gain from what can best be called scams.

Church leaders selected Jesse Carter Little from New Hampshire as their agent and Brannan's replacement in East. In a letter to Little dated January 20, 1846, Brigham Young instructed him to accept any aid he could find to assist the Westward emigration. Young wrote: "If our government shall offer any facilities for emigration the western coast, EMBRACE THOSE FACILITIES [Young's emphasis], if possible, as a wise and faithful man, take every honorable advantage of the times that you can." (Yurtinis 1975, 22).

Jesse Little spent the next several months traveling among the Mormons on the East Coast urging them to follow Brannan to the California Coast and warning them of the dangers of overland travel through borderlands that had proven hostile to Saints. At the same time, he was attempting to garner support from anyone with political contacts who could help his cause.

On May 13th, Congress declared war on Mexico. On that same day, Jesse Little was in Philadelphia addressing a Mormon conference. Among those attending was twenty-four-year-old Thomas Leiper Kane, a non-Mormon and the second son of a very prominent and politically-connected Philadelphia family. Kane's older brother, Elisha, was a renowned Arctic explorer. His father, John Kane, was a politician and lawyer who had been an associate of Andrew Jackson, was a close friend of President James Polk, and was a neighbor of then-Secretary of State and future President, James Buchanan.

Thomas Kane, a lawyer himself, was a sickly young man who wished to make his own mark on American history. The plight of the Mormons, as told by Little, provided him with an ideal opportunity to make a significant contribution. He saw the opportunity to use his political connections to aid the Westward emigration of the Mormons, and at the same time to become an important part of both the war effort and the settlement of the West. Kane met with Little, gained his confidence, and provided him with the political acumen needed to get the badly-needed aid from the federal government.

Bolstered by Kane's guidance, Little traveled to Washington, arriving on May 21st. The next day, in the company of several men, including Congressman Daniel King of Massachusetts, Little attended a reception at the White House and met President Polk. The President did not record the visit in his diary, but noted that a number of people had offered their assistance in the pursuit of the war. On May 23rd, Little met with a politically powerful associate of Sam Brannan's, Amos Kendall, who was the first to raise the possibility of a volunteer force of Mormon men in the Mexican War (Yurtinis 1975, 26). Kendall reported to Little on discussions he had with Polk and on conversations the President was having with his Cabinet. However, no affirmative answer came from the White House. Polk and his senior staff were having detailed discussions on securing the future of New Mexico, California and Oregon for the United States, but the Mormon issue did not seem to be a major topic.

On June 1st, acting on Thomas Kane's advice—and probably with his assistance—Little drafted a letter to President Polk that moved the Mormon's plight to the forefront. In it, Little professed his patriotism and that of the Church leaders; he testified to the moral and virtuous nature of his Church; and described the plight that he and his Church had endured. But before he concluded asking for assistance and stating the Mormon's willingness to defend the new territory against invaders, he inserted a thinly veiled threat. He referred to the thousands who had begun the Westward movement by land

and sea, and the many Mormons throughout the United States preparing to travel westward. Then he stated:

> "We have forty thousand in the British Isles and hundreds upon the Sandwich Islands, all determined to gather to this place and thousands will sail this fall."

Several sentences later he states:

> "We would disdain to receive assistance from a foreign power—although it should be preferred [sic]—unless our government shall turn us off in this great crisis and will not help us, but compel us to be foreigners" (Bigler and Bagley 2000, 34).

His cleverly worded message to Polk inferred that if the United States government did not assist the Mormon emigration, the Saints would be forced to accept assistance from another government if they were to prevail in their new homes. In other words, if Great Britain chose to contest Oregon and that was the area that the Saints settled in, then the Mormons would be compelled, in turn, to support Great Britain. Little's message was clear to Polk: the Mormons were moving West and they would be loyal to whoever assisted them. Unknown to Little at the time, it was a hollow threat; Polk had already resolved the Oregon issue with Great Britain by agreeing to the 49th parallel boundary in the Northwest. Nevertheless, Polk got the message that it would indeed be better to have the Mormons on his side just in case the British had designs on a portion of the Mexican provinces now being contested, or wished to push their fortunes in Oregon.

At the very time Little's letter arrived, Polk and his top staff were discussing securing New Mexico and California by sending Colonel Stephen Watts Kearny and his troops forward from Fort Leavenworth as the Army of the West. The plan called for Kearny to first occupy Santa Fe, where little resistance was expected, and then to move forward to invade California, provided that the Winter weather was favorable.

The day following Little's letter, Polk met with his Cabinet and finalized the plans for the expedition against California. Kearny was to take control of Santa Fe, establish a temporary government, leave enough troops to control New Mexico, and then take the remainder of his troops, plus a contingent of Missouri Volunteers that had already started west to California. In addition, 1,000 mounted volunteers from Missouri were to go to Santa Fe and be at Kearny's disposal. Polk's diary states:

> "Col. Kearney [sic] was also authorized to receive into service as
> volunteers a few hundred of the Mormons who are now on their
> way to California, with a view to conciliate them, attach them
> to our country, & prevent them from taking part against us."
> (Bigler and Bagley 2000, 36).

Little was not aware of this decision when he and Amos Kendall met with President Polk on June 3rd. In his diary, Polk indicates the purpose of the meeting was to determine the government's policy toward the Mormon migration. After Polk assured them that the Mormons would be treated according to the Constitution without regard to their religious beliefs, he asked Little:

> "if 500 or more of the mormons [sic] now on their way to Cali-
> fornia would be willing *on their arrival in that country* [empha-
> sis added] to volunteer and enter the U.S. army in that war, un-
> der the command of a U.S. officer" (Bigler and Bagley 2000, 36).

Little, as Young's representative, had full authority to accept such an offer, and replied in the affirmative. Polk then told them he would meet with them the following day. However, Polk wrote in his journal that did not tell them of the Kearny expedition, and then recorded:

> "The mormons [sic], if taken into the service, will constitute not
> more than ¼ of Col. Kearny's command, and the main object
> of taking them into service would be to conciliate them, and
> prevent them from assuming a hostile attitude towards the U.S,
> after their arrival in California. It was with the view to prevent
> this singular sect from becoming hostile to the U.S. that I held

the conference with Mr. Little and with the same view I am to
see him again tomorrow" (Bigler and Bagley 2000, 36).

On Friday, June 5th, the President again met with Little and Kendall.
Polk explained that during a meeting with the Secretary of War it was decided
that a battalion of Mormons could not be enlisted until they reached California, which meant the Mexican Territory west of the Louisiana Purchase. Once
they arrived, if the Mexican War had not ended, then "500 [would] be mustered into the service of the U.S. as volunteers for 12 months, placing themselves under the command of a U.S. officer who would be ready to receive
them." Hoping to obtain remuneration as quickly as possible, Little proposed
enlisting the Mormons immediately, but Polk declined his offer (Bigler and
Bagley 2000, 37).

After Little left the meeting, Polk continued his conversation with Kendall, explaining privately that Kearny had been ordered to proceed to New
Mexico and then, if possible, continue on to California. He further explained
that because a large body of Mormons now on the way to California might
alarm the current residents, Kearny's combined force could not contain more
than one-quarter Mormon volunteers. Kendall agreed with the wisdom of
Polk's decision (Bigler and Bagley 2000, 37).

The arrangement between Polk and Little, as recorded by the President in his diary, would do nothing to help the plight of the Mormons. At
their prairie camps, the Mormons were more than 700 miles east of the Mexican boundary and the nearest area called California—the land to the west of
South Pass in present-day Wyoming. New Mexico was 700 miles to the southwest. Young's plans called for them to remain near the Missouri until the following Winter had passed. At that rate, no Mormon would reach California
via overland routes until the Mexican War was essentially over and there was
no longer a need for a Mormon Battalion.

Fortunately for Young and the Saints, the written orders sent to the
commander of the Army of the West did not clearly state Polk's plan to delay

the enlistment of the Mormons until they crossed into Mexican territory. Secretary of War William L. Marcy's orders to Stephen Watts Kearny, dated June 3, 1846, instructed him to "take the earliest possession of Upper California" relying in part on his current forces and newly enlisted mounted troops from Missouri (Bigler and Bagley 2000, 38). In addition, he was instructed to proceed to California as soon as possible after the occupation of Santa Fe.

Reflecting the difficulty with communicating over vast expanses of the American West, Kearny was given full authority to use his best judgment with the best available information to obtain supplies, select the proper routes, and reach California in the fastest possible time. Kearny was also instructed to establish civil governments in both New Mexico and California following his successful occupation. Secretary Marcy's order concluded by stating the President directed "that the rank of brevet brigadier general will be conferred on you as soon as you commence your movement towards California" (Bigler and Bagley 2000, 38-40).

Regarding the Mormons, Marcy's order stated:

"It is known that a large body of Mormon emigrants are en route to California, for the purpose of settling in that country. You are desired to use all proper means to have a good understanding with them, to the end that the United States may have their cooperation in taking possession of, and holding, that country. It has been suggested here that many of these Mormons would willingly enter into the service of the United States, and aid us in our expedition against California. You are hereby authorized to muster into service such as can be induced to volunteer; not, however, a number exceeding one-third of your entire force. Should they enter the service they will be paid as other volunteers and you can allow them to designate, so far as it be properly done, the persons to act as officers thereof" (Bigler and Bagley 2000, 38-39).

Thus, from the highest levels of the Executive Office in Washington was given the order to create the Mormon Battalion. Either through omission, confusion or misunderstanding, the requirement to enlist the Mormons after they had reached California was left out of Kearny's orders. Although federal assistance to Brigham Young and the emigrating Saints was on its way, no one other than Jesse Little, his confidants Kendall and Kane, and a few top administration officials were aware of it. The Mormons camped on the prairies had no knowledge of what was coming.

Communication between the War Department in Washington and Kearny at Fort Leavenworth was much easier and faster than it was west of the Missouri. The development and expansion of steam-powered transportation systems in the 1830s meant that people and messages could travel from Washington to the edge of the Western frontier within a week or two. Because of its importance and confidentiality, Secretary Marcy's order to Colonel Kearny probably traveled by military courier using rail (and possibly canal) from Washington to Western Pennsylvania and then west by riverboat down the Ohio, to the Mississippi, and on to the Missouri and Fort Leavenworth. Marcy's order was received by Kearny before June 19, 1846.

On that day, Colonel Kearny issued an order to Captain James Allen at Fort Leavenworth instructing him to go to the Mormon camps and recruit "4 or 5 Companies of Volunteers" each company consisting "of any number between 73 and 109" (Bigler and Bagley 2000, 41). Each company was authorized to elect a captain, a first lieutenant and a second lieutenant, subject to Allen's approval. The officers, in turn, would appoint non-commissioned officers, again subject to Allen's approval. Once organized, he was directed to muster the recruits into the service where they would then "commence to receive the pay, rations and other allowances given to other Infantry Volunteers, each according to his rank" (Bigler and Bagley 2000, 41). Once that was accomplished, Allen was to advance two grades to the rank of Lieutenant Colonel of Infantry. He was also directed to appoint an adjutant sergeant major and a quartermaster sergeant to serve as his aides in the Battalion.

Allen was instructed to take the Mormon volunteers to Fort Leavenworth where they were to be outfitted and prepared for the march that was to follow Kearny to Santa Fe. In typical military fashion of the day, Kearny included instructions to Allen on the protocol to be followed in obtaining the necessary supplies. Kearny also stated:

> "You will have the Mormons distinctly to understand, that I wish to take them as Volunteers for 12 months—that they will be marched to California, receiving Pay & allowances, during the above time and at its expiration they will be discharged and allowed to retain as their Private Property, the guns & accoutrements to be furnished to them at this Post. Each Company will be allowed 4 women as Laundresses, who will travel with the Company, receiving rations & the other allowances given to the laundresses of our Army" (Bigler and Bagley 2000, 41-42).

Like most other regular Army officers, James Allen had spent his seventeen-year career in the military waiting for promotional opportunities. During the years preceding the Mexican War, the Army consisted of fewer than 10,000 troops. The only military actions were against Indian tribes along the frontier. Career officers found that promotions were infrequent and it was difficult to distinguish themselves. That changed with the start of the Mexican War when the Army swelled to over 100,000 troops, and officers had the opportunity to show their skills. For Allen, a two grade promotion and the opportunity to demonstrate his abilities in achieving Manifest Destiny was all he could hope for. With an escort of five dragoons, Allen set off at once for the Mormon camps across Iowa.

While Brigham Young needed federal assistance to help the Saints on their Westward move, it's doubtful that he expected a government grant. He understood the cost of the new war would preclude discretionary expenditures. But it is possible that he hoped that in some way, war expenditures might be used to finance the move. At best, war-related expenditures might prove helpful considering the Mormons history of offering military services under contract. He was about to learn that help was being offered, but its cost in human terms would be high.

Chapter 3

The Battalion is Formed

As Captain Allen approached Iowa's Mount Pisgah on June 25, 1846, Brigham Young and Charles Bird visited the trading post run by Peter Sarpy about eight miles south of Council Bluffs. There, Sarpy informed his visitors:

> "that Major Mitchell (Robert B. Mitchell, the local Indian Agent) had written to the commander of the troops at the fort, that the Mormons were conniving with the Indians and had committed some depredations at the Pottawatomie town, and wanted the Dragoons to come up and keep the peace and prevent their uniting with the Indians to fight the United States" (Journal History of the Church [LDS], June 25, 1846).

The following day, the same day that Captain Allen was arriving in Mount Pisgah, Brigham Young met with thirteen of his closest associates, including members of the Twelve Apostles who were present, to discuss the rumor from Sarpy. They decided to send Orson Hyde and Newel Whitney to speak with Mitchell to determine the accuracy of the report. Hyde and Whitney left immediately. The *Journal History of the Church* states that the

> "Council adjourned to Major Hunt's camp two miles north, where we dined except Elders Hyde and Whitney who retired to visit Major Mitchell. After dinner, Major Hunt went with the council to head quarters, when Elders P.P. Pratt, Heber C. Kimball, Geo. A.

Smith, and Pres Young went to the boat, where we met Brother
Hyde and Whitney, who informed us that Major Mitchell said,
he had not written any letter . . ." (Journal History of the Church,
June 26, 1846).

Thus, the rumor was put to rest.

This incident, however minor, shows the prompt reaction of the Mormon leadership to any perceived threats against the Saints. It also demonstrates the confidence that Brigham Young and the leadership had in Jefferson Hunt. Clearly, the trip to and from Hunt's camp was to enlist his aid
and advice should there be some truth to Sarpy's rumor. It's clear that Hunt
would have taken a prominent role in protecting the Saints if an armed confrontation ensued. Also of note is the reference to Hunt's rank of Major in
the Nauvoo Legion. It appears that Hunt was one of the highest ranking
military officers, if not the most senior officer, in the western-most camp of
the Saints.

Captain James Allen's small group rode into the camp of the Saints at
Mount Pisgah on June 26th. Not knowing that Church leaders arrived at the
Missouri River 100 miles to the west nearly two weeks before, Allen incor-
rectly believed the main Mormon camp was at Mount Pisgah and, accordingly, went there first.

When Allen arrived there was immediate alarm among the Saints.
They did not expect to see uniformed soldiers, and after their experiences at
Nauvoo, Far West and Kirtland, they were suspicious of any strangers—especially those who were armed and uniformed. Some feared Allen's small group
was sent to spy on them in preparation for an attack by a larger force.

Captain Allen met with William Huntington, who was in charge of
the Mount Pisgah camp, and Apostle Wilford Woodruff, the highest ranking
Mormon Church authority present because he was traveling toward Council
Bluffs and happened to be in the camp. Allen explained his mission and requested permission to address the Saints at the camp. Huntington and Wood-

ruff approved and on the following day Allen spoke to the incredulous Saints gathered before him.

In his speech, Allen informed the Saints of the presidential authorization to recruit 500 men for the Battalion and the instructions from the new commander of the Army of the West, Stephen Watts Kearny. Allen also drafted a circular in which he stated that the recruits would

> "receive pay and rations, and other allowances, such as volunteers or regular soldiers receive, from the day they shall be mustered into the service, and will be entitled to all comforts and benefits of regular soldiers of the army, and when discharged, as contemplated, at California, they will be given, gratis, their arms and accountrements, with which they will be fully equipped at Fort Leavenworth" (Bigler and Bagley 2000, 43).

Allen explained that he was looking for able-bodied men eighteen to forty-five years of age and he hoped to complete the recruiting within nine days.

Allen's message failed to inspire the crowd. To most, if not all, it was so outlandish that few believed it to be true. And they had other more serious thoughts on their mind. Rather than volunteering for the Army, they worried about survival for their families and themselves. They were moving across unknown territory toward an unknown location, were destitute, and tired of repeated persecution with no governmental support for their plight. Allen got no recruits at Mount Pisgah. He realized that his success would depend on reaching the Mormon leadership as soon as possible.

Huntington and Woodruff immediately dispatched a courier to Brigham Young and the other leaders at Council Bluffs, advising them of the arrival of Captain Allen and his message. The courier traveled one hundred thirty miles in three days, arriving on June 29th. The following day, Allen arrived at Council Bluffs and asked to meet with Young and other Church leaders, who had already met to discuss the request for the Battalion. Young immediately recognized that the Army's offer would provide badly needed cash to help finance the Westward Migration. They also recognized that Allen could be instrumental in obtaining a solution to their other major problem—where to spend the coming Winter months on the Plains.

Council Bluffs on the eastern bank of the Missouri River was on Indian land, as were other desirable camping sites to the west and northwest. The Mormons could not camp there without government permission. Allen's presence as the representative of the federal government could offer a solution to this immediate need. Captain Allen met with the Mormon leaders on July 1st, and the major topic of discussion was the issue of temporary camps on Indian Lands. In response to a question from Young, Allen specifically stated that he, as a representative of the President, could agree to the arrangement requested by the Mormons, unless otherwise notified by Polk.

The Mormon leadership had the government assistance they had hoped for. Cash would be made available to assist in the emigration. Permission would be granted to camp on Indian lands. Finally, there would be no government interference in either their temporary camps or their migration to the Great Basin. Brigham Young and the other church leaders now had to convince 500 men to enlist in the Battalion.

Just before noon, Brigham Young, accompanied by Captain James Allen, gathered to address the Council Bluffs camp. After Allen explained his mission to enlist 500 men for a battalion, Young addressed the assembled people and told them this was "the first offer we have ever had from the Government to benefit us" (Bigler and Bagley 2000, 46).

Heber C. Kimball of the First Presidency "moved that five hundred men be raised, in conformity with the requisition from the government; the motion was seconded by Willard Richards and carried unanimously" (Bigler and Bagley 2000, 46). The leadership of the Mormon Church demonstrated that they backed the enlistment effort.

The recruitment was not as easy nor as rapid as they had hoped. The events in Missouri and Illinois, along with the failure of either state or federal intervention on their behalf, caused many of the Saints to question the sudden challenge they were now facing. Hosea Stout, whose young son died on June 28th and who had been the Nauvoo chief of police, felt little support for the American cause when news of the Mexican War broke. When he heard the plea to enlist, he stated strongly what many of the Saints felt when he wrote:

> "We were all indignant at this requisition and only looked on it as a plot laid to bring trouble on our people. For in the event that we did not comply with the requisition we supposed they would now make a protest to denounce us as enemies to our country and if we did comply that they would then have 500 of our men in their power to be destroyed as they had done our leaders at Carthage" (Yurtinus 1975, 40).

Like Stout, many feared they had been placed in a very difficult position in which they could face substantial harm whether the Battalion was formed or not. Others feared the hardship that the Battalion formation would bring on both the participants and their families and friends left behind.

At Mount Pisgah, where Allen had originally stopped, the feeling was much the same, except they had not yet heard that the Church leadership was supporting the idea of a Mormon Battalion. Brigham Young, Heber Kimball and Willard Richards, along with Allen and his escort, left Council Bluffs and arrived in Mount Pisgah on July 6th. Shortly before their arrival, the party encountered Jesse Little on the trail. Little, who had left Washington along with Thomas Kane right after Polk's order to form the Battalion, confirmed the discussions that occurred in Washington, along with Polk's attitude regarding the migration and formation of the Battalion.

Not only were there large groups at Council Bluffs and Mount Pisgah, there were large numbers of Saints on the 300 mile trail and at Garden Grove and Nauvoo. Understanding Allen's need to recruit 500 members for the new Battalion immediately, Brigham Young sent letters to the leaders at various locations telling them about the recruitment effort and asking them to send young men from the ranks of those driving the wagons. And to replace those young men, the leaders were to gather older men, boys and others who could work and send them to Council Bluffs where they were needed to drive wagons, cut hay and do other work (Bigler and Bagley 2000, 48).

Sixty-six men were quickly recruited at Mount Pisgah during the first day, and a number more volunteered on the following days. At Council Bluffs, Parley Pratt, one of the Twelve Apostles, was actively recruiting when Brigham Young returned. As the days passed, the Church leadership continued to be very active in trying to recruit the 500 needed by Captain Allen. After suffering years of deprivations at the hands of others and having their welfare ignored by the government, most Saints were reluctant to volunteer to help in the War.

In spite of the need to recruit 500 men, not all volunteers were acceptable to Young. One such case was that of Jonathan Browning, a forty-year-old from Quincy, Illinois. He had been converted and then moved to Nauvoo in 1842 where he pursued his trade as a gunsmith. Browning not only repaired firearms, he was also an inventor who skillfully hand-produced one of the first successful repeating rifles that avoided patent infringements with Samuel Colt's revolving cylinder. This rifle, called a "slide gun" or "harmonica gun," utilized a horizontally sliding bar magazine which held six chambers loaded with powder and ball and capped with a percussion cap. While cumbersome to carry, it was a reliable system that operated from a simple mechanism. It gave the user the ability to fire multiple rounds at a much faster rate than the three or so rounds a minute that could be fired by a trained and experienced shooter using the conventional muzzle-loading musket or rifle.

Browning had stopped at Mosquito Creek in Council Bluffs. When Brigham Young saw him in line to volunteer, he pulled him out and told him his services were needed far more as a gunsmith and master mechanic. Browning, in fact, would not be permitted to emigrate West until 1852. He eventually settled in Ogden. His son, John Moses Browning, born in Ogden in 1855, became the most innovative and prolific firearms designer of all time. His firearms include the Browning .50 caliber machine gun, the Browning Automatic Rifle (BAR of military fame), the Winchester Model 97 shotgun, the Colt .45 ACP Model 1911 pistol, and dozens of other famous and popular firearms.

The criticism of the government expressed by Brigham Young and other Church leaders over the years was fresh in everyone's mind. Now those same leaders were in the awkward position of explaining that the opportunity to form the Mormon Battalion was a godsend and a positive change for the Church. Many of the Saints were bewildered by the sudden change in attitude. Many had suffered deaths of family or friends or other serious hardships in the months since they left Nauvoo. Most men were reluctant to leave their families on the Plains while they marched to California. In the best of conditions, the march of the Battalion would be difficult for both those going and those left behind. However, conditions were far from good. It was going to be a very difficult year for everyone. In the end, only faith in the Church and trust in the Church leadership would convince enough men to volunteer. The key to this was the promise made by Young to take care of the families left behind.

By July 13th, Brigham Young and Captain Allen had been joined by Thomas Kane and Jesse Little in Council Bluffs. They and others met with those of the Twelve that were present before addressing the camp about the recruitment effort. The *Journal History of the Church of Jesus Christ of Latter Day Saints* records that at about 11 a.m. that morning "Major Hunt called out the first company of volunteers" (Journal History of the Church, July 13, 1846). Even though Hunt was not yet officially part of the Mormon Battalion, his new assignment was clear to everyone present. While he called the name of each new recruit and they assembled in the bowery, Young met with Thomas Kane.

Following that meeting, the Twelve Apostles along with Allen, Kane and Little, assembled before the camp and the new company called by Jefferson Hunt. Brigham Young spoke first and renewed his promise to take care of those left behind. He reminded everyone of the importance of the Battalion to the future of the Church by saying:

"The blessings we are looking forward to receive will be attained through sacrifice. We want to raise volunteers. Are we willing to undergo hardships and privations to procure that which we desire?" He explained that he knew everyone had obligations with respect to the emigration, but service to the Battalion was necessary to achieve "the privilege of going where we can worship God according to the dictates of our conscience." (Journal History Church, July 13, 1846).

It is clear from the day's activities that Brigham Young had already given considerable thought as to who should command the various companies being recruited.

Although the Army said the recruits could elect their own officers, Mormons understood such appointments would be made by Brigham Young. When Apostle Orson Hyde spoke to the members, he referred to the company under the command of Dan Davis, announcing it was ready and on its way from Mount Pisgah to Council Bluffs. The *Journal History of the Church* says that the assembly "voted unanimously that Pres. Young and his council nominate the officers for the several companies as far as he thought proper" (Journal History of the Church, July 13, 1846). Captain Allen addressed the assembly and told them that Senator Thomas Hart Benton had sponsored legislation that entitled each man a uniform allowance of $3.50 per month and that each would have to carry his own clothing. Allen told them that they could wear everyday clothing, but that it should be wool which would be more durable. He also told them to obtain blankets which could be purchased at a reasonable price at Sarpy's trading post. Young counseled everyone to take a tin cup with them.

Brigham Young then stated that Jefferson Hunt's company was full and suggested that Jesse Hunter be appointed the captain of the second company. Hunter promptly gathered seventy-three recruits. Orson Hyde gathered an additional seventy-three recruits for a third company. These companies, along with the company coming from Mount Pisgah, meant that the Battalion was fast becoming a reality.

The next day, July 14th, Jefferson Hunt's company gathered to make out the muster rolls showing exactly who was in his company. By the end of the day, there were enough new recruits to fill yet another company. Later, the contingent from Mount Pisgah arrived at Council Bluffs. The *Journal History of the Church* also notes that Brigham Young recommended George P. Dykes to be the Adjutant of the Battalion (Journal History of the Church, July 14, 1846). As Adjutant, Dykes would be on Captain Allen's staff and responsible for the administrative functions of the Battalion. Dykes would provide the Battalion commander and company commanders with advice and information, and would assist the commander in seeing that orders were carried out as intended.

Captain Allen followed Young's recommendation making Dykes, whose official capacity was First Lieutenant in Company D, the Battalion Adjutant. Dykes would prove to be a capable and loyal military staff officer. Unfortunately, his efforts were often in conflict with the desires of the men of the Battalion, and he would come to feel the animosity of many who believed that he had the best interests of the Army in mind and not those of his fellow Mormons. However, an analysis of the success of the Mormon Battalion shows that George P. Dykes' work as adjutant was invaluable. Brigham Young had made a good recommendation.

Young met briefly with his council on the morning of July 15th. Then he crossed the Missouri River to visit his family at the camp which was at the location to be known as Winter Quarters, now part of Florence in the northern part of the Omaha, Nebraska metropolitan area. He instructed the remaining members of the Twelve Apostles to gather and speak to the Battalion recruits regarding their behavior and religious obligations while in service. Young also told the apostles "the next Temple would be built in the Rocky Mountains," a clear signal that the final goal of the migration was not to be modern-day California, but the Valley of the Great Salt Lake. Jefferson Hunt and Jesse Hunter met with the apostles "and received instructions to ascertain how much wages each soldier would be paid at Fort Leavenworth" (Journal History of the Church, July 15, 1846). The day ended with the apostles calling on the camp for more recruits to complete the remaining company.

By July 16th, about 450 men had been enlisted and the time came to prepare for their march to the Pacific. The men gathered, heard from several of the Twelve Apostles and then marched double file from the assembly site in Council Bluffs to Sarpy's, some seven or eight miles away. There they purchased blankets and some other necessary supplies with money to be deducted from their Army pay. With supplies in hand, they returned to Council Bluffs to await the completion of the last company's enlistment and the beginning of the long march. On the same day, Allen—now a Lieutenant Colonel—issued several orders. He first proclaimed the Mormon Battalion to be part of the Army of the West. The second and third orders appointed Allen's staff, which included George Dykes as Adjutant and a Mormon, William L. McIntyre, as assistant surgeon. The other orders provided for passage and camping rights on the Indian land as had been requested by Brigham Young.

The next day, July 17, the men of the Battalion were officially on the payroll of the United States Army, but not all of the companies were complete. Instead of the six days that Allen thought would be necessary to complete the enlistment, nearly three weeks had passed and more men were still needed to reach the 500 authorized. Public meetings, impassioned speeches and promises of spiritual rewards had not been enough. In order to reach the 500 goal, the pressure would have to be turned up by the Church leadership.

Everyone in the Mormon camps had been forced to move from their homes in Nauvoo; many had been forced to flee from Far West in Missouri a decade before; and some had been forced to leave their homes in Ohio before that. Each forced move took a terrible physical and emotional toll, and each was an economic disaster for the Mormons. Now they were facing the toughest move of all. Reaching their new homes would take nearly two years of travel over a rough trail nearly 1,000 miles long. More than ever, each family needed every adult male family member to help. When stationary in camps, everyone had to work at building temporary shelters, growing crops, herding cattle, and taking care of all of the essentials of daily life. When moving on the trail, the work was even harder. Each day, camp had to be set up and later broken down, equipment cared for and repaired, food provided, meals cooked, livestock cared for, and campsites guarded around the clock. It is to the credit of the Mormons in Iowa in the Summer of 1846 that nearly 450 men voluntarily enlisted at the request of the Army and the Mormon leadership.

But simple requests were not going to get the remaining fifty recruits. At 10 a.m. on July 17, Brigham Young and some of the Twelve again addressed a meeting in the bowery set up along the Missouri. The bowery was a frame structure with roof coverings of tree branches that served to protect those underneath from the sun and light rain. Young and Heber Kimball addressed the group and called for another forty to fifty recruits to fill the final company. At 10:30 a.m., the "meeting adjourned a few minutes to fill up the companies" (Journal History of the Church, July 17, 1846). Young and his councilors tried direct discussions with individuals to convince them to enlist. Over the next several days, their personal push to enlist the final fifty would continue.

Henry Standage recorded that during services on Sunday, July 19th, Apostle Parley Pratt again asked for recruits and that he (Standage) "gave my name to Cap. Hunt as a soldier though not without counsel from Elder Benson (Ezra Taft Benson) of the Quorum of the 12" (Golder 1928, 139). David Pettegrew, known as "Father Pettegrew" as he was one of the oldest men in the Battalion, recorded that "I was counseled by President Young to go with the Mormon Battalion, it being a particular request" (Ricketts 1996, 17).

Levi Hancock, the brother of Solomon Hancock who originally brought the teaching of Mormon Prophet Joseph Smith to Jefferson Hunt and his wife Celia, records on July 20th that he also enlisted in the Battalion. As a President in the Council of Seventies, Hancock was a General Authority of the Mormon Church. Accordingly, he was the highest ranking Church official in the Battalion, although he enlisted as a private and was made a musician in Company E. Hancock played the fife and recorded his Battalion experiences in his journal and in numerous songs and poems written on the journey.

The Mormon officers of the Battalion received advice and direction from Brigham Young and other members of the Twelve before leaving on the march. On the evening of July 18th, Young and members of the Twelve Apostles met with the officers and non-commissioned officers in a cottonwood grove near the river. The meeting lasted several hours and consisted of the Church leaders encouraging fairness, honesty and respect in dealing with the men. The officers were encouraged to promote civility, not to permit profanity and to have the men follow the tenants of the Church. Finally, three men were selected to go to Fort Leavenworth to collect the first monies paid to the Battalion (Journal History of the Church, July 18, 1846).

While not specifically stated, it can be inferred that during these meetings Brigham Young and his chief councilors stated the importance of the success of the Mormon Battalion to the Mormon people and their great emigration. What can be said is that the officers and most, if not all, of the troops in the Battalion began the march with full knowledge that their religious leaders expected the Battalion to be a successful demonstration of the patriotism and military determination of the Mormon people. Just as important, they understood that the leaders expected the uniform allowance and pay received by the troops would be made available to help finance the migration to the Great Basin or beyond.

Subsequent events suggest that Jefferson Hunt, and possibly Jesse Hunter, were given a secret assignment—locate potential sites for Mormon settlement in California or other parts of the West, and do what was necessary to secure those locations for a Mormon Theocracy. Samuel Brannan was already on his way to California aboard the ship *Brooklyn* and Brigham Young may have not yet have decided on the Great Basin as his final stopping place. The Mormon Battalion could serve as a forward component for the great Mormon migration if Young eventually decided on California as the permanent home for the Saints.

On Monday, July 20th, the men of the first four companies of the Mormon Battalion gathered at Council Bluffs and completed their final preparations for the long march ahead. Those with families said their goodbyes and reassured their loved ones. They gathered the few items they were able to take with them. The men of Company A authorized their officers, led by Jefferson Hunt, to collect the forty-two dollars that would be due them as a uniform allowance at Fort Leavenworth and to send that money back to the camp of the Saints where they thought it would be distributed to the families left behind. The plan called for the first four companies to begin the march toward Fort Leavenworth with the fifth company (Company E) leaving Council Bluffs as soon as it was filled. The long march was about to begin.

As soon as the fifth company was filled, the Battalion was mustered into the Army, and Jefferson Hunt assumed the rank of Captain in the volunteer army. In accordance with the instructions of Brigham Young, Captain Hunt was regarded by the Mormons as their senior captain, or the most senior of all Mormon officers. Even though Hunt had previously held the rank of Major (one grade higher than Captain) in the duly constituted Nauvoo Legion, his new title accurately reflected the rank authorized by the Army for the position he held.

It is difficult to imagine the daunting task facing the Battalion as it prepared to march. Battalion members were facing the prospect of walking over 2,000 miles from Council Bluffs, Iowa to the Pacific Coast. One year later, after their enlistment ended, they would travel to wherever the Mormons had settled. As it turned out, many had to travel an additional 800 miles east to reach their new home in the Valley of the Great Salt Lake, and some even went another 900 miles back to Winter Quarters. Much of this travel would be across deserts and mountains that were largely unknown to them. The Battalion was ready to begin a very difficult task under very difficult circumstances, and it would succeed—but not without difficulties, both natural and manmade.

Chapter 4

The March Begins

The march included more than the men who enlisted in the five companies. The Army also authorized pay for twenty laundresses—positions that were filled by the wives of some of the soldiers. In addition, other wives joined their husbands, and these families brought their children along. Several teenagers who were too young to enlist traveled as servants to the officers, their fathers. There were others also traveling with the Battalion who may have been teamsters or were in some other way attached to one of the families. The number of volunteer officers and enlisted men was about 500, but approximately ninety additional adults and children began the march with the Battalion as well.

Jefferson Hunt's traveling party was by far the largest in the march, totaling twenty-one men, women and children. Enlisted in Company A in addition to Hunt were his oldest son, Gilbert (age twenty-one), who was first corporal, and his second oldest son, Marshall (age seventeen) who was a private. With his wife, Celia, were their other children: Jane (fourteen), John (thirteen), Harriett (eleven), Joseph (nine), Hyrum (five), and the twins, Mary and Parley who had just reached their first birthday on July 12th. The only family member who did not leave on the march was nineteen-year-old Nancy, who was married and stayed in Council Bluffs with her husband. With Hunt's plural wife, Matilda (age eighteen), were her brother, Peter Nease (eleven), and sister, Ellen Nease (nine), who had been adopted into the Hunt family. Two of Hunt's nephews (sons of his sister, Catherine Hunt Kelley), privates Milton Kelley (Company E) and Nicholas Kelley (Company A) and their families also traveled with the party. Nicholas' wife, Sarah, and their child Parley, and Milton's wife, Malinda Allison Kelley, were part of the group. In addition, the elderly English couple, John and Jane Bosco, also traveled with the Hunts. Some accounts list John Bosco as a teamster for Hunt, but because of his age it is more likely that the Boscos were not employees but rather Mormon emigrants that were traveling with the Hunts as they moved west from Nauvoo. Four of this party of twenty-one did not survive the year, and there was one child (Malinda Catherine) born in El Pueblo to Milton's wife, Malinda.

The Hunt family did not leave Council Bluffs with Hunt because they had much to do in preparation for the trip. Rather, they left several days later and caught up with the Battalion at Fort Leavenworth. They left Council Bluffs for good, taking all of their possessions brought from Nauvoo, along with recently purchased supplies needed on the trail. We can assume that they took at least two wagons and associated livestock. Hunt rode a horse, while Gilbert and Marshall probably walked or drove the wagons. Some of the remaining thirteen members of the entourage rode in the wagons, but most walked all or part of the time. Travel by so many in a few wagons would be a difficult and demanding experience.

Each day on the trail, the Hunt family had to begin by breaking up their camp, cooking the morning meal, gathering the oxen and harnessing them to the wagons, packing all of the camp goods into the wagons and then setting off behind the Battalion, which was marching in front. At the end of a long day's travel, the family set up a new camp, tended the oxen, gathered fuel—wood or buffalo chips—to start the fire, cook an evening meal, and set up their tents and bedding for the night. The following day, the process was repeated. Travel across the plains, mountains and deserts of the West involved a lot of work and effort by everyone old enough to do a job for the family.

The older children—Jane, John, Harriett and Peter—played an important role in caring for the family needs, and the children learned important and useful skills while doing so. Young John Hunt applied his skills nine years later as a teamster and postal courier across the Mojave Desert and Great

Basin, carrying mail and goods between San Bernardino and Salt Lake City for his father.

Companies A, B, C and D began the march from Council Bluffs on July 21, 1846. They traveled only four miles to Mosquito Creek. That day, Brigham Young arrived from Winter Quarters across the Missouri only to find that the companies had marched without finishing the rolls and lists of the enlisted men that he needed to determine who was in the Battalion and how much money might be collected from them for the migration. Allen, however, was leaving much later than he had planned and needed to get the Battalion marching toward Fort Leavenworth.

The following morning, Company E joined the others and the Battalion was complete. The march now began in earnest, with the musicians playing the song "The Girl I Left Behind." The Battalion's first major goal was Fort Leavenworth, about 180 miles to the south. They followed the road along the eastern side of the Missouri River in the state of Missouri.

That second day out, Private Samuel Boley was very sick but continued in one of the wagons. He died later that night, becoming the first fatality of the march. By the fourth day of the march, many of the men were beginning to feel the physical pressure and pain of constant walking. Levi Hancock summed up the feelings of many when he complained that his feet were very sore and that he depended on the support of others to continue (Hancock 2000, 75).

As the Mormons moved south along the Missouri, they were marching uncomfortably close to their enemies who drove them from Far West. At one point, they were within thirty to forty miles of their former homes. In a few instances, they actually recognized members of the mobs that had driven them out of Missouri in the late 1830s. Many of the Missourians who had been so keen to drive the Mormons out of the country were very concerned that such a large body of them were marching through their communities. Fortunately, there were no incidents between the Mormons and their former enemies. The Missourians watched in amazement as the 500 of the Battalion marched smartly through their towns.

Of some concern to the Mormons, however, were the mounted volunteer companies under the command of Colonel Sterling Price, a prominent anti-Mormon Missourian who had proven to be their enemy at Far West and was leading a force toward Santa Fe at the same time. During one incident, a supply of flour being delivered to the hungry Battalion was delayed by Price and was delivered only after Colonel Allen sent specific orders to him. Allen knew of the anti-Mormon background of many of the Missourians and was committed to protecting his Battalion. For this, Allen would be fondly remembered by the Mormons of the Battalion and those at Council Bluffs.

When word of Polk's call for volunteers had reached Missouri in May, Governor John C. Edwards called on prominent Democrats Alexander Doniphan and Sterling Price to recruit volunteers. Both enthusiastically embraced the cause and began to recruit and lead mounted volunteers to join the Army of the West. Both Doniphan and Price were well known to the Mormons from their Missouri days. As was discussed in a prior chapter, Alexander Doniphan, in his capacity as a lawyer, represented the Mormons; then as a general in the Missouri militia, he is credited with once saving the lives of Joseph Smith and other Church leaders. Sterling Price, on the other hand, did not regard the Mormons favorably and was considered to be their enemy in Missouri. As a result, the members of the Mormon Battalion were comfortable with Colonel Doniphan, but wary of Colonel Price and his men.

Doniphan led his regiment out of Fort Leavenworth about the same time the Mormon Battalion arrived. Price and his regiment trained at the Fort and departed Westward on August 10th, three days before the first Mormon contingent left. They arrived in Santa Fe about the first of October, a week before the first Mormons. Therefore, for much of the 850 mile march from Fort Leavenworth to Santa Fe, the Mormons and Price's Missourians were in close proximity. Since the Mormons were on foot and the Missourians were mounted, their daily rate of travel varied, but they occasionally camped near each other and their paths crossed often. Both units were heavily armed and neither trusted the other, creating tension for most of the journey.

The Mormon Battalion marched into Fort Leavenworth on Saturday morning, August 1, 1846. Most of the regular troops had left with Kearny on June 30th, leaving only a small contingent of regular troops at the Fort. Six companies of Missouri volunteers were at the Fort obtaining supplies for the trip to Santa Fe. The Battalion was issued one tent and cooking utensils for every six man unit, called a "mess"; they shared a tent and cooking duties and ate together. Levi Hancock wrote that James Pace was his company's First Lieutenant, Andrew Lytle was the Second Lieutenant and that he and David Pettegrew were part of their mess (Hancock 2000, 25). Hancock, Pettegrew, Pace and Lytle, along with others, were soon to play major roles in the events that nearly led to the dissolution of the Mormon Battalion.

On the following Monday and Tuesday, the men were issued their firearms. Jefferson Hunt's Company A was issued ninety-three muskets and "4 Rifles Half St. Harpers Ferry" (Ricketts 1996, 38). The former referred to the Model 1816 U.S. Flintlock Musket which had a .69 caliber smooth bore barrel forty-two inches long. The latter probably referred to the 1803 flintlock with a .54 caliber rifled barrel 33 to 35 inches long and a stock that went only half-way along the barrel. Daniel Tyler states that "a few cap-lock yaugers for sharpshooting and hunting purposes" were also issued (Tyler 1881, 136). This probably referred to Model 1842 percussion cap muskets which had .69 caliber smoothbore barrels forty-two inches long, which would be more suitable in shooting game, since there was no perceptible delay between the trigger pull and discharge as there was with the flintlock weapons. With percussion cap muskets, it was much easier for the shooter to hold his aim while firing.

Each man was issued a bayonet and scabbard, associated tools, cartridge boxes, belts and assorted items. Two hundred rounds of ammunition (a ball and black powder in a paper cartridge) were issued for each man. The only common item of uniform equipment issued to each volunteer was a large white leather belt that everyone was instructed to keep clean. In the event of a combat engagement, this belt would enable each man to quickly identify his fellow Battalion soldiers. No uniform clothes were issued and each person was free to wear whatever civilian clothes they wished, as long as they wore the white belt.

After weapons were issued, the basic manual of arms was taught and there was some drilling of the companies. Each company was permitted to pool its funds to buy a wagon and mules to carry its tents and heavier equipment. While the wagons lightened their load, each soldier marched carrying the ten pound rifle and associated equipment plus a knapsack, a three pint canteen, extra clothes and a blanket. With more than 1,800 miles to go, the burden of the individual Battalion soldier had gotten heavier.

Brigham Young's emissaries, Parley Pratt, John Taylor and Orson Hyde, arrived in Fort Leavenworth on August 4th to collect the men's uniform allowance, which was paid the following day. Each Battalion member received $42.00: $3.50 per month for a twelve month period, as had been stipulated by Colonel Allen. Young and other leaders assumed that most of the money would be sent back for the benefit of the families left behind and the Saints on the migration. However, of the $21,000 collected by the men, less than $6,000 was given to Pratt, Taylor and Hyde to take back to Council Bluffs. Young was not pleased and expressed his displeasure in many Sunday services over the following months. Much of the money that was taken back was not given to the remaining families but was used to stock Young's store and to finance other parts of the migration. Many of the families justifiably felt they had not received the money sent them by their men in the Battalion.

During the time the Battalion was at Fort Leavenworth, several non-Mormons there enlisted in the Battalion and several Mormons who had not left Council Bluffs with the Battalion also arrived. By August 7th, Jefferson Hunt's family also arrived at Fort Leavenworth (Ricketts 1996, 40).

The march of the Battalion from Council Bluffs to Fort Leavenworth took the men through several small communities where some were able to obtain liquor and drank to excess. Liquor was available at the fort, and once again, some soldiers overindulged. Levi Hancock was concerned by the excessive drinking and asked David Pettegrew to visit each mess and talk to the men. Pettegrew's efforts proved successful; after August 9th the reports of drunkenness decreased.

Near the fort and at various points along the Santa Fe Trail to the west were groups of "sutlers" or traders who prospered by selling to the soldiers and others on the trail. The sutlers main commodity was liquor, but they also sold knives, firearms, ammunition, items of clothing, food and other necessities that might be needed on the trail. The Mormon and Missouri volunteers moving west were a tempting target for the sutlers, so they would shadow the soldiers along the trail. In at least one case involving a sutler named Pomeroy from Missouri, Jefferson Hunt and the Battalion's officers reached an agreement permitting him to accompany and supply the Battalion. Pomeroy, Hunt, and the Mormons again crossed paths in the West before the decade was over.

After two weeks at Fort Leavenworth, the Battalion finally began its march to Santa Fe on August 13, 1846. Colonel Allen was sick and directed Jefferson Hunt to lead the march forward to Council Grove, where he planned to rejoin the Battalion. In the mid-August heat, Companies A, B and E started forward, while the two remaining companies prepared to leave two days later. The heat was oppressive and a number of men were sick. William Coray says that seventeen men in his Company B were sick, as were five in Company E. Hunt's Company A left their sick at the fort to catch up later. The sick rode in wagons whenever possible and the companies traveled at a leisurely pace, strung out across the Plains.

Having moved about fifty miles southeast of Fort Leavenworth, the lead companies stopped travel on August 17th. Two days later, the remaining two companies caught up and the Battalion was nearly complete again. That afternoon, a violent thunderstorm hit the camp, drenching everyone. Lightning and thunder was constant and the heavy rain was punctuated by periods of heavy hail. Fearsome winds leveled nearly every tent and blew over two of the large military supply wagons. William Coray's wife, Melissa, jumped from their wagon as it was blown nearly 150 feet by the windstorm. No one recorded seeing a funnel cloud, but the thunderstorm was so powerful and the wind damage so great that the men named the site "Hurricane Point" (Golder 1928, 148).

Jefferson Hunt's family was not spared by the storm. Daniel Tyler writes:

> "There were many sick in our camp, among whom were Mrs. Celia Hunt, wife of Senior Captain Jefferson Hunt, and her twin babes, who were taken with chills and fever before leaving Fort Leavenworth. They were very sick. The matron lady happened to be in her wagon, while her husband held the babes in the tent, which blew down. With much difficulty the Captain kept the little ones from drowning and suffocating. As everything was wet they were forced to sleep in their wet clothes. Strange to say, with all the exposure, neither the good lady nor her 'dear angels,' as she termed her babes, had any more chills and fever. My recollection is that others, also, were cured by this wonderful shower bath" (Tyler 1881, 140).

Nearly 1,000 miles to the west of Fort Leavenworth, a small group of just less than 100 emigrants were struggling to cut and clear a wagon passage out of the canyons on the western slope of the Wasatch Mountains. Following the bad advice of a promoter named Lansford Hastings, this party spent fourteen days traveling a mere thirty-five miles down the slopes into the Valley of the Great Salt Lake (Morgan 1963, 262-263). While the Mormon Battalion was camped at Hurricane Point, the band of emigrants to California cleared a road used the following year by Brigham Young and the first Pioneers to settle Salt Lake City.

This emigrant group was led by James Frazier Reed and two brothers, George and Jacob Donner. In less than two months, they would be trapped in the snows of the Sierra Nevada Mountains, and the Donner Party tragedy would capture national attention, influencing thousands of gold seekers in 1849 and other travelers for the next two decades. Battalion members escorting General Kearny eastward in the summer of 1847 would be among the first to witness the horrors of the Donner camps at present day Truckee, California.

The snowbound group that became known as the Donner Party was not one homogeneous unit that set out to conquer the Western trails together. As C.F. McGlashan, the first to author a history of the events stated: "The formation of the company known as the Donner Party was purely accidental. The union of so many emigrants into one train was not occasioned by any preconcerted arrangement" (McGlashan 1993, 19). The Donner/Reed Party at one time consisted of several hundred wagons. By the time the decision was made to follow the Hastings Cutoff, only a handful of the original group remained and a few new families and wagons joined as they caught up with the party. The last group to join, the Graves family, did so as the wagons were trying to make it through the most difficult part of the Wasatch canyons.

Along the Humboldt River in central Nevada, three hundred miles west of the Great Salt Lake, James Reed, the acknowledged leader of the Donner/Reed Party, was involved in an altercation with a teamster named Snyder. Reed stabbed the man to death in what appeared to be self-defense. An impromptu court was held by the camp, and Reed was banished from the train. Leaving his family and possessions behind, Reed successfully crossed the Sierras before the snow closed the passes. His efforts to organize rescue parties from Sutter's Fort brought the plight of the stranded to the attention to the Californians and were key to the survival of many early the next Spring.

Wagon train travel was not as organized as it might seem. Different outfits traveled at different speeds, with some wagons and stock moving faster than others. Personality conflicts often caused hard feelings among travelers, particularly when everyone was forced to be together for long periods. Travelers often elected officers for their trains and hired guides, but then chose to ignore both when confronted with difficult circumstances on the trail.

As a consequence, the Westward Migration was constantly reconfiguring itself. Some wagons would pull ahead of others and join new trains to the front; others might drop behind and join trains to the rear. Some travelers tried to find other groups with whom they were more compatible; still others were abandoned by their traveling companions or forced to leave existing groups or trains and fend for themselves. Such instability was the norm. The only major exceptions to this can be found within many of the migrations organized by and for the benefit of the Mormons, and then only because of the commonality of the religion and force of personality of the Church leadership.

But even the resolve and best intentions of the most loyal Mormons would be challenged by the difficulties faced by the Mormon Battalion.

As the Battalion moved west from Fort Leavenworth, each day made communication with the Church Leadership and with military commanders more difficult. East of Fort Leavenworth, communication was facilitated by mounted couriers traveling between communities, riverboats plying the waters of the rivers and canals, trains and an organized postal system. To the west of Fort Leavenworth, communication was limited to the speed that mounted couriers could travel with messages and mail. And that communication was often interrupted or slowed by weather, hostile Indians, and other conditions not common in the East.

For this reason, military commanders in Washington and in the field such as General Kearny, and leaders of other organizations, such as Brigham Young, depended heavily on the ability of their subordinates to carry out instructions and to make day-to-day decisions based on the circumstances at hand. The selection of these subordinates and the delegation of authority were key to the success of any endeavor where communications were slow. Decisions had to be made as the conditions warranted and could not wait weeks or months. The success of any organizational unit operating under these conditions depended entirely on the ability and judgment of the local leaders. The Mormon Battalion was no exception.

When Stephen Watts Kearny selected James Allen to organize the Mormon Battalion and lead it forward to California, he issued orders only one page in length—a sign of confidence that Colonel Allen could get the job done with minimal instruction. Relying on judgment and experience, Allen began to carry out those instructions. When it became apparent that he was not going to raise troops on his own, he enlisted the aid of Brigham Young and the other leaders. After it became apparent that their aid was contingent upon obtaining permission to camp on Indian Lands, Allen reached an agreement on his own without having to contact superiors in Washington or elsewhere. He understood his orders and obligations and exercised his authority to achieve them.

Similarly, it was understood by Young that when Jefferson Hunt was made senior Captain of the Mormons in the Battalion, ultimate responsibility for decisions would fall on Hunt and he would rely on his experience and best judgment to reach those decisions. Unlike Kearny's order to Allen, we have no initial written communication from Young to Hunt. However, we do know they discussed the mission before separating at Council Bluffs, and we can assume that Young made it clear to Hunt and the other officers of the Battalion that he expected the march of the Battalion to be successful.

When Brigham Young selected the captains of each company and recommended George Dykes as Adjutant, he did so believing they were the best and most qualified people available for the successful execution of the assignment. Young did not base his selection on individual popularity or standing within the Church. Rather, his selections were based on loyalty to the Church and First Presidency, ability to carry out the assignment, experience in making good decisions, and demonstrated leadership. Young expected Hunt and the other officers to make difficult decisions when necessary and to implement them as required. He did not expect the officers to win a popularity contest.

Unknown to Jefferson Hunt and the other officers, the stage had been set for the first of several severe tests of the resolve of the Battalion's officers and men. During the first month of the Battalion's existence, seeds of dissent had been sown which were about to surface.

Chapter 5

Dissention and Decision

Once the first of the recently discharged Battalion soldiers reached their new homes in the Valley of the Great Salt Lake in the late Summer and Fall of 1847, they, their families and their brethren in the Church recognized that the march of the Battalion had been a great success and a tremendous accomplishment. Former Battalion members could look back with pride and say they were an important part of the history of both the United States and of the Mormon Church. As the years progressed, the role of the Battalion gained even more importance in the collective memory of the Saints. Eventually, Battalion veterans were universally acknowledged as heroes by their fellow Saints, and their contributions and efforts were seen as nothing short of miraculous.

What was not acknowledged was that dissent was present from the beginning and nearly caused the disintegration of the Battalion. During the first two and one-half months, four major leadership crises hit the fledgling Battalion. If successful, any of the four could have caused the Battalion's collapse. Instead, the dissent was successfully handled by Jefferson Hunt and the other officers as it occurred, and with the assumption of command by Colonel Philip St. George Cooke in Santa Fe, the dissention began to dissipate and no longer threatened the Battalion.

Daniel Tyler, a sergeant in Company C, who wrote the first book history of the Battalion, published in 1881, does not mention the first crisis even though his company was principally involved and he had full knowledge of the events as they occurred. Similarly, other diarists such as Levi Hancock and Henry Standage mentioned other events of the day but did not refer to the crisis. A few writers mention the internal conflicts, especially William Coray, the first sergeant of Company B, whose remarkable journal is one of the best written during the march.

On the evening of the fierce storm at Hurricane Point, the first crisis came to a head. Dissent had begun within Companies C and D shortly after they left Council Bluffs. Many in those companies were dissatisfied with the captains selected by Brigham Young: James Brown of Company C, and Nelson Higgins of Company D. When Companies A, B and E left Fort Leavenworth on August 13th, things began to deteriorate within the other two companies. Captain Brown was ill at the Fort and First Lieutenant George Rosecrans was effectively in charge. The day after the first three companies left the Fort, Adjutant George Dykes, acting on behalf of the ailing Colonel Allen, ordered Lieutenant Rosecrans to have his company clean up the campground just vacated by the three departed companies. Rosecrans refused to carry out the order. When Captain Brown heard this, he, in turn, ordered his company to clean the campground. This set the stage for more trouble.

Recognizing deficits in Captain Brown's leadership skills, Robert Clift, a Lieutenant under Brown's command, attempted to persuade the captain's wife, Mary, to help convince her husband to resign. Obviously, this didn't sit well with Brown and when he heard Clift's comments, he got his pistol and threatened to shoot the Lieutenant. Fortunately, Brown could not find Clift and the immediate danger passed. Clift, however was not about to let the matter drop. He felt that Brown's threat to shoot him was grounds for a court martial and proceeded to file charges. Adjutant Dykes sought to resolve the matter informally and got both sides to agree to a settlement: Clift would drop the charges and Brown would apologize to Clift and the Company. However, the dissenters believed that Captain Brown spoke too long and they reinstated the charges.

This was the status of the dispute when Companies C and D arrived at Hurricane Point just as the storm began to rage. Following the storm, everyone gathered the wind-strewn equipment and attempted to dry out. But Companies C and D did more; they held a "toast meeting" to determine the level of support within their companies for removing Captain Brown and Captain Higgins. With the sutlers nearby and the marchers just a few days from Fort Leavenworth, there was no shortage of whiskey at hand.

William Coray recorded the following in his journal:

> "The secret of the matter appeared to be this: Brown had done wrong and Rosecranse [sic] and Clift wanted to supplant him, which was evident from a toast meeting held in the evening of the 19th instant in Company C, Rosecranse [sic] and Clift being at the head enjoined it upon everyone to drink and give a toast expressive of their sentiments in regard to Capt. Brown and Higgins, the latter being the Captain of D Co. Cyrus Canfield, the 3rd lieu of the 4th co. also craved the place of his capt. The toasts ran like this: Here is to Capt. Brown that he may be discharged and sent back to the Bluffs, he having disgraced himself as an officer and that his place may be filled by Lieut Rosecranse [sic], who raised the co. Here is to Capt. Higgins that he may be discharged and one to take his place, meaning Canfield, who it rightfully belongs to" (Ricketts 1996, 44).

Levi Hancock, the highest ranking ecclesiastical official in the Battalion did not mention this incident, but recorded a rather strange dream which may or may not be related to the attempt to overthrow the captains. Using the date of August 20th, Hancock wrote of the storm and mentioned Melissa Coray's frightening ride in the wind-blown carriage. In his dream, Hancock saw some Mormons cutting their own throats and graphically described the scene. He was very disturbed by this dream and sought out Andrew Lytle, Thomas Woolsey, James Pace and Father Pettegrew to administer to him, which they did. Dimick Huntington, a private in Company D, told Hancock "some of the brethren had defiled themselves and many witnesses had seen it with their own eyes and could witness against two" (Hancock 2000, 37). Hancock took the report of adultery and drunkenness at Fort Leavenworth to mean his dream had merit and something needed to be done to restore the moral character of the Battalion.

Hancock pondered what to do and decided that he could not directly lay hands on the offenders to bless them and drive the evil spirits away for fear that he, himself, would be seized by the same evil. He called on Jefferson Hunt and suggested that the Captain hold some meetings with the Battalion to counter the evil influence that seemed to have overtaken many.

It's unclear if Hancock's dream happened to coincide with the attempt to overthrow the commanders of the two companies or if it was an allegory of the ruinous behavior that the Battalion was facing. We do know that Hancock did take some credit for getting Hunt involved in the resolution of the problems, and that Hancock also used the fear of moral collapse to foster his position as the leading ecclesiastical authority in the Battalion.

On the morning of August 20th, Hunt convened a meeting of the officers of the Battalion to deal with the insubordination in Companies C and D. He was not aware of the "toast meetings" the previous night, but realized the success of the Battalion required recognition of the officers as designated by Brigham Young a month before. Sergeant William Coray recorded the meeting and the firm hand Hunt used to deal with the dissent:

> "Capt. Hunt said this matter had grown completely out of hand. He and the others gave the Capt [Brown] and his subordinates [Rosecrans and Clift] a complete dressing out. Both parties made every acknowledgement asked for and the Capt. [Brown] retained his standing" (Ricketts 1996, 44).

Later that day, the officers met with the entire Battalion to address the moral issues facing the men. Levi Hancock opened the meeting and was fol-

lowed by Daniel Tyler, William Hyde and Jefferson Hunt. William Coray said
of Hunt's speech:

> "the latter [Hunt] told his feelings at considerable length and
> with great animation. He fairly laid the ax at the root of the tree
> and discountenanced vice in the strongest terms, which impart-
> ed a good spirit to the Battalion and checked insubordination
> materially. Capt. Hunt advised the captains of cos. to get their
> men together often and pray for them, and teach them the prin-
> ciples of virtue and to be united with each other" (Ricketts 1996,
> 44-45).

Throughout his life, Jefferson Hunt was regarded as an effective and
influential public speaker. He received requests to deliver messages at funer-
als and church services frequently, and speeches at public events, such as the
Fourth of July or Utah's Pioneer Day. While we know that Hunt frequently
gave speeches, the report by William Coray is one of the few examples which
detail the quality and style of his delivery. Others also recorded that Hunt's
speech was well received; Levi Hancock says "the senior Capt. addressed the
same handsomely" (Hancock 2000, 37).

The dissention in Companies C and D was resolved to the benefit of the
Battalion, and was mostly forgotten. Within a month, Captain Higgins would
leave the Battalion and lead a group of families and sick Battalion members up
the Arkansas River to El Pueblo (Colorado), and Captain Brown would lead
a similar group from Santa Fe to El Pueblo a month after that. With Canfield
and Rosecrans in charge, Companies C and D would be no more troublesome
than Companies A and B. The future problems seemed to be concentrated
with some of the officers and men of Company E.

Jefferson Hunt maintained a long-term friendship with Robert Clift,
who reenlisted for an additional six months in July 1847. At Hunt's request,
Clift later penned a letter to Brigham Young proposing a Southern California
settlement for the Mormons. He would go on to be one of the early colonists,
along with Hunt, of San Bernardino where he served as sheriff. In 1859, Clift
was killed by Indians while employed by Hunt as a mail and express carrier in
Nevada (Leo Lyman 1996, 418-419).

In his desire to reduce the dissention and resolve the moral and religious issues, William Coray says that Hunt called on Levi Hancock and David Pettegrew to "take charge of the spiritual affairs of the camp" (Journal History of the Church, August 23, 1846). This was a reasonable request, since Hancock was a General Authority of the Church and, as such, the highest ranking Church official in the Battalion. Pettegrew was highly respected by everyone, was Hancock's close confident and was often given religious assignments by him.

What was not apparently as clear to Levi Hancock was the role of Jefferson Hunt as both the military leader of the Mormons and as Brigham Young's designated senior leader and representative. Over the next eleven months, Hancock and his associates would take a more divisive stance challenging Hunt's leadership and that of the other officers on a number of occasions. It can be argued that Hancock used his status as a General Authority to attempt to take control of the men of the Battalion. And it partially worked; immediately following the discharge of the Battalion, about two-thirds followed Hancock's leadership. It can be said that the role of spiritual leader given to Hancock would come back to haunt Hunt (Christiansen 1993, 55).

The next day, August 21st, Adjutant Dykes and the sick from Fort Leavenworth arrived at the camp with word that Colonel Allen was very ill. Dykes was upset to find the Battalion had not made it to Council Grove, which was an Army supply point. According to William Coray, Dykes scolded Hunt for not marching rapidly to Council Grove as directed by Allen. The slow start found the Battalion nearly out of supplies and thirty miles from the next re-supply point (Ricketts 1996, 45). Several companies of Sterling Price's mounted Missouri volunteers passed the Battalion and the sutlers continued their thriving business selling liquor, clothes and other supplies to the soldiers from Missouri and the Battalion. The next day, the march resumed, leaving Hurricane Point.

At 6 a.m. on the morning of August 23, 1846, Colonel Allen died at Fort Leavenworth. News of his tragic death reached the Battalion three days later, on August 26th.

During the short time Allen was associated with the Mormons, he became highly respected by both Church leaders and the men of the Battalion. Allen was true to his word, granting Brigham Young access to Indian lands across the Missouri River. He treated the men of the Battalion with fairness and compassion and stood up for them when confronted by Sterling Price's insolence on the march to Fort Leavenworth. In the two short months that he was among the Mormons, he gained nearly mythic status. He was one of the very few governmental agents who supported the Mormons and their beliefs unconditionally. His loss was felt by everyone in the Mormon community who had known him.

Sergeant William Hyde said of Allen:

"This information struck a damper to our feelings as we considered him a worthy man, and from the kind treatment which the Battalion had received from him, we had begun to look upon him as our friend, and a person from whom we should receive · kind treatment" (Yurtinis 1975, 97).

Similarly, William Coray wrote:

"Capt. J. Allen was a good man; he stood up for our rights better than many of our brethren; he obtained for us a good fit out with plenty of provisions, was kind to the families journeying with us, fed private teams at public expense, was never auster [sic] or tyrannical, which is the case with nearly all the regulars. In short, he was an exception among officers of the U.S. Army" (Yurtinis 1975, 97).

The agreement originally made between Allen and Brigham Young stipulated the Colonel would command the Mormon Battalion, and that if anything happened to Allen, command would transfer to the Mormon captains in succession. If Allen ceased to lead the Battalion for any reason, the command would go to Jefferson Hunt as Captain of Company A. This agreement and its implementation led to the second major leadership crisis within the Battalion in ten days.

Lieutenants Pace and Gully and eight men had been sent to Fort Leavenworth to bring the wagons and sick detail back and to inquire about the health of Allen. Pace and Gully were present when he died. Lieutenant Colonel Clifton Wharton was the commanding officer of Fort Leavenworth and suggested that either Pace or Gully return to Winter Quarters to inform Brigham Young and the Mormon leadership of Allen's death. Pace left at noon on August 23rd, rode to the north, and arrived at Winter Quarters at 10 a.m. on August 26th, the same day that Lieutenant Samuel Gully, Quartermaster Sergeant Sebert Shelton, and the others who had ridden to the southwest, caught up with the Battalion near Council Grove, Kansas. Thus, Young and Jefferson Hunt, who were more than 200 miles apart, heard the news of Allen's death at the same time.

Upon hearing the news, Captain Hunt of Company A assumed command of the Mormon Battalion on August 26th. Yet, only three days later, on August 29th, he relinquished the command to a regular Army officer. The reasons for this decision were not known or understood by the majority of the men of the Battalion. Many criticized Hunt for giving up command. Nearly everyone was dissatisfied with the short-term consequences of his decision. However, this one turn of events may very well have led to the eventual stunning success of the Mormon Battalion.

After Allen's death and before departing to rejoin the Battalion, Lieutenant Samuel Gully wrote a letter to be taken by Lieutenant James Pace to Brigham Young at Winter Quarters. In it Gully told of Allen's death and reported that Lieutenant Andrew Jackson Smith of the regular Army intended to take control of the Battalion. Gully questioned the wisdom of that action and asked Young to respond with his counsel when he sent an emissary to Santa Fe to collect the Battalion's pay (Bigler and Bagley 2000, 92). Coincidentally, Surgeon George B. Sanderson, a Missouri physician who had been appointed as the Battalion's surgeon by Allen before his death, also wrote a letter to Young reporting the death and advising that he and Lieutenant Smith were going out to accompany the Battalion to General Kearny at Santa Fe.

In response to Gully's request, Brigham Young quickly drafted a letter. Addressed to "Samuel Gully, Quartermaster and the Mormon Battalion," it is clear that the letter was intended for all of the officers and men of the Battalion. In it Young states:

> "You will all doubtless recollect that Colonel Allen repeatedly stated to us and the Battalion that there would be no officer in the Battalion, except himself, only from among our people; that if he fell in battle, or was sick, or disabled by any means, the command would devolve on the ranking officer, which would be the Captain of Company A, and B, and so on, according to letter. Consequently the command must devolve on Captain Jefferson Hunt, whose duty we suppose to be to take the Battalion to Bent's Fort, or wherever he has received marching orders for, and there wait further orders from General Kearny, notifying him by express of Colonel Allen's decease at the earliest date" (Bigler and Bagley 2000, 96).

Brigham Young instructed the Battalion to inform General Kearny of Allen's agreement. Young also drafted a letter to Kearny informing him of the understanding reached with Allen. When the Battalion eventually reached Santa Fe, Kearny, who by then knew of Allen's death, was on his way to California and had already issued other orders regarding the command. The Battalion did not see Kearny until well after their arrival in California the following year, and his measures resolved the command issue to the benefit of everyone involved.

Since the Battalion was over 200 miles southwest of Young at Winter Quarters, and since they were marching westward each day, some time passed before Young's letter caught up with the Battalion. The letter to Gully and the Battalion was finally delivered by Pace on September 17th, nearly three weeks after the Battalion learned of Allen's death and the officers resolved the command issue.

The day after hearing of Allen's death, the Battalion arrived at Council Grove where they picked up two cannon, a portable blacksmith shop and forty provision wagons. These, along with the twelve family wagons and five private baggage wagons already with the Battalion, were soon joined by a group of traders en route to Santa Fe with thirteen more freight wagons.

That day, August 27th, William Coray recorded:

> "The minds of the brethren were much engaged meditating upon our condition after the death of Col. Allen. To this end the council met and decided that Capt. Hunt should lead the battalion. There were, however, two contrary minds as usual, viz. Lt Dykes and Shelton." (Ricketts 1996, 47).

We don't know what objections Dykes and Shelton had or who they felt should lead. The logical leader and the leader pre-designated by Brigham Young and Allen was Jefferson Hunt. In an interesting footnote, Henry Standage reported that Shelton was arrested the following day "for talking disrespectfully to the officers" (Golder 1928, 152). He was tried the day after that, and was acquitted.

At 1 p.m., following Shelton's trial, Jefferson Hunt assembled the Battalion and marched them with full arms to a grove by Council Grove Creek for Colonel Allen's memorial service. The men formed a square with the officers in the center. Adjutant Dykes delivered the sermon which spoke of the resurrection, and was followed by Hunt who spoke about the Mormons volunteer spirit, loyalty, and duty to the government. He

> "reproved the young men in particular for their disorderly conduct, drunkenness, and profanity exhorting them to conduct themselves in a manner to secure the favor of heaven and the approbation of the community of Saints" (Yurtinis 1975, 101).

Levi Hancock sang a song and David Pettegrew ended the service with a prayer. A number of the ever-present Missouri volunteers and sutlers witnessed the ceremony and were very impressed.

Philip Thompson, the Battalion's guide, attended Allen's service. During the Mexican War, the Army made use of former mountain men as guides for many of the units traveling to California. These men were experienced on some portions of the routes, knew many of the Indian tribes along the way, and were experienced in living and surviving in the mountains and deserts of the West. In unfamiliar territory, the guides used their skills as scouts to locate water, animal feed, and the best road to follow. Thompson was an experienced trapper, mountain man, and horse thief who had traveled along the Arkansas River and had been in California. He had settled in Oregon, but apparently was at Fort Leavenworth in time to be hired by the Army to pilot the Battalion to the West (Hafen 2001, Vol III, 339-347). William Coray recorded that the ceremony "melted the old guide [Thompson] into tears and caused groanings among the Missourians" (Yurtinus 1975, 101).

Not long after the memorial, the entourage of Lieutenant Andrew Jackson Smith and Dr. George Sanderson arrived from Fort Leavenworth. Their party included a paymaster, Major Walker, and several servants, including a man named Pomeroy who had been Allen's servant. Some of these servants may have been slaves or former slaves who served as cooks and valets for the officers. Within hours of their arrival, the second major crisis during the Battalion's march surfaced.

Lieutenant Andrew Jackson Smith, thirty-one years old, was a graduate of West Point's Class of 1838. He had been at Fort Leavenworth with Kearny, but had been instructed to remain and follow with other units. His immediate orders were to escort a "large train of ord[nance] stores" from the Fort to a regiment of the Missouri Volunteers (Bigler and Bagley, 94).

As an experienced cavalry officer, Lieutenant Smith conducted training of the Missouri mounted units, including Sterling Price's, prior to their departure from Leavenworth. He was not impressed with the volunteer units he had seen there. Like all young army officers of the time, Smith saw the Mexican War as a great opportunity to advance his career. In the years before the war, the Army was small and there was little opportunity for advancement. The Mexican War changed all that. However, notice best came to those who were able to distinguish themselves in combat. Lieutenant Smith had little chance to be noticed a thousand miles from the front. When the opportunity came to move to a possible combat area, he was quick to act.

Lieutenant Smith went on to have a distinguished military career. While his service during the Mexican War was not notable, he served in California and Oregon during the 1850s where he was involved in several Indian skirmishes. During the Civil War, Smith was involved in a number of actions and received a temporary field promotion to the rank of Major General in the Union Army. Following the Civil War, he was made commander of the newly created Seventh Cavalry with the rank of Colonel. The Seventh Cavalry, of course, was the same unit that achieved fame under the command of George Armstrong Custer at the Battle of the Little Big Horn several years later. Smith finished his public career serving as the postmaster at St. Louis for twenty years.

Upon Allen's death, Lieutenant Smith saw the opportunity to command he had been hoping for. He drafted a letter to Kearny and the Army's Adjutant General stating that he was on his way to report to General Kearny and "with the consent of the Mormons, take charge of the Battalion at Council Grove & conduct it to Genl. Kearny, or until I receive orders from him in relation to them" (Bigler and Bagley, 95). Lieutenant Colonel Wharton, the commander of the post, concurred with this plan of action.

Dr. George B. Sanderson had been appointed to serve as the Battalion's surgeon by Allen before his death. Sanderson was a volunteer from Missouri who had equipped a hospital wagon with supplies and was at the fort waiting to leave with Allen. Upon the Lieutenant Commander's death, he continued with Lieutenant Smith.

Dr. Sanderson's journal was recently made public after an absence of almost 150 years, when it was acquired by the University of Utah. The journal is complete and detailed in some of his observations, but lacks meaningful discussion of many of the medical issues typically found in a doctor's daily journal. Sanderson makes some derogatory comments about the Mormons, but gives little defense of his position in light of the extensive criticism from Battalion members. In fact, a reader going through the document in one sitting would not get any idea of the seriousness of the view the Battalion soldiers had of their Army surgeon.

The decision that put Lieutenant Smith in command was controversial within the Battalion. News of it was delivered to Young by Hunt's detractors within a few months of the event. It would be nearly two years before Hunt would again see Young and be able to explain in person his actions in deferring command to Smith. Following their arrival in Santa Fe, Hunt and Captain Jesse Hunter felt compelled to write to Young describing what happened after Lieutenant Smith's arrival. In the letter, dated October 17, 1846, Hunt describes how he requested Captain Hunter and Lieutenant Dykes to "examine the Law on the subject that we might be better prepared to decide on the matter for there appeared to be some devission [sic] amongst us" (Bigler and Bagley 2000, 99).

Hunt had previously told the Mormon officers in council that he was prepared to assume command. The day before Lieutenant Smith arrived, the officers again met and

> "Capt Hunter produced the law on the subject—which went to
> show in every respect that it was my wright to lead the Bat & that
> no other could lawfully do it, unless the parties were agreed. . ."
> (Bigler and Bagley 2000, 99-100).

The council of officers agreed with Hunt that he should assume command. Lieutenant Smith arrived the following day and immediately met with Hunt. Smith carried a letter from Major Wharton, commander of Fort Leavenworth, telling Hunt that the government property in the possession of the Battalion "was not receipted for" and advising them to "submit to the command of Lieutenant Smith" which would save them "considerable trouble" (Tyler 1881, 144). Smith told Hunt that the Battalion would be better off if he, a regular Army officer, was in charge.

Hunt told Smith that he was prepared to lead the Battalion to Santa Fe. However, he agreed to put the matter before all of the officers assembled and to follow their decision when the matter was put to a vote.

That evening, the Mormon officers met with the newly-arrived Army officers. The plans at that time called for the Battalion to follow the Santa Fe

Trail along the Arkansas, to Bent's Fort, southwest to Raton Pass, and thence southward to Santa Fe. They expected to be further supplied by provisions placed at Bent's Fort for the Army of the West or by a supply train that was also working its way toward Santa Fe. Accordingly, Lieutenant Smith's first argument to the officers was that the Regular Army officer in charge of those supplies would not know the Mormons and in the absence of any official documentation would not provide them with the needed supplies. However, if Smith and his officers were in charge, they would have the full resources of the Army at their disposal.

Major Walker, the paymaster, then addressed the officers and advised them that they would avoid many difficulties by having the Army officers in charge. Perhaps the most persuasive comment was made by the guide Philip Thompson who told the Mormon officers that "it was the intention of Col. Price, who we all knew was our inverterate enemy, to attach us to his regiment if we did not accept Smith" (Bigler and Bagley 2000, 100).

The only Mormon officer to comment in the presence of the Army officers was Adjutant Dykes, who stated that the Battalion was unable "to make out correct pay rolls and other documents now wanting without some instruction" and, therefore, he favored Lieutenant Smith (Bigler and Bagley 2000, 100). Jefferson Hunt questioned Smith about his intent to "carry out the designs of Lieut. Col. Allen" and stated that he would not relinquish command unless Smith followed those directives. Lieutenant Smith then stated that "such was his intention" (Bigler and Bagley 2000, 100).

Following the presentations by the non-Mormons, they were asked to leave the meeting. The Mormon officers met to discuss who should have command of the Battalion. According to Hunt's letter:

> "The matter was talked over a little, when Capt. Higgins moved that Lieut. Smith should lead us to Santa Fe, which was seconded by Capt. Davis and carried unanimously, Smith was apprised of this and took command the next morning" (Bigler and Bagley 2000, 100).

Daniel Tyler, in his book *A Concise History of the Mormon Battalion* published in 1881, says that three officers, Lieutenants Lorenzo Clark, Samuel Gully and Wesley W. Willis voted against Smith (Tyler 1881, 144). In any case, the second major crisis in the Battalion's short march was resolved. The process that led to the decision was not discussed with the troops and was not understood by all, and that, combined with subsequent hardships caused in part by Smith's command, led to further dissention within the ranks.

The strongest voice favoring Smith was that of Adjutant Dykes, who also felt compelled to write Brigham Young from Santa Fe to explain his actions. In his letter, Dykes stated that he believed Hunt was unable to "fill the station" of commander because he did not know the form to follow in making receipts and requisitions and could not teach others in the Battalion how to do it (Yurtinis 1975, 107). Dykes also reminded Young of his instruction to the officers to learn the ways of the military so that they could be teachers of military tactics and methods upon their return. Dykes felt that the best instruction would come from a West Point-trained officer such as Lieutenant Smith. Dykes made many unpopular decisions as Adjutant, but his strong support for Smith was considered by many in the Battalion to be the worst.

Following the Mexican War, George P. Dykes traveled to Salt Lake City and was sent on the first mission to Scandinavia in 1850, where he was very effective in organizing the first Mormon churches there. Back in Salt Lake City in November 1863, Dykes converted to the Reorganized Church of Jesus Christ of Latter Day Saints. The Reorganized Church, headed by some of Joseph Smith's descendants, split from the original church following Brigham Young's assumption of control of the First Presidency after Joseph Smith's murder. With Dykes' help, the Reorganized Church grew to over 300 members in Salt Lake City in a relatively short time. This desertion and conversion further harmed Dykes' reputation among the Saints in Salt Lake City.

Why did Jefferson Hunt so quickly give up the command of the Mormon Battalion? Everything we know about him leads us to believe that Hunt was a strong-willed, outspoken, loyal servant of his Church and its leadership—especially Brigham Young, who had made it clear to Hunt that as Senior Captain he was to assume command of the Battalion should anything happen to Colonel Allen. Hunt was not a man who would shirk from his responsibilities.

However, Hunt was almost 300 miles from Young and other Church leaders, and about 700 miles away from Stephen Watts Kearny, the overall commander, who was in Santa Fe. Clearly, while he might ask for guidance, the lack of prompt communication meant that any realistic decision would have to be made on the scene and not at some distant location. In fact, the officers of the Battalion sought advice from three sources: Brigham Young, the Army in Washington and General Kearny. And they got three different answers back. Young advised Hunt to take command, but that word did not reach Hunt until September 17th. The Army Adjutant General in Washington directed Captain P.B. Thompson who was stationed in St. Louis to assume command, but Captain Thompson never caught up with the Battalion. They left Santa Fe under the command of Philip St. George Cooke before his arrival. Cooke was Kearny's choice to lead the Battalion to California.

Hunt knew that the difficulty in communicating meant that he and his other officers would be responsible for making the best decision possible regarding the command. He also knew that both Brigham Young and his council and the Mormons in the Battalion strongly preferred that the command go to a Mormon officer following Allen's death. But it is clear from what happened that Hunt realized Smith was best suited to take over the command. As Senior Captain operating under a mandate from both Colonel Allen and Young, Hunt was not obligated to refer the matter to the other officers. In fact, his duty was to assume command unless he saw some overriding reason not to do so.

The process of decision-making in the early Mormon Church usually involved the leader using the counsel of his close advisors and top assistants to reach decisions. The history of the Church is filled with examples of Brigham Young calling together the Quorum of the Twelve Apostles to help him reach a decision. Each was able to express his opinions and arguments. In reality, however, the final decision was that of the leader; the council served to validate that decision and then implement it. So it was with the Battalion. We can be sure that in calling the officers together for a decision, it was understood by everyone that they would follow the lead of their designated leader, Jefferson Hunt, and do his bidding. We can assume that Hunt intended to pass the command to Smith.

Undoubtedly, Hunt would not have given up command and knowingly incurred the wrath of his troops without strong reason to do so. What is the most likely reason for doing so? The lack of ability or knowledge to complete the paperwork is not a strong argument for several reasons. The first is that Army provisioners along the trail at Bent's Fort and at Santa Fe all knew that the Battalion was part of Kearny's Army of the West and expected it. Secondly, it is likely that Smith and/or Walker, both regular Army officers, would have continued on with the Battalion to Santa Fe.

A much stronger reason appears to have been the threat presented by Colonel Sterling Price and his regiment of mounted Missouri Volunteers. Price, the powerful Missouri Democrat and commander of the Second Missouri Mounted Volunteers, was mirroring the route of the Mormon Battalion. He had long been anti-Mormon. Price was the one responsible for chaining up Joseph Smith and his followers in Richmond, Missouri, in November 1838. He actively looked for ways to harass the Mormons of the Battalion—and the Mormons were quite concerned with Price's proximity. In fact, Hunt in his letter to Brigham Young referred to him twice. In addition to reporting the comment made by the guide, Philip Thompson, Hunt closed the letter by saying:

> "We had not provisions to last us more than half way to Santa Fe and should consequently have had to go on one fourth or one half rations, but he [Smith] made a requisition on Col. Price and made him give us about twelve days' rations. This Price would not have done for us under any consideration had we been alone." (Bigler and Bagley 2000, 101).

Thus, Hunt stressed the importance that the nearby presence of Price had on the decision.

It is clear that from the beginning, Brigham Young wanted the Battalion to be a success, both to provide financial assistance, and as a reputation and morale builder. No doubt Young told Hunt that the success of the Bat-

talion was his number one priority. As the Battalion sat on the prairie con-
templating their fate following the loss of Colonel Allen, Hunt had to evaluate
which threat against the Battalion was the greatest. The two biggest challenges
they faced were: first, internal dissention as experienced ten days before and;
second, the possibility of intervention by the strongly anti-Mormon Colonel
Price who was traveling uncomfortably close to them with an undisciplined
force of mostly hostile Missourians. One threat could cause the disintegration
of the Battalion, the other could result in physical confrontation that could
involve injury and death.

The best solution to avoid both threats was for Jefferson Hunt to submit the command of the Battalion to a Regular Army officer—Lieutenant Andrew Jackson Smith. As a non-Mormon commander, Smith would not be influenced by the internal strife and dissention. He could make decisions using
established Army rules and was not subject to internal considerations such as
personal friendships or standing within the Church. Similarly, any attack by a
volunteer regiment commanded by a volunteer officer on a unit commanded
by a Regular Army officer would be a major crime that would not be tolerated
by the Army. In other words, the best way for Hunt to guarantee the success of
the Battalion was to relinquish command to Lieutenant Smith. It appears that
this was his decision, and it was validated by most of the other officers of the
Battalion. By giving up command, Hunt made a major step toward achieving
the success Brigham Young so badly wanted.

The crisis of command was not the only problem Jefferson Hunt faced
during the last few days of August 1846. During the night of August 27th,
Jane Bosco, the elderly English convert who had traveled with the Hunts since
Nauvoo, died at the camp at Council Grove. On the morning of August 30th,
her husband, John Bosco, died. Daniel Tyler says the following:

> "They were very highly respected. They were buried in one
> grave, and a dry substantial stone wall was built around and
> over the tomb, under the supervision of Elisha Averett, to

mark their last resting place and to shield their bodies from the wolves. The covering was of good but unpolished flat rock" (Tyler 1881, 142).

Thus, Jefferson Hunt ended the first full month of the Battalion's march by briefly assuming command—only to give it up a few days later. This was swiftly followed by the grief of losing two close members of his traveling party. The coming month brought even more crises to Hunt and the Battalion.

Chapter 6

Dr. Death

On August 26th, when Gully and Shelton caught up to the Mormon Battalion with the news that Colonel Allen had died, they also delivered a bundle of mail from the Mormon camps and Winter Quarters. One of the letters, dated August 19, 1846, was from Brigham Young and the Twelve and was dictated to Willard Richards, the Clerk for the First Presidency. It read:

> "To Captain Jefferson Hunt and the Captains, Officers, and Soldiers of the Mormon Battalion:
>
> We have the opportunity of sending to Fort Leavenworth, this morning, by Dr. Reed, a package of twenty-five letters, which we improve, with this word of counsel to you all: If you are sick, live by faith, and let the surgeon's medicine alone if you want to live, using only such herbs and mild food as are at your disposal. If you give heed to this counsel, you will prosper; but if not, we cannot be responsible for the consequences. A hint to the wise is sufficient" (Tyler 1881, 146).

One of the standard works, in addition to *The Holy Bible* and the *Book of Mormon*, in the Church of Jesus Christ of Latter Day Saints is the *Doctrine and Covenants*, which is a collection 138 sections of divine revelations and two official declarations. All but three of the revelations and the two declarations were given to Joseph Smith before his murder. Section 42 was given through

Smith on February 9, 1831, in Kirtland, Ohio, and contains 93 verses that can be generally thought of as "Law" given to the Mormons. Section 42, Verse 43 says: "And whosoever among you are sick, and have not faith to be healed, but believe, shall be nourished with all tenderness, with herbs and mild food, and that not by the hand of an enemy." The next verse (44) states: "And the elders of the church, two or more, shall be called, and shall pray for and lay their hands upon them in my name; and if they die they shall die unto me, and it they live they shall live unto me" (Doctrine and Covenants).

Relying on these verses and the teachings of Joseph Smith and his successors, most Mormons believed that herbal medicines were acceptable, while medicines made from minerals were not, and that the laying on of hands was an effective form of treatment. Jefferson Hunt practiced the laying on of hands and was regarded as being particularly effective using this method of affecting a cure for the sick. In retrospect, when considering the medical practices of the time, this Church-approved treatment was probably as effective—and certainly less damaging—than many of the other treatments then used. When composing the letter, Young and the rest of the Twelve relied strongly on Section 42, which was well-known to the soldiers in the Battalion.

In France, a twenty-four-year-old chemistry student, Louis Pasteur, was still several years away from getting his doctorate degree and making his first major discoveries essentially creating the field of crystallography. It would take even more years for Pasteur to firmly establish the role played by germs in diseases. By the 1880s, the medical profession understood that bacteria and viruses caused infectious diseases. Vaccinations were then becoming more common, sanitation practices were being developed and followed, and the first research was being conducted to try to find medicines that would fight infectious diseases. That work eventually led to the development of the first antibiotics fifty years later.

But in 1846, there was no real way to effectively fight an infectious disease, other than to let the human immune system run its course. Doctors in military service were somewhat successful in dealing with wounds using surgical procedures such as amputations or stitching. They did not understand the causes of infections, and therefore could do little or nothing to stop wound infections or contagious diseases. In fact, unsanitary medical procedures in war conditions often spread infections. It is not surprising therefore, that the doctors assigned to military units were called "surgeons," since most of their procedures involved surgery.

In some instances, such as smallpox, tuberculosis and often cholera, people could identify the disease, although they did not know its cause or an effective remedy. In most instances, however, people of the 1840s simply used terms to describe symptoms that might encompass a large number of different diseases. For example "ague" might be used to describe any disease where fever, chills, aches, pains and coughs were present. "Catarrh" might be used to describe a disease where there was sore throat, laryngitis or chest congestion. These terms often encompassed a wide range of diseases from malaria to staph infections, to flu to colds and more. If the disease was hard to identify in the 1840s, its prevention and treatment was even more difficult.

Doctors of the time, however, attempted to treat infectious diseases using some methods we today consider as ludicrous and sometimes even barbaric. One of the most common practices was "purging," which was thought to remove poisons from the body through excretion. The patient was given powerful laxatives to cause the purging process to begin. The most commonly used purgative in the first half of the 1800s was calomel, or mercurous chloride, an inorganic compound. Today, mercury and its various compounds are known to be very toxic, with some forms absorbed by the body faster than others. The most toxic forms of mercury are metallic mercury vapor and organic compounds of mercury such as methyl-mercury. Some bacteria act on metallic mercury or inorganic compounds of mercury to create organic compounds over time.

A dose of any inorganic salt of mercury, including calomel, containing one gram of mercury is considered lethal, although actual amounts needed to kill may vary significantly between individuals and conditions. Since mercury may cause damage to the nervous system or to internal organs such as the kidneys, lethal effects of a calomel overdose may arise over days, weeks or months . . . or not at all. In short, calomel is toxic, but it is not necessarily an immediate killer, and its effects may vary (Toxicological Profile for Mercury).

The use of calomel as a medicine appears to date to ancient times. One of the most important proponents of the use of calomel as a medicine was Dr. Benjamin Rush, a Revolutionary War patriot and signer of the Declaration of Independence. Rush was not only a Founding Father, but with a medical degree from the University of Edinburgh, he was considered to be the pre-eminent physician in America in the late Eighteenth and early Nineteenth Centuries. During a major Yellow Fever outbreak in Philadelphia in 1793, Rush was credited with successfully treating a number of patients using both blood-letting and calomel. He became convinced that fevers could be successfully treated by purging the patient's system. Accordingly, he produced a medicine appropriately called the "Bilious Pills of Dr. Rush" which contained both calomel and jalap, a powerful purgative made from the ground tubers of a plant native to Mexico.

In 1803, Rush sent Captain Meriwether Lewis an eleven-point set of rules for good health. The first rule prescribed his pills as a treatment for fevers. Lewis accepted this advice and took with him fifty dozen of Dr. Rush's pills. With no less of an authority than the famous Dr. Benjamin Rush proclaiming the value of calomel, it is easy to see how any reputable physician of the first half of the Nineteenth Century would place trust in the effectiveness of it.

Levi Hancock reported another dream in his diary entry for August 28th:

> "I dreamed that a night hawk flew over the camp and cried "Peek" over all the tents, back and forth, and then turned as bright as the sun, which awakened me. . . . I then called for the musicians to beat the reveille, and then I heard there was a letter for the Battalion from the Twelve. I then had a peek at it and it said that we must be careful not to take medicine from the doctor. Some had taken sick and Andrew Lytle said, 'Brother Levi

this letter is your night hawk.' I then, after that, told the sick to
peek at that letter when they would ask me what they should
do when were sick and then [have me] pray for them and lay
hands on them, and surely there were many healed. At this time
came the Doctor, Mr. George Sanderson, and surely death and
hell followed after this man. [He] gave his charge to McIntyre,
our doctor, and mercury was crammed down the Saints against
their will" (Hancock 2000, 42, 43).

The Battalion renewed its march on August 31st under the command of
its new officer in charge, Lieutenant Smith. Almost immediately, Dr. Sanderson took charge of the sick. He required all ill Battalion members to report to
him each morning, where he then administered a dose of calomel. Initially,
Dr. Sanderson gave the sick soldier a paper packet containing the drug, but
when he found out that many were simply discarding the medicine, he began
to administer it himself from an old rusty spoon. Those receiving treatment
were permitted to ride in wagons or otherwise be assisted in traveling. Those
sick who did not report for their dose of calomel were required to march with
everyone else. Treatment in the form of calomel was not optional; it was man-
datory and enforced by Lieutenant Smith.

On the morning of August 31st, Dr. Sanderson held his first sick call,
even though he, himself, was not feeling well, attributing his illness to fish he
had eaten the day before. Of the fifty or so men who reported to sick call, he
felt that only ten or fewer were actually sick and attributed their illnesses to
their diet (Sanderson, August 31, 1846).

On September 2nd, Lieutenant Smith pulled several sick men that
had not seen Dr. Sanderson from the wagons they were riding in. Nathaniel Jones, a Sergeant in Company D, attempted to tell Smith that the refusal
to take calomel was based on a religious belief that only herbal medicines
should be used. When Smith asked Adjutant Dykes if that was so, he replied
that there was no such belief, thereby firming up Smith's resolve to make the
soldiers conform to his view of accepted military protocol. When Lieutenant

Smith tried to remove sick soldiers from Sergeant Thomas Williams' wagon, the Sergeant confronted Smith, who drew his sword. Williams responded by threatening to knock Smith to the ground with his whip (Ricketts 1996, 49). The incident was resolved later that day over a drink, but without an apology from either.

William Coray, whose wife, Melissa, was with him and traveling in a family wagon, summarized the problem faced by the men of the Battalion by writing on September 2nd:

> "The sickness increased. The diseases were principally ague and fever and bilious and congestion. I was taken with the ague and fever this day but fortunately better provided for than many others having a wagon to ride in and a man to drive it. The Col. [Smith] turned the sick all out of the wagons this day because they were not under the doctor's care. He said they might stay on the prairie if they would not submit to the order. Such indeed was the straits we were in and a narrower place no people was ever placed in. The Council of the Church one way and the breaking of the commander's orders would be mutiny on the other hand, the church saying if you want to live, don't take medicine and if they didn't take medicine they could not ride" (Ricketts 1996, 50).

We don't know what sicknesses troubled those in the Battalion, but we know that physical examinations as we know them today did not exist in the 1840s. Any pre-existing conditions the Battalion members may have had were usually not discovered until they surfaced during the march. We also know from other records that malaria and influenza were two of the more common illnesses of the time. Dr. Jeremiah Hall Lyford, writing of his experiences as a physician in the Rock Island County, Illinois area said: "The prevailing diseases were fever and ague, Intermittent and bilious fevers and some seasons they prevailed very extensive. The autumns of 1845 and 1846 were the two most sickly seasons that I have known in this country" (Lyford). We can assume from the logs of the Battalion that similar conditions prevailed across the prairies. Dr. Lyford reported that he had some success treating ague with quinine, a common treatment for malaria to this day.

There was limited help to the soldiers from Dr. William L. McIntire, a Mormon member of the Battalion who had been appointed Assistant Surgeon by Colonel Allen before his death. Dr. Sanderson had ordered Dr. McIntire not to administer to the troops unless specifically told to do so. Sanderson continued to administer his calomel, sometimes augmenting it with small doses of arsenic, another poison used in small amounts as a medicine during the 1800s. Those too sick to walk to sick call each morning were sometimes administered to by McIntire, and at other times were forced to either walk or be carried to Sanderson's camp, which was usually a distance from the main camp.

In spite of the sickness among the troops, the Battalion made good time in its westward march through today's Kansas during the first week of September. Some days they made twenty miles and on a few days walked as far as twenty-five or more miles. One sick man was hidden in an empty pork barrel and rode in a wagon to be spared the ministrations of the dreaded doctor. Others were able to treat themselves, thereby bypassing the doctor. William Coray stated on September 8th that he "succeeded [in breaking] the agues by this time by means of quinine and held myself present for duty" (Ricketts 1996, 52).

As they marched along, they also encountered their first buffalo. Some of the Battalion went hunting and they were able to augment their rations with fresh buffalo meat, which they found quite refreshing. Since they were now in territory without suitable firewood, they learned to cook their meals over fires made with dried buffalo dung. They were also entering the territory occupied by the Pawnees and Comanche. For years, Indians—especially the Comanche—preyed on travelers along the Santa Fe Trail. Most Santa Fe traders tried to travel in large groups for self-protection. The size of the Battalion and the nearby Missouri Volunteers meant that they would not be attacked. Nevertheless, the Missourians reported some incidents of Indian harassment.

However, sickness remained a problem. As soon as some recovered, others took sick. Everyone in the Battalion came to detest Dr. Sanderson—or "Dr. Death" as he became known—and their new commander, Lieutenant Smith, who condoned the hated actions of the doctor. The sudden and untimely death of Colonel Allen, the transfer of command from Jefferson Hunt to Lieutenant Smith, and the new routine of long marches and forced medicine caused considerable consternation within the Battalion. This along with new events during the second week of September created another crisis.

General Kearny had assembled a sizable military force and an even larger supply system at Fort Leavenworth during May and June. Since the Army of the West would technically be in American Territory (that of the Louisiana Purchase) as long as they remained north of the Arkansas River, and since little or no opposition from Mexican forces was expected until Santa Fe was reached, Kearny chose to send his Army components westward in smaller groups. Bent's Fort, near present-day La Junta, Colorado, would serve as the Army's primary supply point on the trip West. So the various supply wagon trains, droves of extra livestock, and the civilian contract suppliers headed in that direction. Mounted and infantry units were sent on their way from Fort Leavenworth as they assembled and were ready to leave.

The first of those units, two companies under Captain Benjamin Moore, left Fort Leavenworth on June 6th. Other units left throughout the month. Kearny and his associated units were the last to leave on June 30th, almost three weeks before the Mormon Battalion left its assembly point at Council Bluffs. Although he did not find out about it until August 15th, the War Department in Washington made him a Brevet Brigadier General on the day he left. Kearny and all of those units before him followed the traditional route of the Santa Fe Trail. This took them along the same trail to be followed by the Battalion to the Arkansas River. They then followed the river to Bent's Fort. Another six or seven miles along the river, at present-day La Junta, Colorado, the trail left the river and headed southwest to the present city of Trinidad, Colorado. From Trinidad, the trail headed south and climbed about 1,800 feet over Raton Pass (7,834 feet) on today's Colorado-New Mexico border. From there, the trail headed southward toward Wagon Mound and Las Vegas, New Mexico, where the trail headed westward, through Glorieta Pass, and on to Santa Fe.

This original route of the Santa Fe Trail was well-watered, had ample supplies of feed for livestock, and avoided the fierce Comanche for the most part. It had the additional benefit of passing Bent's Fort, a civilian trading post operated by William and Charles Bent and Ceran St. Vrain. Built in 1833 as a trading post to serve trappers and Plains Indians as well as Santa Fe Trail caravans, it was the only major outpost on the trail between Missouri and the villages of New Mexico. The fort had been the primary resupply point selected by Kearny for the Westward march. When he arrived, the plains around the fort held hundreds of wagons filled with supplies, several thousand soldiers and many thousands of livestock, all waiting for the push toward Raton Pass, then the Valley of the Rio Grande and the Mexican government center of Santa Fe.

At the fort, Kearny met with James Magoffin, a Santa Fe trader who, along with his brother, Samuel, spoke fluent Spanish and were well known to the officials in New Mexico. Magoffin strongly supported the American cause and through Senator Thomas Hart Benton had met with President Polk and Secretary of War Marcy. Polk and Marcy authorized Magoffin to attempt to broker an agreement with Governor Armijo of New Mexico to surrender that territory peacefully. Magoffin bore letters to Kearny from Polk and Marcy regarding the mission. He told Kearny how he hoped to use persuasion or bribery to get Armijo and the military officers in Santa Fe not to resist the American invasion. Kearny assigned Captain Philip St. George Cooke and a detail of twelve men to escort Magoffin to Santa Fe. The emissary and escort left Bent's Fort on August 1st.

On August 15th, two days after the Mormon Battalion left Fort Leaven-worth, General Kearny and his army rode into Las Vegas, New Mexico, and took the small village without resistance. He required the *alcalde* (the munici-pal magistrate), the militia units there, and the citizens in the plaza to swear allegiance to the United States. Following this brief ceremony, Kearny contin-ued on his way to Santa Fe, passing through several other small Mexican com-munities where the same ceremony was performed. At one of these towns, Cooke returned and informed Kearny of a successful meeting on August 12th with Armijo and his military staff. Because of his knowledge of the route to

Santa Fe and the possible defenses in the perilously constricted Glorieta Pass, Cooke was assigned to command the advance guard.

Several days later, word arrived by rider from Santa Fe that Armijo, the principal military officers and the troops under their command had left Santa Fe and the road was open for occupation by the American troops. On August 18th, Kearny and his command arrived in the capital of the Mexican province of New Mexico without firing a shot. Kearny was now able to begin work on creating an American military government, provide troops to control aggressive Navajo and Ute warriors who were harassing Mexican settlements, and to prepare for his march to the Pacific Coast.

Kearny assumed the position of governor of New Mexico and summoned the Mormons' good friend, Colonel Doniphan, and several others to draft the necessary codes and laws needed to govern the new territory. On August 22nd, Kearny wrote to General Wool in Chihuahua that he would send all of the troops he could spare to him as soon as Colonel Sterling Price's troops and the Mormon Battalion arrived in Santa Fe. As Kearny prepared to leave for California, Charles Bent was made civilian governor of New Mexico and Colonel Doniphan was left in charge of military affairs, with instructions to depart south for Chihuahua as soon as he could be relieved by Colonel Price. On September 25th, Kearny left Santa Fe for California with 300 of his dragoons.

General Kearny's plans called for Sterling Price's troops to hold and keep secure Santa Fe and the Rio Grande Valley. Reports that former Governor Armijo and various military officers would try to dislodge the Americans were common. In addition, Kearny was obligated to send Doniphan's troops south to Mexico to augment American forces there. Kearny needed Price and his men in Santa Fe soon, and he needed the Mormon Battalion to follow him on to California. Accordingly, Kearny sent a messenger east from Santa Fe with instructions to both Price and the Battalion that they were to travel to Santa Fe as fast as possible, and to that end, were not to follow the old Santa Fe Trail route past Bent's Fort and over Raton Pass. Rather, they were to take the Cimarron Cutoff which left the Arkansas River west of present-day Dodge City, Kansas, and head southwest. This route shaved over seventy miles off the trail, eliminated the Raton Pass climb and descent and saved a number of days' travel.

On September 10th, Kearny's couriers arrived at the camps of the Battalion and the Missouri Volunteers with word that Santa Fe had been captured and that they were to take the Cimarron Cutoff. This new order presented some immediate problems for the Battalion. The first and most significant was that the new route began with a fifty mile *jornada*—a fifty mile forced march without water. With no rivers or springs, the only available water in the first section was that which accumulated from recent rains. Such sources, if they even existed, were not reliable and were usually stagnant, contaminated pools unfit for humans. Lieutenant Smith had direct orders from his commander to march his soldiers over a long and treacherous route, but he was burdened by sick soldiers and many families.

Two days later, on September 12th, near the point where the Cimarron Cutoff left the Arkansas, the Battalion had a chance encounter with an eastbound group of fellow Mormons led by John Brown, who many in the Battalion knew from Nauvoo. Brown and the others were from Mississippi. They had left from Independence and traveled along the Platte to meet with the Saints going to the Great Basin. They learned from eastbound travelers and mountaineers that the main Mormon camp had remained in Council Bluffs and would not be heading West until the following year. Somewhere between Chimney Rock and Fort Laramie, the Mississippi Mormons met mountaineer and trader, John Baptiste Richard (pronounced and often spelled Reshaw), who advised them to go south with him to a more hospitable place to spend the Winter. They then turned south about 300 miles and arrived at the small trappers' enclave known as El Pueblo on the Arkansas River (present-day Pueblo, Colorado).

The El Pueblo colony had first been established by mountain men in 1842. The location on the American side of the Arkansas River and on the plains east of the Rockies offered a moderate Winter climate, excellent farming, and was about sixty miles west of Bent's Fort, which offered supplies and support. The Battalion learned that there were fourteen Mormon families with forty-three people staying near the confluence of the Arkansas River and Fountain Creek, about a mile east of El Pueblo. Brown and his companions were heading back to Mississippi to gather their own families and additional Mormons to bring them West the following Spring.

This fortuitous meeting provided Lieutenant Smith and the Battalion officers with a partial solution to the problem of having the families on a difficult march with little water and reduced supplies. Most of the Battalion's supplies were at Bent's Fort, which would now be bypassed. We don't know if the suggestion to send the family detachment to El Pueblo originated with Lieutenant Smith or within the Battalion. It appears that it was done with the full cooperation, and probably at the instigation of Jefferson Hunt. However, we do know that the composition of the family detachment was nine women, thirty-three children, and an escort of eleven Battalion soldiers, including Captain Higgins as commander, Jefferson Hunt's son, Corporal Gilbert Hunt, and nine privates. Two of the privates were Hunt's nephews, Milton and Nicholas Kelley. We also know that the detached soldiers were to escort the families, help them get settled by building shelter and then catch up with the remainder of the Battalion at Santa Fe or beyond. However, only two actually returned to the Battalion, dispatched before the others as couriers. By the time Higgins and several of the soldiers reached Santa Fe, the Battalion was well on its way to California. Higgins and his soldiers were sent back to El Pueblo by Colonel Doniphan. He also authorized the El Pueblo detachments to use the Battalion's supplies at Bent's Fort.

Fourteen of the fifty-three members (or more than twenty-five percent) of the first El Pueblo detachment were members of Hunt's traveling family. Included, in addition to the soldiers Gilbert, Milton and Nicholas, were his wife, Celia, and seven of their children, Milton Kelley's pregnant wife, Malinda, and Nicolas's wife, Sarah, and child, Parley. In total, there were three pregnant women in the detachment who delivered children at El Pueblo. Two of the new fathers, Norman Sharp and Milton Kelley, did not live to see their new babies. Kelley died from natural causes on November 4th, and Sharp died as a result of an accidental gunshot wound inflicted on September 28th.

Two of the families in the detachment (Hunt and Shelton) had seven minor children; one family (Higgins) had six children; two families (Brown and Button) had four children; and one (Huntington) had three children. Anyone who has cared for or traveled with children, or who has watched other families of similar size, can attest to the difficulties and work involved. A cross-country journey today with seven children, including two infants, with all of the conveniences offered such as hotel or motel rooms, laundry facilities, fast food stops, disposable diapers and in-car entertainment systems would be an ordeal for most mothers, fathers and children. Imagine compounding that experience with the rigors of trail travel, in wagons or on foot, over deserts or mountains, during war. It is no wonder that the family detachment was sent on a path that would allow them to rest the Winter in protected quarters, with others of their own faith, and travel only one quarter of the distance to their final stopping place that the others in the Battalion faced. The presence of the Mississippi Saints in El Pueblo offered a clear solution for the Hunt family and other large families. By including three adult males of his own family as detachment soldiers, Hunt was able to provide strong family support.

Additionally, the Captain of the detachment was Nelson Higgins, who was at the center of the near insurrection earlier in the march. Sebert Shelton, who had previously been charged with insubordination to an officer, was also in the detachment. Thus, the family detachment's departure served Hunt well in several ways: his family was protected and two of the more problematic members of the Battalion were at least temporarily removed.

The family detachment was the first sent by the Army to Winter at El Pueblo. Two more sick detachments were later sent there by Colonel Philip St. George Cooke. The next, sent from Santa Fe in October, was headed by Captain James Brown and was comprised of ninety-one men (mostly sick), nineteen women and ten children. The last, sent by Cooke from along the Rio Grande, was comprised of fifty-seven men, one woman and no children.

It is necessary here to pause to consider a major inconsistency involving the history of the Hunt family. Norma Ricketts, in her well-researched work on the Mormon Battalion, states that Celia and her children went to El Pueblo with the family (or Higgins) detachment that followed the Arkansas River from this point (Ricketts 1996). On the other hand, Pauline Udall Smith, a Jefferson Hunt descendant who wrote the only book-length biography of him, states that Celia and the children traveled with the Battalion to Santa Fe and went to El Pueblo from there with the Brown Detachment of sick soldiers and families (Smith 1958). Other Hunt descendants concur. A third source, a list compiled by Thomas Bullock who served as a recorder of events for the LDS Church, seems to indicate that all of the Hunt family, with the exception of Jefferson and Marshall, were part of the Higgins detachment (Bigler and Bagley 2000, 459). Which is correct?

The basis for the Santa Fe claim is a statement made by John Hunt, who was thirteen years old in 1846. In a newspaper article published nearly sixty years later in 1905, John Hunt states:

> "My father obtained permission for my mother and the children to go with the Battalion. We went with it as far as Santa Fe, New Mexico. Now the Battalion faced the Mohave Desert where there would be a scarcity of water and great heat, so it was decided to send the sick soldiers and the women and children back to Pueblo, Colorado, where there was a Mexican stockade fort which would be some protection from attacks by Indians. This company was under the direction of Captain Brown. My eldest brother, Gilbert, who was a sargeant [sic] also with this Company, was sent back. Here we spent the winter" (Deseret Evening News, October 7, 1905).

This statement appears to confirm that John, and possibly his mother and siblings, went with Jefferson Hunt as far as Santa Fe, and then went to El Pueblo with the Brown detachment. But there is a more likely third scenario. Just before the quotation above, John says the following: "My father had an adopted son of about my own age, named Peter Nease [Jefferson's plural wife Matilda's younger brother.] He is still living in Idaho somewhere, and he went through most of my experiences with me" (Deseret News, October 7, 1905).

We know that Matilda, along with her brother, Peter, and sister, Ellen, went as far as Santa Fe and then traveled to El Pueblo with the Brown Detachment. It is quite conceivable that John Hunt went to Santa Fe with his father and Matilda, Peter and Ellen, and then traveled with the latter and the sick detachment to El Pueblo where he rejoined his mother and other siblings who had been accompanied by Gilbert in the Higgins Detachment. Bullock, when recording his roster, probably assumed that all of the Hunts traveled together and combined them into the Higgins detachment.

This scenario makes a lot of sense for several reasons. It would explain why John was so clear in later life about visiting Santa Fe, an experience that he would vividly remember. It would also explain why Gilbert was part of the Higgins Detachment. It is highly unlikely that Jefferson Hunt would have assigned Gilbert to the Higgins Detachment if the rest of the family was not part of that unit. His role as eldest son in the family was significant, and he was given a corresponding amount of responsibility toward the family that he would bear for much of the rest of his life. As previously shown, the Kelly families, relatives of Hunt, were also part of the Higgins Detachment.

And finally, Hunt clearly demonstrated a tendency to show his sons the fundamentals of being a frontiersman. In the late Fall of 1848, he took his sons Gilbert, John and Peter Nease to Southern California with a party to get supplies for the Salt Lake settlement. And even later, Gilbert was running the family business affairs while Hunt was away in the Legislature, and John, then in his twenties, was carrying the mail along the Mormon road between Southern California and Utah. Hunt's sons learned their frontier lessons well and performed admirably.

If we accept the logical assumption that Hunt was responsible for deciding who was to be part of the detachment, and if we accept John's statement that he traveled to Santa Fe, then the only logical explanation is that Celia, Gilbert and the smaller children, along with the Kelley families, were part of the Higgins Detachment and that Matilda, Peter and Ellen Nease, and John accompanied Hunt to Santa Fe before being made part of the Brown sick and family detachment to El Pueblo.

On the afternoon of September 15th, the Battalion crossed from the north to the south side of the Arkansas River at a point several miles east of the present community of Cimarron, Kansas, and a little to the east of the several "Middle Crossings" that had to be used when more water was present. The Battalion had left the United States and was in Mexican territory. The river was dry—or so nearly dry that they were able to cross anywhere they desired. Most of the water was below the surface of the gravely streambed where it was accessible with just a little digging. This knowledge of Western streams was remembered by many of the veterans of the Battalion, including Jefferson Hunt, in the years to come.

Dr. Sanderson noted that the Arkansas River, when he first saw it on September 11th, was mostly dry with a small amount of water in places and none in others, and that it had some intermittent flow at times, probably related to storms upstream. Interestingly, Sanderson makes no comment about the family detachment or how they were selected or evaluated. The following day, September 16th, the Higgins Detachment began its journey to Bent's Fort and El Pueblo along the north bank of the Arkansas.

On September 16th, Lieutenant Smith ordered the Battalion to rest and prepare for the difficult jornada that would begin the following day. Since the bulk of the Battalion's provisions had been sent ahead to Bent's Fort and that place would now be bypassed, Smith requisitioned additional provisions from Colonel Price who, true to his long-held animosity toward the Mormons, refused to comply. Smith was outraged and, according to Henry Bigler, sent word back to Price that if he didn't comply, Smith would "let loose the Mormons and come down upon them with his artillery" (Yurtinus 1975, 137). Price sent the requested supplies. This incident and its successful resolution precisely demonstrated the wisdom of having a regular Army officer in command of the Battalion. Had Jefferson Hunt been in command, the results would have been much different.

Levi Hancock did not approve of the departure of the family detachment, believing that the instructions from Brigham Young stated that the Battalion should not be split in any way. Hancock followed a literal interpretation
of Young's earlier instructions and did not consider the factors favoring the
detachment in the same way as either Jefferson Hunt or Lieutenant Smith.
This further caused him to distrust Smith and created additional resentment
toward the Mormon officers of the Battalion. It appears, however, that the
majority of the Battalion saw that their welfare and that of their brethren was
best served by detaching the families.

On the night of September 16th, Sergeant Edmond Brown of Company
E pointed out to Hancock and others a star apparently moving in the eastern
sky. Hancock recorded that:

> "I looked and I saw a star moving up and down between two
> stars as if dancing. I said, 'This is a sign of something, this is
> what was meant when the Savior said there should be signs in
> the heavens. Something will soon follow'" (Hancock 2000, 53).
> A number of others in the camp saw the same phenomenon.
> One, Daniel Tyler, mentions that: "It attracted considerable at-
> tention while it remained in sight, and finally disappeared below
> the eastern horizon" (Tyler 1881, 158).

That same night, Private Alva Phelps died. He had been very sick and
forced to take calomel in the rusty old spoon from Dr. Sanderson earlier
that day. Phelps told his fellow soldiers that he "would live if he did not take
medicine" (Hancock 2000, 53). The general feeling within the camp was that
Phelps had died because of the calomel—and possibly arsenic—he was forced
to take. Henry Standage recorded that he placed Phelps's body in his tent to
prepare for burial, then was called out by others to see the moving star. Standage noted that: "It was directly in the course that we had traveled" (Golder
1928, 165). They believed that "Dr. Death" had poisoned his first victim. Many
in the Battalion felt that Phelps's death amounted to murder. A number of
the troops recalled the oaths made by Dr. Sanderson and Lieutenant Smith,

and therefore, believed that Phelps' murder was intentional. The resentment toward Smith and Dr. Sanderson and their harsh treatment of the sick was at the verge of boiling over.

In his diary, Sanderson did not directly refer to Phelps's death other than to say several days later that one man, who had refused the medicine, had died, and to generally criticize the Mormons for preferring prayer over medicine. He did not comment about the general outcry against his method of medical treatment, even though he was aware of it.

Very early on the morning of September 17th, the Battalion buried Phelps, with Samuel Gully making some remarks. The shallow grave was dug by torchlight on the sandy flats south of the Arkansas River and couldn't be made deeper than four feet deep because of the high water table. The early morning burial was necessary because that was the day the Battalion took the Cimarron Cutoff and began the fifty mile dry march. Because of the heat, the distance, and the lack of water, the march needed to cover as much ground as possible in the best possible conditions. Success called for an early start, few stops or interruptions, and considerable self-sacrifice.

In two months, the Battalion had heard that its beloved Colonel Allen had died; experienced discord that bordered on insubordination or even mutiny; witnessed its elected officers submit command to a relatively inexperienced Lieutenant Smith; faced a schism between the officers led by Jefferson Hunt and the religious faction led by Levi Hancock; saw a portion of its ranks detached to El Pueblo; and faced death at the hands of the officer and doctor who were sworn to lead them. Now they were to depart from the better known, well-watered and provisioned part of the Santa Fe Trail to head into a jornada fifty miles long. This was not what they and the Mormon leaders and Brigham Young had envisioned a short time before. Circumstances and difficult communications with military and religious leaders had complicated their condition.

The turmoil and confusion facing the Battalion badly needed a calming influence. That was not to happen. Matters were about to become much worse and the Battalion would soon face its most serious test yet.

Chapter 7

The Bull in the China Shop

After burying Alva Phelps, the Battalion began its march on the Cimarron Cutoff. They had gone only a few miles, when from the east—the direction of the dancing star the night before—rode in three men from Winter Quarters. The three were: Lieutenant James Pace, returning from Fort Leavenworth and meeting with Brigham Young; Howard Egan, a prominent Mormon; and the leader of the small party, John Doyle Lee.

The eminent Mormon historian Juanita Brooks entitled her 1961 biography *John Doyle Lee: Zealot, Pioneer Builder, Scapegoat.* A zealot he was; as a pioneer builder he was no more remarkable than hundreds of others of his time; but a scapegoat—that is questionable. In his autobiography, *Mormonism Unveiled,* written shortly before his execution by firing squad in 1877, Lee explained himself by saying: "I never willingly committed a crime. I have acted my religion, nothing more" (Lee 1877, 38).

On August 27th, Brigham Young asked Lee to go to the Battalion and collect the next round of pay; Lee was quick to answer in the affirmative and began preparations for his trip. He showed great deference to the top leadership of the Church and quickly charged forward whenever called on a mission. Problems arose when that leadership wasn't directly guiding or controlling his actions. John D. Lee was fanatical, excessive, impulsive, literal, irrational and in his own way, loyal. He always sought attention and command—which he frequently had no right to.

Born in 1812 in Illinois, Lee converted to the Mormon Church at Far West, Missouri, in 1838. As a new arrival in the community, he lived with Jefferson Hunt and family for several weeks as he got settled in. He also joined the Danites and was involved in some of their activities. By his own admission, while living near Far West, Lee participated in raids on "gentile" farms and communities and "took what property we could find, especially provisions, fat cattle and arms and ammunition" (Lee 1877, 74-75). In the 1840s, Lee served several missions, and converted several members of the Pace family, including James Pace. In Nauvoo in 1843, Lee became the seventh member of the newly-created Nauvoo police department. Throughout those years, his faithfulness and fidelity to the Church leadership was noticed and he continued to rise in their esteem. His home was often a gathering place for others. He entertained Jefferson Hunt and his family members on several occasions.

By 1845, plural or celestial marriage was being secretly practiced by some of the higher officials in the Mormon Church, even though it was not to be officially revealed and made available to everyone for seven more years. Early in 1845, John D. Lee was admitted by the Church leadership into the practice. As with most things Lee did, he acted quickly and excessively, taking five new plural wives, marrying one on February 5th, two on April 19th and two more on May 3rd. Lee eventually had nineteen wives and sixty-four children, fifty-four of whom were living at the time of his execution.

In the 1840s, the practice of adult adoptions was instituted among the senior leadership of the Church. This practice was eventually discontinued and was never widely instituted. But for Lee, it further enhanced his perceived standing within the Church. Brigham Young was "sealed" to the murdered Joseph Smith. Young, in turn, "adopted" thirty-eight men. The second such adoptee was Lee. Ever in a rush to partake of the newest practices in the Church, Lee quickly adopted "eighteen or nineteen young men" into his family (Brooks 1973, 73). Among those he adopted was James Pace. To emphasize these relationships, Lee sometimes called himself John D. Lee Young, and referred to his adopted sons accordingly—as in the case of James Pace Lee.

Thus, when Lee departed on his mission to the Battalion marching to Santa Fe, he saw himself as more than a mere representative of Brigham Young: he saw himself as Young's adopted son on a mission with his own adopted son, James Pace.

In later years, Lee became one of the first and most influential settlers in Southern Utah, but not without great controversy. He became prominent in the formation of the Iron Mission at Cedar City, Utah and then the community of Harmony, south of Cedar City. His position was that of Farmer to the Indians (Indian Agent), and as such, he commanded the respect of the Indians in his charge. However, he often offended the missionaries and other Mormons of the Southern Utah communities. Later, he was involved in the horrific events now called the Mountain Meadows Massacre, which we will discuss in a subsequent chapter.

So, on September 17, 1846, just after they began the march on the Cimarron Cutoff, the Mormon Battalion generally, and the officers and Jefferson Hunt specifically, were about to come face to face with the chaos, confusion and furor of John Doyle Lee.

On August 26th, Lieutenant James Pace arrived at Winter Quarters with the first news of Allen's death. The following day, Brigham Young went to Lee's tent and asked him to undertake a "Dangerous though Responsible Mission" to go to the Battalion and receive the payment that was to be paid to them (Brooks 1967, 175). Young told him that he would have two men with him and that they were to take a light wagon, a span of mules and should travel forty miles a day. The small party of Lee, Egan and Pace took along with them a small dog named Trip, owned by Dr. Willard Richards of the Twelve, which was to warn them in case anyone attempted to rob them while they slept. Lee and Egan set off on their mission on Sunday, August 30th and Pace caught up with them on September 3rd. Lee had no doubt about his importance and the significance of the assignment given him. In the opening of his diary entry for the day he says: "Pres Young engaged in fitting out his son (J D Lee) for an expedition to the Western Army Mormon Bat." (Brooks 1967, 176). Lee was on a mission not just from the President of his Church; he was on a mission from his adopted father.

Lee and his party were well-outfitted for the trip. They took a light wagon for themselves and their supplies because it was faster; but it was also more fragile than the more common supply wagon most often seen on the trail. Mules were provided for both the wagon and riding. Food supplies were obtained at Council Bluffs, and additional supplies were purchased at Fort Leavenworth and several other locations on the eastern part of the trail. But most importantly from a security standpoint, they were armed with some of the most advanced repeating firearms available anywhere. Both Lee and Pace—and probably Egan also—were equipped with Jonathan Browning's remarkable "slide guns," or harmonica rifles, with multiple round slide magazines. Each also had additional magazines which permitted them to reload quickly in an emergency. Equipped with these repeating rifles which were cumbersome if carried on a mount, but very comfortable to use if carried in a wagon, two or three men had the firepower of many times that number. These rifles were truly "state of the art" weapons in 1846. Lee also carried a Colt's six shot revolver and at least one single shot rifle.

They reached Fort Leavenworth on September 5th, and were asked by the post commander to wait until the following day to leave so that they could carry the mail west. At Leavenworth, they heard an account of a recent Indian attack on a Santa Fe trading party, and as they headed west, other eastbound travelers told them of the location of the Battalion and reported that Lieutenant Smith was now in command. In spite of a broken axel that delayed them for a day and a half, and another broken axel six days later that delayed them for a half day, they made excellent time and passed several wagon trains filled with provisions for the Army of the West. Lee found the land along the Arkansas some of the best he had ever seen. They were all impressed by the extensive wildlife including buffalo, antelope, wolves and prairie dogs. Lee even found a little time to hunt buffalo (Brooks 1967, 181-191).

The Santa Fe Trail was surprisingly well-traveled. The little party found many sutlers and Army provision wagons traveling in the same direction. They encountered several parties of traders and others returning from Santa Fe. On September 14th, they were surprised to encounter John Brown, William Crosby and the other Mississippi Mormons traveling eastward. Crosby gave Lee a full accounting of the Saints now located at El Pueblo, and probably told Lee of the information that they obtained while camped with the Battalion. Lee promised to inform Young about the intentions of the Mississippi/El Pueblo group when he returned to Winter Quarters following his mission to Santa Fe.

As Lee and his party approached the Battalion, Lee knew there had been changes that did not conform with the wishes of Brigham Young and the Church. He had heard at least two accounts that Smith was in charge of the Battalion and probably heard from Crosby and Brown of Dr. Sanderson's activities. He was probably aware that there was dissention within the Battalion and may have been aware of Levi Hancock's and the other dissenters' positions. And since Lee was carrying letters regarding the assumption of command, he had time to consider what action he should take on overtaking the Battalion. He was probably aware of the change in plans which called for the Battalion to hurry along to Santa Fe by taking the Cimarron Cutoff, but he probably didn't clearly understand the full extent of the difficulty presented by the first fifty miles of the route, since all of his information related to the more traditional and well-watered trail along the north side of the Arkansas River leading to Bent's Fort. Because of his impetuous nature, Lee would not have given much thought to Brigham Young's overriding concern—to make the march of the Mormon Battalion a success.

On Thursday, September 17th, John D. Lee, Howard Egan and James Pace began their travel at daybreak. Not long after starting out, they saw both the Battalion and Sterling Price's mounted units on the other side of the river about five miles away. When they approached the Battalion, they came from the same direction as the dancing star the night before. This fact was not lost on many in the Battalion.

As an emissary and adopted son of Brigham Young, Lee expected the troops to stop and read the letters he carried and listen to his counsel regarding the command and leadership of the Battalion. But that was not to be. The decision of command had been made; orders had been received from Kearny; and, most importantly, the Battalion had begun the critical march over the dry Cimarron Cutoff. To stop now would mean to turn around and return to the Arkansas River several miles to the rear and then begin the march on another day. But to do that would ignore the urgency carried in Kearny's most recent orders to the Battalion.

When Lee caught up with the Battalion, he quickly learned of Phelps' death the night before and was brought current on the other news of the relationship between the troops, Smith and Sanderson. Lee sought out Jefferson Hunt, who confirmed the reports that the command had passed to Smith with the approval of the officers and not at the vote of the entire Battalion. Lee then had Hunt introduce him to Lieutenant Smith. Then both Smith and Hunt got into Lee's wagon and rode with him as the march continued. Lee presented them with the letter from Young and the Twelve and read to them the "views of the council in relation to the situation of the Bat. & the right of command" (Brooks 1967, 191). Lee then requested that they stop and let the troops rest and that they reduce the long marches and give more rest. He then recounted the death of Alva Phelps following Dr. Sanderson's treatment. But Smith's response was to continue the march.

Lee restated the promises of Colonel Allen and how they were not followed by Lieutenant Smith. He condemned the treatment of the troops at the hands of both Smith and Dr. Sanderson. According to Lee's own account written on that date, he berated Smith and enumerated all of his shortcomings, while praising the deceased Colonel Allen's sensitivity to the needs of the troops. According to Lee, "I expected he [Smith] would have chalenged [sic] me for a Duell but instead of that he never resented the first word. . ." (Brooks 1967, 193). According to Lee, Smith agreed with what he said and promised to do better in the future. In any case, Lieutenant Smith did not stop and continued the dreadful march across the Cimarron Cutoff as fast as possible. Thirty years later, in recounting this same conversation, Lee stated that "Captain Hunt got very mad, and jumped out of the wagon. He said I talked like an insane man more than a man of sense" (Lee 1877, 192). Perhaps the thirty-year-old recollection was more accurate than the sedate version Lee recorded in his diary at the time of the conversation.

In any case, the confrontation in the wagon came to an end when the Battalion happened upon a small depression in the desert containing some very poor quality water. It was muddy, and filled with live and dead insects. In the opinion of Henry Standage, the water "could not be compared to anything else but Buffalo urine, as a great portion of it was of the same, yet we were glad to get this" (Golder 1928, 165-166). The day was hot and there was no water except that was carried by the troops. Some of the men reported that the sutlers were selling small amounts of water from the Arkansas at outrageous prices. The livestock and Battalion needed water, and this small amount, no matter how bad, was all some had. The need to quickly cross the desert was clear to those in charge. The Battalion went on its way and covered twenty-five miles, or half the journada, that first day. That night, they had to make a dry camp with very little feed for the livestock.

When Lee caught up with the Battalion, he believed that the letters he carried from the Church leaders, combined with his counsel, would set straight the command issue and the treatment of the troops. He expected the Mormon officers to "stand up for their rights & free themselves from such lamentable Tyrany [sic]. . ." (Brooks 1967, 194). But the issue facing Jefferson Hunt and the other officers was much more basic. Their primary concern was to preserve the Mormon Battalion as an integral unit of the Army of the West and to reach the successful conclusion envisioned by Brigham Young when the Battalion was first formed. John D. Lee did not present a solution to a problem; he became the single most critical part of the problem that needed to be resolved.

Lee recorded that when Lieutenant Gully first returned to the Battalion from Fort Leavenworth, he wanted the Battalion to stop and either wait for Pace's return or to send a message to General Kearny in Santa Fe for further instructions. At that time, the Mormon officers dismissed both ideas. His first night in the camp, Lee again raised the idea of sending a messenger to Kearny asking for instructions, and again, the officers with Jefferson Hunt at the head, refused to do so. They had substantial reasons for their actions, since Kearny had already conveyed to them the need for speed in reaching Santa Fe, they were in the middle of the long march on the Cimarron Cutoff and were in no position to stop. Unknown to anyone with the Battalion or the Missouri

Volunteers, Kearny at this time was very eager to be on his way West and was depending on both units to arrive soon. Colonel Sterling Price would soon suffer Kearny's criticism for being slow, and the Battalion would soon receive an ultimatum to reach Santa Fe quickly.

That night the Mormon officers of the Battalion met to discuss the new developments. The apparent topic of the meeting was how to quiet the dissent being aggravated by Lee's arrival.

Lee recorded that Captains Hunter and Davis and Lieutenant Lorenzo Clark were sent by the officers to meet with him and to tell him that he "had no right to abuse their commander Lieut Smith whom they had appointed" (Brooks 1967, 194). The message to Lee was clear—the Mormon officers of the Battalion were not going to try to undo any of their previous decisions about the command of the unit, and they were not going to relinquish any special authority to Lee.

Lee's diary of his mission to Santa Fe is a very detailed and compre-hensive description of not only the trip, but of the intrigues associated with the dissention within the Battalion. His entry for September 17th, his first day with the Battalion, contains descriptions of the conversations noted above, and also contains a detailed account of many of the events experienced by the Battalion up to that day. He placed the blame for the decision to pass com-mand on the Mormon officers, acting on the advice of Dykes and Shelton. Lee mentions the pressure created by the presence of Colonel Sterling Price and the officers' belief that they needed a Regular Army officer to provide them with provisions and payroll. From these comments, we can see that Lee was very busy that first day in finding out what had transpired during the previous two months.

It is not surprising that Lee made his camp with his adopted son, Lieu-tenant Pace who was part of the mess that also held Samuel Gully, Levi Han-cock and David Pettegrew. It was this group that were the most outspoken opponents of the decisions of the Mormon officers and that led the opposition to the changes that had gripped the Battalion. It is apparent that Lee obtained most of his information from them and quickly took their side in the dispute. Events soon unfolded that show that he strongly supported them in the dissention that occurred in the following days and before Santa Fe was reached.

The troops were awakened at 4 a.m. on the morning of September 18th and began another long march across the Cimarron Cutoff. They covered twenty-five miles and camped at a small stream with more bad water and inferior grass. On September 19th, the march again began at sunrise, and before noon they reached their goal; Cimarron Springs was a well-watered spring with good grass for the livestock. There they camped, rested and let their livestock feed. By leaving earlier than the mounted Missouri Volunteers, the Battalion got to the springs first and occupied the best camping area.

John D. Lee recorded that the sutlers traveling with the volunteer units came to him and requested the mail he had picked up at Fort Leavenworth. Lee demanded ten dollars from them or threatened to return the mail to Leavenworth. They paid, and Lee gave them the mail

Lee had hoped to receive the pay when the Battalion arrived at Cimarron Springs. However, he discovered that the Battalion paymaster would not pay off the troops because it was not lawful to pay more than they were due; the end of the month had not yet arrived. Furthermore, he did not have sufficient small change to make partial payments. They would have to wait until Santa Fe to be paid off. Therefore, Lee and Egan would have to travel on with them. Lee brought up the idea of sending a special letter to Kearny, proposing that he and Egan quickly carry a secret letter in advance of the Battalion. The officers again met in private at Jefferson Hunt's tent and, wisely, the offer was again declined.

At 6 a.m. Sunday, September 20th, Jefferson Hunt told Lee that there would be a meeting at 7 p.m. that evening in the large tent used by Pace, Gully and Lytle and their mess. The Battalion marched a little over ten miles and then camped. The Mormon officers, with Hunt at the lead, met privately to discuss the dissention being aggravated by the arrival of Lee, Egan and Pace. After some time spent in this private discussion, the officers sent for Lee. It was not to be a harmonious discussion amongst peers, but a forceful attempt on the part of the officers to squelch the revolt before it went too far. Hunt recognized that the success of the Battalion depended on stopping the dissention before it got worse. He was not about to let internal strife disrupt what he had worked so hard to achieve. He was intent on following the directions of Brigham Young and the Twelve Apostles to make the Battalion a success.

When Lee and the others, including Egan, Hancock, Pettegrew, Pace and Gully, were escorted into the meeting, Jefferson Hunt began by clearly stating his authority. According to Lee:

> "Capt. Hunt said it [was] customary for the man that appointed the Ball to open it—then proceeded & said that Bro Lee considered he was insulted by not being permitted to meet with us, according to appointment. The reason we did not met at Bro Lee's quarters was the Capt's wished to meet alone. . ." (Brooks 1967, 197).

Captain Jesse Hunter then accused Lee of arriving and trying to dictate to the Battalion and of acting improperly by criticizing and insulting the Army officers who had been properly selected by the Mormon officers. Hunter also stated that if the Mormon officers wanted Lee's help, they would ask for it, but as of then, there was no need for Lee's intervention and he should drop whatever he was doing to foster dissent.

Lee responded by claiming that it was he who should be offended and if they had problems with Smith and Sanderson, it was their own fault since they selected them. Levi Hancock and David Pettegrew again brought up the idea of sending a messenger to General Kearny for instructions.

For the past two months, Jefferson Hunt had resolved problems the "Mormon Way"—that is, by taking counsel from his key advisors and peers (the other officers) and then trying to reach a consensus agreement about what to do next. For the short period that the Battalion had been together, it had more or less worked. Decisions were made with most of the officers agreeing and with the troops of the Battalion consenting to follow their leaders in spite of the hardships they were forced to face. As a consequence, the Battalion was succeeding as a military unit in spite of the unforeseen problems that arose.

But Hunt was a strong, forceful man, committed to his mission, and not willing to accept mutiny regardless of who was behind it. Counsel and consensus had worked all the magic it could; now was the time for forceful leadership if the Battalion was to continue.

Captain Jefferson Hunt, the man designated Mormon commander by Brigham Young and the Twelve and responsible for meeting the changing challenges found on the trail decided now was the time to lay down the law to the dissidents. He told Lee and Egan that they had been encouraging the Battalion to revolt, but as outsiders they had no right to come in and offer any counsel to the either the officers or the men of the Battalion, and that Lee was to stop. Similarly, he then put Lieutenant James Pace and Levi Hancock in their place. According to Lee, Hunt said: "No one has a right to council this but myself & my authority I will exercise in the Name of the Lord & no man shall take it from me" (Brooks 1967, 198). Hunt had told them who was in charge.

The message was clear to those present. John D. Lee responded that he did not want to take over command of the Battalion, but that if Hunt had taken the same forceful stand with Smith and Sanderson as he just had with him then there would have been no problems. Several of the lieutenants present, including Samuel Gully, Andrew Lytle, Elam Luddington, and George Rosecrans, rose to Lee's defense and said that he didn't mean to cause bad feelings or do anything wrong. Howard Egan had been silent and was called on for his view which was that the officers didn't want his counsel so he remained silent on the issues. Lee said he concluded the meeting by saying that the men of the Battalion should remain united and things would get better (Brooks 1967, 198-199). But Lee's opposition was not over.

Having failed to change things with a direct confrontation of Jefferson Hunt and the Mormon and Army officers, the leaders of the opposition settled back and waited for a more opportune time to strike. Since they were approaching New Mexico and Santa Fe, it is unlikely that their goal was simply the removal of Lieutenant Smith as commander; it is more likely that their ultimate goal was the disbandment and return of the Battalion to Winter Quarters.

The Mormon officers realized that John D. Lee would return to Winter Quarters and Brigham Young much sooner than they would, and were very concerned that he would misrepresent the events that took place on the trail. In order to clarify their position, they drafted a letter on October 13 in Santa Fe, and gave it to Howard Egan with instructions to deliver it to Young should Lee not accurately state their position. The officers who signed the letter were: Captains Jefferson Hunt, Jesse Hunter, and Daniel Davis; and Lieutenants George Oman, Lorenzo Clark, William Willis, Philemon Merrill, Sylvester Hulet, Cyrus Canfield, Ruel Barrus, and Robert Clift. The letter so clearly states their position and is quite significant:

> "In consequence of some excitement that has been got up in the Battalion . . . .We have deemed it prudent to lay the facts before you, in a concise and simple manner, from which this excitement springs (it having occurred since the appearance of Brother Lee, Egan & Pace in our midst on the 17th Ultimo [this month].

> "These brethren arrived in the morning just as marching orders were given and the companies were moving off, having a sixty mile paraie [sic] before them without wood or water. In despite of this latter fact & the orders officially issued Brother Lee called a halt and was there and then determined to dispossess Lieut Smith, our commander, of the command of this Battalion. Not being able to accomplish this on the ground he called Smith into his wagon, and as he rode along, gave him a lecture on the Priesthood, as well as making a severe attack on our Surgeon—that it was one of our religious principles to heal the sick by the laying on of hands; he further informed our commander that if the doctor offered to administer a dose of calomel to him he would cut his damned throat from ear to ear. When this became public among the soldiers they took Brother Lee's statement and conduct for their license and the excitement became greater and greater, till a mutiny seemed to be gaining a strong hold in the Battalion, and alarming consequences were

likely to ensue . . . . The four Captains then present in conjunction with Quarter Master Gully got together for the purpose of adopting measures to stop his career. After deliberating on the subject we thought it best to wait upon him by a committee and request him to desist. This only served to insult "his majesty" and increased the excitement in his bosom. We consequently, that same evening, saw it indispensably requisite to call a Council of all the commissioned officers in order to take decisive steps on the matter, Captain Hunt being the Senior Officer of the battalion present laid before the meeting the facts of the case, in a calm, deliberate manner, showing the impropriety of Brother Lee's conduct, and requesting him for the future to forbear urging on and aggravating the excitement of the measure, that had been taken in reference to the command. Brother Lee arose and reproached the remainder of the officers for having given their voice for Smith, also expressing his dissatisfaction at the insult offered him by the officers in trying to silence him. Captain Hunter expressed his mind to the effect, that the officers, and not Brother Lee, had been insulted; and used his influence to allay the excitement with Brother Lee, and convince him of his error. This seemed to infuriate him still more, and he declared that no man had it in his power to stop his mouth. One or two endeavored in vain to calm him a little. Captain Hunt then arose and used his authority informing him that he must from that time cease, or harsher measures would have to be taken . . . . This step seemed to be of much service and from that time, all public mutinous language was stopped, but still something under cover was continued in the same line borne out by numerous revelations, visions, and prophecies, and peace is not fairly restored until this day" (Yurtinus 1975, 150-152).

But this was not the only message that Howard Egan was to convey back to the camps at Winter Quarters. He was also tasked with delivering a personal narrative to a key confidant of Brigham Young, Hosea Stout.

On September 21st, the Battalion continued on. Lee recorded in his diary that Jefferson Hunt and Lieutenant Smith were seen riding together. Hunt was overheard telling Smith that the Mormon officers had given Smith command until Kearny was reached. Lee, Pace, Egan and others could be placed under guard if they continued their disruptive actions (Brooks 1967, 281).

For the next four days, the march continued with Dr. Sanderson still administering his dreaded calomel to the sick, despite the protestations of the sergeants and others. When they reached the Cimarron River, they found that that it was dry on the surface but that water could be reached by digging small holes and letting the underground water seep in. This lesson, like that on the Arkansas, was one that Jefferson Hunt would use on the Mojave River several years later.

On the 26th, they met an express from Kearny heading for Fort Leavenworth, and learned that the General had planned to leave Santa Fe for California the day before. Lieutenant Smith sent a letter to Kearny asking him to await the Battalion's arrival. Also sent, according to Lee, was a letter drafted by Gully asking for instructions and asking to be able to spend the Winter north of Bent's Fort. The dissidents simply did not understand the urgency General Kearny placed on their arrival in Santa Fe. Now that he had created a civil government for New Mexico, Kearny was anxious to get on to California, the ultimate goal of his mission from President Polk. But Kearny had promised the protection of the United States government to the people of New Mexico and they were facing harassment by the Navajos. Kearny wanted to send Colonel Doniphan and his troops to settle the Navajo issue, but could not do so until the arrival of the Mormon Battalion and Colonel Sterling Price's troops. Kearny simply did not have the time or patience to wait to resolve the issues of the Battalion, even if he knew about them. He had more important things to do.

According to Ricketts, on September 27th, "John D. Lee, assisted by James Pace, Levi Hancock, Andrew Lytle, and William Hyde, devised a plan to replace Captain Jefferson Hunt with Quartermaster Samuel Gully. They couldn't get enough support, so the plan failed" (Ricketts 1996, 60). William Coray wrote the following of the incident in his entry dated September 28th:

"This evening I was informed that a secret influence was used against Capt. Hunt at the same time holding up S.E. Gully as the only fit man to lead this Battalion and that Lee was at the head, assisted by Pace, Hancock, Lytle and William Hyde, that they had many dreams which gave them evidence of the justice of their position. In the mean time I heard them relate several dreams and I must say that I could not suppress thoughts running through my mind, but I can keep from writing them" (Journal History of the Church, September 28, 1846).

William Coray's statement of the conspiracy against Jefferson Hunt and the other officers, and his comment about his own feelings is very telling. Coray was no fan of either Lieutenant Smith or Dr. Sanderson, but he was loyal to the officers placed in charge by Brigham Young and the Twelve. He clearly did not approve of the clandestine attempt by Lee and the others to replace them. This feeling was held by the great majority of the Battalion's troops. When the opportunity came to rise up against the officers and support Brigham Young's emissary and the ranking Church Authority present, they chose to follow the original course and pay their allegiance to the original Mormon officers first appointed by Young. The success of the Mormon Battalion depended on their loyalty, and they showed where it lay. This demonstration of fidelity to the original cause of the Battalion and their officers was the definitive statement that they chose to make the march of the Mormon Battalion a resounding success in spite of the forceful opposition thrown at them.

One last test of fidelity would befall the Battalion in the final eight days before the Battalion reached Santa Fe. From the time that Lee, Egan and Pace joined them, the Battalion had moved through what is now the southwest corner of Kansas, the southeast tip of Colorado, across the Oklahoma Panhandle and into the current state of New Mexico. By October 1st, they were well into New Mexico, and Santa Fe was just over 150 miles away. Their first major goal was nearly in sight.

On October 2nd, the Battalion was met by a unit of Kearny's Dragoons heading east from Santa Fe to Fort Leavenworth. They brought orders from General Kearny that if the Battalion was not in Santa Fe within eight days (October 10th), they would be discharged. In his diary entry for the day, John D. Lee states that if they were so discharged, they would receive "1 yr rashion [sic] & pay" (Brooks 1967, 289). No one else recorded this provision. Kearny would never have made such an order since he badly needed the Battalion in Santa Fe and California, and did not have the authority to make such a decision in any case. Reacting to his new order, Lieutenant Smith pressed the Battalion on and told the sergeants to strictly obey his orders. They did as directed and several men were put under guard for not following their orders, including William Follett, who was reported by Sergeant William Coray for calling Lieutenant Smith a "Negro driver" (Ricketts 1996, 61).

On Saturday, the Battalion started out as normal, marched six miles and then stopped. At that point, Lieutenant Smith and the Mormon officers met to discuss the new requirement that they reach Santa Fe by the 10th. Considering that there were many sick and lame, in addition to some remaining families, it was clear that this would probably be a difficult, if not impossible, task. If the Battalion pushed on too hard, the sick would slow them down; and abandoning the sick was not an option to the Mormons. On the other hand, reaching California had been their principle goal since the Battalion began its march over two months before. The four captains present all indicated that California was the goal and that they should try for it.

Adjutant George Dykes came forward with a solution to the problem. His idea was to pick fifty healthy men from each company and they, along with most of the officers and sufficient supply wagons drawn by the best teams, would press on as fast as possible to Santa Fe. The remainder, including the rest of the families, would follow along at the best pace they could. The lieutenants of each company would accompany this unit and the senior lieutenant, George Oman of Jefferson Hunts' A Company, would be in overall command. The officers considered this proposal and agreed that it was the best option. Of the twenty-two officers, only Lieutenants James Pace, Samuel Gully, Andrew Lytle and Lorenzo Clark opposed it. Of these, James Pace was nearly pressed to revolt (Brooks 1967, 291). Needless to say, John D.

Lee, Levi Hancock and David Pettegrew also opposed the idea, claiming again that a division of the Battalion was not in accordance with Brigham Young's instructions.

As sound as Young's instructions may have been, he could not have anticipated the day-to-day contingencies of the trail. The officers led by Jefferson Hunt were delegated the responsibility and authority to make the necessary decisions to deal with those contingencies. Separating the Battalion into two units at that point was the only realistic way to meet the overall goal of a successful march to California. The division was only temporary, since the units were to reunite in a short time in Santa Fe. This option created little threat to the Battalion, and if it was accepted by General Kearny, it presented a solution that would save the primary mission of the march of the Battalion—California.

The officers explained the new program to the men, who greeted it with mixed feelings. Many didn't like the division; others objected to the forced march that would be necessary to reach Santa Fe; others hoped that the venture would fail so that they would be discharged. But when volunteers were called for, 250 men quickly stepped forward. Levi Hancock was asked to assign musicians to the forward unit and complied, but did not volunteer himself. Lee and Egan rode with the forward unit, since their primary mission was to collect the pay and their internal conspiracies could no longer affect the march to Santa Fe. By 5 p.m., the division assignments were complete and the forward unit set out. During the evening hours and under a full moon, they marched another twenty miles and stopped just before midnight near the present location of Wagon Mound, New Mexico.

With the conclusion of that day's march, the threat of imminent collapse of the Battalion died. Santa Fe was a relatively short distance away; Lee and the other opponents had been quieted; Hancock, Lee and other dissidents were physically divided; but most importantly, the men of the Battalion had reaffirmed their commitment to carry out the wishes of Brigham Young and the Twelve Apostles. As John Steele of D Company stated: "We were all very vexed to party, but those who are bound must obey" (Yurtinus 1975, 164).

The same day (October 2nd) that the Battalion received word from General Kearny that they must be in Santa Fe by October 10th, the General received confirmation from Santa Fe that Colonel Allen had died. Kearny, an experienced officer who was seriously depending on the Mormon Battalion to supplement and support his regular Army troops in California, realized the need for an experienced commander to be in charge of the Battalion. Kearny selected one of his best field officers, Captain Philip St. George Cooke, to return immediately to Santa Fe for the purpose of assuming command of the Battalion upon its arrival in Santa Fe. Cooke set out and arrived in the New Mexico capital shortly before the arrival of the first unit of the Battalion.

The forward unit of the Battalion pressed on quickly for Santa Fe. The day following their separation from the rear unit, they reached the first of several Mexican settlements on the trail. For the first time since leaving Fort Leavenworth over a month and a half before, the Mormons encountered civilians living in small towns along the route. They were fascinated by the houses and buildings which were made of adobe. They learned that the structures were comprised of dried mud or large un-fired bricks. They were grateful to find fresh produce and other commodities that were not found on the trail. The forward unit also noted that the local farmers made extensive use of irrigation to grow crops. They were not familiar with irrigation since it was not necessary in the East where rain provided all of the water needed for crops. They also began to see for the first time the snowfields that capped the peaks of the Sangre de Cristo Mountains, the southernmost extension of the Rocky Mountains. They were drawing nearer to Santa Fe and the exotic lands of the West.

Averaging over twenty miles per day, the forward unit reached the mountains east of Santa Fe by October 7th. John D. Lee had come to accept the conditions of command of the Battalion and recorded in his diary of this date that he engaged in friendly conversation with Adjutant Dykes, Lieutenant Smith and others in the hopes of reuniting the Battalion (Brooks 1967, 295).

The following day, a message arrived from General Kearny advising the Battalion that Philip St. George Cooke had been promoted to the rank of Lieutenant Colonel and given the command of the Battalion when it reached Santa Fe. Lee records in his diary that some of the Mormon officers, Adjutant Dykes and Lieutenant Smith were stunned by the news and that this could have been forestalled had the officers written to General Kearny earlier as he had advised (Brooks 1967, 297-298). In this assessment, Lee was wrong. Kearny was a seasoned and well-trained officer and had the success of the Army of the West riding on the decision of who should command the Mormon Battalion. He would not have left that decision to the Mormons themselves. Only General Stephen Watts Kearny could select his subordinate officers.

On Friday, October 8, 1846, the advance unit of the Mormon Battalion crossed over Glorieta Pass and descended northwest into Santa Fe. There they found that the military commander was their old friend from Missouri, Colonel Alexander Doniphan. He ordered a 100-gun salute to be fired by his troops as the Battalion marched through town to their campsite. Doniphan saw that they were immediately given badly-needed food and supplies. Even John D. Lee had to admit that the warm reception foretold "better times ahead" (Brooks 1967, 299). The unit under Lieutenant Oman continued to march, with some grumbling from the troops. Most however, reached Santa Fe on October 12th, and the Battalion was once again reunited.

Eight hundred miles to the northwest of the Battalion, on October 5th, while the two Battalion units were on their final dash to Santa Fe, the Donner/Reed Party was traveling along the Humboldt River, east of present-day Golconda, Nevada. On a particularly difficult ascent of a sand and rock hill near the river, two wagon teams got tangled up. John Snyder, a teamster for the Graves family, got into a verbal dispute with James Frazier Reed, the owner of the other team. Within seconds, the altercation escalated and Snyder began hitting Reed with the butt of his whip. In self-defense, Reed drew his hunting knife and stabbed Snyder just below the collar bone. Very quickly, Snyder was dead, and many of the others charged Reed with murder (Stewart 1936, 63).

An impromptu trail court was held later that day, and with his friends, the Donners and some others traveling well ahead of his group, Reed was found guilty. He was banished from the party and departed the next morning, leaving his sick wife and three children behind with several teamsters and servants. Reed caught up with the Donners, and he and one other man began a forced journey to Sacramento, over 330 miles away. By October 31st, the main Donner party found themselves just east of the crest of the Sierra Nevada Mountains near the lake and pass that today bears their name. Then a disastrous snowstorm hit, slammed shut the pass and the only overland wagon road to the California coast. Of the eighty-nine persons in the party, forty-one eventually died and forty-eight survived the Winter, some of those surviving by resorting to cannibalism.

Reed reached Sutter's Fort (Sacramento) on October 28th, and was able to spread the word about the trapped party, which included his family. Following several failed rescue attempts and some service as a volunteer in the war against Mexico, he eventually was among the first to reach the survivors the following Spring.

Dissention and disruption no longer played a major role in the affairs of the Battalion. That is not to say, however, that all would be quiet. Dissention by Levi Hancock and several of his followers would continue throughout the life of the Battalion and beyond. However, the skills, bearing and authority of Colonel Philip St. George Cooke assured that dissention played no further role in day-to-day operations.

Jefferson Hunt had been successful in quelling any incipient mutiny by first using his fellow officers as counselors in reaching decisions and then by firmly issuing orders when necessary to stop the opposing forces. It is ironic that his two major adversaries organizing and supporting the dissention were both men who had played previous roles in his life. It should be remembered that it was Levi Hancock's brother, Solomon, who first introduced Hunt and his wife, Celia, to the Mormon Church, and it was he who first sheltered the newly-arrived convert John D. Lee, in Missouri. And in the intervening years,

Hunt had known, socialized and participated in Church activities with both men.

Think for a moment of the Battalion's formidable accomplishment in reaching Santa Fe. Five hundred men who had been fleeing for their lives only three months before had enlisted in volunteer service at the urging of their Church leaders. Regardless of physical condition, and without the benefit of pre-service physical examinations, they set out to walk on a two thousand mile journey that would last more than a year, most leaving their families behind to an uncertain future. Nearly all suffered from the trials of sore and blistered feet, sore muscles, inadequate clothing and very little other comforts. Many were terribly ill at some point during the march, and those who were sick were treated badly by Dr. Sanderson and Lieutenant Smith. A few even died. The march pushed them to the limits of their physical and emotional endurance. But in spite of it all, the Mormon Battalion reached Santa Fe on time to play an important role in the Army of the West.

Chapter 8

A New Commander

Philip St. George Cooke was born in Virginia on June 13, 1809. His father, a Navy Surgeon during the Revolutionary War, was captured and sent as a prisoner of war to Bermuda. There he met and eventually married Philip's mother. Cooke's name probably is derived in part from his mother's home city of St. George, Bermuda.

At the age of fourteen, Cooke was accepted into the United States Military Academy, where he graduated four years later. Commissioned as a Second Lieutenant on July 1, 1827, his first assignment was Jefferson Barracks, Missouri. In 1828, he first met then-Major Stephen Watts Kearny on frontier duty. The following year, he was part of a force sent to protect traders on the Santa Fe Trail. Following that, he served in the Black Hawk War, spent time again on frontier duty, and as part of the Dragoons. In 1835, Cooke was promoted to Captain and spent some time recruiting in the East before being sent West to rejoin the Dragoons.

Ironically, during this same period, Philip's older brother John Esten Cooke, a physician and teacher, was noted as one of the major proponents of using calomel to treat nearly every disease.

During the first half of the 1840s, Cooke found himself again protecting Santa Fe traders and participating in excursions in present-day Wyoming, all the while serving under Kearny. By 1846, with the likelihood of war with Mexico, Cooke was hoping for an assignment with Zachary Taylor in Mexico proper. However, Kearny was not about to let one of his most experienced officers out of his grasp. So it was that Cooke became part of Kearny's Army of the West. With nearly twenty years Army service, most along the frontier, Cooke was a valuable resource for Kearny. Cooke had dealt with his share of dissention, desertions and volunteers during his frontier career, and Kearny properly felt that he was ideal to command the Mormon volunteers, who were largely unknown to him. When Kearny received confirmation of the death of Colonel Allen, his first and obvious choice to lead the Mormon Battalion was Philip St. George Cooke.

Cooke's reaction was one of disappointment. For a career Army officer, the most desirable position would be one in an active military campaign where combat was likely and the opportunity to distinguish himself was the greatest. Commanding an infantry unit marching to California to provide strategic backup and support for other Army officers did not seem to Cooke to offer that opportunity. Combat duty was not likely with the command he was given. Cooke, however, was loyal and he gave his full commitment to Kearny's orders. History later showed that in his entire forty-six year career as an Army officer, Cooke was most remembered for his march with the Mormon Battalion.

Philip St. George Cooke was given the brevet rank of Lieutenant Colonel by General Kearny. On October 3rd, he left Kearny along the Rio Grande and returned to Santa Fe, arriving on October 7th, a few days in advance of the first group of the Battalion. Meanwhile, on October 6th, along the Rio Grande below the present city of Socorro, New Mexico, Kearny's Army saw a group of riders approaching them from the south. In one of the significant events of the Mexican War in the West, Kearny was met by the renowned mountain man and guide Christopher "Kit" Carson, and an escort of sixteen men. Carson, who had been serving as a guide for John C. Fremont in California, had been charged by Fremont and Commodore Stockton to carry a very important message to Washington—California was conquered. The feat was accomplished with a small number of Americans in Northern California, friendly Mexicans, Fremont's small group of soldiers and Stockton's modest naval force. They had taken California with very little resistance. All looked well; California appeared to be securely in the hands of the United States.

Kit Carson had traveled 800 miles in twenty-six days on his way to deliver the news to Washington. He still had nearly a thousand miles of overland travel until he could use the steamboats and railroads to hurry the message along. Kearny quickly reassessed his plans. Relying on these new reports, Kearny believed that he no longer needed a large force of Dragoons to fight the Mexicans in California. Rather, he believed that it was essential to assume the role of governor immediately, as directed by President Polk. Additionally, there was a greater need for troops in New Mexico to pacify the Navajo and then to proceed to Mexico to help with the war there. Accordingly, Kearny made a fateful decision to send two hundred of his troops back to Santa Fe and proceed as fast as possible with only one hundred Dragoons to act as an escort.

Kearny also realized that he needed an expert to get him to the California coast as quickly as possible. The most qualified expert of all was Kit Carson, who had just ridden into his camp. Carson had completed several trips across the Great Basin to California with Fremont, knew both the Northern and Southern routes, and was well acquainted with the routes through California itself. The General quickly began his recruitment of Carson as his lead guide. For his part, Carson wanted to complete the mission to Washington as directed by his friend and mentor, Fremont, and visit with his family at Taos, New Mexico. Reluctantly, Carson was convinced to give up his mission and return to California as Kearny's chief guide and scout.

To accomplish this swap, Kearny gave the mission to Washington to another legendary mountain man who was with Kearny as a guide and scout—Thomas "Broken Hand" Fitzpatrick. Fitzpatrick was a long-time friend of Carson and was willing to take on the assignment. With the swap made, Fitzpatrick took the express messages and Carson's escort and headed East. Carson showed Kearny the Gila River route to the Coast that he had just traversed. Two hundred of the Dragoons began the return to Santa Fe to assist Doniphan in New Mexico, and later in Mexico.

Unfortunately, California was not as peaceful as Kearny had been led to believe. His arrival in California was to be marked with a major battle in which he lost a number of his remaining soldiers. Similarly, New Mexico was not to remain as peaceful as when Kearny left. In a short time, a revolt against the Americans broke out and the new governor, Charles Bent, was killed along with a number of others.

Philip St. George Cooke arrived back in Santa Fe on October 7th, the same day that Kearny and Carson began the trail to California and Tom Fitzpatrick began his trip to Washington via Santa Fe. Four days later, Fitzpatrick reached Santa Fe and conveyed the new information to Cooke. Late that afternoon, Captains Jefferson Hunt, Jesse Hunter, James Brown, Lieutenant Lorenzo Clark, plus John D. Lee and Howard Egan met with Cooke, who explained the events in California and told them of Kearny's orders for the Battalion. They would take with them sixty days' provisions and otherwise travel as lightly as possible, since they would be crossing over territory where there were no established roads. For a good portion of the route, they would have to carve their own wagon road out of the wilderness. It would become the first all-weather, year-round road connecting the Pacific Coast with the rest of the United States. Not only would it serve the Battalion, it would have major implications for future military support and commercial enterprise.

Cooke then explained that he and Doniphan had discussed the issue of the sick and the women and children of the Battalion and that they would send (but not discharge) them to winter at El Pueblo so they could rejoin the Westward Migration the following Summer. In an abrupt change of attitude, both Levi Hancock and John D. Lee agreed to this division of the Battalion. Lee wrote in his diary: "This I considered to be a fair & liberal proposal, for I was well persuaded that neither the Sick, Women & children could stand the fatigue & exposures of the Journey to go around with the Bat" (Brooks 1967, 302). It is quite possible that the change in attitude were due to the change in commander, which negated any need for an effort to discredit Lieutenant Smith, Jefferson Hunt or any of the other officers.

With the arrival of Lieutenant Oman's rear detachment the next day, the Battalion was again complete. Cooke lost no time in preparing for his march to California. One of his first efforts was to inspect the Battalion. A substantial number of men were found to be sick or impaired enough to require detachment to El Pueblo. (Dr. Sanderson did not record participating in or providing medical opinion for this inspection.) Cooke's original plan was to issue disability discharges to these men. When challenged on this idea, Cooke took the matter to Colonel Doniphan, who ordered the men to be placed on detached duty with pay. The sick and disabled soldiers, along with several officers, all of the children and all but five of the women, were to be sent to El Pueblo under the command of Captain James Brown. This detachment included ninety-one members of the Battalion. Brown was replaced as captain of C Company by Lieutenant George Rosecrans. Included in those sent to El Pueblo were Hunt's son, John, his plural wife, Matilda Nease Hunt, her brother, Peter, and sister, Ellen.

Some of the men of the Battalion prevailed on Doniphan to assign them to the sick detachment going to El Pueblo. For example, John Hess called on Doniphan when his Captain (Davis) wouldn't agree, and made a plea to accompany his wife to El Pueblo. Doniphan, in turn, asked the opinion of Adjutant Dykes, who agreed. Hess was permitted to go (Hess 1931). Similarly, when the men heard that all of the wives would be required to go to El Pueblo, several men, including Captains Hunter and Davis, and Sergeants Brown and Coray met with Cooke and convinced him to amend his rule to permit their four wives to continue to accompany the Battalion at their own expense (Ricketts 1996, 67). In a short time, orders were issued permitting men whose wives were being sent to El Pueblo to go with them, and about twenty men did so.

Cooke also found that the Battalion was composed of men who were poorly drilled in military matters, but who were obedient and willing to follow his orders. One of his first tasks was to reorganize the Battalion staff. The most pressing problem he had was that of obtaining draft animals and supplies for the march. Kearny had taken nearly all of the serviceable animals left in Santa Fe with him. In addition, Doniphan badly needed good, strong animals for the drive south to Mexico. While supplies had been rushed West at the start of the conflict, some were at Bent's Fort, others were still on the road, and still more had been taken by Kearny and Doniphan. The question of getting draft animals and food was not simply solved. Accordingly, Cooke felt that the matter of obtaining and issuing supplies should be in the hands of regular Army officers with training and experience in that area. He appointed Lieutenant Andrew Jackson Smith, the former commander of the Battalion, to be quartermaster, and Second Lieutenant George Stoneman to be assistant Quartermaster. Stoneman, whose West Point roommate was Thomas "Stonewall" Jackson of Civil War fame, was later elected as the fifteenth governor of the State of California (1883-1887).

This change meant that Samuel Gully, who had served as the Quartermaster since the Battalion's inception, was removed from that position. The change, regardless of how necessary to the mission, was not viewed favorably by the men of the Battalion. Gully was very popular and had been one of the most outspoken opponents of Lieutenant Smith—who was now to replace him. Regardless of how wise a military move this may have been, the personnel change raised many objections. Cooke had neither the time nor the patience to deal with the issue; he had to successfully march the Battalion another thousand miles across unknown deserts and mountains and that need outweighed the politics of the issue and his popularity among the troops. In his diary, Lee goes so far as to lay the blame for Gully's removal with "some of the officers"—meaning Battalion officers (Brooks 1967, 303). Gully was devastated by the turn of events and, thus, was permitted to resign from the Battalion. He returned to Winter Quarters with John D. Lee and his party. One additional man, Roswell Stephens, resigned from the Battalion and accompanied Lee as an escort.

On October 13th, two meetings were held with the Battalion. At the first, held in the morning, the plan to send the sick detachment to El Pueblo was announced and was received favorably by the troops. Jefferson Hunt also spoke and beseeched the men to send as much of their pay as possible back to Winter Quarters. He told them that this would likely be the last opportunity to do so. At the second meeting, held in the evening, Adjutant Dykes read the order appointing Smith and Stoneman to their quartermaster duties, thereby relieving Gully. Lee and others continued to support Gully, and Lee wrote on October 14th that he assisted in preparing a petition to Cooke and Doniphan to reinstate Gully (Brooks 1967, 304). However, nothing came of the effort.

Cooke continued with his reorganization of the Battalion. Several of the sergeants in Company C were reduced in rank and new sergeants, including Daniel Tyler, were appointed to replace them. Sergeant Major Glines was sent with the sick detachment and James Ferguson was appointed to replace him. The changes would continue after the Battalion began its march to California. On November 1st, Adjutant Dykes was made Captain of Company D, replacing Nelson Higgins, who had been sent to El Pueblo. The sergeant major position was then filled by Philemon Merrill. Dr. Sanderson retained his position as Surgeon. However, under Cooke's watchful eye, he was no longer a serious problem to the sick of the Battalion. As they marched south along the Rio Grande, there would be one more sick detachment formed for El Pueblo. But at this point, the major changes in the reorganization of the Battalion were complete.

Meanwhile, back in the camps along the Missouri River, the Saints continued to prepare for Winter. The man charged by Brigham Young with securing the camp was Hosea Stout, who essentially acted in the capacity of the senior police and military official. He posted and checked nightly guards, gathered information about any "mobbers" who might be about, guarded cattle, and dealt with disputes among families and others. Stout was brought into the Church by C.C. Rich, and was in almost daily contact with Brigham Young and the Twelve Apostles. At Nauvoo, Stout had been an officer in the Nauvoo Legion and acted as the head of the police force. Later, in Salt Lake City, Stout became a prominent lawyer and legislator. He was also a close personal friend and business associate of Jesse Hunter, Captain of Battalion Company B. He also had his own run-in with John D. Lee.

On August 1st, only two weeks after the departure of the Mormon Battalion from Council Bluffs, John D. Lee went to Hosea Stout and told him that those persons in the camp at Council Bluffs who were saying that Stout had fallen out of favor with Brigham Young were "put to shame" and that Brigham was satisfied with him (Brooks 1964, Vol. 1, 184). Had Stout ever had problems in his relationship with Brigham Young, he would have immediately known about it, since he and Young were in almost daily contact. Stout's position required near total loyalty and trust between the two men. He was a strong, self-assured leader who did not need a meddlesome intermediary like Lee to tell him of his relationship with the president of the Mormons. It is likely that Stout saw this effort by Lee for what it was—a pompous attempt to ingratiate himself with another close confident of Brigham Young.

In February 1846, Jesse Hunter had worked closely with Stout in setting up the groups that protected the various camps of the Saints on their migration Westward from Nauvoo. And in the Spring of 1846, Stout and Hunter agreed to combine their resources and equipment to form a partnership and move across the Missouri River, west of Council Bluffs. (Stout 1953, 72). Their plans, however, were stalled by Spring rains and, finally, news of the outbreak of the Mexican War. When Hunter left with the Mormon Battalion, he took with him his plural wife, Lydia, whom he had married in February 1846, but left his first wife, Kesiah, and five of their children at Council Bluffs. Hunter's son William, fifteen, accompanied his father's company as a drummer (Ricketts 1996, 30-31).

As the time for the departure of the Battalion to California and for Lee, Egan and their party to return to Council Bluffs grew near, the men wrote letters to friends and families left behind. Fortunately, several of those missives were retained and still exist. One of them was written by Captain Jessie Hunter to Kesiah on October 12, 1846, from Santa Fe. The last paragraph on the two page letter reads as follows:

"A word or two to Capt Stout Dear Sir

I received a few lines from you which was very [??]—things are mooving [sic] off now tolerable well but we have had some considerable trouble in camp in consequence of some geting [sic] religion—but they soon received a thorn in their side lest they should [??] through the abundance of revalations [sic] and visions they received. I have not time to retell these matters if you will call on H Egan he will tell you the whole affair" (Hunter 1846).

It is clear that this paragraph is a thinly coded message from Hunter to his good friend Stout, a close associate of Brigham Young, to seek out and hear the verbal account given to Howard Egan. It is also clear that Hunter, and probably Hunt, specifically met with Egan to give him additional details (not included in the letter) of the difficulties to date, and that they chose not to commit those details to writing where they might be intercepted and/or destroyed. Although there are no diary entries to show that the message was passed on, we can assume that Stout got the message from Hunter, listened to Egan, and passed the information on to Young.

On the evening of October 14th, a fandango—or ball—hosted by the local residents and members of the Missouri Volunteers was held. Cooke felt that relations between the new occupiers and the citizens would best be served by a strong attendance by the Battalion members and their ladies. He encouraged the captains to attend and, in turn, the officers, including Jefferson Hunt, encouraged the others of the Battalion to attend. Most of the officers and about three-quarters of the troops paid the two dollar admission charge—much to the chagrin of John D. Lee, who felt that the money would better serve the poor in Winter Quarters. He also did not particularly believe in socializing with persons of other faiths or different moral standards. Lee was disappointed to see some of the Battalion drinking to excess and gambling their sparse funds (Brooks 1967, 304-305). William Coray reluctantly went, and said that the "accommodations were poor," and the "music was tolerable, but the ill manners of the females disgusted me." He also complained that supper was a "grab game" and that "the man that waited for manners lost his supper" (Ricketts 1996, 69).

Lee recorded that the following night, someone stole Dr. Sanderson's trunk and broke into it, stealing money and a gold watch worth $300. Also stolen was scout Phillip Thompson's gold watch worth $180. Two mules were also made off with. Men were confined to their tents for a while and a search was made for the missing items, but they were never found (Brooks 1967, 306). Thirty years later in his autobiography, Lee recalls the incident and says that after he, Egan, Gully and Stephens started the trip back to Winter Quarters, Stephens appeared with the mules. Lee then says that he believed that Howard Egan and Roswell Stephens were responsible for the theft of the mules, watches and money, even though they did not admit it (Lee 1877, 194). Interestingly, no one else with the Battalion mentioned this event. It is not recorded in Dr. Sanderson's journal, and he would have undoubtedly mentioned such a major event had it taken place. As the military historian, Sherman Fleek, points out: "One must conclude that John Lee was not telling the truth, besides blaming a deed on Howard Egan" (Fleek 2006, 251). Since there is no other evidence that the theft took place, Lee was either casting aspersions at Egan and Stephens or, if there was in fact a theft, was directly involved. Thus, by his own admission, Lee was once again suspiciously close to a major breech of integrity.

The Army in Santa Fe was very short of money to pay off the men of the Battalion. Since trade with Mexico had ceased, there was a major shortfall in cash for use in normal transactions. This problem was not uncommon on the Western frontier for years to come. However, in this case, the Army accommodated the men of the Battalion by writing checks to them for their pay. When it was cashed locally, it was usually at a steep discount of up to twenty-five percent. When Jefferson Hunt encouraged the men to send money back to Winter Quarters with Lee and Egan, many complied by giving both cash and their newly-written checks. Lee records that two who did not give money to take back were Captains Hunt and Hunter. Lee collected nearly $2,500 for return to Winter Quarters. He kept possession of half and gave half to Egan so that should anything happen to either one of them the other might still be able to protect a portion. On the evening of October 19th, according to Lee, Egan stayed in town and got very drunk, but was found in the street with the money safe (Brooks 1967, 309).

Howard Egan was no angel. In 1851, he was tried and acquitted for murdering a man who had seduced one of his wives while he was away in the California goldfields. However, in light of his own failings, we must question whether Lee, in his diary entry on October 19th and his autobiography written forty years later, was accurately reporting the facts or was attempting to discredit Egan for bearing the messages regarding the dissention with the Battalion back to Brigham Young and the Twelve.

After some difficulty in finding mules for their return trip, Lee with Egan, Gully and Stephens began the trip back to the camps of the Saints. The first night out, Lee says that an attempt was made to rob them by three men who were detected by the dog "Little Trip," who was still providing protection for them. The journey home had little else of note happen except that they managed to find several mules which probably had been part of a trader's caravan that had been attacked several days before by Pawnees. They experienced one more broken axel, which they quickly repaired with a spare brought from Santa Fe. Lee's last entry is dated November 19th, when he and his party were in the northwest corner of Missouri, a short distance from Winter Quarters (Brooks 1967, 325).

In Santa Fe, Cooke and his quartermasters struggled to find enough mules and other stock and supplies to outfit them for California. Cooke managed to find 140 mules, though many were in poor condition. Hearing that Kearny had decided to send back the wagons and use pack animals en route to the Coast, Cooke also obtained packsaddles for his mules, just in case they were needed. Similarly, there was a sparse amount of food available in Santa Fe. Most of the supplies were at Bent's Fort or scattered back along the trail; Doniphan's and Price's units needed a substantial amount of food, and Kearny had taken much with him. Accordingly, the Battalion was not able to secure all they needed and spent most of the following months on less than full rations.

On October 18th, Captain Brown and his detachment of the sick and families left Santa Fe for El Pueblo. The detachment contained 121 people—ninety-one soldiers and officers, Dr. McIntire, nineteen women and ten children. Two of the men died en route. They traveled north, over Raton Pass, and nearly to Bent's Fort where they obtained supplies. Then they traveled west along the Arkansas to El Pueblo, arriving near there on November 15th.

The Mormon Battalion left Santa Fe for California just before noon on October 19th. It consisted of nearly 400 Mormon volunteers, five women—including four wives—and Cooke and his staff. To haul supplies and people as necessary, there were nearly fifty wagons, most pulled by mules, but six pulled by oxen. Twelve of the wagons were private family wagons, five were wagons owned by the men of each company to be used to carry personal belongings to cut down on the load they had to carry. The first day, they traveled six miles south along the Rio Grande and stopped to wait for Cooke and others to catch up before the trip began in earnest. The last leg of the trip to California had begun.

In 1846, the names "California" and "New Mexico" meant something quite different than today. Then, New Mexico included the territory in New Mexico, much of today's Arizona and much of southern Nevada around what is now Las Vegas. California included today's California, the states of Nevada and Utah, and portions of Colorado and Wyoming. The men and families of the Battalion knew that the future destination of the Saints was "California." Most did not understand that Brigham Young and the Twelve Apostles were looking more to the western slopes of the Wasatch Range as their eventual home. According to Yurtinus: "From all of these indications, the rank and file soldier believed that the final destination of the Latter-day Saints would be in upper California near San Francisco and the Sacramento Valley" (Yurtinus 1975, 196).

Thus, as the men set out from Santa Fe, many believed quite literally that they were marching to their new home. They felt that they would be discharged somewhere very near the spot where all the Saints would reunite and where they would be free from persecution. It was this feeling that had driven them from the time of their enlistment. It had given them the strength to reject the entreaties from their ecclesiastical leaders and to follow their military leaders during the previous three months.

Again, as Yurtinus has pointed out:

"From their frame of reference, the Mormon Battalion was a 'Military Colony' en route to California at the expense of the American Government. They could not revolt against army authority for fear of losing a gathering place in California and jeopardizing the safety of the body of Mormons at Council Bluffs. Their military services and pay would help all Mormons gather in upper California undisturbed by mobs or older residents. In order to accomplish this goal they owed one year's allegiance to the United States government and would tolerate non-Mormon officers, forced marches, divisions, strict discipline, and other aggravating problems without revolting" (Yurtinus 1975, 196-197).

With a new and substantially more experienced commander in Philip St. George Cooke, and with most of the Mormon officers, including Jefferson Hunt, still in firm control, the Battalion set out on the final leg for what they thought would be their new home—California.

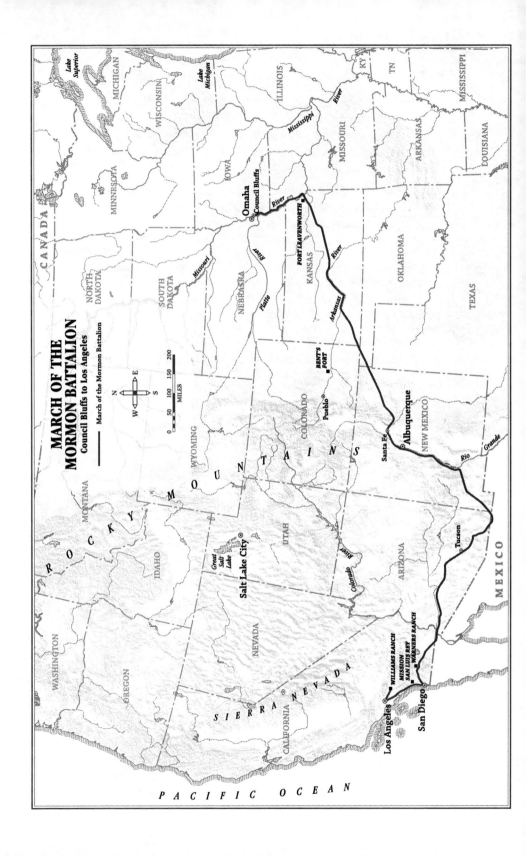

Chapter 9

The March to the Coast

The Battalion left Santa Fe on October 19th and moved six miles to where the animals could graze. When Lieutenant Colonel Cooke arrived at the camp later that day, he found "all huddled in the sandy creek bottom; no grass; many mules without ropes or picket pins, they, and the beeves and oxen were herded under rather difficult circumstances." He continues: "The battalion has never been drilled, and though obedient, has little discipline; they exhibit great heedlessness and ignorance, and some obstinacy" (Cooke 1951, 48). Clearly, the new commander had to take some quick measures to establish control. Beginning then, he enforced stricter discipline and issued a number of orders designed to gain better control. Additional pickets were devised to hold the stock, and the night guard over the animals was significantly increased. Nevertheless, some animals still managed to wander away and had to be gathered up before the march could resume the following day.

The Battalion was not alone with this problem. On October 23rd, they encountered three companies of Price's group, which had left Santa Fe four days before the Battalion. The major in charge complained to Cooke that after each day's travel it took him "two or three [hours] to collect the animals" (Cooke 1951, 49) Near Albuquerque, Cooke had procured twenty good quality mules. Unfortunately, Kearny's orders to him were to provide the best twenty-one mules for Fitzpatrick's express mission to Washington. Cooke was left with only marginal animals to take them a thousand miles to California. He could not afford to lose mules; they had to be taken care of.

One of Cooke's first orders was to have the company baggage wagon precede its company in travel. This caused a dust cloud in front of each unit, which the men disliked intensely. They were not sure about their new commander and began to watch him closely. On the second day out of Santa Fe, Captain Jesse Hunter's mule wandered away and he went in search of it without first obtaining permission from Cooke. When the Colonel discovered this, he ordered Hunter to march at the rear of his company instead of the head for the next three days. On October 23rd, Cooke also met with Jefferson Hunt and the other captains and "earnestly exhorted them to lend me more efficient assistance in requiring the mules to be properly grazed and fed; or else the expedition must soon fall through. They made excellent promises" (Cooke 1951, 50). That same day, Cooke demoted one of the first sergeants for failing to meet his strict standards for forming the company at reveille in the morning. Three days later, Cooke met with his captains again and gave them instructions on how to prepare the mules for packing and pulling wagons.

Cooke's quartermasters were only able to obtain sixty days rations prior to leaving Santa Fe, and the estimated time to California was 100 days. As a result, the Battalion started the march under reduced rations. As they proceeded south along the Rio Grande, Cooke was able to purchase some additional mules and bought 380 poor quality sheep and lambs to take along for increased rations. Some additional amounts of corn and other produce were also purchased. As they progressed south, the road became sandy and the mules had difficulty pulling the wagons, which required the men to help by pushing. In some cases, wagons were double-teamed and as many as twenty men were needed to get them up the sand hills. The rations were sparse, the discipline was strict, the work was hard, and the men were getting concerned about whether they would ever reach California.

Cooke had a difficult task, and not the least of his worries was which route to take to California. Generally, he knew he was to go south along the Rio

Grande to some point, then west to follow the Gila River, then into California. The maps of the time were grossly inadequate and most of the known routes dipped far into Mexico. His intention was to build a wagon road and to keep it within the newly-captured territory. Various portions of the route he expected to take were known—the Rio Grande Valley, the area around Tucson, the Gila River Route, the Colorado River area, and the Coastal Ranges of California. Other trails such as those between the Rio Grande and Tucson and the Gila River were not well known, nor were some of those portions west of the Colorado River. Clearly, Cooke needed guides and scouts to provide him with what information was known and what could be found out about the new territories.

As the senior captain of the Battalion, Jefferson Hunt undoubtedly was in a position to work with and observe the role played by the scouts. On the trail from Fort Leavenworth to Santa Fe, it was a simple matter to follow the tracks of hundreds of wagons and thousands of livestock that had preceded them. But at other times they might be following only ill-defined Indian footpaths or no paths at all. In many instances, water sources were not easily seen and had to be scouted well in advance of the arrival of the Battalion so that sufficient water for both people and animals was found. The scouts used a combination of personal knowledge, information garnered from residents (both Mexican and Indian,) and general scouting skills to fulfill their jobs. Shortly after his discharge and for several years thereafter, Jefferson Hunt would apply these same skills.

Frontier scouts have long been portrayed as wise, loyal and experienced—but rough and uneducated. The Mormon Battalion scouts were a diverse group, and were far from that stereotypical portrayal. There were six or seven scouts, but five of them are of particular note and are discussed here. The first, Pauline Weaver, became a fur trapper in 1830. By 1832, he was married in New Mexico and had traveled to Los Angeles. Before the Mexican War began, in 1845, he applied to Mexican Governor Pio Pico in Los Angeles for land ownership in San Gorgonio east of today's San Bernardino. By the time Cooke enlisted his help, he had made a number of trips along the southern route to California. In later years, Weaver lived among many of the Mormon Battalion members who settled in San Bernardino and his path crossed that of Jefferson Hunt on many occasions.

Another scout was Baptiste Tesson who had been with John C. Fremont on his 1843-44 expedition to California and had traveled throughout California and the Great Basin.

Dr. Stephen G. Foster, twenty-six, who graduated from Yale, had practiced medicine in Missouri. Foster was fluent in Spanish and was used as an interpreter and special emissary for Cooke.

Also enlisted by Cooke was Willard Preble Hall, an attorney who was part of Doniphan's regiment and assisted in writing the new laws for New Mexico. He requested discharge from Doniphan and then signed up with Cooke. Shortly before leaving Missouri with Doniphan, Hall was elected as a Congressman from Missouri. He later served three terms in Congress and eventually went on to be the Lieutenant Governor (during which time he also served as a Brigadier General in the Missouri Militia) and then Governor of Missouri during the Civil War.

Two other scouts retained by Kearny were sent back to assist Cooke. The first, and possibly the most fascinating, was Jean Baptiste Charbonneau. Born in the mountains to a French-Canadian trapper and his Shoshone wife, he spent fifteen years as a trapper and mountain man, yet Charbonneau was one of the best-educated and certainly the most-traveled of the scouts. His father was Toussaint Charbonneau, a guide for the Lewis and Clark expedition, and his mother was the legendary Sacajawea, who played such an important role in that expedition. Jean Baptiste was born on February 11, 1805, and was nicknamed "Pomp" or "Pompy" by Captain William Clark. Portrayed strapped to his mother's back on a United States one dollar coin, Jean Baptiste Charbonneau is the only trapper/mountain man—and the only child—to have his likeness on American money.

Following his mother's death in 1812, he was adopted by Clark and educated in St. Louis. At age eighteen, while on the frontier, he met Prince Paul of Wurttemberg. Returning to Germany with the Prince, he studied languages and traveled to England, France and Africa. He returned to St. Louis in 1829 and became a trapper and mountain man. It appears that Baptiste knew at least five languages and, accordingly, served as an interpreter.

As a mountain man, Charbonneau spent much of his time employed with Bent and St. Vrain at Bent's Fort and the surrounding country. Following his duties with the Battalion, he was appointed *alcalde* at the Mission San Luis Rey in California. He was subsequently accused of supporting an Indian insurrection against the new American authorities, which he denied. In any case, many people felt that because of his mixed heritage, he supported the Indian cause more than that of the government. Accordingly, he submitted his resignation in July 1848.

Antoine Leroux, age forty-five, was of French Canadian, Spanish, and quite probably Indian heritage. In the early 1830s, he became a Mexican citizen and for six or seven years traveled and trapped in much of the area between Santa Fe and the Colorado River, including along the Gila River. Because of his heritage, citizenship and family connections, he was given a land grant of over 400,000 acres in New Mexico, making him by far the wealthiest man with the Battalion. Cooke considered Leroux to be the chief of the guides because of his extensive knowledge of the territory and his connections to the country. In later years, Leroux was a guide of the ill-fated Gunnison Party in Utah, leaving for another assignment a short time before the party was massacred. During the Utah War in 1857, he was a guide for a unit bringing provisions for Johnston's Army, but arrived after a settlement of the issues had been reached.

As the first week of November approached, the Battalion was still moving south along the Rio Grande, but conditions remained difficult and no relief was in sight. On October 30th, they struggled to cross sand dunes with both men and double-teams of animals dragging the wagons across. But Henry Boyle still had time to note the agricultural methods in use:

> "Their land for cultivation is enclosed by ditches, hedges & adobe walls. On account of the dry Seasons in this country, they have to irrigate all this farming land, all their vineyards and orchards, which is done by leading the water from the River through ditches through all their grain and everything else that is raised or produced" (Ricketts 1996, 75).

On November 1st, when it became clear that Captain Higgins was going to remain in El Pueblo, Cooke placed Adjutant Dykes in charge of Company D and moved Second Lieutenant Merrill into the position of adjutant. This move was favorably received by most of the Battalion, since it removed Dykes from a critical position and put him in charge of a company where he could do comparatively little harm. As they continued south, they crossed over the river; the road became very sandy and rocky, and the vegetation became increasingly poor. The men were weak, the teams tired, rations had been reduced again, and Cooke began to wonder how they were going to make the remaining thousand miles to California.

Even though many of the sick had been sent from Santa Fe to El Pueblo, illness remained a problem. The sick still had to make "sick call" and calomel was still administered. However, the outcry was now less than before due in part to Cooke being less tyrannical than Smith, and in part to the fact that most of the men were now committed to reaching California. Levi Hancock continued to assist the sick with prayer as best he could. On November 3rd, forty-year-old James Hampton suddenly became ill and died shortly after. He was buried along the trail the following morning. Dr. Sanderson recorded the death on the day he was buried and attributed it to a heart problem. That same day, Thomas Woolsey arrived from El Pueblo (he had been one of those with the first detachment) and brought news and mail from there. Included in his mail was undoubtedly some for Jefferson Hunt from his family.

At this point in their travels, the Battalion had crossed the Rio Grande and was following a new route close to the river. The older main trail was through a long journada to the east of the river that both Kearny and the Battalion avoided by crossing to the west bank. While they had water and wood for fuel nearby, this route was very rugged and caused them much difficulty in crossing sand hills, rocky ravines and benches. It took its toll on the men and reduced significantly the distance traveled each day.

After marching for seventeen straight days, Cooke called a halt for a day's rest on November 5th. Four days later, after breaking a new road in the desert, they reached the point where Kearny had left the River and headed West. Antoine Leroux returned with a report that he had followed the river and then turned west, where he found a water hole and then, further along, a stream. However, the report was not heartening; Leroux and the guides doubted that the mules could be driven unloaded to California. Cooke had to make some hard decisions.

Cooke quickly decided to lighten the load that had to be carried West. He ordered the three remaining ox teams to return. He also ordered that unnecessary cooking pots and utensils, along with the tent poles and thirty-one tents be left under the charge of a beaver trapping party they found there until another Army unit picked them up. From this time forward, the troops' muskets would serve as tent poles and nine men would share a tent. Some equipment would be carried in packs by the loose mules and the overall loads of the wagons would be reduced. But most importantly, Cooke again inspected the condition of the Battalion and determined "that fifty-five of the sick and least efficient men shall return to Santa Fe" and take with them reduced rations for twenty-six days (Cooke 1951, 55). Dr. Sanderson recorded on November 9th that there were twenty men on sick call and that three of them had measles. The detachment of the sick would further reduce the weight of the transported cargo by 1,800 pounds.

The new detachment for El Pueblo, consisting of fifty-four men and one woman, left the Battalion on November 10th under the command of Lieutenant Wesley Willis. Thomas Woolsey, who had just rejoined the Battalion, was their guide to El Pueblo. That night, Jefferson Hunt and Jesse Hunter went to the Willis camp and ministered to the sick and wished them well for the return trip. Hunt also used the opportunity to mail news to his family. The departure of the ill left the Battalion with 335 of the strongest and most fit volunteers. The total number of the sick and families that had gone to El Pueblo came to 159 men, twenty-nine women and forty-three children (Ricketts 1996, 80). The realignment of personnel meant that an additional eight days of rations were available, and several thousand pounds less of other items would need to be carried.

Cooke immediately noted an improvement in conditions and was able to make twenty-nine miles in the next two days. Even the men's attitudes began to improve. They had hoped that Cooke would abandon the wagons and follow Kearny's lead using pack animals. But when the sick were sent back and

the load lightened considerably, the march began to look more possible. As
Sergeant Coray noted on November 12th:

> "All things go on in the battalion in good order, although our
> hardships are great, such as any other people would not stand,
> half fed, pushing wagons through deep sand. Lt. Dykes of D Co.
> has settled down quietly in his office and contents himself with
> being the object of odium and disgust in the battalion" (Ricketts
> 1996, 81).

Cooke dispatched the scouts to search for a suitable route for the wagons to head West. On November 13th, a note was found on a post a mile or
two downstream from Leroux who also sent two of his men back with instructions to depart the river and begin heading southwest. So began the long
march across the otherwise unknown desert that stretched from the Valley of
the Rio Grande to the northern-most settlement of Sonora—Tucson. On this
date, William Coray described what had become the daily ritual under Cooke:

> "Perhaps it would be well for me to record the history of every
> day occurrences. Our march was attended with very great fa-
> tigue. We had to be up generally two hours before daylight to get
> breakfast. The trumpet would be blown at the first appearance
> of day. This is called the assembly, but the drummers and fifers
> would set in immediately and play reveille, not at full length and
> the men must all be in ranks before it ceased or receive an extra
> tour of guard. The first sergeants called the rolls of the compa-
> nies and detailed the guard under the inspection of an officer.
> Within 15 minutes the sick call was made, 5 minutes before this
> the morning reports must be handed in to the Adjt. 30 minutes
> after sick call guard mounting must be attended to. Immediately
> after guard mounting the signal was to the teamsters to get up
> the teams. All hands laid to help them till we were ready to start.
> Then the companies were divided into equal parts under the su-
> perintendence of officers or N.C. officers to boost at wagons all
> day. These were every day occurrences" (Ricketts 1996, 81).

Over the next several days, the Battalion headed southwest away from the river and into the forbidding desert ahead. Directly west of them was a fairly tall mountain range with snow on the peaks. Toward the southern end of this range they stopped at "a small swampy hole of water near a gap of the mountain" (Cooke 1951, 67). Charbonneau returned to the camp and reported that the gap was easily passed and there was some water on the other side. That same "small swampy hole of water" would eventually be near the location of Fort Cummings, an important fort later in the century. The mountain range was eventually named Cookes Range, and its principal peak several miles north of the gap was named Cookes Peak. Thus, in tribute to his efforts with the Mormon Battalion was Philip St. George Cooke's name memorialized on the future maps of the West. The road created by the Battalion through the gap remains little changed today from what it would have looked like in the late Fall of 1846.

Throughout their march across New Mexico, the Battalion members had been seeing obviously old ruins of buildings, along with broken pottery shards that indicated previous habitation by fairly sophisticated Indians. Since the Book of Mormon is a description of activities in ancient America, the Mormons of the Battalion were fascinated by the evidence they saw of ancient civilizations.

On November 17th, the Battalion got an early start and crossed over the gap. After a short march of about six miles, the Battalion encountered one of those ancient locations. Henry Standage describes it as follows:

> "Close to our camp is some traces or proof of the Nephites once living here. Large entrances into the rocks and several pestles and mortars found made of rock, also some pieces of ancient crockery ware showing that a people has once lived here who knew how to make such things, whereas the Indians who now inhabit these parts do not understand such things. We found a great many hieroglyphics engraven in the rocks, which resembled those found in Pike Co. Illinois. I take this for good circumstantial evidence of the Divine authenticity of the Book of Mormon" (Golder 1928, 184).

A visitor to this site today would find the road made by the Battalion passing between the rock with the petroglyphs and the large flat rock in which the mortars were carved. Because of its fairly open location and lack of other features often associated with habitation, this site has an air of mystery that suggests its use as a ceremonial site of some importance. No wonder many of the Battalion carefully inspected it and noted its unusual features.

The evidence of an old occupation was not the only thing of note. Plant and animal life suddenly changed character as well. New bushes and succulents were seen for the first time, and the California partridge was also first observed (Cooke 1951, 67). Since they had left the Valley of the Rio Grande and crossed over a mountain range, the rainfall and temperature variations that influenced plant and animal life changed. They were still in a desert, but it was a different kind with new and wondrous things to see. The notable exception was Dr. Sanderson who recorded only a general account of Apache depredations in the region.

That the trail discovered by the guides passed by the ancient site was not an accidental happening. Guides and scouts in the Western deserts who were entering new territory for the first time knew of a tool that could often be used to find the next spring or water, or the next pass over mountains or around other obstacles. It was the ancient system of Indian trails that had been used for centuries. These footpaths were developed long before the introduction of horses by the Spanish. At that time, travel was limited by the distance a person could walk in a day and by whatever a man or woman could carry. Since water is so essential to life and it was difficult to carry sufficient water along with other essentials, the trails tended to link water locations at one-day intervals, connecting habitation and ceremonial sites.

Knowing this, a scout would try to find the nearest water location in the direction of travel by following an Indian footpath. The paths were usually quite distinctive and different from those established by horses or wagons or other livestock. Experienced desert travelers knew of this system. Inexperienced desert travelers, such as Jefferson Hunt, were able to learn this system by observing first-hand the activities of the guides and scouts. Hunt used these same techniques in subsequent years as he traversed the southwestern deserts. The members of the ill-fated Jayhawkers party that accompanied him part of the way to California in 1849 also used this technique to try to find a way to the goldfields.

From the camp near the Indian site, the Battalion had to march north-west to the Mimbres River for water; then the route took them a little to the west; and finally they began to head toward the southwest. By doing so, they avoided both the sometimes hostile Apaches to their north and the well-known difficulties of the narrow canyons along the Gila. They were roughly paralleling the known road that ran from the copper mines near present-day Silver City, New Mexico, to the northernmost populated areas of the Mexican state of Sonora. Cooke did not want to get too close to those towns because they were likely garrisoned by Mexican troops, and did not want to engage in fighting there. He had orders to march to California and to make a wagon road while doing so.

On November 20th, when the scouts were unable to find any water, Cooke began to consider making a southeasterly course for Janos in Mexico. But before doing so, he decided to use the well-recognized wilderness distress signal—a large fire built on a high point. He had a fire started on top of a nearby mount, and within a short time, several Mexican traders and several Apaches saw it and came riding quickly into the camp. The Mexicans had some dried beef which they sold, but more importantly, they sold twenty-one fresh mules to the Battalion. One of them agreed to be a guide and translator with the Apaches. While they were stopped, Jefferson Hunt met with Cooke and told him that the men were hungry and the rations insufficient. With that, Cooke increased the rations some, but not enough to fully satisfy the men.

Cooke also called a council with Hunt and Jesse Hunter and discussed with them the possibility of going toward Janos for additional supplies instead of heading directly west. According to William Coray "They told him they would have nothing to say about it, that he must take the responsibility upon himself" (Brooks 1996, 85). Fearing that Cooke might actually deviate from his course and place the Battalion in jeopardy, Levi Hancock and David Pette-grew visited the men at night and urged them to pray for a turn to the West. The following day, not long after starting, Cooke did exactly that. Many of the men attributed the decision to head west a manifestation of the hand of God.

To Cooke, however, the decision was clear—the trail he was following curved southeast and he was headed to California in the west.

That evening, November 21st, Jefferson Hunt called the men together to talk to them. He accused John D. Lee of interjecting himself—an outsider—into the affairs of the Battalion where he had no place. Hunt also stated that he wanted to keep the command of the Battalion when Allen died. Ironically, on the same day, John D. Lee, Howard Egan, Samuel Gulley and Roswell Stevens arrived at Winter Quarters with the collected funds, 282 letters and seventy-two packages and the letters from Hunt to Brigham Young (Journal History of the Church, November 21, 1846). A month after the events, and hard feelings were not yet abated.

The Battalion was now heading into unknown territory. Cooke and the scouts had some knowledge of a good water and feed source at a place known as the San Bernardino Rancho (located just south of the United States/Mexico border and just east of Douglas, Arizona) which was begun as a large ranch in 1822, but mostly abandoned ten years later because of problems with raiding Apaches. However, that ranch was more than a hundred miles to the southwest across two mountain ranges and several very dry playas and valleys. The scouts fanned out and searched for water as the men and animals of the Battalion began to suffer severely from thirst. Not all of the searching was productive. On the night of November 22nd, Charbonneau walked into camp with word that he stopped to rest and feed his mule and when he attempted to saddle it to begin his search, the mule kicked him and ran off. He followed it for several miles before finally shooting it to recover his saddle and pistols, and Cooke suspected, in anger.

On November 23rd, Leroux discovered water and signaled Cooke with a white smoke signal. When the Battalion arrived, Cooke watered the animals first, which required the men to lap up the remaining water or to try to capture seeping water with spoons or quills made into straws. At this point Jefferson Hunt blamed Cooke for marching forward without knowing if there was sufficient water and complained to him for permitting the animals to drink before the men.

Not all of the men could go on, so the officers directed some to remain at the inadequate spring while others went forward. Most were able to cross Playas Lake, a dry lake bed, with good springs and feed and firewood on the far side. Some of the men filled kegs with this good water and went back along the trail to help bring in the stragglers. On November 25th, Charbonneau encountered three grizzly bears and managed to shoot one, which along with several deer and antelope also shot that day, provided the camp with a supply of fresh meat. A Mexican guide hired by Cooke told them that there would be an adequate supply of good quality wild beef when they got to the San Bernardino Rancho.

By the following day, they had crossed into the Animas Valley, which put them only one mountain range away from their goal of the San Bernardino Rancho. Whether they all realized it or not, however, this was a significant day because the Battalion had crossed the Continental Divide, and they were now on the Pacific side of the Continent. However, the Guadalupe Mountains before them presented a major challenge before they could reach the ranch. They knew of Guadalupe Pass, a Mexican road through the mountains that connected several of the more remote Mexican communities in the northern frontier. Unfortunately, they were unable to find the correct pass, missing it by about a mile to the north, but an Apache chief named Manuelita told them that the canyon they were in was the correct route.

On November 29th, they were confronted by a cliff and steep ledges just over the summit of the range. Cooke had the contents of the wagons shifted to 150 pack mules, which Dykes and his company took over the top and down to a suitable camping spot in the canyon beyond. Most of the men, however, spent over a day building a road using picks, crowbars and other hand tools. Then the wagons were let down by ten to fifteen men at the back using ropes to hold the them straight while a small team of mules pulled them forward in front. This strenuous routine had to be repeated for each wagon. Among those involved was Henry Boyle, who commented on the process and used his knowledge and experience two years later to bring the first wagon from Southern California to Salt Lake City by way of the Old Spanish Trail. As an officer, Jefferson Hunt supervised the process while also gaining valuable experience which he too would also use to good effect on the Old Spanish Trail the following year.

After two days of difficult work, the wagons were over the mountains and, on December 2nd, the hungry, tired and thirsty Battalion arrived at the San Bernardino Rancho about midday. Here they stopped to rest and to re-supply themselves by hunting the abundant wild cattle in the area. The men quickly noted that the herd consisted mostly of bulls, the cows and calves having been taken by the Apaches. The bulls were tough and hard to shoot, but the supply was abundant and the men ate heartily, and jerked or smoked the meat for future use.

Their route had taken them just south of the present New Mexico/Arizona/Mexico border. The old ranch site they stopped at is in Mexico, a short distance south of the present San Bernardino Ranch Museum and San Bernardino National Wildlife Refuge, which is in Arizona just east of present-day Douglas. The present Museum dates to the period following legendary Texas rancher John Slaughter's acquisition of 65,000 acres in 1887.

Manuelita and his band of Apaches arrived at the ranch camp and were willing to trade horses and mules for blankets at the rate of one blanket for one horse. The Battalion and the Apaches got along fairly well because they shared a common enemy in the Mexicans to the south. The relationship between the government and the Apaches would deteriorate later in the century as more settlers, travelers and miners descended onto their territory. The resulting battles provided fodder for countless Westerns in the Twentieth Century. But at that time, peace prevailed between the Apaches and Americans in Southern Arizona.

During the brief respite at San Bernardino, Cooke weighed and counted the provisions and discovered that there was less than thought, amounting to only fifty-one days of rations remaining. This discovery, coupled with the fear that there were Mexican troops in the communities not far to the south, caused him to break camp and resume the march at midday on December 4th after only two days rest and before many of the men were able to fully jerk the beef that they had just shot. This upset many of the men. Cooke then ordered that the men were not to shoot at the wild cattle without permission because they had an adequate supply and also probably fearing that a wounded bull could easily attack the marching columns or the stock and wagons of the Battalion. This further annoyed the men.

The aggravation did not stop there. Cooke ordered that men with horses still had to walk and that each man was to carry his own knapsack and not use any company wagons for the purpose. Whether Cooke became more irritable because of his discovery of the short rations or because of the difficulties of cutting a new road out of the wilderness is unclear. What is clear is that his mood changed and his orders became more onerous. William Coray states:

> "... the orders were to kill no more beef cattle till the 9th in consequence of there being so much on hand. This evening the Lt. Col. Told the adjt. Not to receive any on guard who had not their knapsacks on, neither should they ride if they had horses. This I called tyranny in the extreme" (Ricketts 1996, 92).

The following day, however, Cooke granted Coray and several officers permission to hunt for beef and they were successful in killing and recovering two for fresh meat for the camp. For the time being, the Battalion was well-fed and had adequate water.

Chapter 10

To California

General Stephen Watts Kearny may have been surprised at the ease with which he took Santa Fe and New Mexico without any resistance. He may have been even more surprised to learn from his encounter with Kit Carson that California had similarly been peacefully seized and occupied. But his greatest surprise was to come on his arrival at Warner's Ranch, the easternmost American outpost near the edge where California's Coast Ranges meet the forbidding Southwestern desert. Kearny had acted on the best information he had when he returned two-thirds of his force to Santa Fe after meeting Kit Carson. Further accurate information from California did not reach him because of the problems with communication. When General Kearny and his 100 Dragoons arrived at Warner's, they confirmed earlier rumors that a major insurrection had occurred and all of Southern California, with the exception of the Port of San Diego, had been recaptured by insurgents led by General Andrés Pico, the brother of Governor Pío Pico, and the highest ranking Mexican military officer remaining in California. California was *not* safely in the hands of the Americans, and hostilities were far from ended.

Early on the cold, wet morning of December 6, 1846, General Kearny led about half of his Dragoons against a force of mounted lancers commanded by Pico near an Indian community named San Pasqual. That battle site is immediately adjacent to today's location of the San Diego Wild Animal Park east of Escondido, California. Kearny had hoped to surprise the Californian force, but was himself surprised to find Pico's troops mounted and waiting for the Americans. In the ensuing battle, twenty-two of the Americans were killed, including Captain Benjamin Moore. A majority of the remainder of those taking part, including General Kearny, were wounded. The Californian losses are uncertain, but most likely were much less than the Americans. For several days, Kearny and his men were trapped in the area by Pico's forces. Several small parties, including one led by Kit Carson, were sent out to San Diego to obtain assistance from Commodore Stockton, whose Marines and sailors rescued the Dragoons several days later.

Pico's Californians were mounted on strong, fresh horses and were superb horsemen. They were well trained to fight with the lance. Kearny's Dragoons, on the other hand, were not cavalry; as Dragoons, they were trained to dismount and fight on the ground. In addition, they were mounted on mules that were physically worn out from the long journey from Santa Fe. General Kearny and others probably assumed that the Californians would flee rather than fight the U.S. Army. If so, they were wrong. Knowing the strength and condition of Kearny's force, Pico was able to take a stand with superior numbers and deliver a blow for the insurrection. For several days, Pico contained the Americans. But with the arrival of Stockton's reinforcements from San Diego, Pico and his men disappeared into the hills and valleys Southern California.

Historians and military observers have variously called the Battle of San Pasqual a victory for Kearny who held his ground, a victory for Pico who suffered fewer losses, or a draw. But anyone looking at the facts would have to conclude that the battle was won by Pico and the Californians. However, victory was fleeting. Pressured by Kearny and the American naval forces in the south and a military force led by John C. Fremont marching from Northern California, General Andrés Pico capitulated to Fremont on January 13, 1847, at a ranch house in today's San Fernando Valley near Cahuenga Pass. Pico resumed his position as a rancher and leader in the community in Southern California and was elected several times to the California Assembly where he served with Jefferson Hunt. The lesson of the insurrection was not lost on General Kearny and the other military leaders in California. While there were no further major conflicts between the Americans and the Californians,

Kearny was careful to take precautions to show and have ready his military strength. The Mormon Battalion played a major role in that effort upon their arrival on the Pacific Coast.

By December 9th, the Battalion had reached the San Pedro Valley, southwest of the present town of Bisbee, Arizona. They were now heading north along the San Pedro River, which had flowing water in it from the Huachuca Mountains to the west. In addition to the ever-present bulls, there were deer, bear, antelope and even fish. The sutler's price for fish hooks increased dramatically, and the variations in the diet thrilled the men. Mesquite and other trees and bushes grew around the river valley and there was an ample supply of grass for the stock. To some in the Battalion, the abundance of the valley made it appear to be the best location for farming or ranching since they had left Council Grove in far away Kansas.

Some of the men were able to deviate from Cooke's strong marching orders and go fishing or hunting as they traveled along the stream. The difficult conditions had gotten gentler along the San Pedro. Sometime on December 10th, the men passed by what, thirty-one years later, would become the Clanton Ranch, home to Ike and Billy Clanton, Tom and Frank McLaury, Johnnie Ringo, Curly Bill Brocius and others of the famed cowboy faction of Tombstone and the 1881 Gunfight at the OK Corral. As the Battalion moved north they passed within eight miles of the future site of the infamous silver mining town of Tombstone.

No story of the march of the Battalion would be complete without a description of the "Battle of the Bulls" that happened on December 11th along the San Pedro. The march was progressing along the river through tall grass, some trees and numerous bushes. Mixed in along the route were a number of the wild bulls. Some got in with the Battalion's cattle and sheep. Several of the drovers or others then shot a number of the wild bulls. The noise and confusion, coupled with the smell of blood, caused the remainder of the other wild bulls to stampede. Since most of the men were marching with unloaded muskets at Cooke's orders, men scrambled to load their weapons or simply to get out of the way of the wildly charging bulls. Some men hid behind wagons; others climbed nearby trees; still others were able to get shots off at the charging animals—although most missed. Even when hit, some of the bulls were able to continue their charge.

Several of the men were injured by the bulls. Sergeant Albert Smith was head-butted and suffered severely bruised ribs but, fortunately, was spared injury from the horns. Amos Cox was hooked by another bull's horns, thrown ten feet in the air over the animal, and suffered a deep wound in his thigh. Levi Fifield was nearly run down by a bull, but fell to the ground and the beast simply jumped over him (Yurtinus 1975, 399). The Battalion's animals fared worse when two mules were gored. Several wagons were hit by the bulls and were knocked off the road. Even Lieutenant Colonel Cooke was not immune to the threat from the bulls. According to his own account: "I was very near Corporal Frost when an immense coal-black bull came charging at us, a hundred yards. Frost aimed his musket, flint lock, very deliberately, and only fired when the beast was within six paces; it fell headlong, almost at our feet" (Cooke 1851, 77).

Army Lieutenant George Stoneman also fired at the bulls. He was carrying a harmonica or slide rifle that he probably had acquired somewhere on the frontier, and likely had been made by Jonathan Browning. One of the other chambers in the slide of his rifle also discharged and the second rifle ball tore into his thumb, causing a serious wound.

This was not the first such incident involving this type of rifle. On September 14th, three days before joining with the Battalion, John D. Lee recorded that while hunting buffalo with James Pace,

"... my left wrist was seariously [sic] injured by one of the slides being shoved out of its place which let a part of the charge pass to the left—or rather split the charge throwing a part against my left wrist burning it sevierly [sic]" (Brooks 1967, 190).

Jonathan Browning's slide rifle was an innovative yet elegant firearm designed to overcome the major deficiency of cap and ball firearms of the time: the ability to fire multiple shots rapidly without having to reload each time. Samuel Colt's revolvers had more-or-less solved the problem for handguns, and the manufacturer made some revolving rifles, as well. However, Colt strictly controlled the patent rights to revolving cylinder firearms, thereby limiting the number of competitors. The slide rifle resolved this problem without infringing on Colt's patents. While Browning later advertised that the rifle was available in five-, ten-, fifteen-, twenty- and twenty-five-shot versions, it is most probable that those carrying the rifle carried five or six round slides that could be quickly placed into the rifle's firing mechanism. A person carrying a rifle with a slide longer than five or six rounds would have a bulky and unbalanced firearm that was difficult to carry. Thus, it is most likely that when someone referred to a "fifteen shooter," they were talking about a slide rifle with three five-round slides that had been loaded with powder, ball and a percussion cap.

The rifle was in battery, or ready to shoot, when a slide was inserted into the breech mechanism and was locked into place with a cam lever on the outside of the action. This cam engaged a part of the metal on the rear of the slide and forced the slide forward so that an indentation surrounding the loaded chamber fitted into a protrusion around the barrel. This provided a seal that made sure that the slide properly fit the barrel and that no flashback from the discharging load could ignite another chamber—a common occurrence with the hand-loaded revolvers of the time. With this in mind, it is hard to determine why Lee and Stoneman's slide rifles caused injuries. If it was one of Browning's rifles, it is not likely that it was a malfunction of the mechanics of the rifle or a design flaw, but may had been the result of "operator error" which could have occurred under the stress of the incidents.

Imagine for a moment the 350 members of the Battalion walking along next to a stream, in tall grass, in brush and among trees along with several hundred mules and oxen, and several hundred more sheep. Visualize fifty or so wagons and a number of officers mounted on horses also riding along. Then add the confusion of a large number of wild bulls charging aimlessly through the ranks of people, cattle, sheep and wagons. Add to this confused mess dozens of men frantically rushing for cover or loading and firing their weapons. At the time, the Battle of the Bulls must have been terrifying for many of those in the ranks of the Battalion. Later, the story probably took on humorous overtones as it was retold with the knowledge that no one was seriously injured or killed. But at the time, there was nothing funny about it. The

Battle of the Bulls was recorded as the only major battle in which the Battalion was ever engaged.

Cooke had been debating whether to follow the San Pedro north to the Gila River, or to march northwestward toward Tucson and then follow a dry route to intersect the Gila at the Pima Villages. To determine the situation in Tucson, its garrison and the attitudes of the inhabitants, Cooke sent several of his scouts ahead. Leroux returned the day after the Battle of the Bulls. He reported that they had found a small group of soldiers on the way and learned there were nearly 200 Mexican soldiers at Tucson. The scouts then returned in that direction and Dr. Foster continued on into Tucson where he was held as a possible spy.

In the meantime, Cooke was growing apprehensive about the possibility of a shooting conflict at Tucson and decided to drill the Battalion on firing and cleaning their weapons. They had never been properly taught military maneuvers and coordinated weapons use as was common in the infantry at that time. Consequently, at midday on December 13th, Cooke halted the Battalion and spent the afternoon at drilling and firing practice. Cooke himself conducted the drills and found that the men were sorely lacking in experience, but he hoped that the rudimentary instruction in forming lines and line movements would give them the skills needed to follow orders should combat ensue. The officers of each company then conducted the firearms drills and practice. Cooke also issued Order Number 19 to the men, which essentially said that the decision had been made to march to the Gila by way of Tucson because it was a much shorter route. The soldiers must show "justice and kindness to the unarmed an [sic] unresisting" and that "The property of individuals you will hold sacred" (Bigler and Bagley 2000, 158-90).

During the following several days, Cooke conducted negotiations with the garrison at Tucson via several Mexican soldiers that he encountered along the trail. Dr. Foster was released and several of the Mexican soldiers that had been briefly held were also released. No firm agreement was reached, and on December 16th, the Battalion loaded its weapons and marched into Tucson.

There they found that the garrison of about 200 soldiers had fled to the south and forced 400 of the 500 residents to flee with them. The Battalion marched through town and camped along an irrigation canal on the north end of the community. They raised an American flag, the first to fly over the territory that would eventually become the State of Arizona. Thus, Tucson was captured without any confrontation. William Coray noted: "Fruit of various kinds we found here. Gardens were neatly laid out with beautiful irrigation for watering purposes" (Ricketts 1996, 96, 98).

Many of the remaining residents began to trade food for clothes with the Battalion members. Slowly, a number of the residents who fled began to return to their homes. Cooke seized much of the wheat in the public stores of the community. Some of the wheat was fed to the mules and some of it was ground into flour to supplement the meager rations that would have to keep them until the California Coast was reached. As a demonstration of force, the next day Cooke called for fifty volunteers to march south to the Mission San Xavier del Bac, where it was supposed the Mexican soldiers had fled. The small force marched south, but returned after four miles, thus avoiding a potential confrontation with the Mexican troops.

Unable to meet with any Mexican officials, Cooke left a letter for the Governor of Sonora in which he stated that the Sonorans had failed to support the war with the Americans and that their common interest was to protect themselves from the marauding Apaches and not fight each other. He then expressed his belief that the wagon road he was building would benefit both sides.

About midnight on December 17th, two of the on-duty guards, Albern Allen and his son Rufus C. Allen, spotted what they feared was an advance on the Mormon camp by Mexican soldiers. William Coray described the events:

> "About 12 o'clock a body of men came upon our picket guard advancing slowly and cautiously when Bro. Allen of Co. A. hailed and fired. The next to him fired also and ran to camp as soon as they could and informed Capt. Hunt of the fact. My tent being near enabled me to hear the whole story and I thought surely we must fight now. The alarm was given soon public, then the assembly beat and all the men were into ranks

in one devil of a hurry, I tell you, though perfectly calm and without frustration. . ." (Ricketts 1996, 99).

When no enemy appeared, Cooke ordered Jefferson Hunt to take Company A to the town to see if there were any Mexican soldiers present. Hunt returned after finding nothing out of the ordinary in Tucson, other than more of the citizens who had returned home.

On the following day, the Battalion began one of its hardest marches of the campaign. They had to cross nearly seventy miles of waterless plain from Tucson to the Gila River, south of present-day Phoenix. Cooke knew that this was to be a hard march and relaxed the rules. He permitted the men to move forward at their own pace as best they could. He also relaxed the distribution of rations, permitting them to get as much food as they needed. Some men were able to find small amounts of water left from recent rains and that was distributed among the others. Through pure tenacity and by helping each other, the Battalion reached the Gila during the day on December 21st. There they were met by a number of Pima Indians who seemed to prosper along the river.

During this five day period, Lieutenant Colonel Cooke and the men of the Mormon Battalion gained considerable insight into each other. The success of the call for volunteers to march toward the Mission San Xavier del Bac, coupled with the speed and eagerness in which the men responded to the alarm on the night of December 17th, showed Cooke that the men were ready to respond when necessary, even if they did not possess the military skills of the regular Army. Their progress along the dry trail to the Gila showed him that they were prepared to follow him and obey his orders in spite of the difficulties involved. Sergeant William Hyde recorded that he even heard Cooke say: ". . . any other company under like circumstances would have mutinized [sic]" (Yurtinus 1975, 416).

William Coray wrote: "Capt. Hunter observed to the Col. That the mules suffered. Said the Col. 'I don't care a damn about the mules, the men are what I'm thinking of.' . . . I was much pleased at this expression. It was the first humane word I had heard from him. . ." (Ricketts 1996, 101). The actions and hardships of this short period formed the basis of a long period of mutual respect between the Mormons and Philip St. George Cooke.

The Gila River was generally regarded as the boundary between the Mexican areas of Sonora (to the south) and California (to the north). The American military and President Polk were not interested in annexing Sonora, and when the treaty ending the Mexican War was signed, the Gila was the southern boundary of the newly-acquired territory. Along with General Kearny was Lieutenant William Emory of the Topographical Engineers, who was assigned by the War Department to draw an accurate map of the route of the Army of the West. Throughout the trip westward, Emory took accurate measurements of latitude, longitude, altitude and various physical features. Following his return to Washington, Emory prepared his final map and included both the details of a map prepared by Cooke of his route south of Kearny and a possible alternate route (if there was sufficient water available) proposed by the guide, Antoine Leroux.

James Gadsden, the president of the South Carolina Railroad Company, envisioned tying the various railroads in the South into one rail system and then extending it across the Continent along a Southern route. He and others believed that such a railroad would strongly influence the newly acquired territories. They would become commercially dependant on the South and would then support the Southern political agenda with its support for the extension of slavery. A Southern transcontinental railroad route was seen as both an economic issue and a political issue that would benefit the South.

Engineers advising Gadsden and other Southern leaders used information from Emory's map, his reports, along with other information, much of which was garnered from Gold Rush travelers. They believed that the most practical rail route lay south of the Gila River. In 1853, President Franklin Pearce, at the urging of Secretary of War Jefferson Davis, appointed Gadsden as the United States' Minister to Mexico and authorized him to negotiate the purchase of territory south of the Gila River. Not only would this purchase provide a route for the proposed railroad to the West Coast, it would resolve several other issues. The first was the problem of the contested boundary caused when inaccurate maps and descriptions were relied on for the boundary lines in the Treaty of Guadalupe Hidalgo. The second problem was that the United States had been unable to meet its obligation agreed to in the treaty to handle the problems created by the marauding Apaches on the frontier. The third issue was a domestic one created when many believed that the Mexican War was wrong and that the United States should not have seized the Mexican territory in the West.

On the other side of the issue, Mexican President Santa Anna's government was badly in need of money. James Gadsden was able to negotiate a new treaty, signed on December 30, 1853, which granted new territory in New Mexico and a portion of the land south of the Gila River in Arizona to the United States in exchange for $15 million. The U.S. Senate barely ratified the treaty in April 1854, after much contentious debate about adding a potential slave territory to the United States. The Senate also reduced the payment to $10 million. The treaty was strongly opposed by many in Mexico and was a significant factor in the eventual political downfall of Santa Anna.

The new territory was called the Gadsden Purchase and became part of the future states of New Mexico and Arizona. With this purchase of land, the map of the contiguous states of the Union became complete. The Southern Pacific Railroad was eventually built across the area, but not until well after the Northern Transcontinental Railroad was completed, and the slavery issue was resolved once and for all by the Civil War. Portions of Cooke's Wagon Road and other parts of the Gadsden Purchase were used for year 'round roads to California by a number of travelers and commercial operations, including the Butterfield Stage Lines.

Brigham Young may have given Jefferson Hunt another assignment prior to his departure with the Mormon Battalion. While there is no explicit record of it, indirect evidence strongly indicates that Hunt was to scout, locate and then report back to the Mormon leadership any potential sites for future settlement by the Mormons. In 1847, Hunt informed Young of the possibilities of a settlement at Isaac Williams' Chino Rancho, which lead to the eventual Mormon settlement of San Bernardino. Then in 1848, Hunt reported the deposits of iron ore in Southern Utah that eventually became the Iron Mission (Cedar City.) But in 1846, at the Pima Villages along the Gila River, Hunt noted the agricultural potential presented by the soil and availability of water.

On December 21st, Lieutenant Colonel Cooke reported that he met and dined with the chiefs of the Pima and then stated that:

> "I have spoken to the two senior captains [Jefferson Hunt and Jesse Hunter] of the battalion on the subject of their settling near here; they seem to look upon it favorably. Captain Hunt asked my permission to talk to the chief on the subject, and I approved of it." (Cooke 1951, 85).

We have no record of the results of the conversation that may have taken place between Hunt and the chief, and the Mormons did not arrive in the area until they settled the present city of Mesa, Arizona in the 1880s. Most likely Hunt reported back to Brigham Young about the location, but other places were of much greater value and were settled first. What is clear from Cooke's report is that Hunt was on the lookout for locations that would benefit the future needs of the expanding Mormon presence in the American West.

The Battalion intersected a known trail that was first pioneered in 1774 by Father Francisco Garcés and Captain Juan Bautista de Anza from Tucson to Los Angeles. It was also the route that General Kearny had recently used on his way to the California Coast. The trail had not been widely used because of hostile Indians, but its general route was known. Cooke and the Battalion now had the tasks of finding water along the most difficult sections of the route and of making an all-weather wagon road to California as ordered by Kearny. The new road essentially followed the Gila River to the crossing of the Colorado River at present-day Yuma, Arizona, and then followed a route from one well or spring to another across the Imperial Desert near today's California-Mexico border.

As they moved along the Gila, they found there was ample water, but that it was somewhat salty as a result of the confluence of the Salt River. There was not much vegetation for the animals, which caused them to weaken further. While there was a trail, it was not a wagon road, and had to be worked on constantly. Cooke described it as follows:

> "Many miles of road were beaten, with much dust, in a clay formation, where mule tracks were six inches deep; much sand was encountered, and several volcanic bluffs, which required much labor to be made passable" (Cooke 1951, 88).

Cooke again describes the road work several days later:

> "It was found necessary for our wagons to vary much from General Kearny's trail; and a road was cut, in places, through miles of dense thickets, etc. Next day only seven miles could be made; points of stony ridges and clay gullies required much work" (Cooke 1951, 89).

On December 28th, two men from California bearing passports from Kearny—one of whom was Kit Carson—arrived in camp and told Cooke of the battle at San Pasqual. Initially, Cooke considered dividing the Battalion and taking 200 of the strongest men on to California in a forced march to reinforce Kearny. However, upon reflection, he decided not to do so, thereby gaining more respect from the men of the Battalion (Yurtinus 1975, 439). Cooke then sent five of his guides, including Leroux and Charbonneau to find Kearny and advise him of their impending arrival, to obtain additional mules and cattle, and to expect to meet the Battalion at Warner's Ranch about January 21st.

On the same day, Levi Hancock recorded that Lieutenant Dykes approached him for some counsel because "there was considerable feelings existing against him in the Battalion and he would like to do right" Hancock responded that:

> "I told him that I had already had that laid to me and that I had a 'put down' for it when there had never been any cause for it . . . I had concluded not [to] give any counsel to an officer, lest it caused further jealousy" (Hancock 2000, 186-187).

Hancock appears to have stopped giving advice that might divide the Battalion, but the moratorium would not last.

On New Year's Day 1847, they met another group of people from California, and Cooke received additional information about the battle at San Pasqual. It was clear that not all was as originally reported by Kit Carson. Cooke responded to any possible threat by changing the order of the march to have an advance guard in front for defensive purposes.

In this second group were William Money and his wife, who had just given birth, and who were fleeing California for her father's home in Sonora. Money told the members of the Battalion about the arrival in California of Sam Brannan and his group of Mormons on the ship, *Brooklyn*.

Also on January 1, 1847, Cooke decided to try floating some supplies down the Gila on a raft built and guided by Lieutenant Stoneman, who had some previous river experience in the East. While the river appeared to be deep enough to handle such a raft, it was found that wherever there were small rapids, the depth was only three or four inches. Nearly 2,500 pounds of flour and other supplies were loaded on the raft when it ran fast aground on a sandbar after a very short journey. The raft was unloaded and the supplies cached while Stoneman continued on to the Colorado with only the raft, where it could be used as a ferry. Corporal William Muir and a small detachment were given the job of going back, finding, and then retrieving the cached flour and conveying it to the Battalion as it marched forward to California. In the meantime, however, Cooke was forced to reduce the ration of flour to the men even further.

On January 8th, the Battalion finally arrived at the Colorado River at present-day Yuma, Arizona. The Colorado was wide, deep and cold, and the weather had turned very cold for the desert. Ice even formed at night at the river's edge. It took two days to cross with the wagons, livestock and all the men. Each boat crossing took an hour and a half, and was terribly hard work for the men.

Next, the Battalion faced the most grueling march of all; the route from the Colorado to Warner's Ranch. With some of the rations still cached along the Gila, supplies were quickly running out, and rations were again cut. As he continued Westward, Cooke abandoned wagons to reduce the load to be carried. Previously, he had ordered the men not to carry their personal property in the government wagons; however, Jefferson Hunt and the other captains ignored this and kept the private provisions and property hidden.

From the Colorado to the Coast was not far—about 150 miles in a straight line—but the first half of the journey was extremely dry, and the Battalion had to travel nearly 200 miles more before they could see the Pacific Ocean. The first several days of travel took them south of the present California-Mexico border and around the southern end of the Imperial Sand Dunes. Then they turned northwest toward Warner's Ranch and crossed the Yuha Desert just north of the Mexican border and west of the dunes.

The only available water in the Yuha Desert was from a well (Yuha Well) that had to be dug out. Lieutenant Oman was given the task of traveling ahead with a small group of men to find the well and to dig it out for the remainder of the men and animals. The guide Tesson returned from San Diego with thirty-three untrained mules and twelve cattle all worked by four Indian drovers who were able to hitch up the mules to the wagons. The Paymaster, Major Jeremiah Cloud, also returned with the definitive word of the battle at San Pasqual and information regarding the trail ahead.

By January 16th, they had reached Carrizo Creek. Most of the men believed the past five days had been the hardest since they began. By this point, rations were nearly out, their clothing was in tatters and scarcely protected them from daytime heat and nighttime cold. Many no longer had shoes and resorted to making moccasins and sandals from rawhide or wrapping their feet in cloth. The number of wagons had been reduced to five government wagons, three private and no company wagons (Ricketts 1996, 113; Yurtinus 1975, 463; Cooke 1951, 97). By now the men could clearly see the tree-covered peaks of the Laguna Mountains to their left, and the infrequent springs had much more water.

On January 18th, they arrived early in a little valley at Vallecito Creek and rested for most of the day. There was ample water but very little food remained from their stores. They were out of flour, coffee, sugar, and had only beef left. Jefferson Hunt convinced Lieutenant Colonel Cooke to increase the beef ration (Journal History, January 1847). While the food supply situation was desperate, the availability of water had increased and Warner's Ranch was just a short distance away. The Battalion could see the end of their long march fast approaching and a feeling of celebration and jubilation filled the ranks. Nevertheless, fearing that they might still be attacked by Californians fleeing to Sonora, Cooke drilled the men that evening. The anticipation of the end of the march, coupled with the presence of more than enough water, gave the men new hope and they began to relax.

The trail they were following was an established pack route that led from the southwestern desert into the Coastal Ranges and on to the Pacific, but it was not a wagon road. The Battalion still faced their most difficult, and final, challenge in creating Cooke's Wagon Road from New Mexico to the Pacific. The following day, they set out again, and with Cooke still fearing an attack, they marched in close military order with the wagons at the rear. After going only three or four miles, Cooke and the Battalion were confronted with "a rugged ridge in front, some two hundred feet high." Pauline Weaver believed that they were stopped, but Cooke was not to be denied his Wagon Road this close to the finish. Actually, the slope rose 225 feet in elevation over a horizontal distance of 900 feet, a twenty-five percent grade. Cooke ordered the men forward to make the road and "With much active work, I got the wagons over in about an hour and a half" (Cooke 1951, 98).

They followed along a dry creek bed for almost five miles until they came to the biggest road building challenge of all. The trail took them along the gravel and rock-covered bed of the dry creek as it ascended at a six percent grade into a fairly deep and narrow canyon, which continued to narrow until finally it was not as wide as a wagon. Several hundred yards further up was a vertical, dry desert waterfall twenty to twenty-five feet high. In order to complete the final few miles of the road, Cooke had to widen the canyon enough for a wagon to pass through and construct a bypass of the waterfall.

The best of the road making tools had been lost when the raft grounded on the Gila. That left only a few axes, one small crowbar and several shovels. But they would have to do. As Cooke explained:

"Setting the example myself, there was much work done on it before the wagons came; the rock was hewn with axes to increase the opening. I thought it wide enough, and going on, found a hill to be ascended, to avoid a still narrower pass, with a great rock to be broken, before it could be crossed. But when a trial was made, at the first pass, it was found too narrow by a foot of solid rock" (Cooke 1951, 98-99).

Some of the men of the Battalion had to chip away rock outcroppings below the waterfall to widen the road in the bottom of the canyon. Others had to break and clear rocks and level a roadway wide enough for the wagons over several hundred feet of sloping ground around the high and narrow waterfall.

Cooke then had one wagon taken apart and moved through the narrow gap while the men continued to hack away at the rock walls restricting the canyon and the road above. A second wagon was unloaded and partially dissembled and also lifted through. But with less than an hour of daylight left, the work on the narrows was completed "and the last two wagons were pulled through by the mules, with loads undisturbed" (Cooke 1951, 99). The Battalion had just cut a road through an area now named Box Canyon, and it is still visible from a historical marker located on County Highway S2 in east-central San Diego County. The road around the Box Canyon waterfall remained in use for about a decade, when another road at a slightly lower elevation was made for the Butterfield stages that used the same route.

Then they climbed up over the final ridge and found themselves after dark in a valley with three miles to go to yet another ridge they needed to climb before reaching the next water source. Since it was too dark with no moonlight to traverse the next pass—now known as Foot and Walker Pass and located about four miles northwest of Box Canyon—the Battalion camped with good grass for the animals but no water other than what the men had carried with them. Leaving before sunrise on the next morning, the wagons were taken over this ridge and they proceeded on to an Indian village called San Felipi. There they were met by Charbonneau, who had returned with word that they were to proceed to San Diego and that Kearny and his troops, along with Fremont and his troops from the north, were heading to Los Angeles for a final showdown with the hostile Californians who had gathered there. The following day, January 21, 1847, the Mormon Battalion marched about eight more miles and reached their destination at Warner's Ranch. While the march of the Battalion to the California Coast was not quite yet finished, the road building was.

Jonathan T. Warner, owner of Warner's Ranch, was from Connecticut, but went to Santa Fe in 1831 and on to California by way of the Old Spanish Trail shortly thereafter. He decided to stay in California and became a Mexican citizen and was both a merchant and rancher. In 1844, he was granted the land on which he built his ranch. Because of its important location, it was the gateway to California from the southern deserts and as such, played a similar role in Southern California to that of Sutter's Fort in Northern California. Someone entering California from the deserts would know that they reached safety and civilization, such as it was, when they arrived at Warner's. From there, the roads led south to San Diego or north to Los Angeles and the rest of California.

After resting for several days at Warner's Ranch, the Battalion again began its westward march. On January 27th, the Battalion reached the old mission at San Luis Rey and from there, they finally saw the Pacific Ocean to the west. Their goal had been reached. Two days later, the Mormon Battalion reached San Diego. The long march was over. Now the Battalion could begin the work of securing California.

The completion of Cooke's Wagon Road was a significant accomplishment that brought many benefits. The first, of course, was that it was an all-weather road not hindered by the seasonal snowfalls that stopped wagon traffic over the Rocky Mountains and Sierra Nevadas. As such, it meant that government communications and military units could cross into or out of California at any time of the year. Similarly, it also meant that commerce could be carried on between California and the rest of the country throughout the year. The influx of people and commerce as a result of the Gold Rush of 1849 created a steamship route from Eastern and Gulf Coast ports to the Isthmus of Panama—a land bridge across the Isthmus—and then steamship routes up the California Coast to take more people and cargo. But the overland route through the Southwestern deserts, much of which was pioneered by the Battalion, remained in use for twenty-one years. Following the completion of the Transcontinental Railroad in 1869, the commercial importance of the road evaporated and portions of it were relegated to the status of historical curiosities.

The second significant accomplishment was that Cooke's road led to the acquisition of the Gadsden Purchase that created the contiguous United States in its present form.

The third significant series of events centered on the use of portions of Cooke's Wagon Road as part of the Butterfield Stage Route from 1858 until the start of the Civil War in 1861. John Butterfield received a six-year, $600,000 per year contract to provide mail service between St. Louis and San Francisco. The 2,800 mile long route featured a series of stage stations that provided food, water and protection for the stage line. The ruins of some of those stations can still be seen today. In addition to carrying mail, Butterfield also carried passengers and trips were often completed in twenty-five days or less. At the start of the War Between the States, troops were withdrawn for use elsewhere and the unprotected stage service was stopped.

The fourth use of portions of the Wagon Road came in the years following the Civil War when Army troops were again deployed to the Southwest to quell hostile Indian activities. Portions of the road played significant roles in the movement of troops during their actions against the Apaches.

The fifth significant development was that a railroad was eventually constructed across the acquired territory. That, along with today's Interstate Highway System, has made the Gadsden Purchase an integral part of America's transportation corridors.

As for the Mormons themselves, the construction of the road provided very useful experience. Jefferson Hunt eventually used the skills when he and some of the former Battalion members constructed roads serving the economic interests of the San Bernardino community. Hunt also used improved wagon roads along the Old Spanish Trail in Utah. Other former Battalion members similarly applied their skills to developing numerous other roads branching out from Salt Lake City that formed the basis for the rapid growth of the Mormon communities in Utah and other Western States.

One other series of observations along the March would prove to be crucial to the future success of the Mormons in the Great Basin. Most of the people in America in the 1840s, including the Mormons, were farmers. The vast majority lived east of the 100th Meridian where Spring and Summer rainfall were sufficient to raise crops. But west of the 100th Meridian, roughly the north-south line through central Nebraska and the Dakotas, west-central Kansas, and the Texas/Oklahoma border (excluding the Panhandle), rainfall was not sufficient to grow most crops. In this western area, agriculture depended on irrigation. The men of the Battalion noted that extensive—and sometimes ancient—irrigation systems had been constructed by both the Mexican settlers and the indigenous Indians of the West. They had seen and noted the irrigation systems that had been constructed along the Rio Grande, at Tucson, along the Gila River and at the Colorado River.

When these men arrived at their new homes in the basin of the Great Salt Lake, they constructed similar systems to irrigate their new farms and gardens. The community irrigation system quickly became a central feature of each newly constructed Mormon community in the Great Basin and beyond. The remnants of these early irrigation systems can still be seen in cities and towns along the Wasatch Front today.

Chapter 11

California Duty

When the Mormons of the Battalion reached the California Coast, they discovered a strip of lush, green land, about forty-five miles wide that separated the Pacific from the inland deserts. Arriving at Warner's in the middle of Winter, they discovered that the grass had begun to grow, wildflowers were blooming and the land showed its immense productive capacity. After marching 1,200 miles across the barren and forbidding deserts of the Southwest, they were sure they had arrived in a Promised Land. For a group of men, mostly farmers from the Midwest, the East, and England, the bounty that California showed in mid-Winter could not be missed. That they had crossed two-thirds of the Continent through some of most difficult obstacles imaginable was an accomplishment that every man of the Battalion felt.

The importance and success of the march of the Mormon Battalion was not lost on their commander either. On his second day in San Diego, January 30th, Lieutenant Colonel Philip St. George Cooke, put pen to paper and wrote Order No. 1 which was read to the men five days later at their new post in San Luis Rey. That order reads:

Headquarters Mormon Battalion

Mission of San Diego, January 30, 1847.

ORDERS No. 1

The Lieutenant-Colonel commanding congratulates the battalion on their safe arrival on the shore of the Pacific Ocean, and the conclusion of their march of over two thousand miles.

History may be searched in vain for an equal march of infantry. Half of it has been through a wilderness where nothing but savages and wild beasts are found, or deserts where, for want of water, there is no living creature. There, with almost hopeless labor we have dug deep wells, which the future traveler will enjoy. Without a guide who had traversed them, we have ventured into trackless table-lands where water was not found for several marches. With crowbar and pick and axe in hand, we have worked our way over mountains, which seemed to defy aught save the wild goat, and hewed a passage through a chasm of living rock more narrow than our wagons. To bring these first wagons to the Pacific, we have preserved the strength [of] our mules by herding them over large tracts, which you have laboriously guarded without loss. The garrison of four presidios of Sonora concentrated within the walls of Tucson, gave us no pause. We drove them out, with their artillery, but our intercourse with the citizens was unmarked by a single act of injustice. Thus, marching half naked and half fed, and living upon wild animals, we have discovered and made a road of great value to our country.

Arrived at the first settlement of California, after a single day's rest, you cheerfully turned off from the route to this point of promised repose, to enter upon a campaign, and meet, as we supposed, the approach of the enemy; and this too, without even salt to season your sole subsistence of fresh meat.

Lieutenant A. J. Smith and George Stoneman, of the First Dragoons, have shared and given valuable aid in all these labors.

Thus, volunteers, you have exhibited some high and essential qualities of veterans. But much remains undone. Soon, you will turn your attention to the drill, to system and order, to forms also, which are all necessary to the soldier.

By order of Lieutenant-colonel P. St. Geo. Cooke,

P.C. Merrill, Adjutant (Cooke 1951, 103).

The immediate effect of this order from Cooke was to instill in the men of the Battalion a new feeling of accomplishment and a new level of respect for their leader. The March to Santa Fe had been plagued with ill-feelings toward Lieutenant Smith, who unexpectedly became their leader. During the march from Santa Fe to the Coast, many felt that Cooke was too harsh with them and placed them at too much risk from the elements. But Cooke's prompt and forceful recognition of their efforts caused most of the men to quickly regard him as their friend and protector. This attitude only grew with time and a decade later, Cooke was one of the very few officers in the U.S. Army who was trusted by the Mormons. Unfortunately, Captain Jefferson Hunt's standing would not immediately improve; forces were still at work serving to undermine his authority and efforts as leader of the Battalion.

The Higgins detachment containing Gilbert Hunt, who as corporal was second only to Nelson Higgins in rank, Celia Hunt and her children (except for John), the Kelly brothers and their families arrived in El Pueblo in early October after passing through Bent's Fort along the Arkansas. The Brown Sick Detachment which left Santa Fe on October 18, 1846, arrived in El Pueblo on November 17th. This group included Matilda Nease Hunt, her brother Peter and sister Ellen and John Hunt. The Willis Sick Detachment which left the Rio Grande on November 10th and arrived at El Pueblo on December 20th. There were now about 275 Mormons in El Pueblo comprising soldiers, families and those from Mississippi.

El Pueblo was the scene of much activity. Log cabins were built to house the soldiers and families, hunting parties went out to obtain fresh meat and supply runs were made down the Arkansas to Bent's Fort. But many of the soldiers were sick and some did not survive. On November 4th, Hunt's nephew, Milton Kelley, died leaving his wife, Malinda. On November 21st, four days after arriving at El Pueblo, seventeen-year-old Joseph W. Richards, a musician from Company A and a brother of Apostle Franklin D. Richards, died. In his last hours, he had been cared for by Celia Hunt, who brought him food and comforted him. Tragedy then directly stuck the Hunt family, when one of Jefferson's and Celia's twins, eighteen-month-old Parley, died on January 1, 1847.

Twelve of Willis's Detachment had been too sick to travel from Santa Fe to El Pueblo and had been left at Simeon Turley's ranch near Taos. On December 27th, Gilbert Hunt led a small group of soldiers to Turley's to rescue the group of men left there. They returned to El Pueblo by the middle of January, barely missing a tragic attack by Mexican insurgents. In March, Gilbert married Lydia A. Gibson, whose family was part of the Mississippi Mormons. In a few short months at El Pueblo, Hunt's family was transformed; his youngest son had died and his oldest son had married.

In spite of their distance from the New Mexico settlements, the Mexican War caused some stir at El Pueblo. On January 19, 1847, a group of Mexicans and Indians staged a revolt and attacked the government center in Taos, killing Governor Charles Bent and the rest of the non-Mexican/Indian population there. Eight others were killed at Turley's ranch. For some time, it was not at all certain that those in El Pueblo were safe. Finally, in late February, word arrived that Colonel Sterling Price and his troops had resorted order in New Mexico and the danger had passed.

On February 18th, the first rescue party of seven men from Sutter's arrived at the crude shelters at the east end of what is now known as Donner Lake. Acting on the pleas and information from James Reed and several others who had successfully walked out of the snow-bound camps, several relief efforts had been mounted. The snow at the crest of the Sierras was estimated to be at least thirty feet deep and the efforts of the rescuers were a monumental accomplishment. Several of the rescuers continued on to the more distant camp of the Donner families, about five or six miles to the northeast. What they found at all camps was terrible. The living were nearly dead; and some of them had begun to eat the bodies of their fallen comrades. The shelters, clothes and bodies of the survivors were filthy. The sight that met the rescuers was so horrific that it would soon become national news and would terrify emigrants for years to come.

Because of the harsh conditions, they were able to bring only limited amounts of food and were able to lead only a portion of those stranded out. A second relief party, including James Reed, arrived at the lake camps on March 1st. Again, Reed's party was able to leave only a small amount of provisions and to take out only a few of those still stranded. Fortunately, the entire Reed family was rescued by the two groups. But others still remained in the camps and there was still to be more death and cannibalism. The tragedy of the Donner Party had not yet ended.

Once the Battalion arrived back at the Mission San Luis Rey on February 3rd, Lieutenant Colonel Cooke began the slow process of instilling military order into the Battalion. For over six months, the main focus was the march to California. Cooke calculated that the Battalion averaged thirteen miles per day in their march from Santa Fe (Bigler and Bagley 2000, 184). Now preparations could begin to meet any contingency that might arise. While it appeared that all resistance to the American occupation of California had stopped, the threat of future hostilities remained. There also was the possibility that the Battalion might be called to action in other areas, such as Baja California, if Washington decided to take additional territory or to use it as a negotiating chip with the Mexicans. In any case, prudence called for basic military training for the Battalion. The men spent the next month and a half at San Luis Rey drilling and practicing military skills.

Cooke began by ordering the garrison to clean up and restore order to the quarters they would be using and by imposing a new level of military discipline on the officers and men. He then began teaching the officers and non-commissioned officers the basic drills and maneuvers required of a military unit. The Battalion's officers then taught the enlisted men those drills, and afterwards conducted daily drills and exercises. Flour was obtained from San Diego and Indians provided corn to supplement the basic meat diet that had sustained the men for so long. After so many months of marching with reduced rations and the hardships of the trail, the new order of things pleased the men and they quickly adapted to their new circumstances. Several hours of drilling each day seemed of little consequence to men accustomed to much harsher conditions.

The conflict between Levi Hancock and Jefferson Hunt surfaced again on Sunday, February 14, 1847. Captain Hunt called for the first church service for the Battalion in California. He asked former Adjutant George Dykes to preach, and Hunt also addressed the gathering. Predictably, James Pace didn't think much of either man's comments. The apparent slight to Levi Hancock and his position as a General Authority called into question who the religious leader of the Battalion was—Hunt or Hancock. According to William Coray,

> "Lieutenant Dykes preached a sermon on Daniel's Kingdom which very much offended some of the brethren and they would not stay to meeting because Capt Hunt gave out the appointment. After service was over, he [Hunt] gave out the appointment for another sermon on the following Sabbath" (Journal History of the Church, February 14, 1847).

Hancock was not to be easily dismissed. He called a meeting of the men of the Battalion for the following evening.

On February 7th, Sergeant William Coray decided to stop writing daily entries in his journal since they had reached their destination. From that point forward, he only recorded those incidents he felt worth recalling in the future. Coray decided that the conflict between Jefferson Hunt and Levi Hancock was one of those incidents, and describes that meeting and then went on to express his own feelings in some detail "Lest I should forget what my sentiments were at the time regard to the captains and Bro. Levi. . ." (Journal History of the Church, February 15, 1847). In brief, Hancock began by claiming the right to be in charge of the religious affairs of the Battalion. He told the men that Daniel Tyler was the best man to preach to them. He told the captains present that "it was not their place" to handle the men's religious affairs. Coray saw this as a direct affront to the authority of Jefferson Hunt, who had already called for the following Sunday's meeting and designated someone to lead it. William Hyde immediately supported Hancock's comments and said that he would follow him regardless of the consequences. Hunt and the other officers considered this to be an insult to their authority as given by Brigham Young and the Twelve Apostles.

Coray wrote that he was not sure which side was right, but that he had done his duty and felt good about himself and what he had done. He said he was going to record his thoughts so that he could determine if he made the right decision when he found out the feelings of the Church officials on the issue. Coray's summation of his feelings and observations capture what probably many of the Battalion were thinking:

> "When the Battalion was about ready to start as I was one of them, I wanted to know if any man would be sent along to be our counselor or not. I asked Bro Willard Richards if there would be any. He said, 'No, your officers will be your counselors.' After that Bro. Brigham and others of the Twelve met the officers, commissioned and non-commissioned, then give them instructions at which place President Young said, 'Brethren, go and be faithful. Hearken to your officers who shall be over you. Let it be said of you that you are the best men that ever entered the service.' Speaking to the officers in particular, he said, 'Be fathers to the soldiers and counsel them, for you are their counselors and if I hear of your dancing or playing cards, that it will right if your control it. You must have control over everything and all will be well.' There was never anything said about Levi or Wm. Hyde presiding or dictating in any way. Notwithstanding, Bro. Levi Hancock is first counselor to Joseph Young and President of the Seventies and I could do no more than acknowledge his authority over me in spiritual things, but still I thought the course he pursued an improper one in getting up an excitement against the officers and destroying their influence with the men whom they should control according to Pres. Young's instruction. Neither could I justify the officers altogether because some of them set very bad examples and were somewhat tyrannical.

Not so with all, but as little differences should not aggravated, but rather forgotten, I will say no more on this subject" (Journal History of the Church, February 15, 1847).

In his own mind, Sergeant William Coray would stand by Jefferson Hunt and the other officers as the properly designated leaders of the Battalion. It was far from the end of the split between the secular and ecclesiastical leaders of the Battalion. The division continued for the remainder of their enlistment and would even carry on after discharge. Some men strongly took sides; most simply observed the conflict but did not become involved and continued to do their duty.

In addition to learning and teaching drills and squabbling with Levi Hancock over the control of the Battalion, Jefferson Hunt had other duties to attend to. On February 7th, John Borrowman, an enlisted man from Company B who was still feeling the effects of reduced rations and the difficult march, fell asleep while on guard duty. He was discovered by a sergeant and placed under arrest for his dereliction of duty. On February 25th, Borrowman's court martial was heard by Captain Hunt and Lieutenants Oman and Clift. Three other men from Company C, Isaac Peck, John Mowrey, and Ebenezer Harmon, had also been arrested for killing an Indian's cow, and their court martial was heard the same day. All four were convicted and Borrowman was sentenced to six days in the guardhouse with three hours a day in the cell and a three dollar fine. The others were sentenced to ten days, two hours in the cell for five days, and fined restitution of $2.50 each to pay for the cow (Ricketts 1996, 127).

Lieutenant Colonel Cooke took exception to the sentence in Borrowman's case, deciding that it was far too lenient for the seriousness of the offense. Able only to affirm the sentence or reduce it, Cooke showed his displeasure by releasing Borrowman with no further punishment. Cooke commented that he would not trust another court martial to be handled by the Battalion's own Mormon officers (Bigler and Bagley 2000, 196). This incident showed that

Jefferson Hunt and the Mormon officers could be lenient toward their own and improved their standing within the Battalion.

General Kearny had received orders from President Polk dated on June 3, 1846, to take control of California. General Winfield Scott, the senior Army general, wrote Kearny on November 3, confirming that he was to establish a civilian government in California. He then appointed Colonel Richard Mason, or whoever was second in rank to the General, as governor, and required Kearny to return to St. Louis. Additionally, he instructed General Kearny to incorporate Fremont's four hundred or so volunteers into the regular Army. However, the senior military officer in California following the early capitulation of Mexican forces was Commodore Robert F. Stockton of the U.S. Navy. He assumed control, and along with his friend and fellow spirit, Army Captain John C. Fremont, controlled the new territory. Kearny's arrival in California in December with conflicting orders did not persuade Stockton to relinquish his control, and shortly before his departure by sea to Mexico on January 14, 1847, Stockton issued a declaration making Fremont the governor and military commander in California.

Kearny and Fremont were both in Los Angeles and met on January 17th. At that time, Fremont presented Kearny with a letter that stated in part:

> "I feel myself, therefore, with great deference to your professional and personal character, constrained to say that, until you and Commodore Stockton adjust between yourselves the question of rank, where I respectfully think the difficulty belongs, I shall have to report and receive orders, as heretofore, from the Commodore." Further complicating the matter, Fremont signed the letter as "Lieutenant Colonel, United States Army and Military Commandant of the Territory of California" (Walker 2003, 256).

This blatant refusal to acknowledge General Kearny as the military commander and civilian governor of California had repercussions that affected not only the Mormon Battalion, but reverberated across the nation and through the halls of government in Washington.

General Kearny had the authority to arrest Fremont for insubordination on the spot, but chose not to for several reasons. Fremont was popular in California and had commanded volunteers that numbered considerably more men than General Kearny had at his disposal. Doubtlessly, Kearny wanted to avoid any form of confrontation with Fremont supporters. General Kearny was also a friend and supporter of Senator Thomas Hart Benton, Fremont's father-in-law, and one of the most powerful men in Washington. And finally, Fremont, "the Pathfinder," was immensely popular with the American public and any action the General took against him would not be well received. Accordingly, Kearny chose to bide his time and did not confine Fremont. But he didn't dismiss the matter; rather he began to formulate a plan to deal with the situation in the coming months. One of the significant components of his plan was the shift in power that would occur with the arrival in California of his additional troops of the Army of the West—the Mormon Battalion.

The wrangling ended in February with the arrival of Commodore William Branford Shubrick in Monterey with orders to replace Stockton as the chief of Naval Forces. Kearny and Shubrick discussed the matter and referred to the new orders from Washington brought by Colonel Richard B. Mason. On March 1st, Kearny and Shubrick issued a new announcement delineating the authority of each and confirming that General Kearny, as Military Commander, was responsible for administering the new territory of California (Bigler and Bagley 2000, 198).

On the same day, General Kearny issued new orders to Cooke placing him in command of the Southern District of California and putting under his command Fremont's California Volunteers in Los Angeles, as well as the Mormon Battalion and Kearny's own Dragoons. The order instructed him to protect the region from incursions from Sonora and to guard and watch the routes from the deserts, including Warner's Rancho. He further ordered that a company from the Mormon Battalion be sent to guard San Diego, and that Los Angeles be particularly well garrisoned because of the recent history of insurrection there. Cooke was permitted to establish his headquarters where he thought best, but Kearny strongly suggested Los Angeles. General Kearny's adjutant, Captain Henry S. Turner, was given the duty to deliver these orders to Cooke after first telling Fremont in Los Angeles to either put his volunteers into the regular Army under Kearny, or to disband them and to deliver any documents he had to the General at Monterey (Bigler and Bagley 2000, 199-200). Captain Turner arrived at San Luis Rey on March 14th. The Mormon Battalion was soon to be deployed to several different duty stations in Southern California.

The daily routine of drills, inspections, and parades had continued with only limited success. While matters improved, not all of the officers and men became adept at the military regimen being taught. This frustrated Cooke, and his displeasure was shown in the way he treated the men. On March 6th, Lieutenant James Pace sent a letter to Cooke stating that he was "ready and willing to obey" his commands, but that he would like "to be treated with a little more respect" and that he was aware "of our awkwardness" (Bigler and Bagley 2000, 197). The following day, Pace noted a great improvement in the way Cooke treated the men. But with Turner's arrival on March 14th, most of the Battalion was again on the move.

The first unit of the Battalion to leave on March 15th was Company B under Captain Jesse Hunter, which left for San Diego with about two hours notice. Assigned to go with them as assistant to the alcalde in San Diego and as commissary assistant was Lieutenant Robert Clift of Company C. Several days later, on March 19th, the remaining four companies left for Los Angeles, arriving on March 23rd. Thirty-two sick and infirm men remained at San Luis Rey under the command of Lieutenant Oman. They rejoined the others at Los Angles in July. Captain Jefferson Hunt went with his Company A and the other companies to Los Angeles.

But before leaving for Los Angeles, Jefferson Hunt took advantage of the presence of Captain Henry Turner to write directly to General Kearny.

Like most of the other members of the Battalion, Hunt believed that the ultimate destination of the Saints would be near the California Coast. He saw the opportunity to obtain further federal government financial support for the Mormon cause. In his letter to Kearny, Hunt proposed that the Battalion reenlist with him in command, and that he be permitted to return to Council Bluffs to gain the support of Brigham Young and the Church leadership. When Turner left San Luis Rey for Monterey on March 17th, he carried Hunt's letter back to Kearny.

While Hunt's letter to Kearny is not in the military records, there exists a copy of Kearny's response back to Hunt under Turner's signature. That letter states that "the services of the Mormon Battalion will be needed longer than the period of their present enrollment, and that they will be continued in the service of the U.S. should they desire it." But it concludes by stating that "The General does not approve of your going to Council Bluffs at this time as suggested by you" (Bigler and Bagley 2000, 201). It was a good idea, but without the direct support of Brigham Young and the apostles, there would not be enough support within the Battalion for reenlistment, and Jefferson Hunt's idea would only partially be met. In the absence of direct instructions from Young, the dissenting group within the Battalion continued to oppose Hunt and attacked any plans he may have had regarding reenlistment.

In the conflict between Kearny and Fremont, the Mormon Battalion played a quiet, but nevertheless significant, role. The mere presence of an additional 350 armed men of Kearny's Army of the West in Southern California meant that Fremont's supporters, including his California Battalion, no longer held a decided military advantage. This gain further moved to Kearny's favor with the arrival by sea of the Regiment of New York Volunteers during March. At the end of April, some of the New Yorkers were sent to Southern California to help keep the peace in that area. At this time, it was not clear that the war in California was over. Rumors circulated that Mexican forces were massing in Northern Mexico for a move into California, and there was still some fear that the locals in the Los Angeles area might create an insurrection. In fact, no attack or insurrection was forthcoming, but the Mormon Battalion and the New York Volunteers prepared for the worst just in case.

With the exception of thirty-two sick men who remained at San Luis Rey with Lieutenant Oman, the companies left on March 19th and arrived in Los Angeles four days later. Since a number of the California Battalion, which was still garrisoned nearby, were from Missouri, the Mormons experienced some tension at their new campsite outside of the town and away from their suspected antagonists. On several occasions the campsite was moved to more favorable sites—but not near the California Battalion, which still presented some opposition to the Army officers and was suspected by the Mormon Battalion.

After arriving in their camps near Los Angeles, the men began a daily routine of drills aimed at preparing them for action, should the need arise. On evening of March 30th, Jefferson Hunt addressed the men on the issue of the death of Colonel Allen and the assumption of command by Lieutenant Smith. According to Daniel Tyler, Hunt explained that he was willing to assume command but followed the counsel of his fellow Mormon officers and permitted Smith to take over Allen's position. Tyler noted that "This was the first time the facts had been made public. This speech removed some prejudice" (Tyler 1881, 274). The fact that Hunt felt compelled to comment on the matter indicates that the issue was still a major concern within the Battalion. Whether or not some of the grievances toward Hunt were relieved, the greater part of the men soon chose to follow someone else's lead.

It appears that Hunt's discussion of the events of seven months previously aroused further discussions and brought back memories of those days on the plains before Santa Fe. Henry Standage recorded in his diary on April 2nd, that in a conversation that took place on January 28th, Lieutenant Oman told him that Levi Hancock's actions "would have amounted to insurrection had he been left to pursue the same and had not been checked" (Golder 1928, 216). The comments and actions of the dissenters including Hancock, Pettegrew, Lee and others during the first months of the march of the Battalion continued to trouble the officers throughout the period of the Battalion's enlistment.

On April 4th, Jefferson Hunt, as the senior Mormon officer, ordered the men in Los Angeles into formation for a formal dress parade. Unfortunately, neither Hunt nor his men had mastered the commands and precision movements of the formal drills. The parade turned into a comical series of mistakes instead of a smooth display of military skills. In spite of the frequent drills, camp duty was becoming more comfortable for men used to marching and limited supplies. But that didn't mean they would ever make regular Army soldiers.

By this time, supplies had begun arriving from the more adequately stocked garrison at San Diego and from ships docking at the nearby port of San Pedro. Many of the men obtained leather and ordered new shoes and boots to be made by the craftsmen at the Los Angeles Pueblo to replace their march-ravaged footwear.

On April 7th, many of the men signed a petition to their company officers to ask General Kearny for an early discharge, as they felt that the war was over in California and their services were no longer needed. Jefferson Hunt and several of the other officers, knowing that the Army regarded the war as being far from over, and since the petition clearly did not reflect their understanding of the goals as given by Brigham Young, reviewed the petition and discarded it without presenting it to either Cooke or Kearny. James Pace complained on the same day that "Capt. Hunt. . . had been seeking for a second enlistment unbenone [sic] to the soldiers" (Bigler and Bagley 2000, 204). Thus, the rift not only continued, it became even wider.

The Mexican residents of Southern California had been denied the right to possess firearms because of the fear of insurrection. In addition, the turmoil created by the war created opportunities for some aggressive actions by Indians in the territory. To protect the new citizens from raids, on April 11th, Colonel Cooke ordered Company C to march fifty miles east from Los Angeles to the foot of Cajon Pass to protect the ranches there from predatory raids by Indians from the deserts to the north and east. This order set the stage for the events that eventually led to Jefferson Hunt's return to California later that year and the establishment of the Mormon colony at San Bernardino four years later. Those who went east with Company C and future units met Isaac Williams at his Rancho del Chino. They saw for themselves the attractive land and ranches in the San Bernardino, Chino and Rancho Cucamonga areas now known as the Inland Empire. As the men returned from their trek, the word quickly spread within the Battalion of the sparsely populated but extremely productive land.

On April 22nd, Lieutenant James Pace was ordered to take eight men from each company and go to the area of Cajon Pass to relieve Company C. Pace had previously recorded that the departure of Company C was the fifth time the Battalion had been divided, and such a division was contrary to the instructions of the Twelve Apostles (Bigler and Bagley 2000, 204). His new assignment would make the sixth such division. Pace and his unit had just arrived near Cajon Pass when he received orders to return to Los Angeles immediately. Cooke was concerned that Fremont's California Battalion had been getting support from Indians and local Mexicans to attack the Battalion and Kearny's Dragoons. Fremont had returned to Los Angeles on March 30th, and his presence served only to increase the tension.

While no such attack ever materialized, Cooke was sufficiently alarmed on April 25th to order Hunt's Company A to move to a hill that overlooked the town of Los Angeles and to begin the construction of a fort at that location. That same night, Cooke apprised the Battalion to expect an attack and told Hunt "to have the Battalion ready to form a line of battle, at a moment's notice, with loaded guns and fixed bayonets" (Tyler 1881, 279). The Battalion officers did as directed and a number of extra men were placed on guard duty or remained awake awaiting the anticipated attack. While not recorded as such, part of the fear of attack might have been a result of the companies having received six months pay on April 24th and 25th. An extra $16,000 or so, floating around in the hands of the troops, would have provided an enticement to many of their adversaries in the area.

The only combat involving the Mormon Battalion occurred on May 8th and 9th when local citizens asked for help in repelling Indian attacks north of the Pueblo in the northern part of the San Fernando Valley. Lieutenant Samuel Thompson took twenty men and found the Indians. A two hour long battle ensued and six Indians were killed and two soldiers, Benjamin Mayfield and Samuel Chapin, were wounded by arrows (Bigler and Bagley, 2000).

Today's visitor to downtown Los Angeles can find the approximate site where Fort Benjamin Moore was erected by the Mormon Battalion. Located just north of the Civic Center, it occupied the area bounded by the 101 Freeway, Broadway, Hill Street and César Chávez Avenue. The top of the adjacent hill is occupied by the Los Angeles School District. Most of the original hill was removed during construction of Broadway and Hill Streets, and the later construction of the 101 Freeway. Much of the adjacent area has been altered for the construction of other streets and buildings. The location is marked by monuments commemorating both the Mormon Battalion and Fort Moore. A visitor to the monuments or the nearby hilltop can immediately see the strategic advantage the site gave the Army. About 500 yards east of the present Board of Education Hill, and about 100 feet lower in elevation, is the Plaza of the El Pueblo de Los Angeles Historical Monument, the center of the town as it existed in 1847. Troops with cannons occupying Fort Hill could easily command the entire population of the largest city in the southern part of California.

Two previous efforts were made to fortify the hill location. The first occurred the previous August when Marine Captain Archibald Gillespie, who had been placed in command by Stockton, used bags filled with dirt and sand to create a small fortification. The second effort took place in January 1847, when Lieutenant William Emory, the topographical engineer on General Kearny's staff, began work on another fortification on the hill to be used in an emergency. Work on this fortification stopped after less than two weeks when Emory and other officers and men left with Kearny for Monterey. The third and most successful effort to erect a fort occurred when Lieutenant Colonel Cooke perceived the need for a strong fortification in late April.

As laid out, the fort extended for 400 feet along the hill and had emplacements for cannons that were surrendered by Fremont's California Battalion after several requests from Cooke. The rear and north side were protected by a steep ravine that has long since been filled in and built upon. From this commanding site, the view of the Pueblo of Los Angeles and the approaches to the fort was superb. This third and last fortification on the hill was designed and built to be a permanent fixture until the threat from below was deemed to be over. As a result, construction continued through the months of May, June and into July, when the Battalion was set for discharge. Most of the construction material consisted of timber cut in the San Gabriel Mountains and hauled to the site. Trenches were dug around the perimeter. Some adobe may also have been used.

Although Company A began the construction of the fort, by May 1st orders were given "that each company has to work four days a piece, alternately, until the fort is done" (Hancock 2000, 285). As a consequence, everyone in the Battalion at Los Angeles took part in the construction. Their efforts were significant. When the Battalion was discharged in mid-July, the construction was far enough along for the Dragoons and the New York Volunteers to occupy it immediately, although some finishing work continued in the following months. Over the next year or so, the need for the fort diminished as the threat of insurrection faded. With the drop in the number of troops following the discovery of gold in Northern California, the size of the garrison declined. By 1849, the fort was largely abandoned. It was decommissioned in 1853.

The story of the Battalion's involvement with the fort reached a climax on July 4, 1847. Colonel Stephenson of the New York Volunteers, who had assumed the military command of Southern California, wanted a dramatic 150 foot long flag pole to dominate the hill. With help from local residents, two large trees were felled and hauled from the San Gabriel Mountains to the hill. Carpenters in the Battalion spliced the timber and fashioned a 150-foot-long pole, which was raised into position on July 1st. At sunrise on July 4th, the Battalion assembled and paraded within the new fort. The flag was then raised while the musicians of the New York Volunteers played the "Star Spangled Banner." What an imposing sight must have greeted those in the Pueblo of Los Angeles below: The American flag, illuminated by the morning sun, and flying nearly 250 feet above their heads less than 500 yards to the west.

Following the flag raising, the men were dismissed until 11 a.m. when again they assembled for more ceremonies, during which Colonel Stevenson named the new fort after Captain Benjamin Moore, one of General Kearny's officers killed at the battle of San Pasqual six months before (Golder 1928, 233-234). The work of the Mormon Battalion at Los Angeles was essentially over. For most of their remaining eleven days of enlistment, the men prepared for their journey East to rejoin their families and the other Mormons. They busied themselves with acquiring horses or mules and supplies for the long road to their new homes.

By the beginning of May, General Kearny had affairs in California well in control. He was ready to return to Washington, and his plan was to take John C. Fremont with him for court martial for insubordination. Kearny's plan called for him, Fremont, several officers, and a small escort of the Mormon Battalion to travel over the Northern Route to Fort Leavenworth, where Fremont would be arrested and taken to Washington. Colonel Richard B. Mason, the second highest ranking officer in California after Kearny, assumed the role of Governor and Military Commander. Kearny also took Philip St. George Cooke with him. Colonel Stevenson of the New York Volunteers replaced Cooke as the military commander of Southern California and the Battalion reported to him.

Kearny arrived in Los Angeles on May 9, 1847, with Stevenson and several of his staff officers. The General was warmly greeted by a twenty-one gun salute and, in turn, visited the Battalion in camp and spoke with the troops. The following day, Kearny inspected the Battalion and addressed the men comparing their march to that of Napoleon. He praised their good behavior and promised to speak favorably of them in Washington. Kearny intended to make a fast trip East and needed a military escort. Members of Fremont's topographical party would accompany him, but Kearny needed men specifically loyal to him. Since it seemed advisable to leave his Dragoons in California, and since he could not trust members of Fremont's old California Battalion which remained loyal to Fremont, Kearny ordered that fifteen men be selected from the Battalion to serve as his escort. Accordingly, Jefferson Hunt and the officers selected the men from the companies in Los Angeles.

Accounts vary as to the exact number of men assigned to the escort. Some contemporary accounts state that twelve men accompanied General Kearny. More detailed historical research work by Ricketts (Ricketts 1996, 162) and Bigler and Bagley (Bigler and Bagley 2000, 228) indicate that fifteen is the correct number. The latter writers in a footnote indicate that three of the fifteen were discharged on the Bear River on the eastern edge of the Great Basin. This would give some credibility to both numbers at different stages of the trip East. In view of the evidence presented, the author will use fifteen as the correct number of Mormon Battalion members who began the trip.

Who to select to accompany Kearny was an important decision for Jefferson Hunt and the officers of the Battalion. As the commanding officer of the Army of the West, General Kearny was an important figure in the future of the Mormons. What he told his superiors and others in Washington about the loyalty of the Mormons could greatly influence future feelings and decisions regarding them. Since the escort would be in the immediate presence of Kearny for three months or more, it was important to send loyal, dedicated men who would represent themselves well. Who would go to Fort Leavenworth was not a decision to be taken lightly. We must assume that the men who went under the supervision of Battalion Lieutenant Sylvester Hulet and Sergeant Nathaniel Jones were loyal and patriotic and would fairly represent the Mormons.

At this late stage of the enlistment, internal opposition to further dividing the Battalion had ceased. Instead of expressing his opposition, Levi Hancock recorded in his diary for May 11th that: "Last night some men were called to go to the states; the offer was made to me. I accepted it and immediately I felt a darkness of mind and I then said, 'I will not go.' Gave my place to another man" (Hancock 2000, 292). Hancock expressed no opposition to the formation of the detachment.

On May 13th, three of the men left with Kearny to sail up the Coast to Monterey, while the other twelve, under the command of Lieutenant William Tecumseh Sherman, who remained in Monterey for several more years, began the ride up the El Camino Real (The King's Highway) from Los Angeles to Monterey where they joined with Kearny and Fremont for the trip East. The group reached Monterey twelve days later, and Kearny arrived two days after that. There they outfitted themselves further. Since mounted men with pack animals could travel at a rate at least two or three times faster than those with wagons, and since the El Camino Real was not yet a wagon road, no wagons were taken on the trip. The final traveling party consisted of sixty-four men, led by Kearny and his adjutant, Major Henry Turner, and several hundred public and private animals (Clarke 1961, 327). In addition to the officers and escort troops, some discharged military personnel and civilians also made the trip. Included among them was Dr. George Sanderson, the scourge of the Battalion.

They left Monterey on May 31st, and traveled over present-day Pacheco Pass into the great Central Valley of California. The previous Winter had been one of very heavy snowfall and the late Spring runoff had swollen the rivers and streams to near record levels. Much of the low-lying valley was marsh-land and travel was difficult and treacherous. About June 11th, the Battalion members encountered fellow Mormons who were part of Sam Brannan's New Hope Colony at the confluence of the San Joaquin and Stanislaus rivers. They learned that Brannan had gone east to encourage Brigham Young to settle in California. On June 13th, the party camped near Sutter's Fort. On June 16th, they left Sutter's for the trip across the Sierras. Kearny led the march, with Fremont and his party traveling several miles behind—although they eventually traveled together.

On June 21st, the party crossed over the crest of Sierra Nevada Mountains, traveling through snow up to twelve feet deep, and camped at the western end of Donner Lake. The next morning, the party continued to the east end of the lake, where they came upon the cabins and human remains of part of the ill-fated Donner Party. They knew of the tragedy and could tell that many of the remains had been butchered for food. Kearny ordered Major Swords to take a detail of five Battalion members and bury the remains. He then ordered that the cabins be burned. Kearny's party was among the first to reach the tragedy site following the departure of the rescue parties earlier that year. They called this location Cannibal Camp. While the detail was burying the dead, Fremont and company passed and continued on the road down the mountains. Kearny continued on for several miles and camped for the night at a spot now under the waters of Prosser Lake east of modern day Truckee,

California. There they were a little over one mile from the camp where the Donner families had spent the tragic Winter. Some went to see the camp, but no effort was made to bury the remains there.

They then continued on, entered the Truckee Meadows (site of present-day Reno), proceeded east to the Humboldt River and on to Fort Hall. Taking the Sublette Cutoff, they headed for South Pass and the road East. On July 24th, the Pioneer Company of Mormon emigrants entered the Valley of the Great Salt Lake, their new home. That same day, and several hundred miles to the northeast, Kearny's party crossed South Pass. The Battalion members had missed their Mormon brethren who were traveling to the south and west of them. But on August 4th, Nathaniel Jones and others did meet a second party of Mormon emigrants traveling to Salt Lake about twenty miles from Fort Laramie in eastern Wyoming. Jones was pleased to find that they held a letter from his wife, his first word from her in a year. By now, the Battalion escort detachment was aware that the destination for the Mormons was the Valley of the Great Salt Lake.

Finally, on August 22nd, the Kearny party reached Fort Leavenworth. There the Mormon detachment turned in its military equipment and livestock and was discharged. They received their extra pay for the additional month-plus of military service. Jones reported that it amounted to $8.60 (Bigler and Bagley 2000, 251).

Kearny, Fremont and the others continued on to Washington where Fremont was court-martialed. He was convicted and ordered discharged from the Army. President Polk upheld the conviction, but vacated the penalty and ordered Fremont to report for duty. Shortly after, Fremont resigned from the Army. The ever-popular Fremont returned to California, was elected as a United States Senator by the Legislature, and unsuccessfully ran for President on the ticket of the newly-created Republican Party in 1856. General Stephen Watts Kearny died on October 31, 1848. Henry Turner and William Tecumseh Sherman reunited in 1853 when Sherman, as a partner in the St. Louis banking firm of Lucas-Turner, opened a successful bank in Gold Rush San Francisco.

Jefferson Hunt used the opportunity of Kearny's escort to send a letter to Brigham Young. Dated May 14, 1847, in Los Angeles, Hunt mentioned their location and stated that Kearny wanted them to re-enlist. He then went on to say that: "a few unquiet Spirits stirred up mal-contentment and dissension" and that he was the focus of their efforts and that "every good intention [of mine] was construed into evil, and of all characters I was the most vile" (Owens 2004, 60). For details of the march, Hunt advised Young to speak with one of the escorts, Jeremiah Willey, a private in Hunt's A Company. As with Jesse Hunter's earlier message to Hosea Stout at Winter Quarters to consult with Howard Egan regarding details of the dissention, Hunt wanted Brigham Young to be apprised of what was going on, but did not want to commit the details to writing.

At the time Hunt wrote this letter to Young, he was not aware of the final destination of the Saints. Many still believed that Young would lead them to the Coast where he had previously sent Sam Brannan and the *Brooklyn*. Consequently, Hunt ended his letter by saying that: "We have a very good offer to purchase a large valley sufficient to support 50,000 families," and that the purchase of land and 8,000 head of cattle could be made "by paying 300 dollars down and taking our own time to pay the remainder" (Owens 2004, 61). Clearly, Hunt was advocating settlement at the Williams Ranch in present-day Chino.

Hunt's letter also contained a brief request for advice regarding the conditions of discharge as agreed to by Colonel Allen and Brigham Young. He told of the animosity shown to the Mormons by some of Fremont's men who were from Missouri, but stated that the good works of the Mormons had overshadowed any negative talk from them. He also discussed the command of the Southern District under Stevenson and the command of the Battalion which was now fully in Hunt's hands.

Hunt's letter did not immediately reach Brigham Young, since Young's Pioneer Company to the Valley of the Great Salt Lake arrived there at the same time that Kearny's escort was near South Pass in Wyoming. They had missed each other. Most likely, the letter was given to a subsequent Mormon wagon train heading for Salt Lake that was met on the trail. Young did send advice to the Battalion, but they would not receive it until well after discharge and while they were on their way East.

By late May, a number of the Battalion troopers had been sent on temporary assignments to the interior valleys fifty miles east of Los Angeles to protect the ranchers there from attack by Indians coming from the north and east. The returning soldiers spoke favorably of the country and the owner of one of the more prominent ranches, Isaac Williams. His Rancho Santa Ana del Chino, at the site of present-day city of Chino, was one of the first encountered by traders, raiders and Indians arriving in the valleys from the Mojave Desert. Williams had arrived in California more than a decade earlier and had married into the prosperous and prominent Lugo family. His hospitality saved and comforted many travelers arriving from the desert.

James Pace recorded that on May 22nd, Captains Hunt and Davis, and Lieutenant Rosecrans started on a trip to see the Williams Ranch for themselves and to meet Isaac Williams (Bigler and Bagley 2000, 213). Captain Davis, and presumably Hunt and Rosecrans as well, returned to Los Angeles on May 25th (Golder 1928, 223). This trip was more than a simple sightseeing trip; it was an exploration for the benefit of the Church. And it was probably not Hunt's first visit to Williams. Hunt was impressed with what he found and he told others in the Church of the importance of this discovery. During this visit, Hunt and Williams discussed the possible Mormon acquisition of the Chino Rancho as Hunt reported in his letter to Brigham Young. Much of Hunt's life during the next decade would be spent near the Williams Ranch.

During the final month of their enlistment, the issue of re-enlistment again became a major issue within the Battalion. The Mexican War had been going on for over a year and throughout the Army, men were refusing to reenlist. Many had enlisted for an opportunity to leave the cities of the East where they had felt economically trapped, and now that their enlistments were up, they were free to find better lives elsewhere. In Mexico, Texas, New Mexico and California, the size of the Army was dwindling. Nowhere was this more evident than in California, a large land with only a handful of soldiers in the regular Army and volunteers from New York and the Mormon Battalion. The Army needed to reenlist as many as possible to maintain its ranks.

Accordingly, on June 5, 1847, Governor Richard Mason wrote to Jefferson Hunt, with a copy to Colonel Stevenson, asking him to "induce" the Battalion to reenlist and promising Hunt the rank of Lieutenant Colonel if he could raise a battalion of 256 privates plus non-commissioned and commissioned officers. Should he get less than that, his rank would be that of Major. Mason advised Hunt to go to San Diego to talk to the men stationed there also (Bigler and Bagley 2000, 254-255). At the same time, Mason also wrote to Colonel Stevenson, asking him to "use your best efforts to accomplish the object I have herein proposed" (Bigler and Bagley 2000, 256). In that same letter, Mason authorized Stevenson to discharge those that reenlisted in March 1848, should they choose to be discharged then. Even though the minimum enlistment period was one year, Mason could authorize an early discharge. He probably believed that the March date might appeal to the men since it would give them time to travel East to their families.

Jefferson Hunt did not go to San Diego, but Colonel Stevenson did and arrived there on June 22nd. In a letter to Governor Mason dated June 28th from Los Angeles, Stevenson reported that the Mormons stationed in San Diego were highly respected by the local community who desired their continued presence (Bigler and Bagley 2000, 258-262). Not only had the Battalion men provided strong military protection for the city and port, they had worked hard in the employ of the locals digging wells to provide an adequate water supply, making bricks and doing other jobs about the town and surrounding area. The income from these efforts supplemented their military wages. During his visit, Stevenson became aware of the depredations of some of the local Indians, especially at the Mission San Luis Rey, and reported that it was important to select a strong Indian Agent to manage their affairs there. He also accepted the resignation of the alcalde of San Diego and appointed Lieutenant Robert Clift of Company A, who was serving with Captain Hunter at San Diego, to fill that post.

A short time later, Captain Jesse Hunter was appointed to the Indian Agent position. He remained in California following the discharge of the Battalion. Hunter's plural wife, Lydia, had died on April 26th, six days after giving birth to a son named Diego, the first birth to American parents in San Diego. Hunter's appointment not only met the needs of the new American government in California, it met his personal needs as well.

On June 23rd, Colonel Stevenson addressed the Company in San Diego complimenting them and asking for volunteers to reenlist. About thirteen of the men said they would reenlist under the proper conditions. Captain Hunter spoke favorably of the request, but William Hyde and Horace Alexander spoke against it. It was generally agreed that a delegation should go to Los Angeles to hear the views of others, and especially that of Levi Hancock. Accordingly, Hunter, Hyde and Alexander accompanied Colonel Stevenson on his trip back to Los Angeles where they arrived on June 28th.

The following morning, work on the fort was suspended and everyone was told to assemble at 8:30 a.m. That assembly with Colonel Stevenson and subsequent meetings with Jefferson Hunt and some of the other officers would be the final push to get members of the Battalion to reenlist. According to Henry Standage, the assembly began with Stevenson explaining the need for troops until others arrived from the States. The Colonel asked for a battalion-sized reenlistment, but would be satisfied if only a company reenlisted. He explained that they would be under the command of their own elected Lieutenant Colonel or Major, depending on the number that remained. He explained that he understood that those with families needed to return East, but hoped that those without families would heed his advice and reenlist. Stevenson promised them that while the term of enlistment would be for one year, they would be discharged the following February with a full year's pay delivered at Monterey or any other place in California, or on the Bear River in the Great Basin. Stevenson concluded by praising the men of the Battalion for their "good behavior" and other efforts (Golder 1928, 230-234).

The men moved to an area about a quarter of a mile away. Captain Hunter was the first to speak. He stated that he believed that it was the duty of the men to reenlist and gave the reasons why. Jefferson Hunt followed and:

> "endeavored to show the advantages we had gained in point of power during the past year's service in the U.S. He also urged the necessity of maintaining the ground we had gained, in as much as an opportunity now presented itself for our still obtaining more power by having a Mormon 3rd in Command in the Territory of California, and the probability of Col. Mason and Col. Stevenson being removed. In which case our Mormon commander would rise still higher" (Golder 1928, 231).

This statement by Hunt may have reflected his own aspirations for more power, or it may have been what he perceived to be a grand opportunity for the Mormons to secure a powerful position in California. Most likely, it was some of both.

Hunt was followed by others who supported the reenlistment, including Captain Davis, Lieutenants Cyrus Canfield and Dykes. Finally, David Pettegrew rose and said it was their duty to return to the Camp of the Saints, since they accomplished all they had signed up to do. Because of the heat, the meeting moved again to a large tent. Henry Standage summed up the importance of the meeting and the general feeling of those present by saying: "This is certainly a very important crisis in the history of the travels of this Battalion of Latter Day Saints, every one left to be led or walk by faith and the light of the Spirit" (Golder 1928, 232). After some further discussion, it was decided to appoint a committee to draft the terms under which some would be willing to reenlist. The committee consisted of captains Hunter, Davis and "Father" Pettegrew. The meeting adjourned and a document was drawn up, but Pettegrew "didn't help them much" (Bigler and Bagley 2000, 264).

With the new reenlistment articles now drawn up, the meeting resumed and many spoke to the two divergent sides of the issue with Captains Hunt and Hunter, along with Lieutenant Canfield and Sergeant Ferguson being in favor and Sergeants Hyde, Tyler and Pettegrew opposing reenlistment. Hunter, in his remarks, tried to draw out the core of the opposition by saying that "it had been hinted that there was a prophet somewhere in the camp, he believed among the privates; if so, he wished he would come forth and give us the word of the Lord on the subject" (Golder 1928, 232). This probably prompted Levi Hancock to appear at the door of the tent and say that "he had never influenced the men against the officers either publicly or privately. . ." (Golder 1928, 233). Lieutenant Lytle also disclaimed ever trying to turn the men against the officers.

The meeting finally ended with "15 or 16 names being obtained for re-enlisting . . . ." Henry Standage clearly stated which side he chose when he said that Pettegrew's "remarks were in my opinion truly applicable" (Golder 1928, 232).

There were clearly two disparate sides to the issue. It appears that the issue was not one of hostile personalities fighting each other as much as it was trying to discern what the true desires of Brigham Young and the Twelve Apostles might be. From the very beginning, the side led by Levi Hancock and David Pettegrew tended toward a literal interpretation of what they believed to be Young's intentions. Jefferson Hunt, Jessie Hunter and the other officers tended toward a more pragmatic interpretation, which allowed the on-scene commanders to meet the challenges at hand and to make decisions based on their best judgment and the facts available to them.

David Pettegrew summed this up in his description of the events of the day when he said: "Lieutenant Dykes said, 'I believe if President Young was here he would counsel the brethren to remain in the war.' I arose and said, 'I don't believe any such thing, I know better.' 'Well,' he said, 'there is so much difference between us.' 'Time will tell,' said I" (Bigler and Bagley 2000, 263). A little over two months later, the Battalion would unexpectedly hear Brigham Young's counsel.

Over the next several weeks, the Battalion prepared for discharge and the long trip home, wherever that might be. While some work continued on Fort Moore, most of the men prepared for the trip to come by obtaining horses or mules and otherwise outfitting themselves for a long trip. Finally, on Friday, July 16, 1848, the year's service came to an end. At 3:00 p.m., the Battalion assembled in formation by company. Lieutenant A.J. Smith marched among the companies and returned to the front. With no other ceremony, Smith announced "You are discharged" (Ricketts 1996, 159). The original one year enlistment of the Mormon Battalion had ended.

While many of the men moved to a new campground three miles up the Los Angeles River to prepare for departure, others prepared to re-enlist. The next day, Captain Davis and Lieutenant Canfield began signing up those that wanted to stay with a new company. In all, seventy-nine discharged volunteers and three young men who served as aides to officers re-enlisted and were mustered back into the Army on July 20th. The company, known as the Mormon Volunteers, was sent to San Diego, which conformed both to their own desires and the most pressing needs of the Army.

Chapter 12

The Trek Home

From the early 1830s until the mid-1840s, two men played significant roles in the history of the Great Basin. One was a former trapper and mountain man turned explorer named Joseph Walker, and the other was a chief of the Northern Utes named Wakara (sometimes spelled Walkara). To complicate matters, Wakara sometimes adopted the name "Walker" and even "Joe Walker"; and the Californians and the Americans in Utah usually called him by these names.

During the Rendezvous in the summer of 1833, Joseph Walker, the mountaineer, organized an exploration party to travel from the Green River in the Rocky Mountains to California. His goal was to take forty of his compatriots, but by the time the group left the northern reaches of the Great Salt Lake, the number had swelled to nearly sixty men—including prominent mountain men Zenas Leonard, Alex Godey, Bill Williams, and Pauline (Powell) Weaver. During August and September, they traveled westward along the Humboldt River, presaging the travels of the tens of thousands who would come later over the same route. From the Humboldt Sink near present-day Lovelock, Nevada, they headed southwesterly, probably passing the Carson Sink and south along the Eastern Sierras. While they were not the first white men to travel in the Great Basin, they were most likely the first to cross directly and explore the western portion of the Great Basin. After traveling along the Walker River, and near Mono Lake, they were unable to find a suitable pass through the imposing Sierra Nevada Mountains to the West.

About October 1st, with their food supplies fast running out, Joseph Walker finally decided to follow an Indian trail into the eastern slope of the Sierras with hopes that they would be able to cross into California and safety. After climbing the precarious eastern face of the Sierras, they found that the western side over the summit was riddled with rocky peaks, boulder fields and steep canyons that offered little opportunity to descend into the Central Valley of California that they knew to be ahead. Just as the roads do today, they followed along a ridge line between two steep canyons on either side. On October 20th, they probably became the first non-Indians to peer into the great chasm of Yosemite Valley. By mid-November they had reached the tide-water area east of San Francisco Bay.

By December, the party of trappers was camped near Mission San Juan Bautista. Walker presented his credentials to Mexican officials in the Alta California capital of Monterey and asked permission to stay. It was granted, and they remained at San Juan Bautista for the Winter. On February 14, 1834, Joseph Walker's party, now numbering fifty-two men with 315 horses plus cattle and dogs, left for the States (Gilbert 1983, 144). They crossed the San Joaquin Valley, traveled southeast along the base of the western foothills of the Sierras and reached the Kern River north and east of present-day Bakersfield, California. Again following an old Indian trail and with several local Indians as guides, they crossed over the pass that soon bore his name—Walker Pass. They arrived in California's Owens Valley about May 1st, where several of the trappers took to the Southern route across Arizona toward New Mexico.

Joseph Walker and the rest headed northward along the eastern slopes of the Sierras toward their original trail. One attempt to short-cut across the Great Basin failed, and the party continued on to the Humboldt Sink, arriving there about June 8th. They finally arrived at their starting point in July, a year after departing. Walker's explorations were memorialized by having Walker Lake in Western Nevada, the various branches of the Walker River in California and Nevada, and Walker Pass between Bakersfield and Ridgecrest, California named after him. Walker Pass, on the southern end of the Sierra Nevada Mountains, was just below one mile in elevation and was a smooth easy road if the Kern River Canyon was avoided. Accordingly, it was used by a number of emigrants, some led by Joseph Walker himself, and was well known to many Western travelers. Walker Pass will play a major role in subsequent chapters of this book.

Joseph Walker and the Indian chief Wakara also knew each other. In the late 1830s, according to Joseph Walker's biographer, Bil Gilbert, Walker was instrumental in saving one of Wakara's wives and child (Gilbert 1983, 159-160). Thereafter, Wakara treated Walker with much respect and even assumed Walker's name sometimes when dealing with whites. This relationship served Walker well on several occasions and enabled him to settle a dispute between Wakara and John C. Fremont in May of 1844.

Although not now well known outside of Utah, Ute chief Wakara exerted control over a larger geographic area than any other Indian chief in American history. His influence extended from the Green River in Wyoming to the Cajon Pass near San Bernardino, California; from the upper reaches of the Great Salt Lake to northern Arizona; from western Colorado through Utah and well into southwestern Nevada. His extended forays took him even further into southern California all the way to the coast, to New Mexico and southern Arizona, and even to Sonora and Chihuahua in Mexico. He was known to have traveled as far north as Idaho.

Authority within tribal groups, especially in pre-white contact areas, did not follow centralized political authority as we know it today. Most often, several chiefs shared authority within tribes, and the tribes themselves were often dispersed local groups or bands who shared a common culture and language. They affiliated themselves when needed for protection or economic necessity. Within the central and southern areas of the Great Basin there were a number of tribes, including the Northern Utes, Southern Utes, Paiutes, Piedes and Shoshone. Because of the sparse amount of available water and the harshness of the desert conditions, most bands were small. While some lived in relatively settled communities, others led a semi-nomadic life.

In the 1830s, while still in his twenties, Wakara formed a band of aggressive, well-equipped and trained warriors. Excellent horsemen and comfortable in both mountains and deserts, these men provided the backbone of Wakara's authority. He also formed alliances with other chiefs and may have been related to some of them. When convenient, he formed alliances with whites as easily as with other Indians. By the late 1830s, Wakara was fully

involved in the slave trade, capturing Indians and Mexicans in one locale and
trading them in others. He was also involved in rustling horses in California
and driving them hundreds or even a thousand miles for sale in New Mexico
and in the northern and eastern areas of his domain. By 1840, Wakara's power
was so solid that Mexican authorities could not stop his raids and other Indian tribes feared him.

During the Winter of 1839-40, Wakara teamed up with famous mountain men Thomas "Peg-leg" Smith and Jim Beckwourth to conduct a raid that
went as far as San Luis Obispo, California. On many raids, Wakara captured
over 1,000 horses. He once stole about 3,000 horses in California and took
them across the desert for trade beyond Utah. Wakara was the most successful and prolific rustler in American history. His biographer, Conway Sonne,
states that "in 1846 or 1847 Walker collected a group of Piede Indian children
which he intended to sell as slaves in California." He took them to Los Angeles, and on the way home increased his wealth even further by stealing even
more horses (Sonne 1962, 38). Wakara amassed considerable wealth in his
illicit activities.

Following the arrival of the Mormons in the Great Basin, Wakara (or
Walker as he was known to the Mormons) cultivated a cordial relationship
with Brigham Young, which was eventually tested when Young forbade the
slave trade. This, combined with continued encroachment on Indian lands by
the Mormons, increased tensions and led to the brief "Walker War" in 1853.
Wakara died of natural causes shortly thereafter, at age forty.

Among the privates in Company C of the Battalion were Charles Brent
Hancock and George W. Hancock, the sons of Solomon who was Levi's brother and the man who first brought the Mormon religion to Jefferson Hunt.
Unlike their Uncle Levi, George and Charles were quick to enlist. Nearly forty
years after the events of the summer of 1847, Charles recorded some of his
experiences in Los Angeles just before discharge. First he described visiting
a band of Indians that had just arrived near the Pueblo of Los Angeles about
July 1st. He wrote that the Spaniards in the community told him that the group

was hostile and much feared by the people of California and Northern Mexico because they took and traded slaves, stole horses and cattle, and drove them to their mountain retreats to the northeast. Charles said: "This Indian force ware [sic] the Utahs and their war chief was Jim Walker [Wakara] known as the King of the Mountains, a thousand dollar reward was offered for his head in California" (Charles B. Hancock Journal).

Charles also described talking to an "Old Spaniard" who told him about the Old Spanish Trail which led to the upper Colorado River, Utah Lake, the Great Salt Lake and the trail to Oregon. He also had some excellent advice: the desert route was too hot to take in the Summer; the best route was to go north to Sutter's Fort and then take the route over the mountains to the east. In addition, the informant offered to act as a guide for pay, provided the Mormons would provide an escort back to Los Angeles after they found the mountain route. That, of course, was not something the men who were eager to get back to their families were willing to do.

The most commonly used route from Los Angeles to Northern California was El Camino Real, which had been pioneered some seventy years before and extended from San Diego to San Francisco. This historic road connected the California Missions and was developed by the missionaries and soldiers accompanying them. The missions were spaced at approximately one days' travel along the road. However, in spite of years of use, the road was mostly a pack trail and not a developed wagon road as its lofty name might imply. Following the secularization of the missions by the new Mexican government in the 1820s, most missions had been abandoned and fallen into disrepair. Nevertheless, El Camino Real was a well known and proven route over the four hundred miles from Los Angeles to San Francisco.

The route went west from Los Angeles to the coast at Ventura, then along the coast to just past Santa Barbara, where it then crossed over Gaviota Pass into the inland valleys that paralleled the coast. It went past the missions and settlements at locations such as Santa Maria and San Luis Obispo and on to Carmel and Monterey. From there it went north to San Francisco Bay, or to Mission San Jose in the present-day city of Fremont. Spanish and Mexican settlement in California was largely around the missions and, hence, near the coast. Only in Southern California and along the rivers feeding into San Francisco Bay were there some settlements well inland. The great Central Valley was largely unsettled. From Los Angeles to Sutter's Fort was about 500 miles via this route.

A second, and seemingly more direct, route north from Los Angeles was a little-used trail, made by Indians that led directly north over the mountains from Los Angeles into the southern San Joaquin Valley. This route went over Tejon Pass and into the San Joaquin Valley, via the Grapevine south of today's Bakersfield. In the 1840s, the southern part of the San Joaquin Valley held several large shallow lakes fed by the uncontrolled runoff from the Sierra Nevada Mountains to the east. Accordingly, the trail left the course followed by today's Interstate 5 and followed what is now U.S. 99 approximately toward the location of Bakersfield. From there it tended to run close to the Sierra Foothills after the crossing of the Kern River. One downside of this route was that it required the fording of several rivers that could have substantial flow during the Spring and early Summer months. Another drawback was the lack of any settlements along the route that could provide shelter or food for travelers. As long as travelers kept the Sierra Foothills on the right, they would eventually run into the American River near Sutter's Fort at today's Sacramento. Approximately 400 miles long, this route was over 100 miles shorter than El Camino Real's route, but would prove to be no quicker. This was the route discussed with Charles Hancock.

The discharged men of the Battalion were still not aware of their final home destination. They knew that many of their Brethren had settled, at least temporarily, at Winter Quarters along the Missouri River. They were aware that still other encampments were stretched eastward from there across Iowa. Many believed that Brigham Young would lead them West, possibly to the Great Basin or California. But no one was sure where the final home of the Saints would be, or if the Westward movement of the Saints had begun.

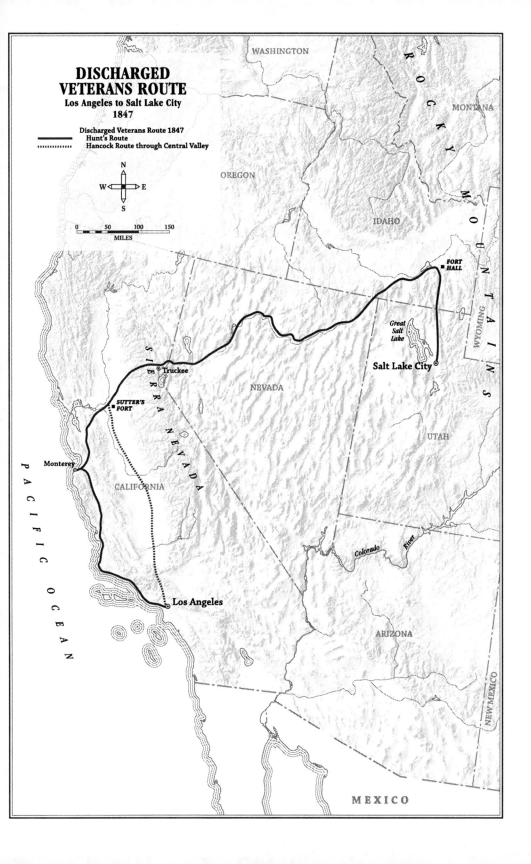

DISCHARGED VETERANS ROUTE
Los Angeles to Salt Lake City
1847

Discharged Veterans Route 1847
Hunt's Route
.... Hancock Route through Central Valley

N
W ← → E
S

0   50   100   150
MILES

WASHINGTON

R O C K Y

MONTANA

OREGON

IDAHO

M O U N T A I N S

FORT
HALL

WYOMING

Great
Salt
Lake

Truckee

Salt Lake City

SUTTER'S
FORT

S
I
E
R
R
A

N
E
V
A
D
A

NEVADA

UTAH

Monterey

CALIFORNIA

P
A
C
I
F
I
C

Colorado   River

O
C
E
A
N

Los Angeles

ARIZONA

NEW MEXICO

MEXICO

What they did know was that they had a long way to travel to reach their families and the rest of the Church. They might have to travel over 2,000 miles, and the season was getting late. Most travelers going from the Missouri River to the Pacific Coast left in mid-April to reach their destination before the weather closed the route and made travel impossible. But the men of the Battalion were still in California in late July. To get to their destination, they would have to travel light and fast. Wagons and oxen would be too slow for the trek home. Most had used whatever resources they could muster to purchase horses or mules for riding and packing. With nearly 225 men purchasing several animals each, the supply quickly began to shrink and the cost to rise. Not everyone was able to buy the required animals; some began to feel that the race home was more than they were willing to risk.

Perhaps this consideration led to some re-enlisting in the volunteer unit that went to San Diego for another six months. It led others to consider staying in California during the coming Winter so they could travel at a more reasonable pace the following Spring. A few stayed and sought work in Southern California; several stopped in Monterey and looked for employment; a few went to San Francisco; some stopped at Sutter's Fort and did not begin the trek over the Sierras. Those that would later choose to continue on from the Salt Lake Valley to Winter Quarters found that their provisions, especially clothing and food, were grossly inadequate. While the march to California was organized with military precision, the trip home was somewhat less organized. However, those traveling Eastward remained in closely organized groups.

At Los Angeles, the Battalion again divided before beginning the trek homeward. About 225 men gathered in Los Angeles before the trip began. The bulk of them, about 175, chose to follow the route through the Central Valley of California with Levi Hancock as their spiritual and trail leader. Their plan was to cross over the mountains north of the San Fernando Valley, descend the Grapevine, find and cross Walker Pass, then head north and east to find where Brigham Young and the rest of the Saints had settled. The remainder under Jefferson Hunt, about fifty men and William Coray's wife, Melissa, took El Camino Real north along the coast. On July 20th, the Hancock group met and organized themselves for travel.

At a time when most overland travelers would form into groups that were tenuous at best and would often disintegrate and reform, the Mormons were resolute in their desire to take care of their own for their mutual benefit and protection. In the tradition of Mormon travel, they organized themselves into groups of hundreds, fifties and tens. Each hundred was headed by a captain; a leader was chosen for each group of fifty; and for each mess a group of ten. Andrew Lytle and James Pace were selected as the two captains, and Levi Hancock nominated the other leaders (Golder 1928, 237).

The following day, the "pioneer" party, led by Elisha Averett with nine or ten other men, left for the northern end of the San Fernando Valley. The rest followed the next day. Everett's group scouted ahead of the main party. By the 25th, everyone had gathered in the Santa Clarita Valley where they purchased forty-five head of cattle at the price of six dollars each, and obtained the help of an Indian as a guide. As they ascended 4,000 feet to the Tejon Pass, they found that the cattle were wild and hard to drive. Eighteen of them were lost. On July 30th, the group stopped and slaughtered the cattle and jerked the beef on racks over fires. The next day, Henry Bigler recorded that the lead pioneer party discovered an inscription on a tree that read: "Peter Lebeck killed by a bear Oct. 17, 1837" (Journal History of the Church, October 16, 1847). A state park is now located at this site.

On the following day, they descended the Grapevine into the San Joaquin Valley where their Indian guide left, saying that he no longer knew the route. By the following day, the main party again caught up with the scouts at the crossing of the Kern River at the location of Bakersfield. The river, which today is dry during most of the year because of heavy agricultural use, was 150 feet wide. Some men built rafts to cross, while others carried their belongings on their heads as they waded the river (Journal History of the Church, October 16, 1847). This description by Henry Bigler conforms to what we know today about the heavy Sierra snow of the previous Winter and the late Summer runoff. Three more days travel brought them to what Bigler described as a "beautiful river" (Journal History of the Church, October 16,

1847). His description of travel points to this being the Kings River, which flowed into the large Tulare Lake to the southwest. The next day, August 11th, they traveled twenty-eight miles over a very dry route to the next river, probably the San Joaquin just northeast of Fresno.

Here Bigler gives us considerable information about the apparent plans of the Hancock party. At this point, Averett, still the designated scout, began to travel eastward along the river in an effort to find Walker Pass. Unknown to the men, the route to Walker Pass was near the Kern River that they had left more than 100 miles behind. On August 13th, the main part of the group traveled about ten miles along Averett's path where they met him returning, not having seen any indication of a pass. The men of the party met and, according to Bigler, "voted to go to Sutter's." Bigler also reported that a map that they obtained in Los Angeles was worthless since it didn't show the rivers and wasn't detailed enough to help them (Journal History of the Church, October 16, 1847). What they didn't know was that the Sierra Crest to their east was formed by a jagged line of mountain peaks between 12,000 and 14,000 feet in elevation, protected by a series of deep valleys that extended for nearly 200 miles between today's Tioga Pass in Yosemite and Walker Pass to the south. One hundred and fifty years later, this imposing mountain structure still has not been crossed by any road.

His comments clearly show that it was the original intent of the Hancock party to find Walker Pass and cross over the Sierra at that point. In reality, they were better off because they did not find it. While the pass was sometimes used to cross the Sierra, the routes eastward from there were not defined and travelers without a guide or knowledge of the area could easily find themselves in trouble very quickly. Had they been successful in crossing over Walker Pass, they would have had to travel north along the eastern slope of the Sierras until they found the known routes over 300 miles away. They would have encountered several rivers, such as the Walker and Carson, which could easily have taken them off course; or they might, as Walker himself once did, attempt without success to find a more southern route across Nevada. In any case, the potential for disaster would have been much greater had they crossed into the Great Basin via Walker Pass.

From Henry Bigler's discussion, we also learn that it was probably not the intention of the two groups (Hancock's and Hunt's) to meet at Sutter's Fort as they eventually did. As we shall see, the Hunt party had a specific set of goals which included seeing Governor Mason at Monterey, while the Hancock party had another, namely getting back as quickly as possible.

By August 21st, it was becoming clear that not everyone was prepared for the long travel still ahead. The group met to discuss how they might provision those brethren who did not have adequate food supplies to make the trip. It was then decided to send four men ahead to Sutter's Fort to obtain the needed supplies. On the 21st, Andrew Lytle and four others left the main party to try to find the Mormon colony of New Hope where some of those from the ship *Brooklyn* had settled. New Hope was located on the Stanislaus River about a mile and a half above its confluence with the San Joaquin (part way between the modern cities of Modesto and Tracy.) Lytle and his group were successful, and visited with the few remaining Brethren at New Hope. They caught up with the main group on the Consumnes River, about twenty miles from Sutter's Fort, on August 24th. Here they also met Jefferson Hunt, who had traveled to the camp from Sutter's Fort with the returning group that had gone on ahead to get supplies. From Hunt and these men, they heard for the first time a report, unconfirmed, from a man named Charles C. Smith who had traveled east with Sam Brannan, that the leadership of the Mormon Church had arrived at the new city of the Saints in the Valley of the Great Salt Lake (Tyler 1881, 310). They now believed that would be their destination. On the following day, August 25th, Hunt and the others arrived at Sutter's Fort.

By August 26th, the remainder of the Hancock party arrived at a campsite about a mile from Sutter's Fort. The Hancock group had traveled over 360 miles and averaged about twelve miles a day since leaving Los Angeles. This might be considered slow for a mounted pack train, but they were forced to cross several large rivers still above normal flow for the time year because of the heavy snow pack of the previous Winter, and they made the ill-fated detour to find Walker Pass. At Sutter's Fort, however, both units of travelers were again together.

Along El Camino Real, Jefferson Hunt's party of about fifty included one woman, Melissa Coray, wife of Sergeant William Coray, who was about to enter her eighth month of pregnancy. This group only used riding and pack animals except for one wagon, that of the Corays. This light wagon was fast becoming one of the most traveled in Western North America.

Why didn't Hunt and the others travel with Hancock's group? Was part of the reason the earlier dissention that tore Hancock and the officers apart? It appears that disagreement was not a primary reason. From his actions in the month following discharge, it is clear that Jefferson Hunt specifically wanted to meet with Colonel Mason, the governor of California, at his headquarters in Monterey. It also appears that Hunt still suspected, or perhaps hoped, that Brigham Young would choose to settle in California. Perhaps he thought word of the future home of the Saints might be found among the *Brooklyn* passengers, or Sam Brannan in San Francisco or Northern California. In addition, El Camino Real was a well-known and often used route that offered no serious impediments to travel. Hancock and his group believed that the Saints would be found to the east and that Walker Pass offered the most direct route to them. The choice of travel routes no doubt played a significant role in the decision for the Battalion to split up. But the tension between the dissenters and the officers still remained and the division offered some the chance to pick the side in which they had the most confidence. Many in the Battalion believed as William Coray did, that Jefferson Hunt was their superior officer in the Military, but that Levi Hancock was the leading religious authority following discharge.

As has been discussed, there were many reasons some in the Battalion stayed in California, having to do with the lateness of the season and the difficulty and expense of acquiring supplies for the journey. A few of the men, including John Barrowman, even went their own way and caught a ship in San Pedro for San Francisco in an effort to get employment and comfort among their brethren in the *Brooklyn* party.

William Coray was clear in his description of his decision to travel with Hunt. He "thought it best to make my way as fast as possible to San Francisco" where he hoped to find work and await the birth of his first child (Bigler and Bagley 2000, 335).

They left Los Angeles on July 22nd and headed north along the better-known and well traveled El Camino Real. From the San Fernando Valley, they traveled west to the coast near Ventura and then north along the coast to Santa Barbara. As noted previously, El Camino Real had been in use for about seventy years, but it was little more than a trail for foot and single-file animal traffic. It was not used for wagon traffic and saw very little use for commerce or trade. This became very apparent to the group a little way beyond Santa Barbara where the trail headed inland over Gaviota Pass. There, according to William Coray, he was forced to disassemble the wagon and carry the parts over the pass. He commented: "Had it not been for Capt. Hunt & two or 3 others who came back 3 or 4 miles to help us through I should have been obliged to stand at the mercy of Indians till I could have made other arrangements for transportation." He then noted that the road didn't improve much over the ensuing hills, since it took the assistance of some Indians with ropes to keep the wagon from overturning along the path (Bigler and Bagley 2000, 335).

From there they continued on past the old and mostly deserted missions, and through the areas where are now located the cities of Santa Maria, San Luis Obispo, Paso Robles, King City, Soledad, and Salinas on their way to the Presidio at Monterey. The records of this group are lacking, but it appears that they did not travel as a single unit. Some of the faster members of the group, including Jefferson Hunt, went ahead and arrived in Monterey on August 9th. William Coray with the wagon arrived there on August 13th. Because of his wife's late stage pregnancy, it is quite likely he, and probably some others, traveled at a slower pace. Since they intended to remain in Northern California, speed was not essential to them.

When Hunt reached Monterey, he immediately set out to find Colonel Mason. Unfortunately, Mason was not there; he had traveled to Southern California, probably by ship. Unable to talk directly with Colonel Mason, Hunt did the next best thing and wrote him a letter which was left in his office for his return. In his note, Hunt asked if Mason wanted him to try to recruit a new military unit. If so, what was the latest date that he would accept them and where should they be gathered and equipped? Hunt also offered to carry mail to the States (the Missouri River landings) if he were unable to organize a new military unit (Bigler and Bagley 2000, 273-274). The letter confirms that Hunt was still interested in raising a new battalion and that he was prepared to try to do so if the Army was interested. It also indicates why Hunt was anxious to take the route to Monterey.

In the same letter, Hunt gave his itinerary for the near term. He said he would be proceeding to the "P. de San Jose," or Mission San Jose, where he would be able to receive Mason's reply. While some authors state that Hunt traveled from Monterey to San Francisco and then to Sutter's, this insight from Hunt himself indicates that he did not go to San Francisco, but took the more direct and shorter route that would take him from Monterey to Sutter's in the Central Valley of California. In 1847, before the Gold Rush, San Francisco was a very small community of little importance, and there was no convenient water transportation from there to the Central Valley, or even to the mainland areas across from the peninsula on which San Francisco sat. All of this would change, of course, in less than two years with the discovery of gold.

Hunt left Monterey on August 10th and headed for the Mission San Jose, which is not in the city of San Jose, but is actually located at the eastern foothills of today's Fremont, California. Not all of the party went with him; some headed north to San Francisco to find work and reside with the *Brooklyn* families and some, including William and Melissa Coray, remained in Monterey. It is also quite probable that several men remained in Monterey to take Mason's response and the mail if any, to Hunt at Mission San Jose or further along the trail.

Hunt's selection of Mission San Jose as a named stopping point is not accidental. Earlier in March 1847, at least two families (and possibly more) of Mormons from the ship *Brooklyn* had settled on the more or less abandoned mission grounds. It appears that a sole padre was left at Mission San Jose when the John Horner and James Light families arrived and settled on the favorable lands at the mission (Mazariegos 2001, 3; Hansen and Bringhurst 1996, 54). Hunt would have heard of their small community while at Monterey and known that he and his party would be welcomed there.

Upon his return to Monterey, Colonel Mason responded to Jefferson Hunt. Mason was critically short of troops in California should an uprising occur. A number of the New York Volunteers had been sent south to Mexico, and many others had deserted or resigned. Fremont's California Battalion had returned to their homes and, in any case, did not feel the same loyalty to Mason they had to Fremont. Most of the Mormon Battalion, with the exception of those in San Diego, had left the service. Accordingly, Colonel Mason was in desperate need of new troops, and immediately responded to Hunt's offer to raise a new Battalion.

On August 16th, Mason wrote Hunt welcoming his offer. He authorized Hunt to recruit three new companies consisting of seventy-five men each; the total complement with officers and others would be 271 men. The commander would hold the rank of lieutenant colonel. He offered the office to Hunt should he be able to recruit three companies with at least sixty-four men each. Otherwise, his rank would be that of major. In addition to the standard pay, uniform allowance, and equipment, Mason offered to pay fifty cents per twenty miles of travel home to the men upon discharge (Bigler and Bagley 2000, 274-276). The new offer was even more attractive than that given the Battalion at their initial recruitment.

There is no record how Jefferson Hunt felt about this opportunity to again command at a higher rank. From his actions during prior recruitment attempts and in later years, we can assume that he welcomed the opportunity to advance in military rank. He would do his best to convince his superiors within the Mormon Church of the advantages of a new Battalion and of a Mormon presence in California. But that was not to happen. Brigham Young had already made the decision that precluded any further enlistments of a new Mormon Battalion. Hunt's military career, such as it was, was put on hold for several more years.

From the Mission San Jose, it appears that Hunt and his remaining band—those that had not stayed in Monterey or gone to San Francisco—headed northeast over the East Bay Hills into the Livermore Valley and past the rancho of Robert Livermore. In the pre-Gold Rush era, this was the major route from the Bay Area and Monterey Bay Area to the upper part of the Central Valley. From there, they took the route through the Altamont Pass over which the Transcontinental Railroad would travel two decades later. They then headed almost directly east and crossed the San Joaquin River near where now Interstate 5 and the railroad bridge the river. Turning northward, they headed for Sutter's Fort, where they arrived about August 24th. From Los Angeles, they had traveled about 480 miles at a rate of about fifteen miles per day.

At Sutter's Fort, Jefferson Hunt soon found the advance party from the Hancock group. He received word from Charles C. Smith, who had just arrived from the east after traveling with Sam Brannan, that Brigham Young had led the Saints to their new home in the Valley of the Great Salt Lake. Hunt quickly turned south and arrived at Hancock's camp on the Consumnes River. There they shared this new information. He also heard from several of the settlers who lived there the details of the cannibalism surrounding the tragic Donner Party.

One of the additional bits of information they received was that John Sutter was very interested in hiring men to work on several of his projects. A camp meeting was held and it was agreed that those men who did not have adequate outfits to continue the journey Eastward could have permission to seek work for Sutter and remain until the following year. Levi Hancock, who, several times during the preceding year had been so vigorously opposed to any division of the Battalion, had come to the opinion that it was a wise to approve some separations. As the ranking Church Authority present and leader of the group, he agreed to permit some to remain at Sutter's. A few short weeks later, he learned that was exactly what Brigham Young preferred to happen.

On the morning of August 25th, Jefferson Hunt and some of the others left for Sutter's Fort and arrived there later that day. This was a momentous event for Sutter, and he recorded in his diary that "Capt Hart [sic] of the Mormon Battalion arrived, with a good many of his Men on their way to great Salt Lake" (Watson 1932, August 25, 1847).

John Augustus Sutter was born in Baden, Germany, to Swiss parents in 1803. Unsuccessful in business and burdened with debt, he left Europe in 1834. After stints as a trader and innkeeper in Missouri and a trader along the Santa Fe Trail, he left for California in 1838. He traveled with a fur trapping party to Vancouver, Washington, and then took a ship to California by way of Hawaii. While in the islands, where he assumed the title of "Captain" in the Swiss Guards, he established some business connections with successful Hawaiian businessmen and hired a small contingent of Hawaiians to accompany him to California. Arriving there in 1839, he soon met with Governor Alvarado, became a Mexican citizen, and was eventually given a land grant of nearly 50,000 acres around the confluence of the Sacramento and American Rivers within the present City of Sacramento. Recognizing his Swiss roots, he named his new property New Helvetia.

His holdings grew with additional land grants and the purchase (on credit) of Fort Ross, on the California coast, from the Russian government. By 1847, he controlled about 150,000 acres of some of the most productive farmland in California. Using help from his small group of Hawaiians and local Indians, he built a substantial adobe block fort that was larger than most others in the West. He planted productive orchards, had substantial harvests of wheat, and owned thousands of cattle, horses and sheep. John Sutter was extraordinarily successful and was well on his way to becoming one of the great land barons in the world in spite of the debts he had accumulated.

When the Mexican War began, Sutter, a Mexican citizen, realized that the future lay with John C. Fremont and the United States. He supported the American cause as soon as it became apparent that the Bear Flag Republic would be successful. Sutter was also deeply involved in the attempts to rescue the Donner Party. New Helvetia served as a welcoming stop for the many emigrants making their way to California from the States. Sutter was courteous, generous and highly regarded throughout the West and beyond.

Having come from a middle-class European background, it is very likely that Sutter saw his future more like that of royalty in the nearly virgin territory of Central California. He had nearly everything needed to make him incredibly rich and powerful. His land produced any crop in abundance; his livestock almost took care of themselves; merchants in places as far away as Chile and Hawaii were clamoring for flour from his wheat and other commodities. He had the vessels to take goods to San Francisco Bay, which had the potential to become one of the greatest seaports on the Pacific. The only thing he was missing was skilled labor to turn his productive land into products for trade. His Hawaiian and Indian employees were unskilled and not very productive. The nearby Mexicans in California and the few Americans that were beginning to arrive in California were either unskilled or unwilling to work for him, preferring to settle their own land for themselves.

Late in the summer of 1847, Sutter was even having problems building a water-powered gristmill to turn his wheat into flour for domestic use. It had been under construction for some months, but little progress was being made. Lumber was virtually impossible to obtain, and he had often discussed a partnership with James Marshall to build a sawmill to provide lumber for his own use and for trade. But without the skilled craftsmen and workers needed for its construction, this and his other projects were only dreams.

All of that changed on August 25th, 1847, when Jefferson Hunt and the two groups of Mormon Battalion volunteers began arriving at Sutter's Fort. John Sutter immediately offered to hire as many of the Battalion members as wished to stay.

James Marshall had explored upstream on the American River and found a location for a lumber mill that offered waterpower, ample supplies of trees and a relatively accessible route to bring the cut timber out of the mountains. These efforts finally resulted in an agreement between Sutter and Marshall that called for Sutter to provide the funding for the venture and Marshall to construct and operate the sawmill, and receive compensation as an active manager. That agreement was signed about August 19th, less than a week before the arrival of the Battalion men. Marshall then hired Peter Wimmer and his family to assist in the project; Wimmer was to be the supervisor on site, and his wife would prepare meals for the work crew (Nunis 1993, 87-88).

Wasting no time to capitalize on his good fortune with the arrival of skilled labor, Sutter's diary noted on August 28th that "Marshall moved, with P. Wimmer family and the working hands to Columa, and to work briskly on the sawmill" (Watson 1932, August 28, 1847). Five months later, Marshall, the Wimmers and the Mormon crew working on the sawmill changed history.

Once again, the former Battalion members did not travel as a single group as they left Sutter's Fort for Salt Lake City. Jefferson Hunt and a small group left Sutter's on August 26th. The following day, a group of about thirty, including pioneers (or scouts) left. The majority of the group under the leadership of Levi Hancock stayed at Sutter's getting their horses shod and preparing for the trip ahead. They left for the eastward journey on August 29th. This traveling arrangement made sense, since the road ahead was over difficult mountains and barren deserts and smaller groups could travel more efficiently and faster when necessary. Over the next several months, the various groups would converge and again separate as conditions warranted.

The various groups all traveled the same route which by now was a fairly well traversed route to California from the east. It was the same route traveled by General Kearny several months before on his trip eastward with Fremont and the Battalion escort. From Sutter's Fort, it led northeast about thirty miles to Johnson's Ranch on the Bear River. Johnson's was the last settlement they would see in California and the last until they arrived in modern-day Idaho. The road—or more accurately trail—followed the Bear River about fifty miles to near the current location of Emigrant Gap on Interstate 80 and old U.S. 40. From there it continued eastward approximately along the route of old U.S. 40 to the crest of the Sierra Nevadas at Donner Pass, and down the east side of the Sierras to the modern town of Truckee and Donner Lake. Perhaps some of the parties, including Levi Hancock's, may have crossed the crest at Roller Pass, about two miles to the south of Donner Pass. This small variation avoided the massive rocks at the summit, but called for traversing a very steep slope at a higher elevation. But as they crossed in late Summer there were still snowfields, a testament to the massive snowfall of the previous Winter.

The first of the parties crossed the Sierra crest about September 5th and encountered the tragic Donner Party camps at the east end of Donner Lake. Henry Bigler noted in his journal that they found tree stumps ten to fifteen feet high indicating where the Donner Party had cut firewood (Journal History of the Church, October 16, 1947). These stumps, some measuring as high as twenty-two feet, indicated the snow depth that previous Winter. The following day, on September 6th, another meeting took place that would again change the future for many of the Battalion.

Sam Brannan, at Brigham Young's direction, led about 230 Mormons on the ship *Brooklyn* from New York to San Francisco in 1846. Brannan had visions of creating a Mormon "state" in the Mexican territory of California. But those plans were dashed when he learned from Commodore Stockton, in Honolulu, of American plans to seize California. In anticipation of his new colony, Brannan created a form of communal organization which each of the passengers subscribed to. When they landed in San Francisco on August 1, 1846, after a six month voyage, the new Mormon settlers formed the larger part of the city's population.

Brannan not only organized and led the Mormon community in San Francisco, he sent settlers inland to form the community of New Hope, and created the first newspaper, the *California Star*, using a printing press he brought along on the ship. Some of his followers took exception to his form of organization and resisted his leadership, which was flawed at best. Nevertheless, Brannan remained resolute in promoting California as the eventual home of the Mormons heading west from Nauvoo.

To further this cause, Brannan decided to travel East in the Spring of 1847 to encourage Brigham Young to choose California as the final settlement. Leaving his newspaper in the hands of his assistants, Brannan set out from San Francisco on April 4th with two or three other men to find Young. Brannan encountered the Mormon leader and the Pioneer Party in central Wyoming on June 30th. In spite of Brannan's entreaties, Young made it clear that his chosen final stopping place would not be California; it would be the Valley of the Great Salt Lake. Once again, Sam Brannan's hopes were dashed.

By late January 1847, there were about 275 Mormons in the village beside the Arkansas River at El Pueblo, Colorado. This included the members of the Battalion, wives and children of Battalion members, and families from Mississippi. Captain James Brown of Company C, who led the sick detachment from Santa Fe, was in charge. Unfortunately, his leadership was lacking; he was harsh and often arbitrary. Dissention and distrust filled the ranks.

When Spring arrived, Captain Brown, other officers and an escort went to Santa Fe to collect pay and received orders on what to do next from the commander, Colonel Sterling Price. Their exact instructions are not clear, but it appears that Price was reluctant to give any orders without instructions from General Kearny. Accordingly, Brown and the other officers concluded to travel to the Oregon Trail in hopes of hearing from either Brigham Young or receiving additional orders from Kearny. The majority of the El Pueblo Detachment began travel on May 24th, toward Fort Laramie on the Oregon Trail in eastern Wyoming.

They traveled northward, passed Pike's Peak and reached the South Platte River near present-day Denver. From there they traveled north along the South Platte, past the trading posts at Fort Lancaster (Fort Lupton), Fort St. Vrain, and possibly Fort Vasquez. Leaving the South Platte as it turned eastward, they continued north and crossed the Cache La Poudre River east of today's Fort Collins, Colorado, and headed into what is now southeastern Wyoming about June 9th or 10th.

At the same time the El Pueblo Detachment was heading north, the Pioneer Company with Brigham Young was heading west toward the Valley of the Great Salt Lake. Also not sure what to do about the approaching end of the Battalion's enlistment, Young decided that the best alternative for the Detachment was to follow him into Salt Lake Valley rather than to have them try to reach California. On June 2nd, Young wrote a letter to Brown to be read to the men. It was to be delivered to Brown by Amasa Lyman, one of the Twelve, who was to be accompanied by three members of the Battalion who had gone to Winter Quarters: Thomas Woolsey, John Tippets and Roswell Stevens. In his letter, Young advised them that Lyman would fill them in on the full details of the travels of the Pioneer Company and the rest of the Saints, and that they should follow behind the Pioneer Company as fast as possible.

Lyman and his small group headed south, not knowing if the Detachment had begun traveling. But on the evening of June 10th, Lyman found the Detachment about eighty-five miles south of Fort Laramie. There, the men heard for the first time their final destination and the instructions from

Brigham Young and the Twelve. They then continued north to the fort and followed along the well-established Oregon Trail just a few weeks behind the Pioneer Company. As they continued westward, a small unit of the El Pueblo group led by Thomas Williams caught up with Young at the Green River. These Battalion members entered the Salt Lake Valley with the Pioneers and immediately set about creating an irrigation system that they learned about in New Mexico (Bigler and Bagley 2000, 325).

From Fort Bridger, the Pioneer Company followed the road (such as it was) made by the Reed-Donner Party the year before. They entered the Valley of the Great Salt Lake on July 24, 1847. The remainder of the El Pueblo Detachment entered five days later on July 29th.

Brigham Young still had to resolve the issue of what to about the Battalion Detachment in his midst. He decided that since their enlistments had expired, the best course of action would be to send a small unit, with Captain James Brown in charge, forward to California to secure the men's discharges and pay. Accordingly, each member of the El Pueblo Detachment executed a power of attorney to be given to Brown. They remained at Salt Lake to build new homes and church buildings, and to begin planting crops to sustain the new community.

Sam Brannan, who was heading back to San Francisco, was reaffirmed as the President of the Church in California and was designated to lead the Brown Party along the same road that he had traveled earlier in the Summer. Brigham Young wrote two letters on August 7th; one to the Saints in California under Sam Brannan and the second "To Captain Jefferson Hunt & the officers and soldiers of the Mormon Battalion." In this second letter, he described the arrival of the Pioneer Company and El Pueblo Detachment at Salt Lake and informed them that others were on the way from Winter Quarters. He invited them to travel to Salt Lake and told them to avoid the Hastings Cutoff across the salt desert, but wrote that: "If there are any men who have not families among your number who desire to stop in California for a season, we do not feel to object; . . ." But as David Bigler and Will Bagley point out, his verbal instructions to Captain Brown were probably more direct. Daniel Tyler wrote that Captain Brown stated: "those who had not means of subsistence" were to "remain in California and labor, and bring their earnings with them in the spring" (Bigler and Bagley 2000, 355 – 357).

About ten men accompanied Brown and Brannan when they left Salt Lake for California on August 9th; several were going as far as the Cache Valley and Fort Hall on a reconnaissance; the rest were going all the way to California. Included as one of the escorts was Gilbert Hunt. Brigham Young was planning on returning to Winter Quarters to prepare for the mass migration the following year. On August 22nd, he held a conference where it was agreed to establish a president and High Council to govern the new city over the Winter. Young and others, including his key counselors, left for Winter Quarters on August 26th. Along the trail they passed a number of organized groups of Saints who were part of that year's migration. On September 9th, Young sent an epistle back to Salt Lake establishing the President and High Council and giving instructions on what should be done over the Winter. In that same mail, he included a letter to Jefferson Hunt regarding discharging the soldiers of the Battalion if that had not already been done (Journal History of the Church, September 9, 1947).

Back at Donner Lake, the advance parties of Battalion members found the camp where their comrades with Kearny had buried the remains of some of the Donner Party victims. Shortly afterward, they advanced the seven miles or so to the Alder Creek camp site near where the Donners themselves had met their deaths. Some of the men went to the Donner camp. The sights there horrified the soldiers. Daniel Tyler wrote that: "It had not only been the scene of intense human suffering, but also of some of the most fiendish acts that man made desperate by hunger could conceive" (Tyler 1881, 314). On September 6, 1847, shortly after leaving the Donner Camp, the Battalion men met Sam Brannan and David Rainey returning to California.

Brannan and Captain James Brown did not get along well during their trip West. Whether it was because Brigham Young had failed to accept Brannan's urgings to settle in California, or because Young had entrusted the important news and messages for the Battalion to Brown, or because both were strong-willed and resented the other, we do not know. But we do know that as they traveled together, they argued and became more and more angry with each other. Finally, somewhere around the Truckee Meadows (present-day Reno) they got into a fight, which prompted Brannan to leave the group and push on ahead with one other companion. He had no more reason to travel with Brown.

On the morning of September 6th, the first group of Battalion members encountered Brannan east of Truckee and the Alder Creek camp. He told them that Captain Brown was traveling just behind him and had important messages from Brigham Young. Brannan then told them his impression of the Valley of the Great Salt Lake which was, in his opinion, quite unfavorable when compared to California. The advance company then returned to their previous camp and waited for the other Battalion groups to catch up and for Brown's arrival. Brannan continued on and repeated the message as he encountered each of the subsequent Battalion groups.

The next day, all of the parties united in camp. From the journal of Robert Bliss, it appears that the campsite was probably near where Alder Creek flowed into Prosser Creek, about four miles northeast of today's Truckee, California, and at or near the same place that the Battalion members with the Kearny party camped several months before (Carter 1956, Bliss Diary September 8-10, 1847). In the evening Captain Brown read Brigham Young's letter to Captain Jefferson Hunt and the Battalion. He then delivered the verbal message he had from Young, and a general meeting was held to decide what to do. Many of the men received letters from family and friends, and for the first time in many months heard news of home and their new destination at Salt Lake.

For Jefferson Hunt, the meeting was even more significant. It's not clear whether Gilbert Hunt stopped at Fort Hall and then returned to Salt Lake, or went on and met his father and the others in the Sierras. In any case, the encounter provided Hunt with the first news from his family in nearly a year. He learned of the death of his youngest son, Parley, nine months before, and of the marriage of Gilbert. He also learned of the death of his nephew, Milton

Kelley, and the status of the rest of the family. He discovered that his family had arrived in Salt Lake; he was one of the lucky ones who would soon see his kin. Many others learned that their families had not yet arrived at Salt Lake or were remaining at Winter Quarters for another year. These soldiers would not soon see their families and friends, but some would rush Eastward all the way to the Missouri River before the weather became too severe to travel.

On the following day, September 8th, occurred the final division of the Battalion. About half the group, approximately 100 men, chose to heed the council carried by Captain Brown and began the return to Sutter's Fort to seek employment either there, in San Francisco or in some other location in Northern California. Some of those who arrived at Sutter's were assigned briefly to work on the grist mill and then were sent on to join the others who were working on the sawmill for James Marshall. This time the division of the Battalion was in accordance with the instructions of Brigham Young and there was no internal opposition.

The hundred or so men continuing toward Salt Lake divided up into groups that would travel at the rate that best suited them. Jefferson Hunt and eight others became the lead group, since they were the smallest in number. Hunt was anxious to determine if another Battalion could be formed. Other groups, including one led by James Pace and another by Andrew Lytle, were formed and followed behind. Since each traveled independently, and since the speed was often determined by illness amongst the men or by difficulties such as those sometimes caused by Indians who stole livestock, the gaps between units lengthened or shortened as they progressed.

The route taken from the September 7th camp followed the now frequently used Humboldt River Route. It bypassed the canyon of the Truckee River west of Reno by first going northeastward and then southwestward again, meeting the Truckee River at today's Verdi, Nevada. From there it followed the Truckee River, went south around a marsh at today's Reno, and then followed the Truckee River canyon to the point where the Truckee turned north at Wadsworth, Nevada. They then crossed the Forty Mile Desert to the sink of the Humboldt River. They followed the watercourse to near Wells, Nevada, where the route then headed north and east into today's Idaho, eventually reaching Fort Hall. It then went east and south into today's Utah, and finally, the Valley of the Great Salt Lake. This route from Truckee to Salt Lake crossed nearly 800 miles of mountains and desert. But it was a well-known and well marked route. Once into the Nevada desert, the travel was fairly easy.

Jefferson Hunt's group was the first of the Battalion to arrive in Salt Lake City on October 11, 1847 (Bigler and Bagley 2000, 365). Other groups arrived later: Levi Hancock arrived on October 18th; Robert Bliss, probably in the last group, arrived on October 26th. Some of the returning veterans had the foresight to realize that crop seeds would be needed in their new home and brought with them from California seeds for wheat, garden crops and fruit trees. Hunt carried with him from California "two bushels of seed wheat" (Bigler and Bagley 2000, 446). Many of those Battalion members with family members still at Winter Quarters immediately set out to the east to reach them before the snows set in. But for Hunt, he was now home with his family in the Valley of the Great Salt Lake. However, his rest would not last long; he would soon be on the trail again.

Part II

Mountaineer and Guide

John Wells Brier, who was six years old in 1849 and was one of the youngest to enter Death Valley, later remembered Jefferson Hunt as follows:

> "The Captain was taciturnity itself. If he possessed the knowledge of a guide, he seemed to wanting in the tact of a leader. This may be fancy of a child, for I confess that I was afraid of the silent man, and wondered if he ever loved anybody and if he slept on horseback" (Werner 1995, 88).

Chapter 13

Aftermath

The accomplishments of the Battalion were many. Some of them benefited the federal government and all Americans in general, and others benefited primarily the Mormons and the LDS Church. Many of those achievements have been forgotten or are little known today. And unfortunately, to some today who know of the Mormon Battalion, the major accomplishments of the Battalion have been reduced simply to making bricks, digging wells and whitewashing buildings in San Diego. The volunteers did those things, but their major legacy is far broader and more far-reaching.

Those achievements of significance to the federal government, the military and the American economy were:

The March: At 2,000 miles, it was one of the longest in American military history. It came at a time when the country was divided about whether or not the United States could secure all of the land across the Continent. The Mormons proved that traditional overland military movements could, in fact, be used to support and defend the new national boundaries. While long marches would soon be supplanted by shipboard transportation and railroads, in 1846-1847 the knowledge that a future threat to the West Coast could be countered by land was an important concept. In addition, the low death rate and low desertion rate of the Battalion demonstrated to military and civil leaders that a higher standard of morale and performance could be achieved by American soldiers.

The Road: The Mormon Battalion broke new trails, cut vegetation, moved rocks and did other things needed to make a road suitable for travel. In some places, such as Box Canyon in the California desert, they even widened the rock outcrops using simple tools to permit wagons to pass. Unlike the more northern routes, the road they made was usable during the Winter months. This meant that Cooke's Wagon Road, as it was called, provided year 'round overland access from the "States" to California—a critical fact for the military and civil leaders of the nation. The road was even used for commercial purposes, including the Overland Stage in the 1850s. Not until the completion of the Transcontinental Railroad in 1869 was another year 'round overland route to the West Coast completed. Finally, segments of the road in New Mexico and Arizona were critical to military operations during the Civil War, against the Apache, and were used through the 1880s.

The Gadsden Purchase: Information provided by Cooke and his staff, combined with information from General Kearny and his people, were used in the early 1850s to support the need for additional land in Southern Arizona. Much of the motivation for the Gadsden Purchase was based on Southern desire to have direct rail access from Texas to Southern California. However, the Battalion proved the value of the land and routes, thus enabling the legislation that provided funds to purchase additional land, and additional compensation to Mexico for the land seized in the Mexican War. The final outline of the contiguous United States was made with the Gadsden Purchase.

Secured California: Not long before the Battalion's arrival in coastal California, General Kearny and the U.S. Army suffered a devastating battle at San Pasqual. In the weeks that followed, it was not clear whether there would be other serious attacks either from the local population or from troops from Mexico. The arrival of the 350 men of the Battalion, closely followed by the arrival by ship of the New York Volunteers, gave Kearny a commanding majority of troops in California. This put to rest any thought of major organized opposition. California was securely in American hands.

Secured Kearny's Command: With the arrival of General Kearny in California came immediate conflict with John C. Fremont—his subordinate officer but a hero to much of California. About the same time Kearny arrived, Fremont led his California Battalion of volunteers, loyal to him, into Southern

California to complete the conquest of the Southland. When Fremont refused to acknowledge that Kearny was to assume military command to establish a government, the stage was set for conflict. Kearny adroitly avoided a direct confrontation, but escorted Fremont East to a court martial for his disobedience. The presence of the Battalion in Los Angeles gave the California Volunteers second thoughts about armed intervention. There was none, and a disastrous confrontation was avoided. In addition, Kearny depended on a detachment of Battalion soldiers to escort him eastward to Fort Leavenworth where Fremont was arrested. Again, the Battalion served to defuse a difficult situation.

Discovery of Gold: The most memorable contribution of the Battalion was providing the workforce that laid the foundation for the discovery of gold, the Gold Rush of 1849, and the subsequent massive American settlement of the Western territory that followed. Several of the first group to enter Sutter's employ went directly to the sawmill site at present-day Coloma. Others in the group that returned to the Fort from Donner Lake first went to work on the nearby gristmill and then were sent to Coloma to work for James Marshall. By January 1848, work was progressing well and many of the Mormons were engaged in digging out the raceway where spent water would exit the mill site. During the day, the Mormons would remove rocks and boulders, and at night Marshall would turn on the water to flush out the smaller sand grains and dirt particles. Unbeknownst to him, he was creating a crude form of a sluice; lighter material was washed away and heavier material sank to the bottom. On Monday morning, January 24, 1848, Marshall shut off the water and looked into the bottom of the race and saw a glittering metallic nugget (Bigler and Smith 1990, 108). Gold had been discovered at Coloma. The Gold Rush was about to start, and the first miners and prospectors of the Gold Rush were the veterans of the Mormon Battalion.

Carson Pass: Many of those veterans heading to Salt Lake City in the summer of 1848 decided to find a less difficult road than the Donner Pass Route over the Sierras. This group scouted and made a new wagon road called the Carson Pass Wagon Road that traveled between Sacramento and the Carson River. This road became the preferred route of travel for a significant number of the '49ers and emigrants who came in later years. Again, the road building and mountaineering skills learned on the march were put to good use. Sadly, three of those who first made and traveled the road were murdered by Indians at Tragedy Springs near the summit of Carson Pass.

Other accomplishments primarily benefited the Mormons. They included:

The wages and uniform allowances paid by the Army to the Battalion members amounted to nearly $75,000. This was augmented by the pay earned at San Diego and Sutter's Fort and by the gold that the Mormons recovered before they left California for Utah. In total, the Battalion contributed $100,000 or more to the Church's coffers. Some of this money went directly to the Church and the rest to the families of the Battalion. In either case, the money went a long way toward financing the Westward movement of the Saints. The magnitude of the contribution becomes clearer when it is realized that the average net worth of a farming family in the 1840s was probably less than $500, and that a convert could be brought from England to the heartland of America for less than twenty dollars. While this money did not offset the losses of the forced sales of property at Nauvoo, it did provide a start for a secure financial future for the Latter Day Saints Church in the West.

The willingness of the Battalion to enlist, to endure the prolonged march to the Pacific, and to remain committed to the Army for their entire tour of duty showed many in the country that the Mormons were loyal and patriotic Americans. The Mormon Battalion had the lowest desertion and disciplinary discharge rate of any unit during the Mexican War (no active Mormon deserted or was given a disciplinary discharge.) In Ohio, then in Missouri and again in Illinois, the Mormons were treated as pariahs and were despised by many of their neighbors. Elsewhere in the country, many, including public officials, saw the Mormons as an outlandish cult with little or no credibility. The experience of the Mormon Battalion changed many of those attitudes, particularly within the military and with influential officers such as General Kearny and Colonel Philip St. George Cooke. This new attitude was very beneficial, at least for a time. It permitted Utah eventually to be granted territorial status with Brigham Young as Territorial Governor, and it eliminated the public charges that the Mormons were disloyal to the United States.

The travels of the Battalion gave the Mormon leadership a new understanding of other areas in the American West that might be suitable for settlement. Insight into those areas gathered by the men and officers of the Battalion led Brigham Young to create new settlements in a number of areas, particularly in Southern California, Nevada and Arizona. Within three years, the first of these settlements were established.

In spite of the dissent within the Battalion, the men remained intensely loyal to both their military commanders and the teachings of their Church. This fact was carefully observed by the Army officers in charge and led them to realize that the soldiers of the Battalion were far more disciplined and organized than most other military units of the time. The Army and governmental officials had every reason to believe that the Mormons would show fierce determination in their opposition to any future mob or military efforts against them. During the so-called "Mormon War" of 1857, these observations served to avoid a direct armed confrontation and helped lead to a peaceful resolution of the issue of the installation of a new governor for Utah Territory. The reputation of the Mormon Battalion served the Saints well.

The soldiers of the Battalion spent a year traveling through and living in country unlike any they had ever seen before. Most were natives of the Eastern United States and some others were natives of the British Isles. Few, if any, had ever experienced the deserts and harsh conditions of the American West. As they traveled and lived in the West, they were required to learn the skills necessary for survival in the new land, and then apply those lessons to their own safety and well-being. This new information, combined with their spirit of adventure, made them ideal candidates for the expansion of the Mormon presence in the West. Over the ensuing years, Brigham Young often called on Battalion veterans to participate in the settlement of new areas in Utah and elsewhere. These veterans were instrumental in the settlement of the Ogden and Cache Valley areas, Southern Utah and San Bernardino.

One of the most important skills learned by the Battalion was the irrigation methods practiced by the Indian and Mexican farmers of the Southwest and California. Most in the Battalion were farmers themselves who had learned their farming methods east of the 100th Meridian, where irrigation was not necessary to grow most crops. In the Great Basin, along the rivers of the western deserts and in the valleys and hills of California, crops would only grow where irrigation was practiced. This information was carefully noted by the soldiers who realized these techniques were essential to the survival of the Salt Lake colony. Within one day of the arrival of the first pioneers into the Valley of the Great Salt Lake, Battalion men began the construction of an irrigation system. The irrigation systems that evolved became one of the most notable hallmarks of Mormon settlement, and those systems can still be seen in parts of many cities and towns in Utah today.

A few additional words are in order about some of those involved with the Battalion. Following the discovery of gold at Sutter's mill, many of the Mormons spent their off days collecting gold from the stream and nearby locations. One of their most fruitful discoveries was at Mormon Island, now flooded by Folsom Lake. They were careful not to spread the word except to other Mormons. One of those who heard about the gold discovery and the relative ease with which it could be gathered was Sam Brannan. He and C.C. Smith had opened a store at Sutter's Fort in October 1847, and heard of the gold discovery not long after it happened. On April 1, 1848, he published the news of the discovery in the *California Star* and began sending copies of the paper to the East to promote California. Word of the discovery began to spread. Brannan went on to become a very successful entrepreneur in Sacramento and San Francisco, but became more and more distant from the teachings of his Church. He died an apostate in poverty in 1889.

John Sutter and James Marshall, who played pivotal roles in the discovery of gold in California, shared similar fates. Neither was able to capitalize on their great discovery. By 1852, Sutter had lost control of New Helvetia, his dream in the West, and died impoverished in 1880 in Washington D.C.— where he had traveled in an effort to obtain compensation for his losses from the federal government. James Marshall spent the final days before his death in 1885 on a small farm. He made spending money selling his autograph for fifty cents a copy.

Melissa Coray delivered a baby son in Monterey on September 2, 1847. He died shortly thereafter, and William and Melissa then went to join the other Mormons in San Francisco. William was one of the first to question Sam Brannan's leadership and his ethics in dealing with the Mormon community in California, and he sent his observations to Willard Richards in a letter in April 1848. Then the Corays left for Salt Lake City with other returning Battalion Veterans. A daughter was born to Melissa in early 1849. William died of tuberculosis on March 7, 1849. Melissa remarried and eventually was honored as one of the very few women who completed the entire travels of the Mormon Battalion. A mountain in the Sierra Nevadas near Carson Pass has been named in her honor.

Captain Jesse Devine Hunter remained in Southern California after he was appointed Indian Agent by Governor Mason. Hunter made a significant impact on relations with the Indians and played a role in future Mormon activities in Southern California. John D. Lee traveled from Winter Quarters to Utah and eventually settled in Southern Utah where he became Farmer to the Indians in the area. We shall hear much more about Lee.

The returning Battalion veterans were warmly welcomed by their families and friends in Salt Lake City, along the trail and in the camps to the east. But the welcome was less than enthusiastic among many of the Saints. Brigham Young, who had quickly endorsed President Polk's decision to recruit 500 Mormons and strongly encouraged men to enlist, began to speak in less flattering terms not long after the Battalion began its march. He accused the men of not sending enough of their pay and allowances back to the Church and admonished the families for criticizing his decision to take much of what pay did come back for the Church coffers. At various times he accused President Polk of intentionally weakening the Mormons by removing 500 of their youngest and strongest men for the war and of conspiring against the best interests of the Mormons.

His comments regarding the amount of money coming back probably reflected his disappointment that the Battalion's efforts were only partially meeting the tremendous financial needs of the Saints in their time of crisis. But his comments regarding Polk and the Army probably didn't reflect his true feelings; rather they reflected his desire to tell the Saints in camp what he believed they wanted to hear. Brigham Young faced tremendous pressure to solidify his position within the Church and to keep his charges safe and their morale high.

Those families left behind were not cared for as well as Brigham Young had promised during the recruitment. Many of their neighbors saw them more as a drain on the limited resources of the camps than as heroic families who were sacrificing for the good of all. Many of the families themselves were disillusioned by the lack of fulfillment of the promises made to them. All of these factors caused many to look at the Mormon Battalion as a bad idea and to dismiss its significance. Some may have even seen the Battalion members as a group of foolhardy men chasing a wild dream or of even trying to escape the hardships faced by those remaining behind. In many cases, jealousy or even envy may have entered the picture.

Just as Vietnam era veterans were often shunned on their return home, many chose to disregard the accomplishments of the Battalion veterans on their return. A number of young men were harshly dealt with for introducing some Spanish customs, such as horseback riding with a person of the opposite sex in the saddle, into the Mormon community. Their welcome home was often lukewarm at best, at least initially. For a returning veteran to claim Battalion status conferred no special significance. But as time wore on, things began to change. The men of the Battalion became known as loyal and reliable members of the Church, and their skills developed in the service became invaluable. Battalion veterans were included in every new expansion outward from the new center in Salt Lake City. From Ogden and the Cache Valley in the north, from Fort Utah (Provo) to the southern communities in Utah's Dixie, and all the way to San Bernardino, Battalion veterans were at the core of the new communities' founders.

The real change began as more and more emigrants traveled through Utah on the way to California and the federal government began to take an increased interest in the affairs in the Mormon-controlled territory. Quickly, the military training and reputation of the Battalion began to take on new importance to the Church leaders and members. Self-protection had again become an important factor, and the Battalion veterans were the core of the needed military resource. By the mid-1850s, the reputation of the Battalion had been rehabilitated and would continue to grow with time.

On February 5th and 6th, 1855, the "First General Festival of the Renowned Mormon Battalion" was held in Salt Lake City. The celebration, hosted by the Church leadership, served both to recognize the efforts of the Battalion and to improve the relations with the veterans. The festival featured speeches, music, food, dancing and toasts. It offered the opportunity for the men to make disparaging toasts to those they disliked, such as Lieutenants Dykes and Oman, John D. Lee, Howard Egan and John C. Fremont. They gave positive toasts to those that they favored, including Colonel Allen, General Kearny, Lieutenant Colonel Philip St. George Cooke and Captains Daniel Davis, James Brown and Jefferson Hunt. Annual reunions were held for nearly fifty years thereafter (Bigler and Bagley 2000, 428-432).

With each succeeding year, the fame and reputation of the Battalion increased within Utah. This feeling culminated with the dedication of the Mormon Battalion Monument on the grounds of the Utah State Capitol in 1937.

Jefferson Hunt did not attend the 1855 celebration; he was in session with the California State Assembly in Sacramento. But we can be sure that he relished the belated recognition when word of the event reached him. He began the Battalion experience as Brigham Young's designated commander, the principle LDS officer. Young had, in effect, delegated the care and safety of the 500 men of the Battalion to Hunt. His was not an assignment to be taken lightly. Because of the lack of communication between the men in the field and the Church leaders, Hunt was expected to use his best judgment and other skills to make the correct necessary decisions. He did exactly that, and often did so by calling on the other officers to be his counselors in reaching those decisions.

During the periods of dissention, some in the Battalion questioned his decisions. But at all times, Hunt's orders were followed and the great majority of the men understood the foundation of his decisions. Just as the Battalion veterans were often shunned in the months and years following their return, Jefferson Hunt was looked upon by some as a leader who failed to follow the directions of Brigham Young by not taking command of the Battalion at the death of Lieutenant Colonel Allen.

Historians David Bigler and Will Bagley noted in their comprehensive book *Army of Israel: Mormon Battalion Narratives* that: "[John D.] Lee's later report, using his diary as evidence, that Hunt, the senior captain, and other Mormon officers had failed to take command of the battalion after the death of Lt. Col. James Allen reflected unfavorably on these men. Perhaps for this reason, Hunt and others never fully realized their leadership potential in the church" (Bigler and Bagley 2000, 109). Hunt's failure to rise to the level of a General Authority in the Latter Day Saints Church is notable, and Bigler and Bagley may well be correct. On the other hand, LDS Church officials, and Brigham Young himself, would call upon Hunt to undertake several important tasks in the years ahead. And it should also be noted that other important figures, such as Jacob Hamlin, Hosea Stout, and others who performed extraordinarily well in early Utah history rose no higher in Church rank than did Hunt.

In addition, Hunt met a number of people and made a number of contacts that would serve both him and his LDS community well in future years. Included, in addition to Colonel Philip St. George Cooke, were Isaac Williams at the Chino Rancho, John Sutter at Sacramento and Governor Mason, Lieutenants William Tecumseh Sherman, George Stoneman and the other officers in California. As a senior officer in the Mexican War in California, Hunt's name became familiar to many of the other important pre-Gold Rush residents of California. These contacts established Jefferson Hunt as a credible politician during his coming years in California politics and played an important part in the future of the LDS Church efforts in California in the 1850s.

Finally, during the fifteen months after he left Council Bluffs until he reached the Valley of the Great Salt Lake, Jefferson Hunt traveled nearly 3,500 miles over prairie, mountains and desert. He crossed long journadas with no water and forded fast flowing rivers. Most of the time he and his companions were following faint pack trails or Indian trails; much of the time, they had to cut their own wagon road along those trails. He had traveled over both of the major routes to California and had traveled through most of the settled parts of the new territory. In short, Jefferson Hunt had become an accomplished western traveler. His new skills were about to be put to use.

Chapter 14

Return to California

Those first arriving in the Salt Lake Valley immediately set about preparing their new home for the future. Everyone was involved in building new homes and a fort for protection. The Battalion veterans from El Pueblo set about creating irrigation systems and built a bowery for community meetings. Others began plowing fields for crops and building fenced-in corrals and fields for the livestock. Lorenzo D. Young planted the first three acres of wheat in the Valley. George A. Smith planted seed potatoes, while others planted what they could and prepared the land for farming. The Pioneers had only a bare minimum of food supplies to last them through the Winter. They and the next Summer's emigrants desperately depended on the following year's crops for survival.

Those in the Valley of the Great Salt Lake recognized that the supply of food was critical. When Captain Brown left Salt Lake City for California, several men traveled with him as far as Fort Hall in modern day Idaho for the purpose of scouting the route and seeing if they could trade with the fort for needed supplies. Unfortunately, they returned with only a small amount of flour and the news that the fort did not have enough food supplies to engage in regular trade with the Saints. The issue of supplies for the coming Winter and the following year was looking bleak.

Prior to his departure to Winter Quarters, Brigham Young appointed a High Council, which in Mormon style was quickly ratified by the Pioneers. The High Council was composed of a president with two councilors and twelve other members. As President, Brigham Young selected John Smith, the uncle of the Prophet Joseph Smith. He was highly respected and his councilors and the other council members were similarly well-regarded senior members of the Pioneers and other arriving groups. The High Council was given the authority to act in both Church and civil matters in the Valley and throughout the Mormon-controlled West in the absence of the First Presidency and the Twelve Apostles. They adjudicated disputes, conducted trials, presided at divorces and issued directives as needed. The High Council was the final word in all matters until Brigham Young returned the following Summer.

George A. Smith, son of President John Smith and cousin of the Prophet Joseph Smith, also returned to Winter Quarters. On October 2, 1847, his father wrote to him:

> "that the crops are all eaten off by cattle, and I am afraid we shall not be able to save, but few if any potatoes for seed, as the tops are all eaten off, and I think it would be wisdom to send on all kinds of seeds as soon in the spring as possible" (Journal History of the Church, October 4, 1847).

George's efforts to get a head start on the following year's potato crop had been in vain. Clearly, the head of the High Council was concerned about future food supplies. If anything, that concern was reinforced on November 1st when a blizzard hit the Salt Lake Valley.

By November, there were over 3,000 people in the Salt Lake Valley and thousands more would be traveling there the following year. Those in the Valley probably realized that the growing season at their new home was shorter than they were used to and that seeds from the East might not arrive in time to be useful during the next growing season. Perhaps reliance on support from Winter Quarters would not be successful in supporting them during 1848-1849. They needed to do what they could to ensure survival.

When Jefferson Hunt arrived at Salt Lake in early October, he still had unfinished business in California. Prior to his departure, Governor Mason and Colonel Stevenson had made it known that they wished he could recruit a new Battalion for service in the new territory. But the instructions from Brigham Young and the High Council were clear. The new home of the Saints would not be in California; it would be in the Valley of the Great Salt Lake and surrounding areas. Any new military commitments would take men away from the badly needed tasks of building a new city and raising crops that were essential to the survival of the Mormon community. Hunt would not be granted authority to create and lead a new battalion as he may have hoped. But he undoubtedly felt compelled to complete his assignment by personally explaining the situation to those in power in California.

On Saturday, November 13, 1847, about one month following his arrival in Salt Lake, Hunt met with the High Council and "stated his reasons for wishing to go to California with a small company of men. Leave was granted him to go, and the clerk was ordered to draft an epistle to send to the brethren in California" (Journal History of the Church, November 13, 1847). Three reasons for the trip were discussed: the issue of reenlistment of the soldiers; the need for crop seeds and livestock; and the need to communicate with those Mormons still located on the Pacific Coast.

Over the next several days, plans were made for the trip, and the travelers prepared for departure. On November 15th, the High Council appointed Asahel A. Lathrop, Orrin Porter Rockwell and Elijah K. Fuller as representatives with authority to negotiate and contract for the needed supplies. Rockwell, one of the first of the notorious gunmen of the American West, was fanatical in his religious beliefs and support for the leaders of the LDS Church. He was described by non-Mormons as a "Destroying Angel" ready to use murder against the enemies of his church. In 1842, he shot former Governor Lilburn Boggs of Missouri in an assassination attempt at the latter's home. Rockwell was arrested and jailed, but never indicted or convicted. At the time of his death in 1878, he was awaiting trial for two murders allegedly committed in 1857. Many attributed a number of other murders and assaults to Rockwell. However, in 1847, he was an experienced guide and mountaineer in his own right and was considered a key player to have along on a mission as important as the one to California along an unknown trail.

On November 16th, a letter was written by the High Council which explained to Californians that their three representatives were authorized to enter into contracts for supplies and that they had the full financial backing of both the LDS Church and the individual members of the High Council. The letter would serve as an introduction to potential suppliers and would demonstrate the sincerity of their wishes to obtain credit. In addition, the reputation of Jefferson Hunt with the Southern Californians would enhance their mission (Journal History of the Church, November 16, 1847).

In a second letter written the same day to Mormons still in California, the High Council made several important points. They stressed that the new home of the Saints was the Valley of the Great Salt Lake where they would be safe from the dangers of the past and that those still in California should take steps necessary to rejoin their brethren as soon as possible. They then advised the Battalion members not to reenlist but to come to Salt Lake where they would be available to plant crops to aid the following year's emmigration. Jesse Hunter was specifically told to remain as Indian Agent or to appoint a subagent if he chose to go to Salt Lake. Finally, they asked the California Saints to provide the "means" necessary to enable the supply mission to be successful. It's clear that their meaning included an indirect request for funds and support for credit in addition to assisting the appointed officers in their mission.

Captains Hunter and Davis were specifically asked for their assistance in carrying out the mission and getting the brethren out of California and on their way to Salt Lake City. From the standpoint of the High Council, everything was set for trip to begin.

Organizing the trip was one thing, but actually traveling to California was another. Because of the time of year, the northern route along the Humboldt and over the Sierras was out of the question. The party would have to travel the southern route, but no Mormon had ever been over it. However, they knew that the Northern Ute chief, Wakara, routinely raided and traded using a route from Utah to California through the Mojave Desert, since some in the Battalion had met him in Los Angeles and knew of his reputation there. They knew that there was some trade and communication between Santa Fe and Southern California over the Old Spanish Trail which covered a good portion of the route. They had heard that John C. Fremont and Kit Carson traveled over much of the route in 1844. They knew the general direction of the trail, but didn't know the specifics of it or the difficulties that would be met. Jefferson Hunt had also very likely talked with Baptiste Tesson, one of Cooke's guides in the Mormon Battalion and a man who had traveled with the Fremont party along most of the route. It is possible that Hunt knew of Tesson's travels, but unlikely that he got any specific trail information from him. However, help was at hand in the person of a former trapper and mountain man named Miles Goodyear.

Goodyear was a young man who had joined the fur trade during its latter years and who remained in the Utah region. He had settled at the present location of Ogden, Utah, just after James Frazier Reed and the Donner Party passed through Fort Bridger in 1846. The following year, he met Brigham Young and the Pioneer Party. Young left instructions with his High Council to purchase, if at all possible, Goodyear's fort and property in the valley about forty miles north of Salt Lake City. The arrival of Captain James Brown from California on November 16th with about $5,000 in Battalion pay provided the funds needed (about $2,000) to purchase the property, livestock and improvements. But the most important fact for our story is that Goodyear had taken the trail to Los Angeles the preceding Winter and traded over $1,200 worth of dressed deer and elk skins to Fremont's California Battalion in January 1847 (Hafen and Hafen 2001, Vol. II, 185).

Concurrent with Brown's return to Salt Lake, Miles Goodyear and his brother also arrived in Salt Lake City on November 16th. Patty Sessions, a renowned Mormon midwife and conscientious diarist recorded his arrival on that date (Journal History of the Church, November 16, 1847). The following day, Sessions recorded attending at the birth of a daughter, Mary Ellen, to Lydia and Gilbert Hunt (Journal History of the Church, November 17, 1847). It is possible Sessions noted Goodyear's presence at the Hunt household or heard of a meeting between Goodyear and Hunt. It is likely that Hunt and some or all of the other leaders of the California expedition met with Goodyear in an effort to determine the direction, nature and specifics of the route.

In any case, the expedition, composed of nineteen packers, left for Isaac Williams' Rancho del Chino on November 18, 1847. (*The Journal History of the Church* says eighteen packers were included, but it lists nineteen names with one added in later.) Included, in addition to Lathrop, Rockwell and Fuller, were four members of the Hunt family—Jefferson Hunt, Gilbert (now a first-time father with a one-day-old baby at home), and the teenagers John Hunt and Peter Nease. The primary account, however brief and incomplete, of this expedition is a report printed in the *Deseret News* in October 1905, as related by John Hunt (*Deseret News*, October 7, 1905; Journal History of the Church, November 18, 1847). He reported that the travelers had one saddle horse each and twenty pack animals. Jefferson Hunt recalled two years later that they began the trip with eighty animals (General Church Minutes, August 20, 1849). No wagons were known to have yet traveled over the Old Spanish Trail.

The roots of the Old Spanish Trail lay in the desire to create an overland route between the established Spanish communities in New Mexico and the newly created ones in Alta California. In July 1776, the same month that the Declaration of Independence was signed in Philadelphia, Spanish friars Dominquez and Escalante and eight other men began a trip to discover an overland route between Santa Fe and California. Knowing that the Grand Canyon and hundreds of miles of dry deserts lay to the West, the party traveled generally northwesterly through what is now northern New Mexico, then Colorado and finally into Utah. They arrived at Utah Lake (near modern Provo) via Spanish Fork Canyon on September 23, 1776.

The Dominquez/Escalante Expedition then headed south and slightly westward, roughly paralleling today's Interstate 15. For the most part, they had Indian guides and undoubtedly followed along existing Indian foot trails. About 150 miles south of Utah Lake, the expedition crossed the Beaver River and bore to the southwest into the large valley that would eventually bear one of their names—the Escalante Desert. Winter was setting in and the group had been on the trail over four months. They realized they were still a very long way from their final goal of Monterey on the California Coast. The leaders wanted to turn back, but many of the others in the party wanted to continue on. To settle the issue, lots were cast and the decision made to return to Santa Fe.

This decision on October 11, 1776, occurred at a place on the eastern edge of the Escalante Desert, about seventeen miles southwest of Minersville, Utah, and is now known as the "Casting of Lots Site." Conditions in the Escalante Desert were not particularly bad for the expedition, since rain and snow made plenty of water available to them and provided feed for their stock. As we shall see, the conditions Jefferson Hunt faced near the same place in 1849 were far different. Dominquez and Escalante turned southeast to the area of modern Cedar City, then over the mountains to the valley of the Virgin River near St. George. Their return from there to Santa Fe is itself a remarkable story but is beyond the scope of this book. These adventurers became the first Europeans to travel the northernmost 200 miles of the general route that would be followed by Hunt and his Southern California-bound travelers seventy-one years later.

That same year, 1776, another friar, Francisco Garces, traveled from the Mission of San Xavier del Bac near present-day Tucson, Arizona, to Southern California. Garces, led by Mojave Indians from the Colorado River area and following existing Indian trails, took a route across the Mojave Desert where he hit the Mojave River at its sink near present-day Baker, California. With Garces, the westernmost 150 miles of what would be known as the Old Spanish Trail was completed.

The longest and most difficult portion of the Old Spanish Trail followed by Jefferson Hunt had yet to be established. That effort began in the Fall of 1826, when the mountain man and trapper Jedediah Smith left the Rendezvous in the northern Utah's Cache Valley with fifteen men and set out to explore the country to the southwest and California. His approximate route took him south past the Great Salt Lake, Utah Lake and into the general area previously traveled by the Dominquez/Escalante Expedition. Like them, he went through the area now occupied by Cedar City and on to the Virgin River near Hurricane, Utah. He then followed the Virgin through its very narrow and steep gorge and into modern Nevada. He followed the Colorado River to the Mojave villages (north of present-day Needles, California) and then followed the trail previously used by Garces to California. Smith became the first person to record a successful transit of a route from the Great Salt Lake to California.

Smith returned to the Rendezvous the following year, and again in 1827 set out along his old route to California with eighteen men. This time, he made a few adjustments in the route, including a more westerly path around the gorge of the Virgin River, which took him into the area of Beaver Dam Wash near the Utah/Arizona border. Unbeknownst to Smith, hostilities had broken out earlier between the Mojaves and other trappers. While crossing the Colorado River at the Mojave villages, his band was attacked and ten men were killed. But Smith escaped and reached California.

During the next several years, other trappers followed essentially the same route to California. Included in that number were Thomas L. "Peg-leg" Smith in 1829, Peter Skeen Ogden with thirty men in 1829, and William Wolfskill and George C. Yount and about twenty men in the Winter of 1830-31. But the route they followed, which was that of Jedediah Smith, still lacked the shortcuts that would more directly take travelers across the Mojave Desert.

The improvements in the route were pioneered by a Santa Fe trader named Antonio Armijo, who led a pack train during the Winter of 1830-31. Armijo took blankets and other woolen goods to trade for livestock in California. Rather than simply following the Virgin River to the Colorado and thence to the Mojave villages, Armijo sent out scouts a number of days in advance to find a more direct route. Departing from the Virgin River above where Las Vegas Wash meets the Colorado River, his scouts headed west and discovered the route that essentially became the Old Spanish Trail from Las Vegas to the Mojave River. They found the new route to be difficult but quite viable if not traveled in the hot Summer months. As with many of those who would follow them, they found themselves running out of supplies and butchering a few of their own animals for food. Armijo successfully traded for mules and horses which, on his return to Santa Fe, were found by the New Mexicans to be of superior quality and inexpensive. As a result, a regular trade began between Santa Fe and Southern California over the Old Spanish Trail.

Throughout the rest of the 1830s and well into the late 1840s, Santa Fe traders, mountain men and others continued using the Old Spanish Trail as the main trading route between the Rocky Mountain West and the California Coast. Not only were goods brought to California and traded for horses and mules, some simply stole the livestock and took them east. Others remained in California. Among those who made the trip partially or entirely along the Santa Fe Trail were Kit Carson, Alex Godey, Dr. John Marsh, Peg-leg Smith, John and William Wolfskill, Jim Waters, James Beckwourth, Miles Goodyear, Joseph Walker, and the Ute Chief Wakara. Few left records of their exploits. For many it was simply a matter of not keeping journals or publicly sharing information; the travel was just part of their lives. For others, such as the rustlers, not publicizing their travels was very intentional.

The notable exception was "The Pathfinder," John C. Fremont, whose five trips through the West were extensively reported. We have already met Fremont and seen his involvement in the seizing California during the Mexican War. However, the trip that concerns us here occurred two years earlier in the Spring of 1844, when he returned East from a successful trip to the northern part of California and Oregon. With such notable Mountain Men as Kit Carson, Thomas "Broken Hand" Fitzpatrick and Alexis Godey, and with Charles Preuss serving as a map-maker, Fremont crossed the Tehachapi Mountains from the San Joaquin Valley and intersected the Old Spanish Trail where it followed the Mojave River, not far from present-day Victorville, California. He described the river as "A clear bold stream, 60 feet wide and several feet deep. . ." (Hafen and Hafen 1954, 287).

On April 22nd, Fremont and his party, which included over 150 head of horses, mules and cattle, but no wagons, began travelling along the Trail and followed the Mojave River for about twenty-five miles. Fremont, by now no stranger to deserts, noted how "the River, instead of growing constantly larger, gradually dwindled away, as it was absorbed by the sand" (Hafen and Hafen 1954, 288). They then left the Mojave and began to travel over the cutoff pioneered by Armijo fourteen years before and regularly traveled by the traders since then. Now the trail jumped from spring to spring or small stream for the next 225 miles or so between the Mojave River and the Virgin River, near the present location of the Nevada/Arizona border.

Along this stretch were eight water sources ranging from six miles to fifty miles apart. The first water Fremont reached about twenty-five miles after leaving the Mojave was Bitter Spring, now inside the Fort Irwin. As the name suggests, the water from this spring was alkaline and foul tasting. But it was drinkable and irrigated a small portion of the surrounding desert where some grass grew. For Fremont and other desert travelers, reaching these verdant areas before larger herds of livestock grazed away what small amount grass was available was extremely important. From Bitter Spring, the Trail crossed over the mountains and deserts and then traveled north along today's Highway 127 to Salt Creek Spring (also called Amargosa Spring) nearly forty miles away. Again, as the name suggests, the water at the major spring there was not drinkable; a very small potable spring was there, but was not obvious and easy to miss.

From there, the Trail went first north and east about five miles to the Amargosa River (which, roughly translated, means bitter water). The shortest route to the Amargosa skirted a portion of the Dumont Sand Dunes—most diarists commented about the difficulty presented by the sand. This small stream usually has some water in it, but again as the name implies, the water at low levels is alkaline. As they traveled north from Salt Creek Spring, Fremont and his men were just to the east of the southern-most end of Death Valley. As they looked to their left they could see this forbidding area. To the northwest about sixty miles they saw the lofty summit of Telescope Peak in the Panamint Mountains that form the western side of the lower half of Death Valley. The Amargosa River drains into the great sink of Death Valley, which at 282 feet below sea level, is the lowest point in the Western Hemisphere. As near as they and other travelers were to Death Valley, there is no confirmed evidence of any non-Indian entering it until the end of 1849.

The Trail then followed along the bottoms of the Amargosa River for another ten miles or so. It appears to this author and others that the trail followed by Fremont then left the Amargosa and followed a small canyon past the location of present-day China Ranch and Willow Spring to the higher tableland to the east of present-day Tecopa, California (LeRoy Johnson and

Tom Sutak, paper presented at the Old Spanish Trail Association Conference, June, 2011, Pomona). From there, the trail went nearly straight north to the famed Resting Spring. As the name implies, this is a fresh water spring that irrigated a substantial area, providing much feed for horses and other livestock. Very often travelers would stop for a day or two to permit their animals to eat well and rest for the rigors of the trail ahead.

From Resting Spring, the trail went east over the aptly named Emigrant Pass in the Nopah (no water) Range and down into the Pahrump Valley along the California/Nevada border. Shortly after crossing the future location of the California/Nevada border and at about twenty-five miles from Resting Spring, they stopped at Stump Spring, which more accurately could be described as a shallow well dug into the desert floor. From there, the Trail continued east, crossing over the Spring Mountains at Mountain Springs Pass. Here they stopped at the aptly named Mountain Springs after traveling about twenty miles. From there the next spot, about nine or ten miles away, was at Cottonwood Spring at the location of today's Blue Diamond, Nevada, just to the west of Las Vegas and just south of Red Rock Canyon.

Traveling east and then north for about twenty miles, they arrived at the great flowing springs called the Vegas or meadows from which the city of Las Vegas derives its name. These springs, located just northwest of downtown Las Vegas, discharged thousands of gallons of fresh water each minute and were considered a marvel to the tired and thirsty desert travelers. For Fremont and other desert travelers of the time, the most difficult and driest part of the journey was yet to come.

Of course, we now know of Las Vegas as a large city with millions of visitors a year. However, in 1844 and for over a decade after, the only people living along the Trail through the Mojave Desert were a few Indians. Fremont and his men encountered only a few between Bitter Spring and Resting Spring when Kit Carson and Godey exacted vengeance upon several Indians they tracked down following the tragic murder and kidnapping of several members of a party of traders ahead of them on the Trail. This famous story is beyond the scope of this book but provides a quick glimpse of how Indians were regarded in the 1840s and for sometime thereafter. Fremont's next watering stop along the Trail was different; it was the location of the most heavily populated part of the trail between San Bernardino and Southern Utah.

But to reach that location along the Muddy River at present Moapa /Glendale, Nevada, required crossing more than fifty miles of desert—the longest and driest stretch of the entire Trail. When they arrived after sixteen hours of continuous travel, they found the river bottoms occupied by a number of Paiutes who lived on the agricultural bounty provided by the ample water of the stream. Even today this location, the Moapa Indian Reservation just north of the town of Glendale on Interstate 15, is home to many Paiutes.

Here, as in most locations along the various trails through the Great Basin and surrounding areas, the indigenous peoples expected what amounted to a toll for the intrusion into and through their lands. This was often seen by whites as begging or even thievery, but it was nothing more than an expectation of gifts of food or other desired items due to those who lived marginally on the land. Fremont handled the situation by posting guards, remaining alert for theft or attack and by giving them several horses to slaughter for food.

From the Muddy River, Fremont then traveled easterly about twenty miles to the eastern rim of what is now known as Mormon Mesa west of Mesquite, Nevada. The trail went over the precipitous edge and down a very steep slope to a ravine that they followed for about three miles to the Virgin River. This descent—or ascent when coming from the other direction—was the hardest single location to traverse along the entire Old Spanish Trail. It would cause much work for future travelers with wagons, and would even be difficult or unsafe for those, like Fremont, using only pack animals. In 1849, travelers with wagons first broke away ten feet or so of the rock rim to make a road, and then used multiple teams to pull wagons up and over the difficult lip of rock.

Along the Virgin River, the hardship of jumping from one desert water source to the next was nearly behind them. The Virgin River in the Spring was fairly high with snowmelt runoff as it tumbled along towards its confluence with the Colorado River. The trail went along the river for about twenty miles to the site of present-day Littlefield, Arizona. Then it headed north from the point where Beaver Dam Wash meets the Virgin River to avoid the steep narrows of the Virgin River Canyon. This cutoff, pioneered by Armijo, then went northeast over the Beaver Dam Mountains about twenty-five miles to the Santa Clara River west of today's St. George Utah.

They were now out of the Mojave Desert. One more day's travel of about twenty-five miles along the Santa Clara River and Magotsu Creek took them to Mountain Meadow, a lush green expanse of spring-watered grass that was used as a major resting place for traders and other travelers along the Old Spanish Trail. Mountain Meadow became infamous in 1857 as the site of the Mountain Meadows Massacre which will be discussed later. As a result of floods which devastated much of the West in 1862, Mountain Meadows (or Mountain Meadow, as it is officially known) today does not have the same lush greenery as it had in the 1840s and 50s. But it is very accessible, and a visitor today can easily imagine the advantages it offered to desert-weary travelers. At Mountain Meadow, the famous mountain man, Joseph Walker, who had been with another group following behind, caught up with Fremont and was added to his list of experienced guides and associates. Fremont now had the premier explorer of the Great Basin and one of the most experienced of all the mountain men guiding him northward.

As they continued north through the upper end of Mountain Meadow, they crossed a nearly imperceptible point at which water would flow north into the Great Basin and not south into the Colorado River drainage. At this point, they were at the rim of the Great Basin and over one mile in elevation. From the famous meadow, they began descending along Holt Creek toward today's Newcastle, Utah, about fifteen miles away to the northeast.

Between Holt Canyon and Newcastle, the Fremont party had a full view of the great Escalante Desert before them: from near present-day Enterprise, Utah, on their left to the distant mountains, the desert extended about 100 miles in a generally southwest to northeast trend. Ranging from twenty-five miles wide in its lower end to seven to ten miles wide in its upper areas, it resembled a major causeway. In fact, today it is an important transportation and communication corridor with a major railroad line, power line, multiple underground pipelines, and cable lines running through it on the route between Northern Utah, Southern Nevada and California. Normally dry and threatening to travelers during most of the year, it can be deceiving. When visited by the Dominquez/Escalante Expedition, it had just snowed and rained and the friars found no problems with their journey into the desert. When the author drove through the Escalante Desert in August 2004, recent monsoon rains had left multiple pools of water and turned normal dirt and gravel roads into mud holes that had to be bypassed; the availability of water was no problem, an excess of water was. The Escalante Desert can experience major swings in surface water availability during the course of a year.

Fremont did not pass directly through the Escalante Desert. Rather, the Trail took him north from Newcastle, then around the Antelope Range where he headed east to Iron Springs on the western edge of the Cedar Valley. Traveling north of the present location of Cedar City, the trail next led to springs near the present community of Enoch. From there it appears from his map that he traveled on the western side of the Red Hills to the Parowan Gap where they turned east to the location of Little Salt Lake. Near there, the Old Spanish Trail cut over the mountains to the east and then went on through Utah and Colorado to Santa Fe in New Mexico.

Fremont was not going to Santa Fe; he was heading back to the United States and continued in a northerly direction crossing over the Black Mountains, southwest of present-day Beaver and south of Greenville, on the same trail that others would soon follow. In any case, Fremont was no longer on the well-traveled trail to Santa Fe and was likely following Indian and trapper trails. He quickly noted the change and in his entry for May 17, 1844, says the following: "After 440 miles of traveling on a trail, which served for a road, we again found ourselves under the necessity of exploring a track through the wilderness" (Fremont 1970, Vol. 1, 695).

On May 20th, two years before the Mexican War began and four years before the region would become part of the United States, somewhere north of the Beaver River near present-day Kanosh or Meadow, Utah, a most remarkable meeting took place. Fremont The Pathfinder was introduced to the great Ute war chief Wakara by his namesake Joseph Walker—the first American to traverse the Great Basin—in the presence of Kit Carson and several other noted mountain men.

With the guidance of Joseph Walker, Fremont continued on to Utah Lake, then began his eastward journey through Utah and Colorado, eventually reaching El Pueblo and the Arkansas River and then on to the Missouri River.

From where he reached the Old Spanish Trail at the Mojave River on April 20th, to Utah Lake where he arrived on May 26th, Fremont spent thirty-six days.

His report and an accompanying map were submitted to Congress in March 1845. These were then printed and were well known to those with an interest in the West, including those in the leadership of the LDS Church and many emigrants. The report and maps were very popular with the American public and many had or read copies. We can safely assume that Jefferson Hunt and others in Salt Lake City in November 1847 knew about John C. Fremont's travels—but the account and map would not have reached Salt Lake City at this point.

Unlike Fremont who had Joseph Walker and other notable Mountain Men as guides, the 1847-48 Jefferson Hunt pack train to California had no experienced guides. Also, they were traveling north to south—from Utah to California—instead of from California to Utah. That fact alone made considerable difference in the ease and speed of travel. At the southern or California end of the route, the Old Spanish Trail was distinct and the only trail of comparable size that was evident. Once a traveler found it on the Mojave River, the Trail could easily be followed. But from Utah Lake or the mountain ranges to the south, there were other trails trending in the same southerly direction. There was no single trail heading south. There was a general route with numerous branches heading into other valleys or through mountain passes or toward nearby streams or springs. Simply heading south by southwest would not necessarily take a traveler to the most obvious trail. A traveler on the trail for the first time could easily be misled and take the wrong branch for some distance until the error became obvious and was corrected.

Only two accounts of the Mormons' trip to California exist. The primary one is by John Hunt and was published in an article in the *Deseret Evening News* on October 7, 1905, about fifty-eight years after the event. The only other account comes from comments made by Jefferson Hunt to the migrating gold seekers on August 20, 1849 (General Church Minutes, August 20, 1849). The article about John Hunt by an unnamed author is titled "Mormon Pathfinders Guests of Senator Clark" and is subtitled "Startling Story of the First Trip From Salt Lake to Los Angeles" (Deseret Evening News, October 7, 1905). Senator Clark was William Andrews Clark, a wealthy mining magnate and industrialist, who was a United States Senator from Montana during the years 1901 to 1907.

To enhance his mining operations and profit from land he and his brother Ross owned in Los Angeles, Clark built the San Pedro, Los Angeles and Salt Lake Railroad that began operation in January 1905. That railroad traveled the general route that followed the Mormon road from Salt Lake City to Southern California. One key location along the route was the springs at Las Vegas, where a town was built at the site of a former Mormon settlement. Clark County, Nevada, home of Las Vegas, was named after Senator Clark.

Prior to the ratification of the 17th Amendment to the Constitution in 1913, senators were elected by state legislators. Clark was known for his attempts to become a senator in 1893, 1898 and 1899. In the latter year, he attempted to buy his senate seat, but was thwarted when one of the bribed legislators showed his fellow legislators the money that had been offered for the vote. This incident was one of those that fostered support for direct election of senators and led to the 17th Amendment. Nevertheless, in 1901 Clark was finally elected to the Senate. He was a man in need of image enhancement.

Following the completion of his railroad to California in 1905, Clark saw the publicity benefits of honoring those early Mormons who had pioneered the cities of San Bernardino, Las Vegas and the Salt Lake/Southern California Road. Accordingly, he devised a plan to host those pioneers from fifty years before by taking them on a railroad trip from Salt Lake to California and back. About twenty-five of those pioneers were found and invited to join the excursion. John Hunt, who was living in Snowflake, Arizona, but was in Salt Lake City attending the Fall General Conference of the LDS Church, saw a newspaper article about the recently completed trip and contacted the paper with the details of his trip of 1847-48. Thus, a firsthand account of the trip was made, even though it wasn't written down until fifty-eight years later.

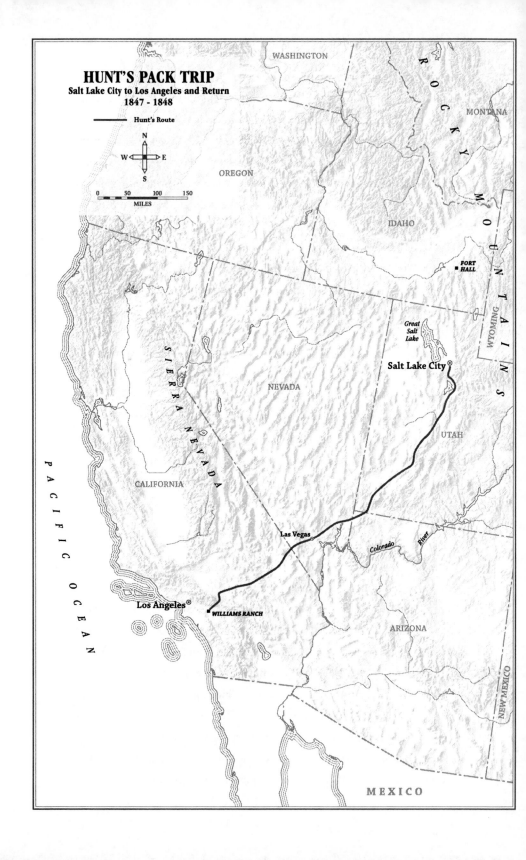

John Hunt in his 1905 recollection describes what happened:

"We took provisions for 30 days, which we estimated would be ample time to reach our destination in. But we found the directions *of Weber* very hard to follow, and lost the trail so often and spent so much time hunting it again, that we finally ran out of provisions before we had reached the vicinity of Las Vegas" (Deseret Evening News, October 7, 1905).

Author's comment: The words "of Weber," italicized above, are in the *Deseret Evening News* account but are not included in the same paragraph copied in the Journal History of the LDS Church under the date of November 18, 1847, which gives the same account of the trip. Furthermore, the author of the newspaper article says elsewhere in the story:

"That party started out with a map, or set of directions, furnished them by a trapper named 'Duff' Weber, after whom Weber river and Weber county are named. Weber had crossed over the trail with Kit Carson several years previously, and had only imperfect recollections of the trail"

This is incorrect on several accounts. The Weber River and Weber County at present-day Ogden, Utah, are named after John H. Weber, a trapper and fur trader with William H. Ashley's American Fur Company, who spent some time in the Bear River and Great Salt Lake areas in the 1820s. During the period of the pioneering efforts in Salt Lake City in 1847, Weber lived in Bellevue, Iowa. Duff Weaver, brother of Mormon Battalion guide, Pauline Weaver, was well known to the Mormons in the San Bernardino colony. As we shall see in Part III, Duff Weaver was a significant thorn in the side of Jefferson Hunt and the other senior members of that group of colonists. It is quite probable that either the article's author or John Hunt or both confused Weaver with Weber and with Miles Goodyear who was another former trapper and who had settled along the Weber River at what would later become Ogden in Weber County. When the *Journal History of the Church* account was recorded, the compiler clearly understood this error and deleted any reference to Weber. We can assume, as stated previously, that the information about the trail was, in fact, provided by Miles Goodyear.

Why did the party take provisions for only thirty days? First of all, food supplies in Salt Lake City were low; that was one of the main reasons for the trip. Those members of the Pioneer Party who were there were able to bring only a limited amount with them, and what they did bring was going to have to keep them supplied until the following year's harvest. In addition, their numbers had been increased by the arrival of the Battalion veterans and a number of other companies from Winter Quarters who had also brought only limited amounts of food with them. By mid-November when the party left for Southern California, over 3,000 people had settled in the Salt Lake Valley (Bagley, 2010, 371). Everyone knew that the next year was going to be a difficult time due to the shortage of food. Further, they knew the approximate distance to Southern California was about 700 miles. They no doubt reasoned that a small group of mounted men leading pack animals would be able to average about twenty-five miles a day over that distance and that thirty days' provisions would be adequate. They did not calculate on the lost days due to inadequate directions and the need to rest their animals.

In total, John Hunt says that it took forty-five days to travel from Salt Lake City to Isaac Williams' Ranch at Chino. If his time is accurate, they arrived on January 2, 1848. If Fremont had traveled the same distance (Chino to Salt Lake City) he would have added at least three days to his travel time, making the trip in thirty-nine days. So the Mormon party was only about six days off the time taken by Fremont and his experienced band of mountain men who were traveling in the opposite direction.

Fremont logged the distance from the point where he arrived at the Old Spanish Trail to Utah Lake as 620 miles. Adding the distance from Salt Lake City to Utah Lake and from the Mojave River to Chino would have increased that to over 700 miles. To travel that distance in thirty days would have required an average daily travel of about twenty-five miles. On the surface, that might appear to be realistic. But with the experience of Jefferson Hunt and some of the others in the party, it would have been reasonable to add additional time to rest and feed their animals and to account for contingencies. We can assume, therefore, that they likely were relying more on verbal descriptions of the trail and distances than on written information. The trading party did not have sufficiently accurate information about the trail ahead to accurately plan for their trip.

As they progressed south from Salt Lake City, the route to Utah Lake was known and evident. Beyond there, the trail was probably less clear and the path they were following split at a number of points. For example, about fifty miles south of Lake Utah—today's Provo—the trail hit the Sevier River near where it changes direction from a northern flowing stream to a westerly direction as it heads to its sink in the Sevier Desert to the west. The correct route left the stream and headed southwest along present Interstate 15 toward today's communities of Scipio, Holden and Fillmore. But in 1847, a very inviting-looking path headed upstream (south) into the fertile Sevier Valley.

Another confusing point would have been further south near today's Summit and Enoch, Utah. Here, the correct trail heads to springs to the west as traveled by Fremont. But other trails used by Indians and some other early travelers such as Jedediah Smith headed south to present-day Cedar City and on to the Virgin River near today's St. George. At points like these, it is clear that new travelers on the trail could have easily mistaken the route and would have been forced to either backtrack or cut over mountains to hit the desired trail. From John Hunt's narrative, it appears that this was exactly what happened either at these and/or other points along the route.

In addition to Jefferson Hunt, there were three other Mormon Battalion veterans in the pack train: his son, Gilbert, who had left the Battalion along the Arkansas River to go to El Pueblo; Thurston Larson and James Hirons, both members of the Brown Detachment who left Santa Fe and went to El Pueblo. Thus, the only person with extensive desert travel experience and who closely watched scouting operations in the deserts was Hunt himself. Therefore it is quite likely that much of the scouting for the pack train was conducted, or at least directed, by Hunt. This would not be the last trip where he would engage in scouting a new trail along the route.

As John Hunt stated, the party underestimated the amount of time required and took only thirty days worth of provisions with them. As a consequence, John writes that: "We then did what I think no other party of "Mormon" emigrants ever had to do—we killed and ate our horses" (Deseret Evening News, October 7, 1905). Two of the horses belonged to John Y. Greene (a nephew of Brigham Young—the "Y" stood for Young) and one belonged to William Cornogg. The first horse was butchered at Mountain Springs to the west of Las Vegas Valley; the second at what John Hunt called "Amargosa springs," in the Salt Spring Hills near the southern end of Death Valley. The third was butchered near the Mojave River.

John Hunt may or may not have been correct in his assessment of Mormon travelers having to kill and eat their working livestock. However, along this route it was a common occurrence. The trail was long, dry and difficult, and it presented many challenges to those who travelled it.

We know from events that were recorded in 1849 that Jefferson Hunt carefully noted the correct route as it was discovered, and that at least twice in 1849 he made—or attempted to make—improvements to the route. Historians Edward Leo Lyman and Larry Reese called the route *The Arduous Road: Salt Lake to Los Angeles, the Most Difficult Wagon Road in American History* (Lyman and Reese 2001). But in 1847, no wagons had yet traveled the route; only pack animals had been used. Pack trains were able to negotiate difficult sections of the route much more easily than wagons. However, in some places, even the pack trains had difficulty with the route. One such place was the crossing of the Black Mountains from the Beaver River to Little Salt Lake. Here there were steep inclines and thick groves of trees that impeded travel, and the distance to water was well over twenty-five miles. Jefferson Hunt noted this area as one to be bypassed, if possible, in the future.

John Hunt concluded his description of the travel by saying that when the pack train got to the location of present-day Barstow, California, on the Mojave River, two of their "strongest men—Shaw and Cornogg—rode ahead to get provisions" at Isaac Williams' Ranch. "They sent a Mexican to us with beef and fresh mounts, and we moved on again, arriving at the Chino Ranch after 45 days on the trail" (Deseret Evening News, October 7, 1905). This would not be the only time that Isaac Williams sent relief to travelers stranded without provisions in the Mojave Desert. In fact, it would become a common occurrence and would earn Williams much gratitude from desperate desert travelers.

When the party arrived at Chino, Isaac Williams became the perfect host, treating them to all the food they needed and letting them and their animals rest. Lathrop and Fuller began discussions with Williams for the needed livestock, seeds and cuttings. According to John Hunt, Williams "furnished us with wild cows which we milked after strapping them down. . ." (Deseret Evening News, October 7, 1848). Most of the livestock at the ranch were allowed to roam freely over the territory and were not used to being handled.

Other men began to carry out their personal assignments. Who did what is not clear, but we have some indication as to the scope of some of their actions and travels. It should be noted, however, that the group of men who returned to Salt Lake City with the needed supplies was not the same group that made the original trek to Chino; some remained in California and others joined.

Jefferson Hunt had been absent from Southern California for less than six months. He was still well known and well thought of there from his role as the senior captain of the Mormon Battalion, and many were glad to see his return. Hunt's first priority after introducing his companions to Isaac Williams was to get the message regarding a new Mormon Battalion to the military authorities and Governor Mason as he had promised. The United States and Mexico were still technically at war and civil and military authorities still feared an attack from Mexico. Governor Mason and Colonel Stevenson still desperately hoped that another Mormon Battalion would be raised to help protect California from invasion, from insurrection within and from Indians and bandits who might try to take advantage of the lack of troops in the area, since many had been moved south to Baja California and the Mexican mainland.

Hunt and Orrin Porter Rockwell, and possibly others, soon left the ranch at Chino and met with Colonel Stevenson in Los Angeles several days before January 12, 1848. In a letter from Stevenson in Los Angeles to Governor Mason dated January 12th, Stevenson said that he had met with Jefferson Hunt and was told that he:

> "expresses much regret that your terms had not been more liberal and a longer time allowed for him to enroll and bring in a Battalion of his people which he could have readily obtained and which he assures me he can yet do if you desire it" (Bigler and Bagley 2000, 383).

Clearly Hunt was still hoping to be able to raise a battalion in spite of the instructions from the High Council in Salt Lake City to the contrary. Upon his arrival in California, Hunt probably heard that a number of troops had been sent to Mexico and that the military was desperately in need of additional troops. He may have hoped that Governor Mason would make such a lucrative offer that the High Council and/or Brigham Young would accept.

Such was not to be however. Governor Mason directed Lieutenant William Tecumseh Sherman to respond to Stevenson, which he did in a letter dated on January 25th. In it, Sherman first indicated that Mason was piqued at Hunt's statement that the terms of enlistment were not liberal enough. He went on to say that the Army was bound by federal law and that had recently been changed to become more liberal for volunteers. Stevenson had copies of those changes which could be shown to Hunt. Sherman went on to say that Governor Mason still wanted a new Mormon Battalion of four companies with about 360 men and he was anxious to have them in Los Angeles by April if possible (Bigler and Bagley 2000, 385-387).

But things in Mexico were deteriorating. There was an urgent need for more troops to support the military efforts there. Consequently, Governor Mason acted to further encourage the formation of a new Mormon battalion. On January 31, 1848, he ordered Lieutenant William H. Warner, a topographical engineer on his staff, to go to Los Angeles to meet personally with Hunt, and if necessary, to travel on to Salt Lake City to recruit a battalion (Bigler and Bagley 2000, 388-189). In the letter Lieutenant Sherman wrote on his behalf,

Governor Mason expressed the hope that the Mormons still wanted to migrate to California and that Hunt possessed strong enough influence to form a battalion. Warner was given detailed pay information and was authorized to muster the battalion in Salt Lake City and give travel pay to the troops.

Warner found Jefferson Hunt at Williams' Rancho on February 12th, only two days before Hunt and his party were set to leave on the return trip to Salt Lake City. The news that Warner received from Hunt was not what the Lieutenant or the Governor wanted to hear. Basically, Hunt said that "there was no prospect of raising a battalion among the Mormons for Lower California, or the coast of Mexico" (Bigler and Bagley 2000, 390-391). However, he then said that he "thought they would cheerfully come to Upper California, & that their leaders would give their consent." Hunt remained optimistic that the Saints might still settle some people in California.

But Jefferson Hunt did not totally dismiss the idea of a new battalion. He told Warner that approval needed to be obtained from the Church leadership, and that he thought it would be granted. He went on to say that he would send a courier to the leadership on the Plains to secure that permission, and that he should be able to return "by the middle of June." Lieutenant Warner was not impressed by Hunt's timeline and told Sherman that he believed that no battalion could arrive "before the middle of August." Governor Mason responded to Warner, who in turn wrote to Hunt in Salt Lake City on March 12th repeating Mason's desire to have a battalion arrive as soon as possible.

All of these efforts toward a new Mormon battalion would end. The Treaty of Guadalupe-Hidalgo ending the Mexican War was signed on February 2, 1848. When word reached Governor Mason, his need to increase the number of soldiers in California ended, at least for a time. But by August 1848, the discovery of gold had changed everything in California. In an August 25, 1848, letter to his former fellow officer, Major H.S. Turner, Lieutenant Sherman complained that:

> "Our soldiers are deserting, and we can't stop it. . . all have gone to the mines. The sailors desert their ships as fast as they come on the coast, and we have been waiting a month to send an express to the United States, but no vessel can get a crew to leave the coast" (Thorndike 1894, 46).

With the end of the threat from Mexico no further attempts were made to recruit a new Mormon battalion.

There is no indication in the record that Jefferson Hunt or any of the three designated to deal on behalf of the High Council had any conversation with Isaac Williams about the future of his property. However, the subject likely came up. This was Hunt's second visit with Williams, and he was certainly aware of the bounty that the ranch provided its owner. Hunt and the others had shown that the Williams Ranch was reachable from Salt Lake City and that it provided a trading gateway into California. Subsequent events indicate that this was an important consideration to Hunt and those with him in their future reports to the Mormon officials.

Lathrop and Fuller had been successful in obtaining the needed supplies from Isaac Williams. In addition to obtaining seeds for wheat and other crops and fruit tree cuttings, the party purchased 200 milk cows at a price of $6.00 each. They also acquired an unknown number of additional mounts and pack animals. For the milk cows they paid $230 cash and promised to pay the additional $970 in twelve months. In addition, Lathrop, Fuller and Jefferson Hunt spent $227.91 which they billed to the High Council upon their return (Journal History of the Church, May 15, 1848; Journal History, May 18, 1848). Isaac Williams also allowed them to catch and take as many wild bulls as they could round up; they eventually rounded up forty bulls giving them a total of 240 head. They would be difficult to drive the 700 miles to Utah.

The return party consisted of Lathrop and Fuller who were "accompanied by nineteen persons, including five hired Indians" (Journal History of the Church, May 15, 1848). However, Lathrop and Fuller met with the High Council and the handwritten minutes state that: "19 persons including 3 hired Indians came through with the cattle" (Salt Lake High Council Minute Book, May 16, 1848). Whether three or five were hired, it is clear that the packers needed additional help with the animals. Orrin Porter Rockwell and James Shaw did not begin the return trip with the Hunt party. The route of the return trip was now well-known to Hunt and the others. They fully understood the locations of springs and feed and had a good idea of the amount of time that would be necessary the traverse the distance, including time for resting and feeding the animals.

They set out, again with Jefferson Hunt acting as guide, from Williams' Ranch on February 15, 1848. They had the seeds, the cuttings, the 200 milk cows and the forty bulls. However, they had missed the earthshaking news from Northern California—that gold had been discovered on the American River three weeks before while they were resting at Williams' Ranch. Chino was too far away and the report was too new to reach them.

Authors Comment: Several writers including Howard Schindler, Rockwell's biographer, suggest that Rockwell did not return with the Hunt party because of a falling out between the two men, although there is no record of such an incident. But Porter Rockwell was not the kind of man who would skulk away from a confrontation with anyone. More likely, Rockwell did not return with Hunt because he traveled with Shaw to Los Angeles and San Diego to visit other Saints, was attempting to secure a mail route, and had been arrested for counterfeiting.

The travelers returned to Salt Lake City sometime before May 15th after a little less than ninety days on the trail. The *Journal History of the LDS Church* says that Lathrop and Fuller reported to the High Council about their trip on May 15th (Journal History, May 15, 1848). Another account written by Eliza Roxey Snow says that she "met the California boys, 7 of them" on May 10th and bought six or seven small potatoes which she used for seed potatoes (Bigler and Bagley 2000, 396). This account would put the group back in Salt Lake by May 10, 1848, about eighty-five days after they began the homeward journey.

They brought back the seeds and cuttings successfully, but success with the milk cows and bulls was another story. John Hunt says that all but one of the bulls and half of the cows died from thirst or an occasional Indian attack (Deseret Evening News, October 7, 1905). This is not surprising, considering that it was probably the first time that cattle were ever driven over the 700 plus mile trail. Previous use of the trail had been for pack trains and driving herds of horses, which could travel much faster. Prior to the arrival of the Mormons in the Great Basin, there was no market for cattle, and hence, no need to drive them such a great distance.

It is also very probable that most of the bulls were considered to be part of the provisions for the returning party. Based on their observations of the trail on the trip to California and their knowledge that cattle traveled at a rate of about ten miles per day except under the most unusual circumstances, such as long distances between water locations, they knew that their return journey would take far longer than their trip out. A simple calculation would have shown them that 700 miles would equate to about seventy days, plus time needed to recruit (rest and feed) the animals at some of the locations where good water and feed could be found. They would have estimated that they would spend an additional day or two, or even three, at locations such as the final camp on the Mojave River before heading to Bitter Spring at China Ranch; or Resting Spring with their flowing water and lush greenery; at Las Vegas before the long push to the Muddy River; at the Muddy River before tackling the next push over Virgin Hill to the Virgin River; at the Virgin River before heading north into Utah, and at Mountain Meadow after leaving the inhospitable Mojave Desert. Clearly, they knew they were looking at a trip of eighty days or more.

As an experienced Mormon Battalion officer and desert traveler, Jefferson Hunt would have recognized that the daily food requirement for each man, in addition to meat, would have been about two pounds of flour or biscuits, potatoes or other easily transported vegetables, sugar, dried fruit, cooking oil or fat, coffee, baking soda and salt and pepper. In addition, each man would be expected to consume about a pound to a pound and a half of meat each day. The food supply for the party would amount to about 3,600 pounds of non-meat products and an additional 2000 pounds of meat. The total food compliment for an eighty-five day trip would approach 6,000 pounds. Considering that the recommended load for a pack animal is about 150 pounds (200 pounds maximum under difficult conditions), the provisions for the travelers alone would have required over forty pack animals.

But their primary reason for making the trip was to carry back seeds and cuttings for use in the next growing season. Every pack animal loaded with provisions was one less animal packed with the needed supplies. We must assume that they were acutely aware of this and did as much as possible to reduce the amount of provisions they would need to take in order to pack more supplies to their final destination. Using cattle on the hoof as a traveling supply of meat would have cut their need for pack animals for provisions by half, and by increasing their diet of meat, in lieu of other foods, they could lower their need for provisions even more. In addition, the cattle were the only readily available supply of meat in California—unlike in the Eastern and Central United States where pork products such as bacon were frequently taken as provisions. It is quite probable that the bulls were taken expressly for the purpose of providing food on the trip and that it was never intended that most of them would reach Salt Lake. They would be butchered as needed along the trail. This method of providing fresh meat was commonly used for decades by cowboys on cattle drives and by emigrants traveling to California and Oregon and other Western places.

Most likely, they butchered bulls when necessary, but resorted to also butchering cows when they weakened and could not continue. As for the Indians along the route, subsequent accounts from nearly all the Western trails indicate that they highly prized the fresh meat provided by cattle and would take the opportunity to bargain for animals, or would steal them, or, if all else failed, would wound or kill an animal so that it would be abandoned. Providing some animals to the Indians along the route was part of the cost of passage through their lands. Harold Schindler, Porter Rockwell's biographer, criticized the Hunt party for losing so many animals while Rockwell, who followed in another party that contained mules but no cattle, lost no animals (Schindler 1993, 174). However, John Riser, a member of that party, stated that Indians stole "in one Haule [sic] from us Eleven Horses and mules" (Bigler and Bagley 2000, 399).

That Jefferson Hunt and his party reached their destination with half of the cattle they began with is a credit to their efforts and not a derogatory comment about their abilities.

On the return trip, Jefferson Hunt carefully evaluated the trail the group traveled. As we shall see, he was able to give a detailed and accurate description of the route in the Summer of 1849. He reported the long water-less stretches across the Mojave, accurately judged the miles between watering holes and amounts of available stock feed at the various springs and streams. He described with care the difficulty and amount of time taken in crossing over obstacles such as Virgin Hill between the Muddy and the Virgin. He noted the ample sources of feed where livestock could be rested and fed at places like Resting Spring, Las Vegas and Mountain Meadow. He evaluated the attitudes of the Indians along the route in places like the Muddy and along the Wasatch Mountains in Utah.

He was also careful to note which locations were likely to support a colonization effort, such as Las Vegas, the Santa Clara River area, and the well-watered valleys south of Utah Lake. Hunt also observed the location of other natural resources such as timber, firewood and mineral deposits. At Iron Springs, he noted the location of the iron ore deposits that led to the naming of the springs. And he considered the ramifications of taking the route through difficult terrain such as the dry, heavily timbered, rocky and steep stretch between the Beaver River and Paragonah. It's quite likely that he also considered alternative routes that might avoid some of these difficulties.

The Mormon Volunteers under the command of Captain Daniel Davis, the remaining unit from the Mormon Battalion, was discharged in San Diego on March 14, 1848. At that time, they were paid off and given cattle in lieu of rations to sustain them on the trip East. Orrin Porter Rockwell, who had remained in California, and likely delivered the High Council's letters to the Volunteers and Jesse Hunter, was involved in a minor escapade worth noting prior to his return to Salt Lake City.

Thomas O. Larkin, who for years was the United States Consul in California, and who from 1847 through 1849 served as naval agent and store-keeper for the United States, kept copies of his correspondence and summed up the incident in a letter. On April 14th he wrote to B.R. Buckelew, a printer that he knew, the following:

"Much excitement exists at the Angeles and San Diego in consequence of the circulation of false gold coin, purporting to
be from the New Orleans Mint. It is supposed the pieces were
brought from the Salt Lake and issued immediately after Major
Rich paid off the troops at the South. These Mormons who came
in with the last company from the Salt Lake are arrested in San
Diego for the circulation of this coin. There was a quantity of
it found in their possession" (Hammond and Larkin 1960, Vol.
VII, 225).

Another account written in a letter dated April 2, 1848, by William A.
Kennedy, a member of the New York Volunteers, to his friend James Ferguson, the former Battalion Sergeant Major, then living in Northern California,
provided addition information. Kennedy names the participants as Lieutenants Cyrus Canfield and Ruel Barrus, Sergeant Samuel Myers and Porter
Rockwell (Bigler and Bagley 2000, 404-405). Governor Mason instructed Dr.
Stephen C. Foster, alcalde of Los Angeles and one of Cooke's guides with the
Battalion, to conduct a trial. Rockwell was apparently released before any trial
took place. Only Barrus was convicted, and his sentence was reduced to one
year at hard labor by Governor Mason (Bigler and Bagley 2000, 400-407).

Within a week of the arrival of the Boyle/Rockwell party in Salt Lake
City, the counterfeiting issue came before the High Council. On June 10th, a
charge was made against Rufus Beach for sending counterfeit money to California, but the case was postponed until the High Council "saw fit to call it up
again" (Salt Lake High Council Minute Book, June 10, 1848). The following
day Patty Sessions wrote that Rockwell appeared before the congregation at
church services (Sessions, June 11, 1848). The *Salt Lake Stake Minutes* give
further detail about what happened. Apostle John Taylor criticized those who
sent and distributed the counterfeit coin in California. Rockwell then spoke
and essentially said that he had learned from his mistake. But then he said that
no one had been hurt by his action; he hadn't passed any of the money; and
that he should be treated the same as in California (Salt Lake Stake Minutes,
June 11, 1848). In typical Rockwell fashion, he showed no repentance.

Many of the Mormon Volunteers discharged in San Diego on March 14th decided to go directly to Salt Lake City over the Southern route they had heard about from Porter Rockwell and James Shaw. They left San Diego on March 21st and arrived at Williams' Ranch on March 31st. They purchased supplies there and in Los Angeles, and with Rockwell and Shaw acting as guides, began the trip to Salt Lake on April 12, 1848. Under the command of Henry G. Boyle, the group consisted of thirty-five people and 135 mules and horses. Most significantly, it included one wagon, that of Captain Daniel Davis, his wife, Susan, and young son, Daniel Jr. (Bigler and Bagley 2000, 397). Just as the Hunt party was the first to take cattle over the trail, the Boyle party would be the first to take a wagon over the route to Salt Lake City. Their demonstration that a wagon could make the journey was very significant.

While Captain Davis' Mormon wagon was the first to travel the entire route between Southern California and Salt Lake City, it probably wasn't the first to travel from Utah Lake and cross the difficult mountains and deserts of the Mojave. That honor may have belonged to wagons in the party of Isaac Slover and William Pope in 1837-38. Antoine Leroux, the mountain man and guide, wrote to Senator Thomas Hart Benton in 1853, that they had used wagons (Robinson 2005, 177; Hafen and Hafen 1954, 181). Perhaps Jefferson Hunt had learned from Leroux that wagons could traverse the Old Spanish Trail since the written record did not appear until after 1849.

Because of the number of pack animals in the party, it is quite likely that they also obtained seeds and cuttings for planting upon their return. It is possible, although not confirmed in any account, that they carried with them the news of the discovery of gold in Northern California. There had been ample time for the Mormons in the north to get the word to their brethren in the south.

Two brief accounts of this trip exist, one by Boyle and the other by John Riser, another Battalion veteran (Bigler and Bagley 2000, 397-400). In addition, Thomas Morris, also a member of the group, made a few brief references to the trip in his later journal of an 1849-50 trip along the trail (Morris 1849-1850.) They arrived at Salt Lake City on June 5, 1848; the trip took fifty-five days, ten days longer that the outbound trip. Rockwell, also having previously been over the route, probably used the same strategy as Hunt to rest and feed the animals before and after difficult drives. The difference between the speed of travel of horses and mules versus cattle accounts for the thirty days' difference in return travel time between the two groups.

According to the *Journal History of the LDS Church*, they traveled:

> "across the Mohave Desert to Las Vegas, up the Muddy Valley and across the Escalante Desert to Beaver Creek and onward to Chalk Creek (Fillmore, Utah); thence to Salt Creek (Nephi) to Spanish Fork River and Timpanogas River (Provo) thence via American Creek to Great Salt Lake City" (Journal History, June 5, 1848).

In this description "Muddy Valley" refers not to the valley of the Muddy River in Nevada, but to the Santa Clara River in Utah. (Dr. Steven Heath, personal communication). Descriptive names given to features such as streams often changed. Many early accounts describe today's Muddy River in Nevada as the "Far Muddy" implying that another stream closer to Salt Lake City was also named "Muddy." A number of accounts of the time also refer to the present Coal Creek that flows through Cedar City as the "Muddy" or "First Muddy." One such account is that given by Jefferson Hunt in his speech to the immigrants on August 20, 1849 (General Church Minutes, August 20, 1849).

John Riser's account of the trip says that: "Passing up into the Utah Basin from the Santa Clara River, and through little Salt Lake valley we found the Indians very numerous and troublesome nearly the whole way" (Bigler and Bagley 2000, 398). This account seemingly implies that they followed what essentially was either the normal route of the Old Spanish Trail or the Fremont route that went through Little Salt Lake Valley. However, Dr. Steven Heath, who has done extensive research on the Southern Utah trails, believes that the Boyle party followed the Escalante Desert and not the Old Spanish Trail route to the Beaver River (Heath 1995). Rockwell and Shaw, knowing the difficulty in crossing the Black Mountains south of Beaver, especially with a wagon, very likely elected to take a different route for about fifty miles.

The accounts of the Rockwell trip are sufficiently confusing on the names to render a precise reading of the route impossible. However, Jefferson Hunt's statements in 1849 point to the fact that Rockwell and his party traveled through the Escalante Desert and, thus, bypassed the Little Salt Lake Valley and the Black Mountains south of Beaver.

From a point very near where the Jefferson Hunt Monument commemorates the splitting of the 1849 wagon train, which is the subject of a later chapter, and near the road connecting the present Utah communities of Enterprise and Newcastle, Rockwell and the others could see nearly the entire length of the Escalante Desert extending to the northeast. From his experience on the southbound trip, Rockwell knew that there was a twenty-five mile waterless stretch that took them up and over the Black Mountains south of the Beaver River. He was aware that it was a very rough and rocky road and was heavily timbered, and that this would make it difficult and time-consuming to clear a road for the wagon. On the other hand, he also knew that his horses and mules could easily do a forced fifty mile drive—or less depending on the availability of water—across the Escalante Desert to the Beaver River, which he had seen flowing westward. It is also quite probable that Rockwell scouted a portion of the Escalante route and determined that it was very doable for his party.

Based on his information regarding the known route and the alternative through the Escalante Desert, it is most likely that he chose to pursue the enticing Escalante Desert trail, thereby avoiding the difficult pass over the Black Mountains. Earlier, his route east of the Muddy River in Nevada and toward the Virgin River had taken him over Mormon Mesa and over the lip of Virgin Hill. There was no road for the wagon and only a difficult trail for the pack animals. At this point, the party lowered the wagon over the rim of the mesa using multiple teams of animals and ropes and chains. But the Black Mountain problem was not so easily surmounted. To go over that route would have required cutting and clearing trees and using multiple teams over the summit.

The Rockwell/Boyle party probably followed the known Old Spanish Trail north from the Jefferson Hunt Monument, past today's Newcastle, and along the west side of the Antelope Range. Where the trail turned east toward Iron Springs (west of Cedar City and Enoch), they continued to the northeast and into the broad, flat, and mostly waterless Escalante Desert. Thirty miles or so northeast of that point, they turned eastward and met the Beaver River somewhere near present-day Minersville, Utah. Had they stopped at Antelope Springs, the distance from there to Minersville would have been a little over forty miles without water.

From there they continued east along the Beaver for fifteen miles or so until they intersected the known trail near today's community of Greenville, several miles west of Beaver, Utah. They followed the trail northward to Salt Lake City. With only horses and mules (no cattle or oxen) and with ample water at either end of the route, they could have easily made this forty or fifty mile journey. If their travels put them on the Escalante Desert during the period between May 13th and May 22nd, which is very likely, they would have had adequate moonlight to assist them in night travel and could have made the forced march in less than twenty-four hours.

Since Jefferson Hunt knew most, if not all, of those on this trip, he undoubtedly heard multiple accounts of the journey and of their success in avoiding the difficult Black Mountain section of the Trail. And even more importantly, he heard confirmation that a wagon had completed the trail. The road from Salt Lake City to Los Angeles was now open for wagon travel.

Jefferson Hunt, in a little less than two years, had accomplished an astounding feat. He had traveled more than 5,000 miles in the American West and had been on all three of the major trails to California. He had become an accomplished road builder, explorer and trailblazer, had demonstrated his leadership along the trails and had established solid relationships for himself and his Church with citizens and military officers in California. There were very few men in the West who could boast as much, and nearly all of them were either mountain men or military officers. And Hunt was the only one in Salt Lake City.

Finally, while any aspirations Jefferson Hunt may have had about leading another Mormon Battalion had been dashed, he had gained a good understanding of the value of California and its productive land for both himself and his Church. He had established the relationships that could benefit the

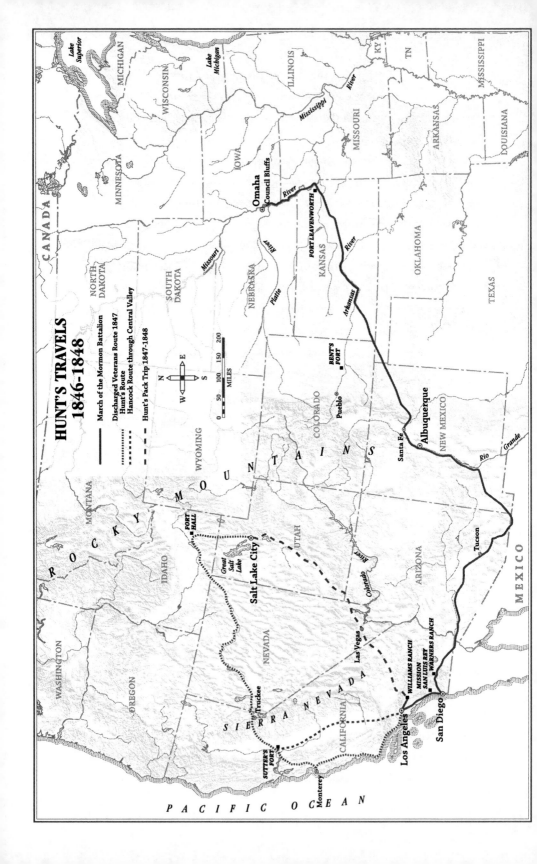

Saints and the Church if a move to California was to be made. All he had
to do now was to persuade Brigham Young and the apostles of the value of
California.

Chapter 15

Interlude

For the first time in two years, the Hunt family was reunited and settled in one place. In the new city of Salt Lake City, Jefferson Hunt could get about the normal duties of civilized life, such as it might be on the frontier. Presumably, Gilbert, who arrived with the El Pueblo detachment very shortly after the Pioneer Company, began building the Hunt family home and preparing the ground for the family crops. Marshall Hunt, who arrived with his father, likely continued the family's work, while Hunt and Gilbert traveled to Southern California.

The home was in the southeast corner of the old fort, now Pioneer Park in Salt Lake City. The Hunt family was not too busy to extend a welcoming hand to newcomers, and hosted George W. Bean and his sister, Sarah Ann, when they arrived in October 1847. Bean was able to make his own home over a several week period with the help of the Hunts (Bean 1992, 54). The Beans would also be neighbors of the Hunts at Utah Lake; two of Bean's sons would eventually marry two of Hunt's granddaughters.

The seeds and cuttings provided by the trip to Southern California were distributed and planted. As May progressed, all looked good for a fruitful season that would support the Pioneers, as well as the flood of Saints headed to the Great Basin from Winter Quarters and beyond. Many of the Veterans were even surprised to find that rains were frequent and that they did not have to irrigate the crops as they expected. Then about the end of May and the first week of June, things changed. First, several nights of abnormally low temperatures drove the temperature below freezing and damaged some of the crops. Then immediately after that occurred one of the most fabled incidents in the early history of Salt Lake City.

A letter written on June 9, 1848, to Brigham Young (now heading Westward from Winter Quarters) by John Smith, Charles Rich and John Young contains the essence of that occurrence:

> "As to our crops, there has been a large amount of spring crops put in, and they were doing well till within a few days. The crickets [locusts] had done a considerable damage to both wheat and corn which has discouraged some, but there is plenty left if we can save it for a few days. The sea gulls have come in large flocks from the lake and sweep the crickets as they go. It seems the hand of the Lord is in our favor" (Journal History of the Church, June 9, 1848).

In another letter written to Brigham Young on June 21st, the same writers add more detail:

> "The brethren have been busy for sometime watering their wheat and as far as it is done the wheat looks well, and the heads are long and large. The crickets are still quite numerous and busy eating, but between the gulls and our efforts and the growth of our crops we shall raise much grain in spite of them. Our vines, beans and peas are mostly destroyed by frost and the crickets; but many of us have more seed and we are now busy replanting and feel assured that we will still raise many pumpkins, melons, beans, etc. Some of our corn has been destroyed, but many large fields look very well and the corn now is growing very fast, as the days and nights are warm, and on the whole we think there is as much good corn growing as we can till and irrigate, though we are still planting early corn" (Journal History of the Church, June 21, 1848).

The threat of famine caused by the locusts was averted and the story went on to legendary status. But in the end, hard work, good planning and the expedition to California provided the bounty needed to sustain the fledgling Salt Lake City past its first critical year of existence.

As the Spring weather improved, the great Mormon migration Westward from Winter Quarters began. By pre-arrangement, it had been decided that the Saints in Salt Lake City would send as many wagons and teams of oxen as possible Eastward to assist the migration. In addition, there had been little communication between Salt Lake City and Winter Quarters during the Winter months. With news from California from both the Hunt and Rockwell parties and the Great Salt Lake, the High Council took steps to communicate with Young in the on-coming migration.

The June 9, 1848, letter to Brigham Young from Salt Lake Counselors Smith, Rich and Young mentioned above begins by saying: "Brethren, as Capt. Hunt and Lieutenant Rosecranze [sic] start to meet you in the morning, it seems good to us to send a few lines to let you know how we get along" (Journal History of the Church, June 9, 1848). From this we can infer that Jefferson Hunt and George Rosecrans were beginning a trip East to meet the migration. However, there is no indication in the record that they ever reached them. Brigham Young and Thomas Bullock, his secretary, were careful to log all important events, and the arrival of Hunt at the camps would certainly have been significant. However, there is no notation of their arrival in either the records of the Church or in the journals of those with the migration. It would be reasonable, therefore, to assume that they never carried the mail Eastward.

The June 21st letter is a different matter. Again, the letter is to Brigham and the Twelve from Smith, Rich and Young in Salt Lake and begins by saying " . . . we again send you a few lines by Orrin P. Rockwell, who starts to-day, in company with Captain Davis and a few others" (Journal History of the Church, June 21, 1848). This letter appears to be an update of the earlier June 9th letter in that it doesn't recount the full story of the "crickets" and gulls, but updates the current status of the crops. Additionally, they state that they "expect more teams will start soon to meet you." This letter expands on content of the June 9th letter, but does not seem to replace it. It appears quite possible that the June 9th letter was carried back, either by Hunt and Rosecrans or by someone else, but there is no record of it having been received or its contents read or discussed.

On the other hand, the June 21ˢᵗ letter was delivered by Porter Rockwell to Brigham Young on July 20ᵗʰ at a camp near Fort Laramie. Thomas Bullock and others recorded that Young read the letter to the camp on July 21ˢᵗ.

Earlier on May 22, 1848, John Taylor sent Young a letter indicating that the Saints in the Salt Lake Valley were sending wagons and teams with a group that included Young's nephews John Y. Greene and Joseph W. Young. This group, with eighteen wagons, arrived at Young's camp near Ancient Ruins Bluffs (north of present-day Sidney, Nebraska) on July 11ᵗʰ, nine days before Porter Rockwell and his party, traveling without wagons or oxen, arrived. They also had with them the official correspondence from Colonel Stevenson and Governor Mason regarding the recruitment of a new battalion, as well as letters from Isaac Williams and Jesse Hunter (Journal History of the Church, July 12, 1848).

Taking advantage of the arrival of Greene, Young and the wagons, Brigham Young wrote an epistle on July 17ᵗʰ to the Saints at Salt Lake and instructed Greene, Benjamin Rolfe and Cyrenus Taylor to take it to Salt Lake City, along with 259 letters plus newspapers and other documents for information. They probably departed on July 18ᵗʰ and shortly thereafter encountered Rockwell and his party, who hastened the short distance to the camp. Young's letter outlined the events at Winter Quarters, the happenings at two Conferences and referred to the arrival of mail from Salt Lake in December 1847, and again on May 2, 1848. He also asked for additional teams and wagons to leave Salt Lake to meet the migration about August 20ᵗʰ at the crossing of the Green River (in Wyoming.) He suggested they include one wagonload of salt.

Similarly, the diaries of John D. Lee and Heber Kimball do not mention either Jefferson Hunt or the June 9ᵗʰ letter. Thus, in all of these notations about the arrival and departure of mail and of personages from Salt Lake City, there is no mention of Hunt or of the contents of the June 9ᵗʰ letter. Again, from this we can infer that Hunt did not make a trip back to the migration in 1848.

During the Summer and Fall of 1848, there was much activity in the Valley of the Great Salt Lake and along the trails leading to it. Several thousand acres had been planted, and the crops were successfully harvested. Building continued in the new community, and a grist and sawmill were completed. From the East, thousands of emigrants were on the trail to Salt Lake from Winter Quarters and other places. And from the West, many of the remaining Battalion veterans began the trek toward their new homes in the Great Basin.

In January 1847, Brigham Young had his only divine revelation as the successor to Joseph Smith, and that dealt with the organization of the Westward migration. In Section 136 of the Doctrine and Covenants, the organization of the migration was spelled out. Several companies would be formed and then organized into "hundreds," "fifties," and "tens"—each with a captain. On the trail, Young further organized the order of travel by spacing the companies out to simplify travel and conserve their resources. Young reached Salt Lake on September 20, 1848. Other arriving companies followed closely behind. Once he returned to the Valley, Young continued to organize the new city by stepping in and giving instructions and directions as if he had never left. Allotments of land were made, work was assigned, and work began on the Church infrastructure. Brigham Young was poised to show more of the managerial, organizational and administrative genius that would distinguish his tenure as President of the LDS Church.

Many of the remaining Battalion veterans and some Mormons from the ship *Brooklyn* began the trip to their new homes in Salt Lake by pioneering a wagon road over the Sierra Nevada Mountains at Carson Pass. In spite to the tragic deaths of three of their advance scouts in an Indian attack, they were successful. With them they brought not only news of the wonders of California, but gold that would soon be put to use in strengthening the Church. They also brought with them two cannons they had purchased from John Sutter for $512 after raising the money from within their ranks, and from several non-Mormons. The veterans began arriving in Salt Lake about the same time as Brigham Young, and continued to arrive well into November.

These same months were also eventful for Jefferson Hunt. His wife, Matilda, gave birth to their first child, a girl named Sophronia Elizabeth, on August 27th. The young men of the family, Gilbert, Marshall, John (now sixteen) and Peter Nease were busy with their assignments. For the Hunts, the Summer and Fall of 1848 was a peaceful interlude with little travel and time for domestic duties.

Hosea Stout, the diligent recorder of events and head of the police in the Valley, mentioned the Hunt family on several occasions. As more people began arriving in the Salt Lake Valley, livestock became a troublesome issue when they got loose in the fields or ran astray. Some young men would gather them up and then return them to the owners for a reward. Stout recorded on October 11th that Marshall Hunt, William Boren and Jesse Earl brought in cattle for a reward, but that they were suspected of "freeing" them first. Marshall and the others confessed to doing exactly that, and Stout required them to "acknowledge the same to President Rich & upon their promise to do better let them go" (Brooks 1964, 333).

Stout and his police were assigned to enforcing the stray animal laws passed by the High Council. Each day, the rounded up strays would be redeemed to their owners for fifty cents each in an effort to curtail the stray problem. On October 21st, Stout recorded that:

> "Capt Hunt whose oxen were taken out of the fields today, when he came for them swelled very largely denouncing the law & swore he would send some of us to eternity if we put any of his cattle in again &c" (Brooks 1964, Vol. 2, 333-334).

Jefferson Hunt was not afraid to express his feelings when angry. The following day, the High Council repealed the stray cattle law and instituted a new procedure in which any damage done by stray animals would become a matter for the courts to resolve.

Throughout December 1848, the weather was cold and snowy; not only did it snow frequently, it didn't melt. As the Winter progressed, it became harder and harder for the livestock to find food under the snow, and there was growing concern about their fate. To this was added the threat to livestock and future crops by the wildlife in the Valley: wolves, foxes, coyotes, minks, bobcats, mountain lions, bears, eagles, ravens, owls, hawks, crows, and even magpies were threatening their sustenance. To counter this threat, Brigham Young acted decisively.

He appointed John D. Lee and John Pack to lead two teams of men to act as hunters and compete against each other in an eradication program. On December 23, 1848, Lee and Pack met with Thomas Bullock, Young's clerk, to formulate the rules and select the men for each team. Each animal was given a score: a raven was worth one, a wolf was worth ten, a bear fifty, and so forth. At the end of the competition, the team with the lowest score would treat the winning team to a feast. Jefferson Hunt was selected to be on Lee's team. Perhaps some of the animosity of two years before was forgotten. The competition began on Christmas Day and continued until March 1, 1849. The thirty-seven men in Lee's team bested the forty-seven in Pack's. The total kill included two bears, 783 wolves (and coyotes,) and 1,026 ravens, and was regarded as a great success in protecting their food supply (Journal History of the Church, March 5, 1849).

Some thought that there might be less snow on the ground in Utah Valley to the south. On January 6, 1849, a party of thirteen, including Amasa Lyman, Porter Rockwell and Dimick Huntington was organized to travel to Utah Valley and determine the feasibility of moving the cattle, and to assess the potential for establishing a fishery at Utah Lake. They reported back on January 20th that there was also snow on the ground in Utah Valley, and that there was no advantage to moving the cattle. But they found that it was an inviting place to settle.

Brigham Young was very busy during the first three months of 1849. All along the frontier, currency was in very short supply and, accordingly, the Mormons were forced to create their own money supply for their own use. To authenticate the money, Brigham had to sign each bill. A system of weights and measures was instituted, and a tax system for community infrastructure was established. Public projects such as a bridge over the Jordan River were begun. The Nauvoo Legion was re-instituted to provide military protection against marauding Indians and whatever other enemies might find their way to Utah. Indians from the Utah Valley stole cattle and had to be chased down and punished. The new city had to be surveyed and land allotted to residents.

Citizens were encouraged to develop needed businesses such as a tannery and foundry. The seeds of government for the State of Deseret were sown when a convention was held; a state constitution was drafted, and officials were elected.

In addition to these civil matters, Church matters also were attended to. Four new members filled vacancies in the Twelve Apostles. The city was divided into nineteen wards and construction was begun on meeting houses. Planning commenced for the construction of new buildings in Temple Square. But most ominously, the harsh Winter with is extensive snowfall caused some of the new residents to question whether they should remain in Salt Lake Valley. That, combined with the news of gold in California, caused some to prepare to leave and head West with Spring. Young was faced with a new challenge—defections of the faithful.

All in all, Brigham Young faced the tasks with determination and energy with his magnificent skills of organization and management. Within six months of his return to the Valley, Salt Lake was transformed from a frontier village to a thriving city set 700 miles from its closest neighbor.

Right at the same time as the constitution for the State of Deseret was being drafted, the council (at Brigham Young's direction) voted to establish a colony in Utah Valley. This decision taken on March 10, 1849, directed that thirty men and their families be sent to this new location on the Provo River near Utah Lake about forty-five miles south of Salt Lake City. Their assignment was to build a fort for protection, establish farms, fish the lake and streams, and work on civilizing the local Indians. This colony became known as Fort Utah. Eventually it was moved a short distance to the east and renamed Provo after the river—named after the trapper Etienne Provost, who was one of the first to visit this part of the Great Basin.

On March 17th, the names of thirty-three men were read as the new settlers of the Utah Valley. They soon set out and their families joined them shortly after that. The elected leaders of the new colony were John Higbee as President and Isaac Higbee and Dimick Huntington, a veteran of the Mormon

Battalion, as his counselors. Jefferson Hunt was one of the settlers. Just as he had at Far West and Nauvoo before, and would be the case in San Bernardino, Huntsville and Oxford in the future, Hunt chose not to live in the main city of Mormonism, but in one of the more distant settlements.

Because of the previous hostilities with the Utes that inhabited the Utah Valley, the first order of business was to build a fort. Homes were constructed in a square with their back walls forming the outside of the compound. A military unit was organized with Jefferson Hunt, an obvious choice because of his prior experience in the Nauvoo Legion and the Battalion, as commander. All able-bodied men and older boys were made part of the militia unit. In the center of the fort, on top of an old mound (probably an ancient Indian midden), a structure was built to house one of the cannons brought back by the veterans from Sutter's. This impressive gun was periodically fired to impress watching Utes of the power of their new neighbors.

The location of the fort provided ample farmland that could be easily irrigated from the Provo River and other nearby streams. As Spring arrived, the settlers once again broke the land to plant crops for their food supply for the ensuing year. But the first order of business was to contact the Utes to establish peaceful relations and to simultaneously expand the fort. Work began about the first week of April. The effort gained urgency when Brigham Young received a letter from Jim Bridger at Bridger's Fort telling of threats by the Utes to attack the Utah Valley settlement. Reportedly the Ute chiefs, Old Elk and Wakara, were "badly disposed towards the whites, in consequence of some difficulties and fighting with Americans" (Journal History of the Church, April 17, 1849).

The following day, Brigham Young sent that information south to Fort Utah "advising them to speedily complete their fort" and to make other preparations in case of trouble (Journal History of the Church, April 18, 1849). One day later, April 19th, Dimick Huntington, who subsequently became well known as an Indian translator and negotiator, wrote to Brigham Young that there was no sign of hostilities between the Utes and the settlers but that there had been some trouble between Ute bands. Jefferson Hunt carried the letter to Salt Lake City and provided additional details to Young. In addition, Huntington asked Young to send rifle cartridges (paper packets containing both gun

powder and a ball) to the settlers since they discovered they were short. He
stated that Hunt would be able to bring them back on his return trip (Journal
History of the Church, April 19, 1849).

Sometime during the six months between Brigham Young's arrival
in Salt Lake City and Jefferson Hunt's departure for Fort Utah, the two men
met, probably on several occasions, to discuss the events of the preceding
two years. There is no record of any such meetings or conversations, but subsequent events can give us some indications of the content. Hunt may have
discussed his side of the events during the conflict within the Battalion, especially since Young earlier had heard the version from Levi Hancock and John
D. Lee, among others. In any case, Young knew that he could still count on
Hunt for difficult missions.

Hunt also told him in some detail about the possible locations for future settlement that he had seen. Specifically, he no doubt told him about the
area along the Gila River and about the areas in Southern California. Hunt
also told him about the route he developed between Salt Lake and Southern
California, and the potential it offered as access between an ocean port and
their new inland city. It is very likely that Hunt pointed out that travel time
and distance to and from the Pacific Coast was much shorter than from the
landings along the Missouri River to Salt Lake. At that time, virtually all of the
migration, including converts from England who sailed to New Orleans and
then up the Mississippi and Missouri Rivers, traveled overland from the East.
Hunt's route to the Pacific would cut time, and possibly expenses, for both
people and goods en route to Salt Lake.

Since Isaac Williams' rancho was at the gateway to the Pacific and was
a lush and productive area, Hunt told him about the advantages of securing a
colony or settlement there or in the immediate area. He'd had some preliminary talks with Williams about the possibility of selling the land necessary for
a colony and discussed this opportunity with Young. In addition, Hunt told
the president about the warm reception he and the rest of the Battalion had
gotten in California, and about the reputation that they gained with both resi-

dents and governmental officials. He possibly raised again the issue of a new battalion, even though the war was over, and received the same answer of no.

Finally, Hunt informed Young of the condition and features of the southern route to California. He would have described the warmer and fertile valleys of Southern Utah and informed Young of the specimens of iron ore he had seen at Iron Springs near present day Cedar City. Soon, Young used this information to begin his own exploration and settlement of Southern Utah and California. Whether or not Hunt had begun his tour with the Battalion as Young's emissary to scout out new locations and opportunities, the information he brought back would help shape the Mormon's expansion over the next several years.

While the Mormons were getting settled in the Valley of the Great Salt Lake and Jefferson Hunt and his friends were settling in Utah Valley, several thousand Mormons were beginning the trek Westward to their new homes. But more significantly to the future of the nation, tens of thousands of others were massing along the Missouri River to begin the great race to California—the Gold Rush of 1849. By the middle of the Summer, thousands passed through Salt Lake City. The heretofore isolated community of the Saints found itself in the middle of the greatest movement of people in the history of the United States.

The '49ers came from all over the country. Some were families that had sold all of their property and put everything into one or two wagons to take West. Others were men who were leaving their families behind until they made their fortune; many were young men out on the greatest adventure of their lives. Some began alone or with one or two other family units. Others organized themselves into companies that usually ranged in size between ten and twenty-five men, agreeing to remain together until they reached the gold fields or even later. Still others pooled their money and outfitted themselves into a traveling company that shared wagons and stock and agreed to stick together for mutual safety and security. They came from cities in New York and along the East Coast or from small communities in Mississippi, or Georgia, and Virginia, or from farming areas in Illinois, Ohio or Iowa. They came from everywhere, including other countries, and they had one goal—to get to California as quickly as possible.

Before the '49ers even began their long trek, thousands of others had already arrived in California. They mostly came by ship from the East Coast, from Chile, from the Sandwich Islands (Hawaii,) or even from as far away as Australia. Others came from Mexico or Oregon, and thousands left the coastal cities of California such as Los Angeles, San Diego, Monterey and San Francisco for the Mother Lode. Many of these men had already been mining and prospecting for a year or more by the time '49ers began their trek. Many of the good claims had already been taken and in many areas, the readily available gold had already been removed. To those just beginning the long road West, time was of the essence. They had to get to California safely, and they had to get there soon or they might miss out on getting their share of the fabulous riches.

Most of the '49ers left from the frontier towns of Independence, St. Joseph or Council Bluffs and planned to take the Northern or Humboldt Route. Their goal was to travel to the Platte River and then follow essentially the same route taken by the Mormon Pioneers through Nebraska and Wyoming. Some decided to take the well-known route north of the Great Salt Lake to Fort Hall, while others decided to go first to the new city of Salt Lake. They all then expected to follow the Humboldt River across Nevada, then cross over the Sierra Nevada at one of several well-known passes and arrive at the gold fields on the western slope before the Winter snows began.

Most of the '49ers formed wagon trains with others. But since different outfits could travel at different speeds and conflicts often developed between members of the trains, individuals and groups often broke off or were left behind. As a consequence, traveling groups of wagons frequently realigned themselves. Only the small groups who set out as an organized company from the same community sometimes made it to the end of the trail as a coherent unit. Many of the animals and some of the people who began the trip died along the way. Wagons that began with a full load of family possessions often had to be lightened. The Plains and Western deserts were littered with discarded possessions. Sometimes the wagons themselves had to be abandoned and people continued on foot or with pack animals. The groups that reached the Sierra Nevada did not look like the same group that began: sickness, deserts, heat, cold and Indians all took their toll.

Many of the '49ers left us accounts of their travels. Some kept journals and others wrote reminiscences in later years. Some journals were detailed throughout the trek; others became more labored or stopped completely as conditions worsened toward the end of the trail. From these accounts we are often able to piece together a sense of the difficulties faced by the thousands heading, they hoped, for a new prosperous life in California. One of the best accounts was written by William Lewis Manly and is entitled *Death Valley in '49*. First published in 1894, this book has gone through multiple editions and is readily available today. Manly's story is of the first group of non-Indians to enter Death Valley and is filled with accounts of hardship, heroism, tenacity and hope.

Manly was a twenty-nine-year-old who had lived in Vermont, Michigan and Wisconsin and worked as a woodcutter, professional hunter and miner. He was one of the tens of thousands with gold fever who decided in the Spring of 1849 to join the Gold Rush to California. Manly had hoped to meet and travel with his friend Asabel (or Asahel) Bennett, who had agreed to take Manly's goods in his wagons. Unfortunately, they did not meet at the Missouri River as hoped, and Manly signed on as a teamster with Charles Dallas, who was heading West with five wagons. Another of the teamsters with Dallas was John Rogers, who shared the following months' adventures with Manly.

When the traveling party crossed over South Pass in Wyoming, Manly discovered that it was too late to attempt to reach California before the Winter snows set in, and that Dallas would most likely discharge them in Salt Lake City. The prospect of being stranded in the Mormon town and delaying their arrival in the gold fields until the following year was not good news for Manly and the other teamsters. After some discussion and virtually no knowledge of the consequences, Manly and six other of the young men set out in an old ferry boat to float down the Green River to its confluence with the Colorado River, and then on to California. This ill-advised attempt predated John Wesley Powell's great exploration of the canyons of the Colorado River by twenty years.

Very few men had ever gone on the river before, and no one had made it through the Grand Canyon. The seven quickly discovered that the rivers and canyons were much different than those in the East. Here they found that the rocks that fell from the cliffs above or were washed down the tributaries formed dangerous rapids and falls that were difficult or impossible to navigate. The small ferry boat they began their journey with was soon smashed to pieces; Manly supervised the construction of several makeshift canoes out of tree trunks. The further they went, the more difficult the river became. At one point in Flaming Gorge, they found William Ashley's 1825 inscription on a rock. Further down, they found a deserted camp and a note from some others who also tried to float the river, but had given up and were going cross-country toward Salt Lake City. Thus, Manly and his small band joined the ranks of the very few who had ever tried to float down the Green River.

After several weeks of travel, they noticed an Indian camp on the banks and landed to see if they could get more information. In one of the more remarkable coincidences in Western history, it was the small camp of the one man who could most help them—Chief Wakara. They camped with the friendly Wakara and, using sign language and a rough map drawn in the sand and piled rocks, he told them about where they had been and what lay ahead along the river. Manly's detailed description of this conversation demonstrates that Wakara's knowledge extended well above the point where they entered the Green River at the trail crossing in Western Wyoming and extended well below where they were on the Green. Wakara showed them that he clearly knew and understood the rapids and cliffs that they had already experienced and that even worse cataracts lay ahead. Worse yet, the chief told them of very hostile Indians ahead. He made it clear that if they continued their journey along the river, they would die. Historian Michael Kane has determined that this meeting occurred at the ford of the Green River, just upstream from present-day Green River, Utah (Kane, 2008.) After studying the account of travels of two of Manly's companions, the author concurs with this assessment.

Accordingly, Manly and four others decided to travel overland from the Green River to Salt Lake City; the other two men initially decided to continue with Wakara, but eventually changed their minds and went over the Uinta Mountains to Fort Bridger. Manly and the four men traded Wakara some clothes for two ponies to use as pack animals and set out following the chief's directions to the Mormon city. Nine days later, they descended into the Valley of Utah Lake, where Manly found his friend Asahel Bennett. The river adventure would have been an adventure of a lifetime for anyone. However, in light of his later adventures in Death Valley, the Green River trip is hardly a footnote in Manly's history. Only in 1869, two decades later, would Major John Wesley Powell fill in the last major gap in the geography of America by completing his exploration of the Colorado River through the Grand Canyon.

The best of intentions and planning didn't always hold together the emigrating companies. Personality conflicts, disagreements over the best route to follow, differing rates of travel, adequacy of supplies, equipment or livestock, and even fear of the unknown ahead took their toll on the solidarity of the companies. Some companies broke up on the eastern reaches of the trail; others near the Green River where a decision had to be made whether to go to Fort Hall on the Northern Route or to the new city of Salt Lake. Many decisions, however, occurred in Salt Lake City itself. There, some believed that the Northern Route was best, while others believed the little known Salt Lake to Los Angeles route was best. Some thought it was best to stop and rest over the Winter, while others were in a hurry to push on. A few, especially those from areas such as Missouri where the Mormons had been persecuted in the past, feared for their safety (with some justification) if they remained among the Mormons.

One case in point was a group of twenty-five men known as the Colony Guard, which had been organized in New York City. At Salt Lake, the group broke up and some went by the Northern Route, others waited to try the Salt Lake/Los Angeles route, and a few even stayed in the city. In another instance, that of the Gruwell family, the adult men traveled the Northern Route while the rest of the family went on the Salt Lake/Los Angeles Route. Jacob Gruwell and one of his brothers were known to many of the Mormons in Salt Lake as mob members who had burned Mormon buildings and crops near Nauvoo. Jacob and at least one of his brothers fled Salt Lake via the Northern Route as soon as they were recognized. The rest of their party, including wives and children, at least twenty-three people, waited to go with their wagons via the Southern Route. This group had to depend on the older children and possibly a third brother to manage the difficult trip ahead. Jefferson Hunt eventually assisted this family on the lower reaches of the trail (Lyman 2004, 47.)

The concern some had about hostilities by the Mormons toward their former enemies in the East was not unfounded. When the Pomeroy brothers from Missouri arrived in Salt Lake City with twenty wagons carrying thirty tons of trade goods bound for California, they were detained and put on trial. Very soon it was discovered that one of them was the same sutler who Jefferson Hunt had permitted to travel with the Battalion on the road to Santa Fe and that he was highly regarded by the veterans. They were immediately released and treated like visiting dignitaries.

Many of the '49ers themselves used the improvised Mormon court system. They sought to rectify internal disagreements with their traveling companions by taking their complaints to justices of the peace for judicial resolution. This process became so extensive that Brigham Young lamented the time and effort that was being taken by Saints in the Valley to resolve issues that had occurred on the trail. Those in the Westward migration were not one big happy family of travelers.

As the emigrants arrived at Salt Lake City in late July and into August, many of them began to fear that they would not successfully pass over the Sierra Nevadas before the snows fell. Failure meant being trapped like the Donner Party. Consequently, many of the '49ers began to question the wisdom of continuing along the Humboldt or Northern Route across Nevada. This concern worsened when reports began to trickle in from eastbound travelers arriving at Fort Hall that cholera was rampant along the Humboldt River. Matters were made worse when word spread of conditions along the terrible Forty Mile Desert at the western end of the trail before the Sierras. They learned that many had abandoned their wagons and were continuing on the remaining 150 miles on foot. So much of the livestock had died along the desert that travelers had to skirt the dead carcasses. In some instances, people learning of the conditions ahead turned around and returned to Fort Hall for sanctuary or traveled to Salt Lake City to winter.

Cephas Arms, a farmer from Knox County, Illinois, who was a leader of the Knox County Company of '49ers, kept a journal and sent many letters to his hometown newspaper. In Salt Lake City on August 13, 1849, he recorded that an "emigrant has just arrived here to spend the winter, from Fort Hall. He gives a sad account of the emigrants on that road which is enough to make the stoutest heart quail. The road is full of dead cattle and left wagons" (Cumming 1985, 81). For many arriving in Salt Lake City, the remaining 700 miles of trail was terribly frightening. The easy miles from the Missouri were hard enough on the people, livestock and wagons. They knew that the deserts and mountains ahead would be much worse.

One other issue troubled Brigham Young and the leaders of the LDS Church; some of the Saints in the Valley of the Great Salt Lake were trying to defect. Some of the emigrating Saints found the difficult travel from the East, and especially from Europe, to be too much. Others were uncomfortable with the new city in the Great Basin. Still others were reluctant to do the work necessary to develop a new society and economy. Still others didn't approve of the tight control exercised over everyday life by the Church leaders. There was also the expectation of great riches if only they could get to the California gold fields. And finally, some of the Saints—especially the younger ones—were developing friendships or relationships with those gold seekers now stuck in Salt Lake.

As some of the Saints became dissatisfied with their conditions in Salt Lake City, the Gold Rush presented a solution. Those who wished to leave could simply travel with or follow the '49ers. Some asked Brigham Young for permission to leave; others simply packed up and left. While some trusted residents were being sent by the Church leaders to California or to foreign missions beyond California, many others simply wanted out and the migration provided further impetus for this movement.

Of the 8,000 plus people in Salt Lake City in August 1849, over 1,000 or more were non-Mormon gold seekers trying to get to California. It appears that the agricultural production was more than adequate to provide for the Saints, those who continued to arrive, and many of the visitors. However, it was clear to the City's leaders that it was not in their best interests to house and feed the migration until the following Spring and Summer when the Northern Route was again open for travel. Brigham Young and the other leaders saw a real advantage to get the gentiles—the '49ers—on their way safely to California as soon as possible. For their part, the gold seekers wanted nothing more than to get to the gold fields as quickly and as safely as they could.

Thus, the stage was set for what was to come next. The Southern Route to California would be used to solve everyone's problem. And the man best able to guide the travelers along that route was Jefferson Hunt.

Chapter 16

The Jefferson Hunt Wagon Train of 1849 Is Formed

Jefferson Hunt's introduction to the '49ers came on the morning of Sunday, August 12, 1849, when he briefly addressed the LDS services at the Bowery. As was customary at the time, services were attended not only by Church members but also by visitors who were curious about the beliefs of their hosts. Many from the migration attended along with the Saints in Salt Lake City. Services were open and gave everyone a chance to hear the news of the day and to meet with others.

Thomas Bullock, the Church Secretary, was charged with keeping a contemporary record of the proceedings at services and formal meetings. Fortunately, those records have been preserved. It appears that Bullock attempted to write a verbatim record of the proceedings. However, a comparison between his record, the comments of others present and the *Journal History of the Church* indicates that, while he captured the essence of what was said and sometimes was able to record what he heard in detail, there were comments made that he did not. He simply couldn't write as fast as the speakers spoke, but his recorded minutes still provide us with a wealth of information.

The services were held in the Bowery, a wood and brush-covered shelter capable of seating 1,500 people on benches, with a raised platform at the front, in today's Temple Square. Typically, services consisted of the reading of announcements and/or letters and articles, followed by prayers, hymns by the choir, and addresses by Brigham Young, members of the Twelve Apostles or other ranking Church officials or members. Occasionally, other Church members who did not hold high office within the Church would speak. Clearly, such appearances were done at the request, or at least with the approval, of Brigham Young. Since Jefferson Hunt was then living at Fort Utah, he had to travel forty-five miles to be present at the service. Clearly, he was speaking with the full backing of the Church President.

Hunt was highly regarded by his contemporaries as an orator. For many years, he was called upon to deliver addresses at Church services and at various public events, such as Independence and Pioneer Day celebrations; the latter held on July 24th commemorated the Mormons arrival in the Valley of the Great Salt Lake. This was at a time in history where good public speaking was regarded as an Art and enjoyed by most of the population. Reports from contemporaries indicate that he had a commanding presence and spoke convincingly about the topic at hand. Hunt was called to speak not only for his message, but also for his delivery.

His address on the morning of August 12th lasted less than five minutes. The first half of his remarks reflected his own personal testimony, and he cautioned his listeners to repent and hear the message of salvation. He warned those who didn't: "Don't you know you are going right into the jaws of hell?" He then spoke of the Mormon's expulsion from the East. He concluded his remarks by speaking directly to the migration and saying: "You that are visiting us—make peace in your midst as you are going among the Emissaries of Darkness," a clear reference to the conditions they would find in California's gold fields (General Church Minutes, August 12, 1849). Following these comments, the Apostle John Taylor reported on the findings of the commission that investigated the trader, Pomeroy, from Missouri.

The following is a reprint of Thomas Bullock's record of Jefferson Hunt's comments at the morning services on August 12, 1849:

"Jefferson Hunt—I used to call myself a preacher of righteousness
& preached the power of salvation. But for the last 3 yrs there has

been no injunction for me to preach. 15 years ago I was called by the great Jehovah to preach the gospel. In the course of time I was called to lay hold of the sword handle. My philanthropy to the nations of the earth has been in a great measure & [illegible]. I [illegible] to repent my past follies. I thought I was the master of the [sun?] & I did think I [could?] be a great big [load or loss?] but I am now satisfied & rejoice in the midst of the mountains. We were driven by the U.S. to a place where they expected we should starve and be suffocated. To you who are now hearing this & who have not yet heard the treasure of [Salvation?] hearken to the councils of the Pres. Don't you know you are going right into the jaws of hell? If you don't, I do, for I've been there. You who have driven us out, you thought you were killing us. But you were doing God's service. But you prepare bread for yourselves when you [should be] in need of it. But you sow it not. It is thus & of the God that has brought us here and sustains us here. I feel as Jethro says—come go with us and we will do you good. We [illegible] [illegible] [stole?] your [breads?] if you could. But who stole first. [illegible] as the Emissaries of Darkness—the Emissaries—and they killed the Prophet of God for bearing record of the things he knew. &c &c You that are visiting us—make peace in your midst as you are going among the Emissaries of Darkness" (General Church Minutes, August 12, 1849).

During this address at the morning services, Hunt made no reference to the Southern Route. That would come in the afternoon services on the same day. This time he only addressed the migration. He began by saying that "it is 700 miles to Los Angeles" and described the gentle road between Salt Lake City and the Santa Clara River. He then said that the next portion of the route would be more difficult and gave some mileages and cautioned them that they would have to use axes to cut a wagon road. Then for the first time, he mentioned that he would be willing to guide them, but that they couldn't leave until October 1st when the weather cooled. He apparently urged them to prepare themselves by resting their livestock at the good feed and grass near the starting point of Fort Utah. He concluded by saying that they could take the Southern Route in the Winter, but if they wished, they could wait for the Northern Route next summer.

The following is a reprint of Thomas Bullock's record of Jefferson Hunt's comments at the services on the afternoon of August 12, 1849:

"Jefferson Hunt says it is 700 miles to Los Angeles. 350 of this road has plenty of water and ¾ of road is level. Gave a table of distances. No rocks on the low roads. Plain is level from here to Sevier River 350 roads. Over mountainous hill you come to Little Salt Lake. Then go 80 miles to Santa Clara that is rough enough. It is the roughest between here and California. Then to Virgin River and down 40 miles covered with verdant brush. Want axes to cut road. Then 20 miles to much water. Then 50 to cactus spring. 12 miles to 12 miles. Over rocky 30 plains and level to Cal but dry. I live at the Utah. If they will make a deposit till the 1st Oct. Have places where plenty of grass and feed. The road is rough enough. I tell you—you can't go before 1st Oct only about 200 miles. The winter season is neither storms nor rains. The grass is uninviting and as [illegible] in difficulty. You can go the south in winter. You can go the north road if you please. There will be plenty of grass on the road within the next 18 months" (General Church Minutes, August 12, 1849).

Hunt's talk to the migration stirred them to think seriously about taking the Southern Route. The urge to move on to California was tempered by the realization that this new route was not as well known as the Northern Route and, by some, distrust of the Mormons. For the next week there was considerable talk about what they had heard and what they should do. Those choosing to go the Northern Route lost no time to begin their journey. Many companies that had traveled together across the plains now began to split up, with some starting immediately on the Northern Route and the others remaining in Salt Lake City to test the Southern Route.

At the afternoon services a week later, August 19th, Jefferson Hunt made a brief announcement to the '49ers present. According to Bullock:

"Jefferson Hunt wants to the say to the immigration present. I expected to make arrangements today. But tomorrow morning at 8 o'clock I will be present and give you a list of the route south. I am not afraid of your pilots and will give you the truth. If I go,

I go for the money. And, bring along your men who say they know the route. And, what I tell you, I will face you with in the mountains" (General Church Minutes, August 19, 1849).

Clearly, Bullock's accounts are not the exact words spoken, but they give us the essence of the announcement. Bullock's account also tells us that there was some criticism of the proposed endeavor along the Southern Route by other expert "pilots."

At eight o'clock the next morning, August 20, 1849, Jefferson Hunt, Brigham Young and the '49ers again assembled in the Bowery to discuss the Southern Route to California. Hunt spoke first and "called for Mr. Waters and Tim Goodale and Mr. Kinney—mountaineers—(not present) to come and contradict his statement" (General Church Minutes, August 20, 1849). The three mountain men were probably the "pilots" referred to the day before. James Waters, Tim Goodale and Charles Kinney had all spent time in El Pueblo, and probably had met the Mormons there. Waters traveled to California in 1849 with a party of other mountain men led by John Brown, They had stopped in Salt Lake City on July 4th. They arrived at Sutter's Fort via the Northern Route on September 15th. Tim Goodale was also probably in the area, since he spent time at Fort Bridger and met the Pioneer Company there in 1847. Charles Kinney guided a party of '49ers from El Pueblo to Salt Lake City. He found that to be a very lucrative job for which he received $700, two wagons, and his choice of three mules (Hafen and Hafen 2001, Vol. 4, 171). Perhaps these men had disparaged the Southern Route in hopes of collecting fees for guiding the migration along the Northern Route.

To establish his credibility, Hunt then described his 1847 trip to Southern California for supplies. His description of travel along the western half of the Old Spanish Trail is second only in detail to Fremont's journal of his 1844 trip. Bullock says he went with "19 men and boys and 80 animals and was 46 days going. Staid [sic] a few weeks. Got 200 cows and 160 animals and we returned [illegible]. I left here 19 Nov [illegible] Come back about 1st May"

(General Church Minutes, August 20, 1949). Hunt then described the route for the first 200 miles saying that there "will be plenty of grass and water" and there was "no trouble here to Sevier River," and that "the way is tolerable rough from Little Salt Lake [illegible]"

Then beginning at a point near present-day Cedar City, Utah, Hunt described the trail to Isaac William's rancho at Chino in some detail, giving fairly accurate mileage between the water sources along the way and descriptions of the conditions along the route. In fact, the detail of his description suggests that he was using a log, journal or diary that he had recorded on his trip. Unfortunately, no such document is known to exist today. To better understand what the migration heard that morning, we should review what Hunt told them.

He began his description of the lower part of the route at some point just west of today's Cedar City, (near Enoch), Utah, and described the road as going eight miles along the "1st Muddy," the name then used for Coal Creek, to a spring with plenty of grass [Iron Springs.] He then described going twelve miles with a "spring on left (a mile off)," a very accurate description of Antelope Springs which is about one mile from the main trail.

Hunt then said it was twenty-four miles to a divide with "Oceans of water and grass on divide." He further stated that half way there the route went in a "dry creek" (Holt Canyon near Newcastle, Utah). The divide he spoke of is the southern rim of the Great Basin and the grass and water is the infamous Mountain Meadow, the site of the massacre of 1857. This location was a much-favored resting spot before beginning the difficult drive into the Mojave Desert that extends from the southwestern corner of Utah, across Nevada and well into California. For decades, pack trains and wagon trains stopped here to let their cattle and pack animals feed and water before the long trek ahead. But the majority of the wagon train that Hunt would soon guide left the known trail just before Holt Canyon to head into the unknown desert to the West.

From Mountain Meadow, Hunt described traveling twenty-four more miles along the rough road down the canyons to the Santa Clara River near Shivwits, Utah. He then described the road going another twenty-four miles, over the divide of Utah Hill six miles from Shivwits, to the Virgin River where

Beaver Dam Wash intersects it at the present location of Littlefield, Arizona. Up to this point his mileages have been nearly exact. However, at this point, his description fails to account for about half of the forty-two miles or so from Littlefield to the Muddy River near Moapa/Glendale, Nevada, called the Far Muddy by Hunt and others to distinguish it from the "1st Muddy" near Cedar City.

While the mileage may have been off, his description of the steep and difficult road up Virgin Hill to the top of what is now known as Mormon Mesa was not. Bullock recorded that Hunt said: "Here is the Buggaboo. A precipice of 6000 feet." The mesa is actually about 500 feet above the bed of the Virgin River and about 2,200 above sea level—but to someone trying to get pack animals or wagons up the sandy slope and over the rocky rim, it must have seemed like 6,000 feet. The next stage of the route, from the Muddy to Cache Spring [Las Vegas], is fifty miles, and Hunt described it as such, but apparently did not stress that it was dry the entire way. At Las Vegas, Hunt mentioned the flowing stream and ample grass.

Hunt then talked about the trail from Las Vegas to Cottonwood Spring near today's Blue Diamond, west of Las Vegas and to Mountain Springs on the summit of the pass between Las Vegas Valley and Pahrump Valley. Bullock's reported mileage from Las Vegas to Cottonwood Spring is twelve miles, rather than the actual eighteen miles, but the mileage from there to Mountain Springs is off only two miles (twelve instead of ten). From there he describes the trail west to Stump Spring, through the California Valley, and over Emigrant Pass (just beyond the present California border) to the lush grass and ample water at Resting Spring not far from today's Tecopa, California. On the flat parts of this route, his distances are overstated—thirty miles rather than the actual twenty miles from Mountain Springs to Stump Springs, for example. But in the mountains and canyons over Emigrant Pass, his reported thirty miles is closer to the actual twenty-three miles.

He next described the route from Resting Spring to Salt Spring near the southern end of Death Valley. The route of the Old Spanish Trail generally recognized by historians today goes from Resting Spring to Tecopa and then along the Amargosa River and through its canyon to the area of Dumont Dunes and then to Salt Spring. Hunt's description sounds tantalizing like his route might be several miles shorter by going to Willow Spring near today's China Ranch, about one and one-half miles east of the upper part of the Amargosa Canyon. If taken, the trail would have then entered the Amargosa Canyon about one-third of the way down and then followed the small stream to the Dumont Dunes, the same route followed by Fremont. Or he may have entered the Amargosa Canyon via Cowboy Canyon as he did in 1849. In any case, the mileage recorded by Bullock, six miles from Resting Spring to ample grass and then fifteen miles to the hills by Salt Spring is very near exact if the route was through China Ranch. And Hunt's subsequent travels along the trail certainly took him along a route that did not enter Amargosa Canyon at Tecopa.

Hunt stated that he stayed at Salt Spring for two days before heading on the long stretch to Bitter Spring. Much of the water at the Salt Spring Hills is non-potable, but a hard to find small spring in the hills is potable and this resource was used to prepare men and animals for the nearly thirty-five mile push without water to Bitter Spring over Red Pass. He then described pushing on the Mojave River and following it to Cajon Pass and then on to the final goal of Williams' Rancho at Chino. He stated it was 150 miles from Bitter Spring to their goal, which again is very close to the actual mileage.

Hunt then concluded his remarks by offering to guide them for ten dollars a wagon. He commented that the weather was mild except that the summer was hot and, therefore, they should not begin before October 1st. He estimated that they would reach Southern California in sixty or seventy days.

The following is Thomas Bullock's record of Jefferson Hunt's comments on the morning of August 20, 1849:

> "Meeting of immigrants at 8 AM when instructions from Jefferson Hunt.

> Hunt called for Mr. Waters and Jim Goodale and Mr. Kinney—mountaineers—(not present) to come and contradict his statement.

> Gentlemen, I am going to give a detail, once for all. I hear many miraculous reports but no nothing of [honor?] I went by the S route to the Pacific. 19 men and boys and 80 animals and were

46 days going. Staid [sic] a few weeks. Got 200 cows and 160 animals and we returned mostly same route. I left here 19 Nov and went to Cal: the snow was here a foot deep. Arrived at Williams' Ranchero at latter end of Dec. Staid 3 weeks. Come back about 1ˢᵗ May. There is no trouble from here to Sevier River. I have no hesitation to say there will be plenty of grass and water. The difficult job is little hills. The way is tolerable rough from Little Salt Lake to a creek about 200 miles. A spring about ½ way among Indians.

[Then follows a list that has miles beyond the 200 miles above. It appears that this list is of the road from about Cedar City to Chino.]

1ˢᵗ Muddy to a spring 8 plenty of grass

spring on left (a mile off) 12 little grass in Nov

to Divide 24 ½ way in dry creek about 300 yards above X. Good water. Oceans of water and grass on divide

head of Santa Clara 24 Pass Ridge. Rocky. Water about ½ way. Good camping. Sure rough country. Gullies, [illegible] Road is round the point. Good coming out of the creek.

Mouth of Santa Clara 24 Spots good grass. Indian farms. Plenty of timber.

Up canyon and divide 6 Plenty of grass. Then descend.

To Rio Virgin 24 Without water, plenty of grass to Beaver Dam. Plenty of water. Go over road 3 miles

Over to Far Muddy 20 Plenty of grass and water (interlined.) Here is the Buggaboo. A precipice of 6000 feet. A mile above is good going up and down 7 miles down is not any trouble. 10 miles is water and grass.

To Cache Spring 50 [Las Vegas] Up canyon 6 miles. Sandy [illegible] table land. Then level to the spring. Plenty of grass and water. Up spring 5 miles.

To water 12 Plenty grass and water. Level plain.

Mountain Springs 12 Rough and rocky. Not much grass. ½ mile further plenty of grass.

Water 30 across level plain.

½ river slough 4 Plenty water and grass.

Spring 30 A bad hill to go over. Plenty of grass and water. [Resting Springs]

Spring 6 Moderate grass. Then down a saleratus creek 6 miles.

A mountain 15 Staid 2 days. [Salt Creek]

A Bitter Spring 50 Over level plain about 6 miles rocky. Little grass.

Mahaugy [Mojave] River 40 No grass. Some sage. Sandy plain 10 miles. See Cal mountains. Plenty of grass and water.

Mahaugy River 50

Cahon Pass Close to settlement 20 miles.

The season is mild except summer is hot. About 12 or 1500 animals—3000 stock and 600 cows in our caravan. I will secure men to go and show you that country at 10.00 a wagon. You work the way with me. I'll find it. We ought not start before 1ˢᵗ Oct. and go through in 60 or 70 days.

825 miles to Los Angeles"

(General Church Minutes, August 20, 1849).

Brigham Young then took the stand, and again Thomas Bullock recorded the essence of his message (General Church Minutes, August 20, 1849). Young began by saying that "Major Hunt [his rank in the Nauvoo Legion and highest military rank yet attained] I have been acquainted with many years." He then expressed his belief that they should continue on to California via the Southern Route since there was a shortage of supplies in Utah and the Northern or Humboldt Route was too dangerous. He added that Hunt had not measured the exact mileages on the Southern Route but that "his mileage chart is his recollection."

Young then gave some very prophetic advice: "I beg to give you a little council. We labor together in union. Travel together. If union does not prevail [you will be] over come with problems. Let me council you to nurture and cherish a state of union. If you don't you are in imminent danger . . . ." Within a month of starting their journey, nearly every one of the travelers ignored his advice. Many of the '49ers suffered major hardships, and some died because of it. A number of unforeseen factors persuaded them to discard the sage advice of Brigham Young, a man who had directed several migrations himself.

Young then suggested that they organize into companies, each with a head, and that each company contribute manpower to a small pioneer unit that would go ahead of the main group to find the best routes for wagons and build roads as needed. He indicated that this procedure would lessen the efforts of the livestock and that they would be in better condition as a result. Left unsaid was the fact that any road improvements would greatly benefit the Mormons in future years. He also echoed an earlier comment of Hunt's by indicating that some additional Mormon men would accompany Hunt. Young implied that he was going to use the wagon train to convey a limited number of Mormons to California and possibly beyond.

He concluded his remarks by telling those assembled that Jefferson Hunt was a "poor, honest and humble man," and that he "would be willing to give him what he asks" or his fee of ten dollars per wagon. Finally, he urged them not to trade their already worn livestock for fresher ones but to take them to good feed and let them replenish during the five or six weeks until they left for California. His last plea was again for remaining together as a cohesive unit: "If you go in union, you will act out Mormonism."

Bullock's last entry tells how well the messages of the day were received: "An immigrant motioned that we the immigrants return our hearty and warm thanks to the President of this Society for his warm wisdom and advice this morning. Seconded! Carried." The gold seekers had discovered a safer and faster way to California; the citizens of Salt Lake City would be freed from the obligation of caring for large number of interlopers; and Brigham Young and the Church leaders would be able to extend their knowledge of the route to the Coast.

The following is Thomas Bullock's record of the comments made by Brigham Young following Jefferson Hunt's presentation on the morning of August 20, 1849:

> "You are strangers to me. I represent him [illegible] Major Hunt I have been acquainted with many years. He has proffered his services to go South route. We are poor from marches and we shall be flooded with many. We wish all who can to proceed on their journey. If we had a surplus of provisions we would advise you to stay all winter. We have been offered .50 a pound for flour. If we should say (yes) we have nothing for ourselves and neighbors. It would be hard. All who have started for gold regions have hopes of deliverance. They feel they need it and are anxious to get where it is. To recommend any man to go the northern road it would be bordering on taking their lives. And it would be marvelous to go by the north road. We have detained our own families from going that route. We have not much confidence in going that N. route this fall. But there is plenty in spring. I should have no hesitancy in going the S. road. It's perfectly safe all the time. Major Hunt has not measured the road and his mileage chart is his recollection. I beg to give you a little council. We labor together in union. Travel together. If union does not prevail over come with problems. Let me council you to nurture and cherish a state of union. If you don't you are in imminent danger. I have had to use all skills and luck to hinder men from going there. Form into companies. Have a pilot to each company with a horse. Search round and [count?] up camp grounds. Let there be a united effort and you can go easy. There is no necessity of having broken down cattle. There is no necessity of having any wagon or animal injured. If I were traveling in a company and had any difficulty I would not leave that wagon till it was through. If you have 4 companies draw out 10 extra men as Pioneers then go through with light teams

and work the canyons. When main train comes on there is no hindrance and your cattle will be as good as when they leave this place. Hearken to the advice of a stranger, patience and perseverance will go through. When we came here 2 years ago, we never lost our [eye?] and laid off a city and worked with same teams same year. Major Hunt proffers his services to go there and some young men will go with him. I want [illegible] for it. He is a poor, honest and humble man. He arrived here having nothing for himself or family. I would be willing to give him what he asks. 10.00 with all my heart. Instead of trading off your worn cattle, put them in good feed, recruit them and go on. If you go in union, you will act out Mormonism. An immigrant motioned that we the immigrants return our hearty and warm thanks to the President of this Society for his warm wisdom and advice this morning. Seconded! Carried" (General Church Minutes, August 20, 1849).

Some of the emigrants also recorded information given by Jefferson Hunt and Brigham Young that expands on Bullock's notes. William Lorton noted that Hunt offered to take 100 wagons for $1,000, and that he also said that only one wagon, belonging to Captain Davis, had crossed over the road before. He mentioned that the Davis party had found packers who had apparently been killed by Indians along the route. Lorton noted that Brigham Young told the emigrants that he would not permit any other company to follow the road made by them, since any following companies of emigrants would have not paid their share and would be benefiting from the work and money of the first group. Lorton recorded that the assembled emigrants thanked Young for his efforts (Lorton Diary, August 20, 1849).

Jacob Stover later wrote that the leaders of his group from Iowa City considered it a positive recommendation when they discovered that Jefferson Hunt was a Mason as were they, and his Masonic ties gave him a considerable amount of credibility within the emigrant groups (Ressler 1964, 189).

A number of others commented in their journals that they were told to take their livestock to the lush grass at the southern end of Utah Valley, just beyond the new Mormon settlement of Fort Utah. There they were to rest and prepare while their stock fed. They would begin their journey from there about October 1ˢᵗ.

Some of the emigrants wanted to get to the gold fields of California as soon as possible. Others wanted to avoid the cholera and deserts of the Humboldt Route. Still others feared the snows that trapped the Donner Party. Whatever the reason, they decided to follow the advice of Jefferson Hunt and Brigham Young to take the Southern Route. About 500 people with approximately 100 wagons and over a thousand head of livestock committed themselves to take the new route. Nearly all of them had confidence in Jefferson Hunt as their guide, at least for the moment.

Some began the fifty mile journey to the Utah Valley almost immediately. Others, such as William Lorton, remained in Salt Lake City for a while before going south. Still others, such as William Lewis Manly, were still on the way to Salt Lake City and wouldn't find out about the new arrangement until they arrived among the Mormons and emigrants. Over the last two weeks of August and throughout September, the '49ers prepared for the desert trip.

Many began to lighten their loads for the long trip ahead. Some in the emigration had discarded heavy or unneeded items on the road to Salt Lake. Having discovered that the road ahead was going to be even more difficult, they began to sell or trade many of their household and personal items for whatever they could get in the form of money, animals or food. To the citizens of Salt Lake who had arrived with very little, this was a great boon. The cost and availability of goods was even better than in St. Louis. Household items like furniture, dishes, silverware and personal comfort items such as feather beds and new clothing were suddenly available in the wilderness. However, many of the '49ers still continued on with more than they needed to carry.

Just as the emigrants were preparing for the trip, Jefferson Hunt and many others in the Mormon community also readied themselves. Hunt returned home to Fort Utah to begin his preparations. It is likely that he traveled the day-long trip to Salt Lake City once or twice more during September to meet with Brigham Young and others.

On September 1, 1849, George Washington Bean, a young man and friend of the Hunt family, was returning from work on his family's farm plot at Fort Utah when Lieutenant William Dayton of the local militia asked him to help fire the cannon at the top of the small hill in the middle of the fort. As mentioned previously, the cannon was periodically fired for training purposes and to impress nearby Indians and even emigrants. The two climbed the ladder to the muzzle-loading cannon, loaded it, and fired one round. Procedures for firing a muzzle-loading cannon required that a wet swab next be run down the barrel to extinguish any embers of the last cartridge before the next charge was loaded. A cannon powder charge was pre-measured by weight and placed into a paper container that became the cartridge. Burning embers of the paper or powder of the last cartridge could burn through the paper and prematurely ignite the next cartridge.

Whether they failed to run the swab through the barrel at all or simply didn't have it wet enough or failed to reach the far end of the barrel is unknown. Dayton and Bean loaded the next charge and both had their hands on the ramrod driving it home when the charge ignited. Both men were in front of the muzzle, gripping the wooden ramrod when the explosion occurred. Both men were blown off the bastion to the ground below. The ramrod was splintered and fragmented. Jefferson Hunt was the first person to run to their aid. He found Dayton bleeding to death with a severed vein. Bean lost a hand in the explosion and suffered other major injuries from the splintered wood, the concussion and his fall to the ground (Bean 1992, 76). He survived the accident, and was later recognized as an influential pioneer, Indian interpreter and judge. His son, George Teancum Bean, married Jefferson Hunt's granddaughter, Celia Evelyn Hunt, who was the daughter of Joseph Hunt.

Jacob Stover, one of the '49ers waiting to leave for California, wrote an account of this incident many years later. He claimed to have been on the scene and said that two doctors from his group amputated Bean's lower arm. Stover's account claimed that the firing of the cannon was in honor of Brigham Young who was present (Ressler 1964, 190). However, Young did not arrive at Fort Utah for another two weeks, so Stover's remembrance was partially in error.

From the Mormon's point of view, ridding Salt Lake City of the emigrants was not the only objective of the Jefferson Hunt Wagon Train. The journey to Southern California would serve two other important objectives. One would be to provide transportation for missionaries en route to various Pacific islands, new emissaries to the Saints in California, and a small group of selected men who would mine for gold to increase the income for them, their backers and the Church. The other objective would be to provide support for the political and infrastructure goals of the Church and its leaders. Often ignored by history, the latter will be discussed first.

When the Saints began arriving in the Valley of the Great Salt Lake during 1848, there was no governmental support for them. The territory was new to the United States and the nearest non-Mormon population was either 750 miles to the west or 1,000 miles to the east. There was no military, no law enforcement, no courts and no representative government. This suited Brigham Young and the Church elders just fine. The absence of federal oversight gave them the opportunity to establish their own government and their own control. It permitted the Saints to create what David Bigler has called "the Mormon Theocracy in the American West" (Bigler 1998).

Faced with Indian attacks, coupled with the influx of emigrants and the desire to expand their control over much of the Great Basin and beyond, the Mormon leaders set about forming a government that would be closely coupled with the Church leadership. A convention was held in March 1849 to discuss the political situation. It was decided to petition Congress for a territorial government, and a committee was formed to draft a constitution. The committee met on March 8th, 9th, and 10th and drafted a constitution for the State of Deseret. The name Deseret came from the Book of Mormon and meant "bee," which described the industriousness of the new residents of the area. Two days later, a provisional government was elected with Brigham Young as governor. A militia was organized for protection and Charles Coulson Rich and Daniel Wells were made general officers in charge.

The original boundaries in the constitution included most of the Great Basin and incorporated all of the current states of Utah, Nevada and considerable portions of Wyoming, Colorado, New Mexico, Arizona, Idaho and Oregon. Most importantly for our discussion was that it also included the entire area of California east of the Sierra Nevada mountains and a corridor to the Pacific Ocean that included the coastal area from Mexico north to present day Santa Monica. This corridor would have placed a route from Salt Lake City all the way to the Port of San Diego under Mormon control. As we shall see, this ambitious plan for a Mormon corridor would be kept alive until 1857.

There is no doubt that Brigham Young and the LDS leaders wanted to control their own destiny for the first time, and that meant providing the shortest and most secure possible access to ocean transportation and distant markets. It also meant that the overland route to Southern California needed to be secured—and where possible—settled by the Mormons themselves. The plan was to be implemented over the next several years. Clearly, the information from Jefferson Hunt and the other Battalion veterans regarding Southern California and the road there was heavily relied upon in making this decision. Hunt and other Mormons traveling with the 1849 wagon train would be able to gather more information and provide the foundation for future travel and settlement.

The General Assembly of the State of Deseret met on July 2, 1849. A petition to Congress was prepared and given to Dr. John M. Bernhiesel to take to Washington. This time, the boundary lines were adjusted to exclude Oregon but to include more of the area of Wyoming and even portions of today's South Dakota and Nebraska. Additionally, the Pacific Ocean corridor was moved northward to near Santa Barbara. The land area included within this boundary was even larger than the first.

At the same time these ideas were being formulated in Salt Lake City, others were coming from Washington D.C. Mexican War general and hero, Zachary Taylor, assumed the presidency of the United States on March 5,

1849. Although he was a Southerner and owned slaves, he was committed to holding the Union together—by force if necessary—and believed that slavery should not be permitted where it was not possible to grow cotton or sugar cane. His approach to resolving the issue was to let states decide whether or not they should be slave states. He believed that the new areas of New Mexico and California should be admitted to the Union and that the residents should have the right to determine the slavery issue. He hoped that in this way the issue of balance between slave and non-slave states could be resolved.

To further his goal, President Taylor had his friend General John Wilson, newly-appointed Indian Agent for California, stop in Salt Lake City and present a proposal to the Mormon leaders. Brigham Young summarized the proposal and his response to it in a letter to Amasa Lyman, the apostle who was then the leader of the Saints in California (History of the Church, September 6, 1849). According to Young, the President proposed that Utah join with California to form a new state. Taylor believed that the anti-slavery Mormons would guarantee that the new state would be non-slave.

Brigham Young rejected that proposal but counter-proposed that he would accept the offer provided it was guaranteed that in 1851 the State of Deseret would automatically be created. Young authorized Lyman to be a delegate to the California constitutional convention representing the Mormon interests in achieving this counter-proposal. But the California convention began before the arrival of the letter to Lyman and nothing came of it. Young also asked Lyman to try to determine if the citizens of Southern California, particularly in San Diego and Los Angeles, would favor a boundary that included them in the State of Deseret rather than California. He then told Lyman that he would remain in charge of the California Saints until the arrival of Apostle Charles Coulson Rich, who was a member of the Quorum of the Twelve Apostles and, therefore, one of the senior leaders of the LDS Church. Rich was also a good friend of Jefferson Hunt, and both had been at the battle of Crooked River in Missouri some years before. Their lives would be intertwined in California for most of the next eight years.

The importance of this discussion of political events is to show that a month before the departure of the Jefferson Hunt Wagon Train, the LDS leadership had a clear political goal in mind. That included the creation of a new state with a transportation corridor extending from Salt Lake City to the Pacific Ocean. And it points out why Rich and others joined Hunt on the Westward migration.

When Brigham Young traveled to Mormon communities outside of Salt Lake City, he did so with an entourage. Usually included were other Church leaders, friends and staff members. On September 14th, he and his group began a trip to Fort Utah. Included were his top two lieutenants, Presidents Heber Kimball and Willard Richards, and the apostles, Erastus Snow and Franklin D. Richards. That evening they stopped at Cottonwood, now in the southern part of Salt Lake City; the following day they traveled to Fort Utah. On September 16th, Brigham Young held services and probably had informal meetings with some of the residents. On September 17th, the party located and roughly laid out the City of Provo, which would be built to replace Fort Utah. They also followed the Old Spanish Trail up Spanish Fork Canyon for a short distance.

That evening the *Journal History of the LDS Church* records that:

> "At early candle light the Brethren [Young, his party and others] met in Capt. Hunt's house to converse about the southern country and the prospects of settling it. Many questions were asked in regard to route, traveling, location, incidents, etc, and the prospects before the saints caused quite a good feeling. About 9 o'clock the company separated when a dance was commenced at Bishop's [sic] Higbee's which was continued till midnight" (Journal History, September 17, 1849).

Before the meeting ever took place, Young and his fellow leaders already had heard from Jefferson Hunt and others about the potential locations for communities along the Wasatch Front, about the potential of the iron ore deposits near Iron Springs, about the hazards of the trip through the deserts, and about the productivity of Southern California. If they were going to develop the corridor to California, they needed more specific information such as exact locations of springs and wells along the route, distances between stops, and where they might locate support facilities to assist the migration of Saints from the coast that they hoped to develop. They needed to flesh out their plans, and the wagon train offered them the opportunity to do just that.

One of Brigham Young's strongest management attributes was his ability to delegate and assign tasks to his loyal followers. In 1849, much was going on in Salt Lake City and Young had much work to do. The Bowery was being rebuilt into a stronger and larger facility that predated the Tabernacle, new residents were arriving from the East daily, the City was being developed and commerce and industry were being established. Work on establishing the Corridor would have to be done by others. Clearly, the September 17th meeting was held to discuss, make plans and assign duties related to the securing of the Southern Route for the benefit of the Mormons. Part of the discussion probably dealt with possible areas in Southern California, such as Isaac Williams' Rancho, where the Mormons could establish their most distant outpost. Jefferson Hunt and the others going on that trip were assigned to gather information and carry out Young's instructions.

The next day Brigham Young and his entourage, along with Jefferson Hunt, returned to Salt Lake City. On September 20th, Thomas Bullock recorded that a council meeting was held with Young and the apostles and that: "Instructions were given to Captain Hunt in regard to his mission with the emigrants and to measure the road. Charles C. Rich, Addison Pratt, James S. Brown and Hiram H. Blackwell were counseled to go with Captain Hunt the following Monday" (Journal History of the Church, September 20, 1849). The planning continued.

Charles Coulson Rich was to play one of the most significant roles in the Church's California endeavors over the next decade. For now, his assignment was to replace Amasa Lyman as the head of the Saints in California, but he had a number of other items on his agenda—including political moves that might still secure a Mormon Corridor to California. On September 29th, many of the top leaders, including Young and Rich, met with some Mormons just

returned from California and received over $4,000 in gold from them. They
then "discussed California" for four and one half hours (Journal History of the
Church, September 29, 1849). The following day, another meeting was held
regarding California. This meeting probably included both Saints returning
from California and some of those about to leave. In any case, a considerable
amount of intelligence was shared among those going to California.

On September 30th, Brigham Young wrote a letter to Amasa Lyman,
to be delivered by Rich, which asked Lyman to determine if the Mormons in
California wanted to stay or not. If so, they were to be "gathered into communities," or if they did not, they should travel back to Salt Lake City. Young
also instructed Lyman to gather as much information as possible about where
settlements could be placed along the road from Utah to Southern California
(History of the Church, September 30, 1849). No doubt Young gave the same
instructions to Rich and Hunt to consider on their way to California.

On October 1st, the day the wagon train was preparing to leave Fort
Utah, Brigham Young was preparing documents for Rich, Brown and Blackwell to use in their endeavors in California and in the Society Islands. Addison Pratt, James Brown and Hiram Blackwell were going on the mission to
the Islands, but some of these men had to stay in Salt Lake City for another
week before departing.

On September 30th, William Lewis Manly and his small band of '49ers
reached the area of Fort Utah and found the groups of wagons preparing to
gather into the great train. One of the first emigrants he met was William
Lorton, who had watched Manly and his group descend into the Utah Valley
from Spanish Fork Canyon and learned the story of the Green River raft trip.
Nearby, Manly was surprised to find Asahel Bennett, his friend whom he believed was well ahead on the Northern Route. Bennett offered to hire Manly
and his friend John Rogers to assist his family wagons on the Westward trek.
They gladly joined forces.

Others, such as William Lorton, who had stayed in Salt Lake City longer than most, also began to gather south of Fort Utah. In all, about 500 people

and nearly 140 wagons were about to begin the final stage to their travel to California.

At the August meeting with the emigrants, Brigham Young had said that he would not permit others to follow the Hunt Wagon Train. Those unwilling to pay Jefferson Hunt as guide would not benefit from those who did. But he did not say that he would prevent others from going before Hunt. And that is exactly what happened.

During the last week of September, approximately 130 wagons and about 500 emigrants had gathered at the south end of Utah Valley preparing for the departure. One of those was Vincent Hoover, who left a detailed journal of his trip to California. In an entry on September 26th, he stated that: "There has been a great deal of contention between the emigrants as to who they should go with & this evening they had a meeting to that effect." He then mentioned Jefferson Hunt and a second man named Antonio "who is compelled to go through anyhow as he is a Mexican and brought through a train of pack mules from Santa Fe." Hoover then explained that Antonio "offers his services for carrying his baggage" (Hoover Journal, September 26, 1849).

Very little is known of the identity of Antonio. It is possible that he was a Santa Fe trader, as stated by Hoover, who went to Salt Lake City for some reason. But there was only limited trade between Santa Fe and Salt Lake City at that time, and only a few traders had made the journey. Also, there was limited contact with traders and travelers from California prior to the 1850s. Another possibility is that Antonio was actually one of the drovers that came to Salt Lake City from Southern California with Hunt in 1848, and was returning home. In that case, he would have traveled the trail but would not have paid that much attention to the exact details of the route, since others were in charge and were guiding the pack train. If this was the case, Antonio may very well have silently been put up to guiding this first company so that this smaller, non-paying group would do much of the work of breaking the wagon road. Whoever he was, it is hoped that Antonio's full identity will be discovered in the future.

From Hoover's perspective, there were two competing guides: Hunt who was going to charge $10 per wagon, and Antonio who would charge nothing except board and transportation. According to Hoover, twenty-five wagons accepted Antonio's offer and more than one hundred accepted Hunt as their guide. Those going with Antonio called themselves the "Independent Pioneer Company" and prepared to leave the Utah Valley on September 27th (Hoover Journal, September 26, 1849). This company has often been called the Gruwell-Derr Wagon Train after the Gruwell family and Peter Derr. Jacob Gruwell and at least one of his brothers took the Humboldt Route to Northern California after they were recognized as having been part of the mobs that harassed the Mormons in Nauvoo. Their families went the Southern Route with adult children and other relatives in charge. The Gruwell brothers had decided to travel to northern California, then traverse the state to the South and meet their families when they arrived.

William Lorton, who arrived at Fort Utah on September 26th, was supposed to travel with a Mr. Burnett, but found out on September 27th that Burnett had been involved in the organization of the Independent Pioneer Company and had already left. Lorton attempted to catch up with him, but turned back and eventually agreed to travel with a Mr. McDermit in exchange for work (Lorton Diary, September 26 & 27, 1849). The Gruwells and many others would depend on assistance before completing their travel through the Mojave Desert.

While Antonio may have been over the road before, he did not do a good job guiding the wagons. Several times during the relatively easy Utah portion of the trip, they failed to camp at places with water and grass. Antonio was unsure of the route and made several mistakes in guiding them south. He misdirected them at the Sevier River crossing and they spent valuable time retracing their steps back to the trail. Within a short time, the train began to break up into smaller groups that traveled alone. The inexperienced Antonio was not the guide that his followers had hoped (Lyman 2004, 48-50).

But the Independent Pioneer Company did perform an important service. Since they were the first wagons to travel the trail in a group, they were forced to make a wagon road out of a pack trail. This involved cutting back brush and trees, moving rocks, breaking down stream banks and forging roads over the most difficult areas such as the Black Mountains and Virgin Hill.

Several pack trains preceded the Independent Pioneer Company and Jefferson Hunt's wagon train. One of the more significant and interesting groups of packers was the Ithaca Company from New York. Trying to avoid cholera that they heard was rampant along other trails, they decided to take a circuitous route. From Independence, Missouri, they headed southwest to the Arkansas River, then up the river to Bent's Fort and El Pueblo (Lyman 2004, 44-45; Hafen and Hafen 1961, 15-26). There, they hired former mountain man George Kinney to guide them to Salt Lake City and California. They traveled north, basically following the Cherokee Trail into Wyoming, then west to Salt Lake City, arriving about July 4th. There the group split up, with half going on the Humboldt Route and the other half on the Southern Route.

From Salt Lake City, those who went south traveled the Southern Route to California, arriving at Chino about mid-October. Other mountain men from the El Pueblo area had joined this group to go to California. It appears that those included Alexis Godey—who had previously been on the Old Spanish Trail with Fremont and Carson—Valentine "Rube" Herring, James W. Waters, John Brown and Lancaster Lupton (Hafen and Hafen 2003, Vol. VII, 50). Some of these men, including Waters, Brown and Herring, knew the Mormons who wintered in 1846-47 at El Pueblo, and eventually settled in or near the Mormon colony at San Bernardino.

Judge H. S. Brown, a member of this party, recalled in an 1878 memo to the historian Hubert Bancroft that they had one wagon with them to serve as an ambulance to assist sick or injured men. He describes an incident in which one man became seriously ill and the wagon was used (Hafen and Hafen 1961, 24-25). It is not clear however, if that wagon traveled the entire way along the Southern Route, went along the Northern Route or was left along the trail. If it did go along the Southern Route, it would have preceded the wagons of the Independent Pioneer Company, and the Ithaca Company would have done much of the work clearing the trail for wagons.

On Sunday, September 30, 1849, most of the migration gathered on Hobble Creek, a few miles south of Fort Utah near the location of present-day Springville, Utah. As prearranged, at eleven a.m., Reverend Lewis Granger, a Baptist minister, delivered a sermon and at the end, called for a meeting to begin the organization of the wagon train. A Mr. Cox was made chair of the meeting and Adonijah Welch was made recording secretary. A committee of Reverend Granger, Welch and Thomas Marshall were selected to draft a constitution and bylaws for the organization. At the same time, William McCormick, Henry Baxter and Chauncey Swan were delegated to count the wagons. This meeting adjourned until four p.m. when it reconvened (Welch Journal, September 30, 1849).

At the second meeting of the day, the committees reported back. A constitution was discussed and adopted. Welch reported that it called for the election of a colonel who would be in overall command, and an adjutant who would assist the colonel. The constitution further called for creating seven divisions, each to be under the direction of a captain. The colonel, adjutant, guide (Jefferson Hunt), and the seven captains would form a council "for deciding all matters of importance on the route" (Welch, September 30, 1849). A committee was also created for the purpose of gathering the fee and setting the final arrangements with Hunt.

Thus, from the very beginning, the command and decision-making for the wagon train was in the hands of the officers elected by the emigrants. Hunt, as the guide, certainly would be able to exercise significant influence, but he would not be in a position to dictate matters to the train.

The following day, October 1st, another meeting was held and the same three men (McCormick, Baxter and Swan) were appointed as a permanent committee to handle the arrangements with Hunt. Several changes were made to other parts of the constitution, and then everyone set about preparing to move out the next day. Jefferson Hunt came to the camp and collected his fee before he returned to Fort Utah to say goodbye to his family. The plan in camp called for the emigrants to move about six miles to Spanish Fork Creek the next day to complete their organization.

Jefferson Hunt returned to see his family at Fort Utah after collecting his fee from the wagons. He would not see them for more than fifteen months. While there is no record showing that he intended to be gone that long, we can assume that he knew he was going to remain in California after his arrival. Similarly, we can assume that he was going to assist Rich and the others in their mission to the California Saints.

His absence from his family would not be unlike that during the Mexican War. His wife, Celia, would serve as the family matriarch and his eldest son, Gilbert, also living at Fort Utah, would serve as the elder male in the family. Sons John Hunt and Peter Nease, now sixteen, would be able to do their share for the family. There are strong indications that Marshall, now twenty, accompanied his father on this trip to California, but there is no reference to him on the trip to or in California.

The separation of the Hunt family patriarch was nothing new. Hunt had been away from his family for twenty of the preceding thirty-seven months. His devotion to his church, its leaders and his sense of responsibility again called him away. Fortunately for Hunt and his family, he was richly compensated for his work and his absence during the trip to California.

Chapter 17

The Wagon Train Begins

Twenty-eight-year-old Adonijah Welch was a graduate of the University of Michigan. He had studied law and was admitted to the bar, but decided on teaching for his career. He joined the Fayette Rovers group in order to go to California. In 1868, Welch became the first president at the newly created Iowa State College in Ames, Iowa. His journal of the trip, which covers less than a month, is detailed and clearly shows his education and intellect.

On October 2nd, most of those present began the first stage of the move south. They found the grass at Spanish Fork Creek to be inferior, so they continued another six miles or so to what they called Election Creek—now Peeteneet Creek—at the present town of Payson. That same day, Welch returned to Fort Utah to finish some business affairs and locate a lost ox. While there, he heard a report from returning California Mormons that told of the conditions in the gold camps and of the horrific conditions along the Humboldt Route. What he heard confirmed his decision to take the Southern Route. Welch tried to return to the train, but arrived at Spanish Fork Creek late in the day. He camped there with a group of fifteen additional wagons that were heading to meet the train at Election Creek.

On October 3rd, Welch and the fifteen wagons headed south to catch up to the others. When he arrived, he found another seventy wagons camped along the creek. There was some politicking going on for the top position, some supporting E. Ewing and others supporting Henry Baxter. At two p.m., two hundred or so emigrants met and elected Henry Baxter as colonel or leader, Dr. William McCormick as adjutant. Seven division captains were then selected, and the group broke up to organize each division after celebrating the election of Baxter and McCormick. In his entry this day, Welch, for the first time, called the wagon train the "San Joaquin Company" (Welch, October 3, 1849). In a short time, as they traversed the desert this would be corrupted by many into the "Sand Walking Company."

At this early stage, there appears to have been only eighty-five wagons in the train. Most accounts eventually list 104 or 107 wagons. Clearly, other wagons were added as they arrived or caught up with the train. Similarly, we don't know if the counts included only fee-paying wagons, or also included "free" wagons accompanying the Mormons. In either case, it is safe to assume that the number of wagons eventually reached between 105 and 110.

Similarly, we don't know the exact count of people or animals in the train. Welch refers to 200 people at the election, but that probably does not include women, children, servants or some of the hired teamsters and others. In some instances, wagons traveled only with family members. In other instances, a small group of men organized as a traveling company—such as the Georgians or Mississippi Boys—who rode on horseback and may have had one or more wagons in the group to carry supplies and possessions. Others may have been packers with no wagons at all. In still other cases, a family may have had more than one wagon and hired teamsters to drive those wagons and care for the livestock. It would be a safe assumption to say that the total number of people in the wagon train was between 400 and 500, with the latter number being more accurate.

Similarly, the total number of livestock is hard to estimate, but with two or three yokes (four to six animals) of oxen per wagon plus horses, spare oxen and additional beef cattle, the total probably approached 1,000 head—or possibly more. By any standards, the San Joaquin Company was a large train and that fact alone would place stress on their ability to move, overall organization and control of the train. Within weeks, the train would begin to break up into smaller groups going their own way.

A key part of the organization of the wagon train—the creation of seven divisions—was designed to facilitate travel along the trail. Each division rotated duties through a seven day week. One day, one division would lead and do the work needed to prepare the trail ahead for wagon travel. The next day, that division would drop to the end of the line and the next division would move forward and do the obligatory work. Similarly, each division would serve as a night guard to herd the livestock and protect against theft or attack by Indians. Groups of men or families traveling together would all be placed in the same division, but others traveling without a group would be added to a division so that each division had the same number of wagons in it. At the start, each division had ten or eleven wagons, but as more arrived, the number of wagons in each division was increased to fifteen.

Each year, then and now, the LDS Church holds two conferences which serve both to give information to the members and to fill administrative obligations. The General Conference is held during the first full weekend of April each year. The Semiannual General Conference is held during the first full weekend of October. In 1849, the Semiannual General Conference was held at the Bowery on October 6th and 7th. As an apostle, Rich had to stay for the Conference, as did Addison Pratt, James Brown and Francis Pomeroy. Francis Pomeroy—not to be confused with the Pomeroy brothers from Missouri who were also in Salt Lake City at this time—was about to lead a pack train south along the trail shortly after the departure of Hunt's wagon train.

During the Conference session of October 6th, Rich gave the benediction. Later that day he and Amasa Lyman (via a letter), who was already in California, were officially instructed to gather funds from the California Saints for the Perpetual Emigrating Fund that was to pay for travel of Mormon immigrants to Salt Lake City. Rich was then directed to assist Lyman until he left for Salt Lake City. At that time, Rich would replace Lyman as the head of the Mormons in California. At the same session Pratt, Brown and Blackwell were directed to go to the Society Islands. During the Conference, Pomeroy was directed to assist Rich.

Finally, on October 8th, now a week behind the wagon train, they left Salt Lake City to overtake them. But they were not alone on the trail. Others were also heading in the same direction as Jefferson Hunt's wagon train. They traveled with a pack train headed by James Flake that left Fort Utah about two weeks after the wagon train and a week after Rich.

The story of George Q. Cannon was typical of some of them. While a teenager in England, Cannon's family was converted to the LDS faith by Apostle John Taylor, who became the third President of the LDS Church following Brigham Young's death. He had married Cannon's aunt. Cannon's mother died at sea and his father died when George was seventeen. Cannon lived with John Taylor in Nauvoo and Salt Lake City and learned the printing trade from him. Because of his own beliefs and his uncle's status within the Church, Cannon could be expected to remain loyal to his faith and return in an appropriate time. Any gold mined would help the family and support the Saints in Salt Lake City. Other young Mormon men were sent to California on similar missions by close friends and relatives.

Another one of the men in the later wagon trains was Henry Bigler who had been a member of the Mormon Battalion and was present at Sutter's Mill when gold was discovered. He too was being sent to California to mine gold. His sponsor was "Father Smith," or John Smith—uncle of martyred Joseph Smith and father of Apostle George A. Smith. He provided the expenses of the endeavor. Smith and Bigler were to each get fifty percent of the gold after expenses had been paid (Landon 1999, 6).

When the camp awoke and began to prepare to leave Peeteneet Creek on the morning of October 4th, they found that many of the cattle had wandered off during the night. Two hours were spent rounding them up. The emigrants learned a quick lesson on the need to be vigilant in protecting their cattle. Before they finally started out for the day, Adonijah Welch and Reverend Granger were appointed to act as scribes or secretaries to record the activities of the train. That night they camped at the site of the present community of Santaguin.

Jefferson Hunt became concerned about the Mormons who had said they were joining the wagon train but had not yet arrived, including his friend Addison Pratt. He decided to return on the trail to discover what had happened.

On October 5th, Hunt was back at his home in Fort Utah when Addison Pratt and Hyrum Blackwell arrived with their wagon, equipped with a roadometer to measure distances. Most likely it was one of Mormon design and provided by the Church leaders to get accurate information about the distances along the Southern Route. Pratt dutifully recorded mileages along the entire route and this information eventually made it back to the leaders in Salt Lake City.

Pratt and Blackwell left Salt Lake City on October 2nd, but experienced several delays. The night of October 5th, the emigrants camped near the present location of Starr, which is currently a railroad siding. On October 6th, Pratt, Blackwell and Hunt set out to catch up with the wagon train. Since Hunt was on horseback and unencumbered by a slower wagon, he went on ahead and caught up with the wagon train at their camp at the present location of the town of Nephi. On both October 5th and 6th, Welch and several others climbed mountains where they could explore the country and see great distances from the heights.

October 7th was a Sunday and the camp leaders called a halt for the day. In the 1840s most Americans were very religious and honored the Sabbath. In addition, the day of rest helped both the people and the animals for the week ahead. While this was a very common procedure during the Westward migration, not all members of wagon trains appreciated such a stop, believing that they should be on the way to the gold. Every day spent sitting around camp meant that one more day would be lost in reaching the gold fields. Sermons were given by Reverend Ehlers, Reverend James W. Brier and a German identified as Crow. Welch wrote that Hunt had arrived. He reported that another twenty wagons were behind them and would join them soon. Some of the camp entertained themselves by going hunting in the surrounding valley and mountains.

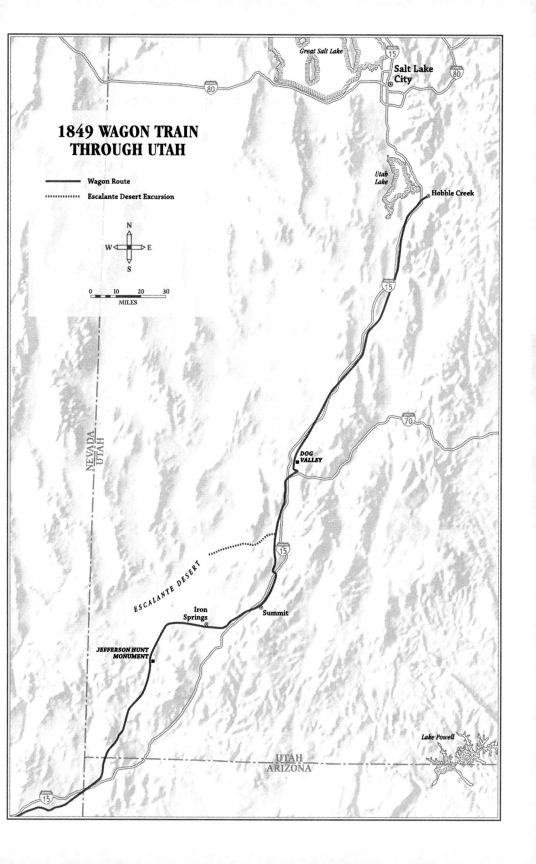

1849 WAGON TRAIN
THROUGH UTAH

——— Wagon Route

·············· Escalante Desert Excursion

N
W ◄——■——► E
S

0   10   20   30
MILES

Great Salt Lake

Salt Lake
City

Utah
Lake

Hobble Creek

NEVADA
UTAH

DOG
VALLEY

ESCALANTE DESERT

Iron
Springs

Summit

JEFFERSON HUNT
MONUMENT

Lake Powell

UTAH
ARIZONA

On October 8th, they continued to a camping spot west of present-day Levan, Utah, with springs that had been previously dug out to resemble cisterns. On this day, Charles Coulson Rich, Francis Pomeroy and James Brown began from Salt Lake City on horseback headed for the wagon train.

On the 9th, the wagon train continued to the Sevier River, where they camped for the night. Here, as at several stops before, they were visited by Indians who wished to trade, offering horses for items such as firearms. On the morning of October 10th, the wagon train started again and began to ford the Sevier River. But because they did not water the oxen first, the animals would stop in midstream to drink. This slowed down the crossing a great deal and they made only two miles before stopping again along the Sevier River.

After only a week on the trail, dissention began to occur on October 11th. That day, two men were so sick Welch reported that the doctors in the train recommended they not travel. The council met and decided to stop for the day. That evening, Captain Marshall of one of the divisions proposed to the council that the wagon train be divided. After discussion, the proposal was rejected by a vote of seven to two (Welch, October 11, 1849). This early in their travels, a number of the emigrants realized that the train was too large and could only travel at the rate of its slowest or weakest members The rate of travel was at the mercy of the officers' decisions, whether good or bad.

Addison Pratt and his fast-traveling group caught up with the wagon train at the camp on the Sevier River. He reported that they joined with the division headed by Captain Town. (Town would eventually be one of the Death Valley '49ers and Townes Pass from Death Valley to Panamint Valley is named after him.) At the same place, an additional fifteen wagons caught up with the wagon train, bringing the total, according to Welch, to ninety-nine.

Knowing that they had their first long stretch with little or no water on the next segment of the trail, everyone filled their water containers and began on the morning of the 12th. That day they traveled south, past the present location of Scipio, over Scipio Pass, and on to a spring near some cedar trees at present-day Holden. The difficult travel of nearly twenty-four miles was made without stops or water other than that they carried. As they progressed, many fell behind and some arrived at the spring hours before the others. Lorton relates that he walked the entire way, leading his horse. The last wagon did not arrive until ten p.m. The early arrivals at the spring lit a fire beacon on the hill in order to guide the stragglers into camp. Lorton summarized the feelings of many by saying, "Everybody out of humor" (Lorton Diary, October 12, 1849). Addison Pratt commented that the number of wagons now totaled 106 (Hafen and Hafen 1954, 64). On October 13th the emigrants moved about eleven miles to the site of present-day Fillmore (which served as the Territorial Capital for a while in the 1850s).

October 14th was a Sunday. Colonel Baxter again called a halt for the Sabbath, and to let the sick men recover. There was an immediate outcry from some of the emigrants. A Dr. Downer presented the wagon train leadership with a written request that they continue to move that day or that they convene a general meeting to decide what to do. Baxter called a meeting and said that he made a mistake in calling a halt since the constitution did not give him specific authority to do so. He explained, however, that common custom gave the commander the right to make such decisions.

The level of dissent was rising. For the second time in four days, the decisions and command of Henry Baxter were being challenged, and this was the easiest part of the long road to California. With the deserts and horrible travel conditions still hundreds of miles away, Jefferson Hunt decided to take action. According to Welch:

> "The meeting was then addressed in a short pittey [sic] speech by Maj. Hunt [Here Welch referred to him correctly using his highest rank—major in the Nauvoo Legion.] in which he urged the absolute necessity of subordination and submission to the standing authorities. The only safety said he on our long and dangerous journey is perfect unity and obedience. We are in advance of the season, have plenty of time for delay and moreover shall by moving slowly save the strength of our oxen which will be needed on the deserts. No motion was made that the train should start and the people returned satisfied to their tents" (Welch, October 14, 1849).

This time the emigrants heeded the words given by Jefferson Hunt and by Brigham Young several months before when he cited the need for unity.

William Lorton, in reporting the same speech, put a more religious touch on it by saying that: "Captain Hunt in a stump speech remarked in regard to the dissatisfaction on account of laying up Sundays, said God on his throne with 300 angels couldn't frame an arrangement that would please everybody" (Lorton, October 14, 1849). Jefferson Hunt was addressing both the dissent and need for discipline, and his own religious beliefs.

His experiences with the Mormon Battalion were clear in his mind as he addressed the assembled wagon train. But unlike the Battalion, the members of the wagon train did not share a common heritage or belief to bind them together.

On October 15th, the wagon train headed southwest and camped on Corn Creek near present-day Kanosh, and very near the small community of Hatton. Here, the trail as used by Fremont and Hunt on his round trip to California in 1847-48, bore to the west, then south, then east to Immigrant Spring next to present-day Interstate 70, and about two miles east of present-day Cove Fort, Utah. This was also the route followed by the Independent Pioneer Company a week earlier on October 7th and 8th. Hoover reported that they traveled thirty-four miles between Corn Creek and the springs near Cove Fort. They had no water and poor feed and were forced to make a dry camp on the night of the 7th. Because of this, they decided to rest on October 9th. It had taken them three days, with one thirty-six hour period of no water and poor feed. Wagons pulled by oxen could not travel as fast as horses and mules without wagons.

Welch's journal is missing entries for the period of October 15th through the 19th, but William Lorton provides us with entries for the period. He wrote that on the 15th, "Three wagons and a number of horsemen follow the pack trail to the southwest" (Lorton, October 15, 1849). Thus, the first defections from the San Joaquin Company were noted. Apparently, they went on ahead on the old route followed by the Independent Pioneer Company—which was

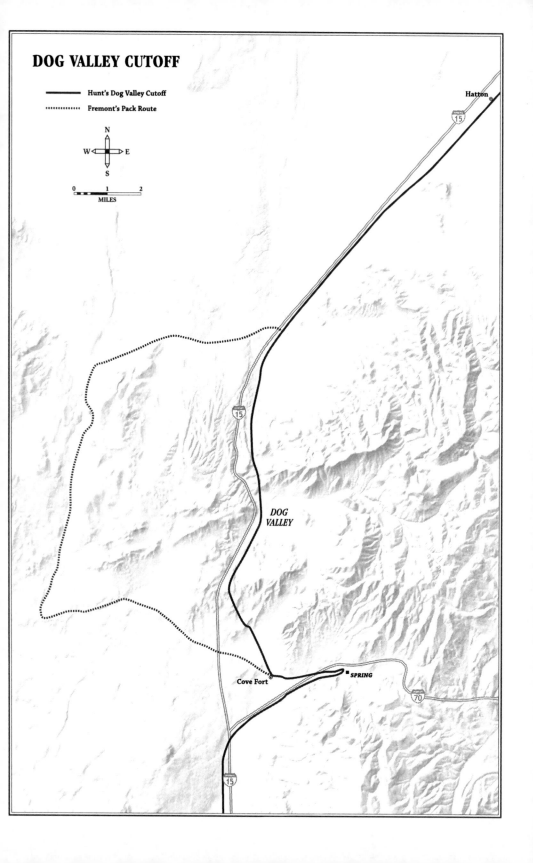

not without its own problems. Near Cove Fort, they tried one of their own, a Mr. Hall, for refusing to share some of his water with others on the thirty-four mile dry trail from Hatton to Cove Fort.

As they left Corn Creek on October 16th, Jefferson Hunt was aware that the circuitous route he had taken in 1847-48 could not reasonably by made by his wagon train in one day. However, he reasoned that if a road could be made by going nearly straight south, he would be able to shave over ten miles off the trail and save a full day in traversing that section.

Accordingly, he led the wagon train on a route that nearly parallels today's Interstate 15 toward Baker Canyon and Dog Valley. According to William Lorton, Hunt directed the wagon train to remain for his signal at the base of the hill (Dog Valley Mountain), while he and several of his assistants went up to the top to scout out the feasibility for a road and to begin preparing the way. When convinced that the wagon train could make it, Hunt signaled them and they ascended the hill.

Lorton again described that they went on a rough road through sage, scrub oak and rough rocks. The ascent just before the summit was steep, but the descent was steeper, and they had to lock the wheels of the wagons to control their downhill speed (Lorton, October 16, 1849). They then entered Dog Valley, a small basin encircled by mountains. The crossing over the next range to Cove Fort was more gradual, but they still had to follow rocky ravines and cut a road when necessary. They arrived at Immigrant Spring, about two miles east of present-day Cove Fort, after dark, but they had gone from water to water and good grass in one day and effectively saved two days over the time taken by their predecessors.

Like hundreds of explorers, scouts and guides before and after, Hunt had improved on an existing trail and reduced the distance between water from thirty-four miles to about twenty-one. His new Dog Valley cutoff saved time, distance and uncertainty. One unusual feature about his cutoff was that it was shorter and quicker than the older pack route. On western trails it is common to see pack and wagon trails diverge at points. Usually, the pack route takes the shorter, quicker, steeper and more difficult route because the pack animals are better able to negotiate more difficult terrain. In this case, however, the Dog Valley cutoff was better for both pack trains and wagon trains and the cutoff became the standard route for everyone. We will see several future instances where the pack and wagon routes diverged to the advantage of the packers.

Hunt's Dog Valley cutoff was, in part, a result of the experience and skills he picked up while in the Mormon Battalion and it was a resounding success.

The next day, October 17th, was another long, waterless drive of twenty-two miles because the steam beds were dry. They camped in Wildcat Canyon and were now approaching Beaver Valley. Then on October 18th, they went about five miles to Beaver Creek and camped west of the present town of Beaver, at today's Greenville. South of them was the Black Mountains, and Beaver Creek flowed to the west. From there they could see before them some of the straggling wagons of the Independent Pioneer Company climbing into the tree line on the Black Mountains.

From their perspective on Beaver Creek, the Black Mountains did not seem too daunting. They were not as high as many of the peaks in the surrounding mountains. They had seen much higher peaks and steeper roads in the Wasatch Mountains near Salt Lake City. From Beaver Creek, the road led about six miles up a six percent grade over the Greenville Bench to the tree line. Just beyond that were some steeper looking mountains with canyons. But from their vantage point, these mountains did not seem too difficult.

Jefferson Hunt, however, had been over these mountains twice before and knew that they were covered by a thick growth of smaller juniper trees that would impede their progress. There were several steep grades near the crest and on the down slope on the other side. He realized that some of the traveling would have to be in a streambed over large rocks, and they would likely have to cut trees to widen the road. More importantly, he knew the next reliable source of water was over the crest, through a small valley, down another descent and, finally, into the Valley of Little Salt Lake beyond—about twenty-five miles away. The large wagon train would have difficult traveling and would probably need to make a dry camp before reaching water.

What Hunt and the others did not know was the condition of the road after the Independent Pioneer Company went through. Had they significantly improved the road, or would it need time-consuming major work? To answer these questions, the camp stopped for the day and a party of scouts, probably including Hunt, some of his men and some of the emigrants, went ahead to survey the condition of the road and to give those in the wagon train an idea of what obstacles were in front of them. For the other emigrants, October 19th was a day of rest and exploration.

On October 20th, Welch's journal continues. In it he describes a morning meeting of the council in which it was decided that Colonel Baxter, Adjutant McCormack and Jefferson Hunt could decide when to order that the livestock be placed in a corral. This would require additional work moving the wagons into a corral formation, but would simplify the process of rounding up the livestock on the following morning. Welch then discussed the results of the previous day's exploration. He noted that the road was rough, that it actually headed to the east of south, which was opposite from the direction of California, and that Jefferson Hunt said that they would have to go twenty-eight miles to water (Welch, October 20, 1849).

How rough was the road over the Black Mountains? Vincent Hoover provided a description of his experiences when his group of the Independent Pioneer Company went over on October 13th, a week before the San Joaquin Company arrived. Hoover traveled less than fifteen miles that day, and had to go through heavy timber that was so close to the road that many wagons suffered torn covers and broken bows that held up the covers. They had to make a dry camp that night, but it snowed and was very cold. The next day, they left before breakfast and made it to present-day Paragonah. Their total travel for the two days was twenty-seven miles. Hoover noted that it was the fifth dry camp they had made so far on the trip (Hoover, October 13 & 14, 1849).

Late in the morning of October 20th, three men, including Adonijah Welch, volunteered to explore Beaver Creek to the west. They left at noon and went ten miles to the mouth of the canyon where Beaver Creek enters the Escalante Desert, near the present-day community of Minersville. They could see that Beaver Creek turned north, not the direction they wanted to travel. They also saw the vast expanse of the Escalante Desert in front of them and could not see its southern end. Welch and his small party returned to the main camp at ten p.m. (Welch, October 20, 1849).

Sunday, October 21st, was not a day of rest for the emigrants. Welch and his explorers reported their findings to the council. Jefferson Hunt, mindful of Porter Rockwell's cutoff through the Escalante Desert the previous year, told the council that he believed that they could reach the Old Spanish Trail by going down the Escalante Desert and that they would find plenty of water at its "further extremity." According to Welch: "Acting on his [Hunt's] advice the council determined to try the experiment. . ." (Welch, October 21, 1849).

The emigrants began the trek westward along Beaver Creek toward the mouth of the canyon at present-day Minersville, Utah. They traveled twelve miles and camped on the creek with its abundant trout. It is not clear exactly what route Hunt had in mind from there. From his earlier travels, he was likely aware that the Escalante Desert was forty-five to fifty miles long and trended in a northeast to southwest direction. Welch commented that Hunt mentioned that the "Little Muddy River [Coal Creek near Cedar City] runs across its further extremity" (Welch, October 21, 1849). Perhaps he was thinking of a route directly south from Minersville to Coal Creek. If so, that route would have taken them over a series of rolling hills and not out into the flats of the Escalante Desert where they ended up. But the availability of water would have been no less of a problem.

Whichever way he was trying to go, Hunt had not been on this portion of the route before. He did not know the location of any water that might be there. But he was aware that the hundred wagons in his train were not realistically able to make the same forced march that Porter Rockwell, the discharged Battalion packers, Captain Davis and his family with the wagon had made the year before. In several weeks, there would be the need for such forced marches across portions of the Mojave Desert, but that was not the case here.

On Monday, October 22nd, the camp prepared to leave Beaver Creek. But first, they had to find many of the cattle and horses that had wandered off during the night. This took a lot of time and the wagons left later than they wished. The wagons were to travel a distance of ten to fifteen miles where they expected to find water. A small group of scouts, including Jefferson Hunt and Colonel Baxter, set off earlier in search of water for the next camp. After twenty miles, they were unsuccessful and Baxter sent word back to the train to stop and set up camp. Unfortunately, most expected to go to water that day and had not taken adequate water with them from Beaver Creek. Welch, Dr. McCormick, the adjutant, and Henry Skinner also set off to explore, but were unsuccessful in finding either water or a better route to Little Salt Lake. Hunt and the other scouts returned late at night and reported that they had gone an additional twelve miles but had not found any water (Welch, October 22, 1849).

That day's camp was located on the plain of the Escalante Desert about twelve miles, just south of west, of the present location of Minersville. Although there is a hot spring four or five miles to the northwest, it was not known to the emigrants and was in the opposite direction of travel, and so was not discovered. The emigrants were camped nearly a day's journey from water, and there was no prospect of any in front of them.

On Monday, October 15, the Mormon packers heading for California left Fort Utah. This group of about twenty included several men who left detailed accounts of their travel. The journals of George Q. Cannon, Henry Bigler and William Farrer are particularly important. James Flake was chosen as captain of the group. Leaving Fort Utah at about the same time was a second group with about the same number of packers. This group consisted of mostly non-Mormons and was headed by Orson Kirk Smith from New York. The two groups traveled together or in close proximity.

O.K. Smith was returning to California with supplies he had obtained in Missouri. He had previously been in California, and had left there in April by ship for the Isthmus of Panama and then on to the Mississippi River. Obtaining goods for trade, livestock and ten other men as packers, he left Missouri in August, arriving at Fort Laramie on August 27th. When he got to Salt Lake City, he brought news of other Mormons and the general conditions in California. Part of the news he carried was that a group of fifteen Mormons were in Los Angeles and would be bringing cattle and a "good deal of gold dust" back to Salt Lake City (Emigrant Rosters, 1849).

The packers, relying on horses and mules, and without wagons or cattle, were able to travel much faster than the wagons. On Monday, October 22nd, after just one week on the trail, the Mormon packers arrived at Beaver Creek and there found a note from Apostle Charles C. Rich telling them to follow Beaver Creek to the west. Both groups then headed west and camped that night on the bench near the mouth of the canyon at Minersville. They could see the wagons camped in the distance.

O.K. Smith had with him a map purporting to show a shortcut from the Old Spanish Trail to Walker Pass. The map had been given to him by Elijah "Barney" Ward, a former mountain man, who was living with the Mormons and would soon join the LDS Church. Ward probably had operated a trading post near the site of Fort Utah for ten years before the arrival of the Mormons and was thoroughly familiar with the Utah region. In 1844, he likely had traveled the Old Spanish Trail with others on a trading venture that included returning to Fort Laramie with a supply of Abalone shells (Hafen and Hafen 2003, Vol. VII, 343-351).

Barney Ward's map showed a route across the desert from a point just north of Mountain Meadow to Walker Pass in California. It showed the location of springs and streams and seemed to show that there was ample water and feed along the entire route. This seemed quite plausible to those who saw the map, because it conformed in many ways to John C. Fremont's map published the year before. It showed a mountain range stretching from east to west across what is now Nevada. Fremont's 1844 map, published in 1848, showed a mountain range extending east to west from about Mountain Meadow to the Sierras. But a notation on the map says: "These mountains are not explored, being only seen from elevated points on the northern exploring line" (Fremont 1970, Map). Fremont had seen snow-covered peaks, which were the southernmost mountains on north to south trending ranges, to his north, and erroneously interpreted them as possibly being part of an east/west range. Many of those traveling had read Fremont's report and had the map, and Ward's map apparently corresponded to the Fremont map in many ways.

Lending additional credibility to the Ward map was the fact that he had lived and traveled around the area for many years. He was known to be an experienced desert traveler, and since he was married to an Indian, it was probably assumed that he had additional information from the various South-western tribal groups. O.K. Smith, who probably got the map directly from Ward, certainly believed in its accuracy, as did many others who saw it.

Why did Barney Ward offer up a bogus map to Smith? We don't have a definitive answer, but several things are certain. First of all, the map was not given to Mormons or to those with Mormon guides. Ward was probably care-ful not to antagonize his friends and neighbors. Secondly, there is a record of Ward trying to deceive other travelers only two months before. An emigrant named Joseph A. Stuart recorded that his party met Ward on the Bear River, near where Idaho, Utah and Wyoming meet today, on August 13, 1849. At that time, Ward told the emigrants that there were no provisions at Fort Hall and that the feed had been burned off along the Humboldt Route. He advised them to travel with him to Salt Lake City for re-supply. These emigrants went on to meet with mountain man and adventurer Peg-leg Smith (no relation to O.K.) at his home twenty miles away and found the report false.

It appears that Ward was trying to divert those on the Northern Route to Salt Lake City. Whether he was trying to do that for personal gain or for the benefit of his friends in Salt Lake is not certain. Nor is there any report that Ward sold the map to O.K. Smith, but that is quite possible. It appears the Ward map was part of a scheme to divert emigrants or to obtain money from the '49ers. In any case, the Ward map in the possession of Captain O.K. Smith was fraudulent and probably based on the Fremont map or report. It would have disastrous consequences for many in Hunt's wagon train.

The morning of October 23rd began with the camp learning the bad news that there was no water nearby. Since they had not brought sufficient water with them and there was no prospect of water ahead, the emigrants were angry and agitated at their situation. Some began to blame Hunt, as the guide, for getting them into the situation. Others blamed the Council who decided to take the unknown route. Addison Pratt, Hunt's good friend and traveling companion, reported that: "Slurs were frequently thrown out about the Mormons, and some even went so far as to threaten the life of Capt. Hunt, if they did not get through safely, and the greatest unreasonableness was exhibited by them" (Ellsworth and Pratt 1990, 384). Pratt noted that many were blaming Hunt, even though it was not his doing.

The Council met and decided that the cattle should be driven back to the creek and each division should take a wagon to get water to return to those in the camp. Most of the livestock were driven back to Beaver Creek unyoked. There they remained overnight while some were used to take water twelve miles back to the camp. Many of the emigrants accompanied them but did not take their wagons, tents or other comforts and were forced to spend a cold night along the banks.

However, Captain Thomas W. Marshall and his division decided to continue on to California on their own, and left with their wagons and livestock. Thus, the wagon train suffered its first major defection when one-seventh of the people, their wagons and livestock separated and continued on alone.

But just as Marshall and his division left the train, the two groups of packers led by James Flake and O.K. Smith arrived at the point Beaver Creek exited the canyon (Minersville). According to George Q. Cannon, they quickly learned of the troubles ahead from returning emigrants and stopped to await more information. Rich, Pomeroy and Brown soon arrived and told the Mormon packers about the conditions at the camp on the Escalante Desert. In turn, the packers told Rich and his group about the map of the shortcut in Smith's possession. Cannon described the map as "Walker's Cut off" and said it went south of the line of mountains described by Fremont as going East to West (Landon and Cannon 1999, 20-24).

The Mormon packers, Rich and his group discussed the implications of Smith's map. Rich and Flake went to see Smith about taking the same route. While James Flake was the captain of the packers, Charles C. Rich was an apostle of the LDS Church, and as such, was regarded by all of the Mormons present as their senior leader. While Rich might have sought input from others in the group, his decision was considered the ultimate one to be followed without question.

At this point it is important to note that Brigham Young and the leaders in Salt Lake City were very interested in measuring, recording and, if possible, improving the route between Salt Lake City and Southern California. Any opportunity to find an alternative road and to take advantage of the experiences of a mountaineer such as Barney Ward had to be seriously considered.

Jefferson Hunt was not yet through with his exploration of a possible route that could bypass the trail over the Black Mountains. On October 23rd, while some went back to Beaver Creek for water, he again set off on one final scouting trip to the south. With him went four men from the company: James D. Martin, G. Wiley Webster, David Switzer and Peter Acker. They took two horses with them but planned to walk the entire distance. Their plan was to go twenty-five miles from camp, and if water was found, they would notify the others and the cattle and wagons would go forward. Welch added that they took very little water with them and it was consumed by ten a.m. (Welch, October 23, 1849).

By nightfall, they reached their stated distance but had not found any water. Welch recorded that "their thirst was almost intolerable and their position consequently somewhat perilous." Hunt and the others then conferred and decided that Peter Acker would return with Hunt on foot, while the other three with the two horses would continue on to known water sources to the south or southeast along the Old Spanish Trail that were now closer to them than was the camp on the desert west of Minersville (Welch, October 24, 1849).

What exactly was Jefferson Hunt looking for? Some indication is in Welch's entry for October 27th where he says Hunt was trying to find a "valley contiguous to" Little Salt Lake (or Parowan) Valley, but that there was a small valley between them (Welch, October 27, 1849). Hunt had probably taken the wagons too far west into the Escalante Desert and was unable to reach

Cedar Valley by simply going straight south. Cedar Valley, with its springs and streams, was to the southeast of their position. The assumption has been that Hunt was trying to retrace the route of Porter Rockwell in 1848. But it should be noted that Fremont's map of his route show him coming north from the springs near Enoch, along the west side of the Red Hills to Parowan Gap, where he crossed into Parowan Valley. Perhaps Hunt was trying to find this route.

Hunt and Acker arrived back at the camp at 9 a.m. on October 24th, not having had any water in twenty-three hours. Exhausted and unable to speak, they heartily drank water, ate and rested. The message to those in the camp was clear; there was no going forward from this point. As the wagons turned around, they aptly named the Escalante Desert "the Valley of Errors" (Welch, October 25, 1849).

James Brown, who wrote of his life fifty years later, described the incident in some detail. Unfortunately, he has some of his timing wrong in that he says that they entered the Escalante Desert from the Beaver River in search of the map's cutoff, which is inaccurate since they did not learn of the cutoff from O.K. Smith until they retreated from the desert. In any case, Brown's description of Jefferson Hunt is worth noting:

> "Sometime in the night Captain Hunt came into camp, so near choked from the lack of water that his tongue was swollen till it protruded from his mouth; his eyes were so sunken in his head that he could scarcely be recognized. His horse, too, for the need of water, was blind, and staggered as he was urged on. Their stay had been thirty-six hours, on the sands, without water" (Brown 1900, 134).

They had to backtrack to Beaver Creek and cross over the Black Mountains to the Little Salt Lake.

They had arrived at Beaver Creek on October 18th, and a week later, were no closer to California. They had lost a full seven days travel time and ex-

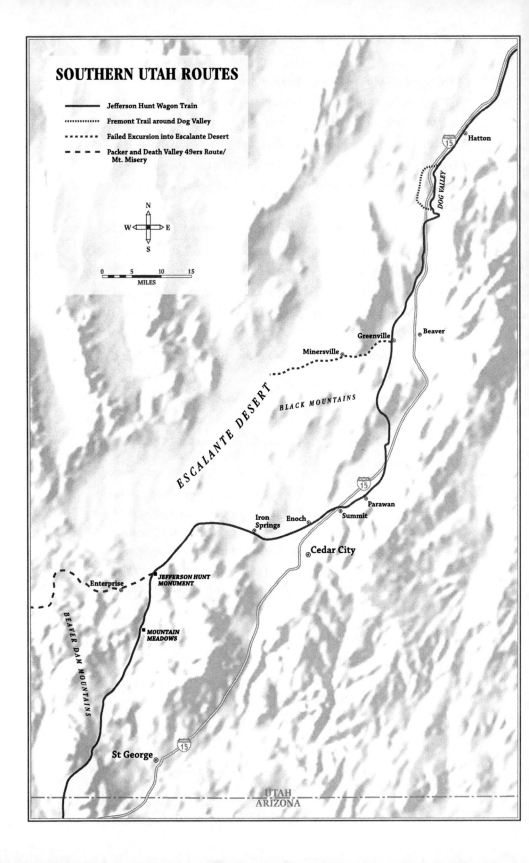

SOUTHERN UTAH ROUTES

———————— Jefferson Hunt Wagon Train

·············· Fremont Trail around Dog Valley

▪ ▪ ▪ ▪ ▪ Failed Excursion into Escalante Desert

— — — Packer and Death Valley 49ers Route/
Mt. Misery

N
W ✦ E
S

0   5   10   15
MILES

Hatton

DOG VALLEY

Beaver

Greenville

Minersville

BLACK MOUNTAINS

ESCALANTE DESERT

Parawan

Iron
Springs   Enoch   Summit

Cedar City

Enterprise   ■ JEFFERSON HUNT
MONUMENT

■ MOUNTAIN
MEADOWS

BEAVER DAM MOUNTAINS

St George

UTAH
ARIZONA

pended a lot of effort and supplies in the process. The camp was disillusioned and rife with discontent. Already one division had set out on their own. With all of the anger at Hunt and the officers of the company, the appearance of the wagons with O.K. Smith and the map created the same effect as kicking a hornet's nest.

The first group that decided to follow Smith were the Mormon packers under James Flake. However, Charles C. Rich, who had joined Hunt in the wagon train, stepped forward to exercise his leadership role as an apostle. Rich recorded that, on October 25th, he, the packers and Jefferson Hunt met to discuss the option of taking the cutoff, and that the packers were "anxious to go by the way of Walkers pass" (Hafen and Hafen 1954, 183). Rich decided to leave the wagon train and join the Flake packers. Shortly thereafter, Rich declined the offer to replace Flake as the captain; rather he suggested that Flake continue as leader with himself as counselor. Francis Pomeroy accompanied them, but Pratt, Blackwell and Brown continued with Hunt and the wagons. Subsequent events show that part of the discussion included instructions from Hunt for them to travel south and intercept the Old Spanish Trail if they got lost or found the route to be impractical.

Why were Rich and the packers so eager to try the cutoff? Part of the answer lies in the desire to explore a new route to California, if one existed. A faster, easier route would benefit the Mormons in Salt Lake, and it is clear that part of their mission was to develop the road to California and for the Mormon Corridor. Another part of the answer is that the proposed shortcut would save hundreds of miles and weeks of travel for them. By dividing, they could still document and refine the Old Spanish Trail route and explore a possible better alternative.

A second reason might have been to focus attention on the newly-described cutoff in hopes of drawing the rest of the train away from Jefferson Hunt—who felt considerable hostility from many of the '49ers. While this is plausible, it is unlikely because it was more reasonable for the Mormons to stand together behind Hunt if there was a belief that the hostility might turn violent. The twenty packers combined with the other Mormons in the wagon train would have been a formidable force of about forty men that would have easily discouraged any violent attack. This author believes that exploration was the primary reason for the Mormon packers to take the cutoff.

When they returned to Beaver Creek, they abandoned the wagons Rich and his associates were using and obtained pack animals to take the rest of the way. Not all of the goods could be packed, so some was cached along Beaver Creek. It is possible that Jefferson Hunt also took charge of some of the goods, especially tools that could be used in the road construction over the Black Mountains.

At this point, it became clear that if Rich and the packers were successful, they might end up at the Southern Mines (near Mariposa) and not in Southern California with Hunt, Pratt and the others. Another of the duties that the group had been charged with before leaving Salt Lake City was obtaining signatures on petitions to Congress endorsing the State of Deseret, the Mormons' proposed government for what is now Utah. To facilitate the petition-gathering in Southern California, George Q. Cannon wrote out a copy of the constitution of the State of Deseret to be taken by Hunt and circulated among the Mormons and their friends in the Chino-Los Angeles-San Diego areas. Cannon occupied himself with this task on October 25th and 26th.

Well-known as he was among both Mormon and non-Mormon residents of California, Hunt was the ideal person to circulate such a petition and to encourage support for Brigham Young's new state. It would be Hunt's first—but not his last—effort in California and Utah politics.

On October 25th, the emigrants and Mormons left what Adonijah Welch called the "Valley of Errors." Most camped near Minersville, but Captain Goddard's company with thirteen wagons continued on, leaving the main group behind. The wagon train continued to dissolve and two divisions had left. The next day, the wagons returned along Beaver Creek to the trail that led over the Black Mountains. Here both Addison Pratt and Welch described following the creek to where the pack trail continued to the south. William Lorton, however, wrote of striking "over the base of the mountains" through sage brush and "up hill and down dale" until they reached the ravine with the pack trail (Lorton, October 26, 1849). Lorton's description differs enough from the others to indicate that he was not on the same path as Pratt and Welch, but that he was traveling on the bench south of Beaver Creek.

As the wagon train traveled and camped, Smith's map was the main topic of discussion. According to Welch, the map showed water, feed and firewood every twelve to fifteen miles. Barney Ward told Smith that he had been on the road twice and it was suitable for wagons. They calculated the cutoff went straight west and stretched about 400 miles from where they were to the San Joaquin Valley. If successful, the Smith/Ward map would save about 300 miles of travel to the gold fields.

From Beaver Creek, they traveled south along the established pack trail and wagon road made by the Independent Pioneer Company before them. Their route took them up the Greenville Bench and into a canyon now named California Hollow, which leads to the summit of the Black Mountains. On the night of October 26th, the remaining divisions made a dry camp within this ravine, about seven miles south of Beaver Creek and about one and one-half miles short of the ridgeline. They kept the livestock within the confines of the ravine (California Hollow) and placed their guards on the ridge on both sides and at the lower end to prevent the animals from returning to the water at Beaver Creek. Lorton commented on the numerous campfires that he could see from his lofty perch above the ravine (Lorton, October 26, 1849).

The next morning, October 27th, they set out, crossed over the top of the Black Mountains, through a pass at the upper end of California Hollow, descended into Little Valley and then into the Valley of the Little Salt Lake via Little Valley Hollow. Lorton described the road as "the devil's own pass, and descending is very steep and tedious," with thick "fir trees" and "ground very stony" (Lorton, October 27, 1849). Welch described the same stretch as "a bad hill to climb and descend" and "quite rough with loose stones" (Welch, October 27, 1849).

Two weeks earlier on October 13th, the Independent Pioneer Company crossed over the same pass and Vincent Hoover said that: "Wagon covers &

bows have suffered. There has been several wagon covers & bows torn to pieces" (Hoover, October 13, 1849). Hoover, on his way to Salt Lake City, had obtained copies of William Clayton's and Joseph Ware's guides to Salt Lake City, Oregon and California. Hoover was inspired by these guidebooks and was making notes for a road guide along the southern route to Los Angeles. Using mileages from a roadometer in his wagon train, he kept detailed notes that he hoped to eventually publish. In his notes, he specifically says that anyone crossing the Black Mountains would "have bad roads besides two bad cedar groves to go through" (Hoover, Guide, 20). The "cedar" and "fir" trees referred to by the various writers are actually juniper trees that were not familiar to those from the Eastern States.

Both Lorton and Welch commented on the rocks and steep grades that marked the road over the pass, but neither commented about the thick growth of trees that caused damage to the wagons in the Independent Pioneer Company. We can assume that most of the overhanging limbs were cut back from the pack trail to widen it, and that the trees presented no unusual problem for the San Joaquin Company wagon train. It seems they were easily able to do what remaining work was necessary to widen the road for their wagons.

Today, it is possible for a four-wheel drive vehicle to go south from Greenville, over the Black Mountain summit, through Little Valley to the south, and intersect with Interstate 15 at Highway 20, about seventeen miles south of Beaver. Today's road closely follows portions of the old trail in some places, but does not go through California Hollow, rather on the ridgeline to the west of it. Most of the route from Greenville to the summit of the Black Mountains can be described as an improved or graded dirt road much of the year. But the portion from the summit down into Little Valley is, at best, a Jeep or ATV trail where any vehicle traversing the road will experience serious paint damage from the trees and branches alongside the trail. The heavy tree and brush growth now extends for almost six miles along the improved roads. It is very easy to imagine the conditions experienced by Hoover and the others who took the first wagons over this route.

It is possible, however, that the trees experienced by travelers in 1849 were not as dense or as extensive as they now are. One hundred years of fire suppression in the area likely has permitted thicker and more extensive tree growth. A longtime resident of Beaver told the author that the current tree line and density did not form until after extensive sheep grazing in the late 1800s, followed by a severe drought at the turn of the century. According to this account, these events significantly altered tree growth patterns. Whether or not the extent and density of the trees in the mid-Nineteenth century equaled today's, the obstacle was formidable to the wagons.

October 27th brought the wagon train over the Black Mountains, through Little Valley and into the Little Salt Lake Valley, at which point they intersected the Old Spanish Trail. Hunt would now follow that trail the remainder of the way to Southern California. The few springs at the north end of the valley were sulphurous, so they continued on to either Little Creek or Red Creek at or near present-day Paragonah. Addison Pratt noted that they were twenty-seven miles from Beaver Creek. They came upon Captain Goddard and his 7th Division, which had left them on the Beaver. Also they found Martin, Switzer and Webster, who had started on the ill-fated search for water with Jefferson Hunt four days before. The three reported that they had traveled another fifteen miles after Hunt left and reached Antelope Springs. From there, they followed the Old Spanish Trail north until they reached their comrades. From Beaver Creek to Paragonah, the train had traveled almost thirty miles and spent one night at a dry camp. It was a taste of what was to come.

On Sunday, October 28th, the camp moved only about five miles to the stream at present-day Parowan. The camp took advantage of the water and grass to stop and let their animals rest. The Council met and addressed disciplinary matters that had come up and punished several men accused of theft. The Mormon packers, still under the command of Captain Flake, and now known to us as the Flake-Rich Company, continued on past the wagon camp. They trekked another six miles to Summit Creek at the present site of Summit, Utah.

George A. Cannon made an interesting observation on that day noting
that O.K. Smith was also camped there but that "he had crossed the Mountains from Beaver Valley & came on the North side of the Lake [Little Salt Lake
which was just to the northwest of them] ... we came down the South side"
(Landon 1999, 28). It appears from this comment that Smith and his packers
may have headed straight south from near Minersville along the approximate
route of today's Highway 130. This may have been the very route that Jefferson
Hunt was looking for when he became lost in the Escalante Desert.

From Parowan, the camp then moved another short distance of about
six miles on October 29th to a location near the present community of Summit. Most of them remained at Summit Creek on the 30th also. There was
much discussion of the new route shown on Smith's map. Some thought it the
best way to go; others were unsure. Compounding the issue was that some of
the emigrants were already showing signs of running out of provisions, and
some of the ox teams and horses were showing the effects of travel. Colonel
Baxter estimated that a quarter of the wagon teams were not capable of continuing on to California and should return to Salt Lake City for the Winter.
Welch noted that many of those people with adequate provisions were concerned that those without might prove to be a burden in the weeks ahead on
the desert (Welch, October 29, 1849).

William Lorton recorded that he had twenty-five pounds of flour stolen, and that Charles McDermit (with whom he was traveling) decided to give
up his wagon and pack from there. Lorton described the incident by saying
"I am set out upon the prairie; come near having blood shed." He called on
the Council to try to settle these matters, but his flour was not recovered—although he did get a ride in another wagon. Lorton summarized the conditions
in camp by saying: "Devil in Man. Provisions getting scarce" (Lorton, October
29, 1849).

The map showing the shortcut to California, the lost time in the Escalante Desert, the shortage of provisions, the general anxiety and breakdown
in discipline, all contributed to much confusion and dissention. They would

soon reach the place that the map showed as the beginning of the shortcut, so all attention was focused on whether or not to go that way. In his book, William Lewis Manly described the scene: The map (or possibly a copy of it, since Smith had probably continued on) was frequently displayed and passed around. Speeches were made about the matter and everyone talked about it.

According to Manly, the map clearly showed the route and the locations of water, grass and obstacles that could be easily surmounted. The more it was discussed, the more support arose for the wagons to take the shortcut. Finally, a general meeting was held and one of the speakers was Jefferson Hunt. According to Manly, Hunt said: "You all know I was hired to go by way of Los Angeles, but if you wish to go and follow Smith I will go also. But if even one wagon decides to go on the original route, I shall be bound to go with that wagon" (Manly 2001, 66-67).

Privately, Hunt held a different view. His good friend, fellow Mormon, and traveling companion, Addison Pratt recorded that:

> "Here Bro. Hunt came to me and told me that his life was at stake as there was a party that intended to kill him if their cattle died in crossing the deserts and he thought there was but one way to escape and that was to have the company voluntarily take the intended cut off and leave a few wagons of us to go where we were of a mind to. He wished me and all the brethren to ask the Lord for his delivery. We told him we would" (Hafen and Hafen 1954, 77-78).

On one hand he had an obligation to the emigrants, but on the other, the dissention had gotten to the point that dissolution of the wagon train was in his best interest.

And that breakup was at hand. At the Summit camp, the Jay Hawkers (Jay Hawks or Jayhawks) under Captain Doty left at ten a.m. on October 30th. The Buckskin Company under the command of Cephas Arms decided to leave early the next morning. Colonel Baxter, the elected leader of the San Joaquin Company, and Adonijah Welch, the recorder, were members of the Buckskins, and accordingly, resigned their positions. The San Joaquin Company effectively had dissolved. Everyone was free to decide on their own whether to try the shortcut or to continue to follow Jefferson Hunt.

While most of the camp at Summit Creek debated the merits of the shortcut, Hunt was busy doing something else. During the previous days and at the Summit camp, Hunt and his Mormon companions had been collecting various tools and similar equipment discarded or abandoned by the emigrants. Perhaps some tools were left along the road in the Escalante Desert and others were discarded on the steep grades over the Black Mountains. More was probably left in wagons that were being abandoned as people decided on packing. Iron tools such as shovels, picks, saws, carpentry tools and similar items were heavy and not needed on the route.

Since Hunt knew he was coming back over the same trail, he decided to cache those tools. There was no better place than the Summit Creek campground. Relying on his Mormon Battalion experiences from the Santa Fe Trail, he knew that the proper way to cache such desirable items was to dig one or more holes, dump the resulting dirt into a stream to dissipate any evidence of such digging, to bury and cover the tools, and then place the livestock over the area for a day or so. He would have known that such actions would eliminate any sign of the cache to others such as local Indians or other trail travelers.

Meanwhile, on the evening of October 30th, the packers were very near the present site of Newcastle, Utah. They met—and at the suggestion of Apostle C.C. Rich—voted to have James Flake continue as the captain, with Rich serving as his councilor. They also voted to take the shortcut on the following day (Hafen and Hafen 1954, 149-150).

When dawn broke on the morning of October 31st, the Flake-Rich group and the Smith packers were several days ahead of the main group; the Jay Hawkers were one day ahead. The 7th Division under Captain Goddard was somewhere behind them. Even before daylight, the Buckskins and several other wagons from other divisions left ahead of the main body. The rest of the wagons followed later. By the end of the day, the Flake-Rich and Smith packers were beyond the present location of Newcastle and very close to the start of the cutoff (near a point now known as the Jefferson Hunt Monument), the 7th Division was behind them, and the Buckskins and others were at Iron Springs, west of present-day Cedar City. The main group was along Coal Creek, north and west of Cedar City. The various groups extended for nearly thirty-five miles along the trail.

On November 1st, the main camp advanced on to Iron Springs in a small gap west of Cedar City. It was here that Jefferson Hunt had previously noted the presence of iron ore. The advance group of wagons were about twelve miles ahead where they proceeded south off the trail about a mile to Antelope Springs.

November 2nd brought the advance group of wagons to Newcastle, while the main body of wagons stopped at Antelope Springs. Lorton, and possibly others, noted that Table Butte, the mountain that many of them saw twenty-five miles to the south of their earlier camp in "Retreat Valley" (the Escalante Desert or Welch's "Valley of Errors") was now not far to the north of Antelope Springs. Lorton commented that they could have reached water and that Retreat Valley might be the road sometime in the future (Lorton, November 2, 1849). At the same time, the packers were still about thirty-five miles ahead on the cutoff and had descended into Headwaters Wash and Beaver Dam Wash, very close to the current Utah-Nevada border.

On November 3rd, the wagon train reached present-day Pinto Creek at Newcastle, Utah. They could see the cutoff a few miles ahead, toward present-day Enterprise, Utah. The time had come for the remaining emigrants to decide which way they were going to go. Some had probably decided to take the new route while others were undecided, and a few were content to go on with Jefferson Hunt.

That evening, another meeting was held to discuss the cutoff. Again there were many speeches and much debate. One of the strongest advocates for the new trail was Reverend James Welch Brier, a Methodist minister who was traveling with his wife, Juliet, and three young sons, and "was very enthusiastic about this matter and discussed learnedly and plausibly about it" (Manly 2001, 66). According to Addison Pratt, it was Brier who spoke first and "took the opportunity to fire the minds of the people with a zeal for the cut off. . ." (Hafen and Hafen 1954, 78-79).

Recognizing Hunt's experience as a mountaineer, the emigrants asked him for his opinion on the proposed cutoff, and according to Manly, Hunt replied that he knew nothing of it and "doubted if a white man ever went over it." He believed that in might be safe for fast-traveling young men, but should be avoided by families. Hunt concluded by saying: "If you decide to follow Smith I will go with you, even if the road leads to hell" (Manly 2001, 66-67).

At the end of the meeting, a vote was taken and again according to Pratt: "Nearly all of them voted in favour of it to the great satisfaction of Capt. Hunt." Also according to Pratt, Hunt came to him before the meeting and said: "It is a time of vast importance to me, and let us put up our united prayers to the Lord for my delivery." At the end of the meeting, Hunt "expressed great satisfaction at their decision and hoped they would hold to it" (Hafen and Hafen 1954, 79).

After traveling six miles on November 4th, the main group came to the place where those before them had turned to the west on O.K. Smith's Walker Pass route, as shown on the map drawn by Barney Ward. They had reached the cutoff. One by one, the wagons turned off the Old Spanish Trail and into the unknown. A few hesitated and then turned to follow the cutoff when they saw that the majority were going that way. When all had turned, only seven wagons remained with Jefferson Hunt.

Both groups stopped to say goodbye. Some, such as William Lorton who had become friends with Addison Pratt several months before in Salt Lake City, were sad to see the last of their friends. Others, according to Pratt had developed "a strong attachment" for Jefferson Hunt. He went a short distance with those who turned off and again spoke to them. Appearing almost ready to shed tears, he reminded them that he was obligated to go the Old Spanish Trail route as long as only one wagon continued on that route (Hafen and Hafen 1954, 80). The breakup of the San Joaquin Company—or the Jefferson Hunt Wagon Train—was complete.

Most of the emigrants were exuberant about the new trail. They were so confident in the map and new route that they rejoiced in the opportunity to bypass the dreaded Mojave Desert and reach the California gold fields much sooner than they expected. But no one was happier than Jefferson Hunt, himself. Addison Pratt wrote the following in his journal after the separation:

> "Not long after he [Jefferson Hunt] came on and over took us I laughed at him a little for his crocodile tears. 'Ah.' Said he, 'It was policy for me to affect something before them for many of them have treated me very kindly and I would to God I could get them out of the trouble they are now going into. They cannot get through with their wagons that way and I hardly think Bro. Rich with the horsemen can, but they stand by far the best chance, but I told Bro. Rich if he found mountains that they could not pass to be sure to slide back into this trail quick as possible and come on and overtake us. 'This,' continued he, 'is the happiest day of my life. I cannot recollect the time when I made so lucky an escape from death before as I have in getting rid of this company. There is a certain set of mobocratic spirits among them that were determined to take my life before we should get through the deserts. Now we will travel on fast as possible and get out of their way for they will soon be coming on after us when their cattle begin to die for there is neither grass nor water that way" (Hafen and Hafen 1954, 80-81).

In an account of his travels written later, Jacob Y. Stover, one of the emigrants who followed O.K. Smith on the cutoff, recalled that Jefferson Hunt addressed those present just before the split and said: "Gentlemen, I agreed to pilot you through and if only one wagon goes with me I will go with it. If you want to follow Captain Smith, I can't help it, but I believe you will get into the jaws of hell; but I hope you will have good luck" (Hafen and Hafen 1954, 278).

Lorenzo Dow Stephens whose book, *Life Sketches of a Jay Hawker of '49* published in 1916, recalled the separation: "When we started on Captain Hunt called out to us 'boys if you undertake that route you will go to hell.'" Stephens further expressed his belief that the map was sent out by Brigham

Young and the Church leaders because: "Brigham and the church wanted a short route to the Pacific Coast, and here was the opportunity of having that route prospected" (Stephens 1916, 33). Stephens went on to explain that Hunt knew this but tried, in vain, to warn them. In retrospect, it is clear that there was no such conspiracy, but that the Mormons in the train did want to explore any possible shortcut if it existed.

The emigrants who hired and welcomed Jefferson Hunt as their guide only one month before disregarded his experience and advice and set off on their own, with only a vague, second-hand map as a guide. They had given up the services of an experienced leader and mountaineer to go alone into an unknown region of the Great Basin. Why?

Several reasons undoubtedly contributed to this decision. It is hard to weigh the importance of the factors, but enough evidence exists to put a measure of relative importance on some of them. First of all, by November 1st, there was a high level of dissention within the wagon train. Part of that resulted from what the emigrants saw as a slow rate of travel south from Salt Lake City. Early on, several days were spent in camp to accommodate a few of the sick. Some Sundays were taken off. A full week was lost by the aborted attempt to find a short-cut through the Escalate Desert. Another factor contributing to the dissention was the large size of the wagon train—over 100 wagons, nearly 500 people and over 1,000 animals. It was unwieldy and slowed down the overall progress. This fact was not lost on Hunt and the Mormons, and they would avoid this problem in future uses of the same trail.

Second, there was certainly a loss of confidence in the abilities of Jefferson Hunt as a guide. While he was successful in making a new road through Dog Valley to the area of present-day Cove Fort, he was unsuccessful in trying to avoid the Black Mountains. Everyone knew of the difficulties and dangers of the Mojave Desert ahead, and some probably felt that he might not be successful there. After all, his previous trips through had been with pack trains and herds of livestock and they were able to travel faster and longer distances than wagons. Some undoubtedly believed that he might not be successful in getting them to water and feed in a timely and efficient manner while going through the desert.

Third, the wagon train was not a cohesive body. It was composed of a number of different groups traveling together and a number of individual family units. They had formed an organizational structure and elected officers, but the strength of the wagon train government was only as strong as the willingness of everyone to comply with the leaders' decisions. The history of the Westward migration is filled with wagon trains forming, then reforming and then reforming again. The experience of the San Joaquin Company was no different than that of most other similar groups on the trails.

Fourth, the Barney Ward map, as presented by Orson K. Smith, appeared to most people to be authentic. It conformed to what they thought they had read in Fremont's report and map of his Great Basin travels. It came with some level of credibility, since it was drawn by a mountain man who claimed he had previously traveled the route. No one seems to have asked the question of why Fremont himself, with experienced guides like Kit Carson and Alex Godey, had not taken the route if it was known to experienced trappers and mountain men. Nor does it appear that anyone questioned why Joseph Walker, the eminent Great Basin explorer, never used or discussed the route. Some may have even known that Wakara had not used the route in his trading and raiding trips. The map of the cutoff to Walker Pass was not supported by any evidence other than the second-hand assurance of its absent author.

Finally, one of the most significant contributions to the breakup was human nature itself. The desire (and greed) to get to the gold fields as quickly as possible was paramount in their minds. The persuasive comments by eloquent speakers, such as Reverend Brier, were given credibility beyond what was deserved. And many probably decided on the cutoff because others were going that way. Human history is filled with circumstances in which groups of people did what no single individual would do on his or her own. This was no exception. When Jefferson Hunt spoke of "mobocratic spirits" he may have been more accurately describing the dynamics within the emigration than even he believed.

When it came time to make a decision about the route to take, the emigrants tended not to use known facts or common sense, but to rely on hope and a belief that all would be better. Amazingly, some continued to believe in their decision even after confronted with overwhelming facts showing they were wrong. A few would die, a number of others came very close to death, and many would endure hardships that they could not yet imagine.

Chapter 18

On to California

On November 4th, Hunt and those who remained with him—seven wagons with eleven men, two women and three children (Brown 1900, 136)—continued on the Old Spanish Trail. They traveled nine miles to the approximate point where it intersected the small stream (Meadow Creek) in Holt Canyon where they made camp. The next day, following a snow storm the previous night, they continued south and soon reached Mountain Meadow, site of the infamous Mountain Meadows Massacre of 1857. That tragedy will be discussed in Part III.

Mountain Meadow was a lush valley with springs and an ample supply of grass. For many years, travelers stopped there to allow their livestock to graze in preparation for the difficult deserts ahead. Today, Mountain Meadow still looks inviting, even though its topography and ecology changed considerably as a result of over-grazing and flooding in 1862. In 1849, it was the last great "rest stop" before pushing on to the Mojave Desert only twenty miles or so ahead. On the north side of Mountain Meadow is the Rim of the Basin, the point where water flowing to the south flows into the Colorado River drainage and water flowing to the north goes into the Great Basin with no outlet to the sea.

Hunt and his small group continued on past Mountain Meadow and descended into the canyon of Magotsu Creek. This they followed for about five miles and camped without water for their animals, although they carried enough for their own use. On November 6th, they continued down Magotsu Creek, past its confluence with the Santa Clara River for eleven miles, and camped about one mile north of the present community of Gunlock, Utah. On November 7th, they went nine miles and camped at what is now known as Camp Spring, about a mile and a half beyond where they left the Santa Clara. Here they remained for one additional day while they prepared for the desert ahead.

On November 9th, they climbed up the grade from Camp Spring to the summit of the pass over the Beaver Dam Mountains. The road they followed from Camp Spring to the Virgin River is virtually the same as the current Highway 91. In fact, until Interstate 15 was built over 100 years later, the main route from Salt Lake City to Las Vegas was the same section of Highway 91 which was the Old Spanish Trail. That night after traveling seven miles, they made a dry camp at the very summit of the pass. Before them was the Mojave Desert of Arizona, Nevada and California. Addison Pratt noted that: "This is very barren country" (Hafen and Hafen 1954, 82).

The wagons that took the cutoff followed the trail left by the packers for about three days. This took them west through the present town of Enterprise, Utah, along Shoal Creek, through Nephi Wash, then south along Jessie Tie Wash (or perhaps Wide Hollow or Rock Hole Wash just to the east), past Pine Mountain to Roundup Flat, and then southwest into Headwaters Wash which, and in turn, drained into Beaver Dam Wash. Here the packers had continued with some difficulty, but the wagons were unable to follow. A few wagons descended part way into Headwaters Wash and some of those packing with the wagons descended further, but it became clear to all that the wagons would not be able to continue behind Smith, the Flake/Rich party, and the other packers.

The route into Headwaters Wash is clearly established by the descriptions of several of the Mormon packers, especially Henry Bigler and William Farrer—who described the route to and through the entrance to Headwaters Wash (Hafen and Hafen 1954, 202-203). Both Bigler and Farrer recorded the initial descent into the wash as being in a southwesterly direction, which it is. In addition, Bigler wrote that he "cut the 3 first letters my name on a Rock &

the date" (Hafen and Hafen 1954, 151). In 1938, the noted historian Charles Kelly, reported seeing those initials carved into a white ash rock formation within Headwaters Wash just as Bigler described (Kelly 1939).

Stopped by the forbidding and difficult terrain and with no knowledge of how to proceed, the wagons set up a camp that some called Mount Misery and others called Poverty Point. While the exact location of Mount Misery is still being debated by historians, the most likely place is on the several square miles of plateau that extends south from Headwaters Wash to Pine Park in Washington County, Utah (LeRoy Johnson, personal communication). An observer standing today on the rim of the ridgeline looking south into Pine Park or on the western promontory looking west to the mountains of eastern Nevada can certainly understand the desperation of the emigrants, why they called their camp what they did and why forward progress to California was stalled.

For several days, scouts went out to find a wagon route that would take them West. Some decided to abandon their wagons and pack onwards along the route taken by the packers, others held out for word of a wagon route that they could follow Westward. Provisions were running out and many of those who decided to pack did not want emigrants with families or without adequate supplies with them, fearing that they would have to assume responsibility for them. Most decided that the folly of the cutoff had run its course. Manly says that: "The enthusiasm about the Smith cutoff had begun to die and now the talk began of going back to follow Hunt" (Manly 2001, 68).

On the third day at Mount Misery, scouts were still out looking for a Westward passage when, according to Manly, a Mr. Rynierson addressed the crowd and said, in part: "My family is near and dear to me . . . . I, for one, feel in duty bound to seek a safer way than this. I shall hitch up my oxen and return at once to the old trail" (Manly 2001, 68). As Rynierson left to backtrack to the Old Spanish Trail, others followed. When some scouts began to return with no word of a Westward passage, more followed. Nearly everyone was ready to leave when several scouts returned with information that it was possible to continue by first going north and then west. By then, only twenty-seven wagons remained at Mount Misery. Nearly all of the 500 or so emigrants began the cutoff, now about three quarters of them had decided to return and follow Hunt's original trail. The remainder, including Manly, John Rogers, the Bennett and Arcan families and their teamsters, Reverend J.W. Brier and his family, and other groups, including the Jay Hawkers, continued west. Others, including William Lorton, were attempting to follow the packers or to find a new and better pack route.

Any semblance of organization or authority had disintegrated by this point. The officers of San Joaquin Company had resigned and Colonel Baxter was very ill from mountain fever. Adonijah Welch, who had kept an excellent journal of the travels for a month, made his last entry on November 5th. Everyone was now free to do as they pleased, but most of the support structure for those with worn and tired animals or low food supplies was also gone. The better prepared simply did not want the burden of caring for those who needed help. In one month, the emigrant wagon train had gone from a well-structured organization to chaos and anarchy. They had not heeded Brigham Young's admonition to them that unity was essential, and many of them would pay the price.

History remembers many of those who continued west from Mount Misery as the "Death Valley '49ers," since it was they who were the first non-Indians to enter Death Valley and to give it the name. By November 12th, there were at least seven different groups of emigrants scattered throughout the region where the current borders of Utah, Arizona and Nevada meet. About 500 people were spread out in an area of more than 2,500 square miles. Some were on known trails, some were trying to find a trail, and some were on their way to becoming hopelessly lost. Some would arrive in California one or two weeks after Jefferson Hunt; some would arrive in California almost two months after him; a few would never make it. Only the Flake-Rich packers would catch up with Hunt and make it to California before him and his wagons.

When the Smith and Flake-Rich packers had traveled about thirty-five miles west and southwest from where they left the Old Spanish Trail, they descended into Headwaters Wash and then into Beaver Dam Wash. From there, they followed Beaver Dam Wash to the current location of Motoqua, where they arrived on November 7th. At that point, they were only about sixteen miles northwest of Hunt's camp at Camp Springs, but neither group knew that.

Had the packers continued on south along Beaver Dam Wash, they would have intercepted the Old Spanish Trail at present-day Littlefield, Arizona, in about seventeen miles—but they didn't. Instead, true to their original plan, they headed west, in part to avoid deep, rocky canyons they saw ahead. They traveled across a sagebrush desert to Meadow Valley Wash and then down that. They had been joined by a group of packers who had left the wagons and reported to them that most of the migration had followed their trail but was stuck at Mount Misery.

The packers endured long dry days and had great difficulty finding water and feed. Both men and animals were showing the effects of the desert conditions. A number of animals were lost, including Cannon's horse, which drowned in one of the few streams with water. Finally, on November 15th, Rich and three other men climbed a mountain to the west to get a better view of what was ahead. It was not good. There were higher mountains to the west and no sign of good grass for grazing or of water. Late that night, Rich and his group returned to camp. There, Apostle Rich assumed leadership and announced that they would head south for the Old Spanish Trail. George Q. Cannon recorded that: "Upon mature consideration he did not think it would be wisdom for him to take the company thro' & he thought he would strike for the Spanish Trail. The brethren were unanimous in their feeling to go the Spanish Trail" (Landon 1999, 52).

The response of some of the Smith packers, who were camped nearby, was to threaten the Mormon packers if they did not divide their provisions before departure. Smith himself derided Rich's decision and swore to continue his westward travel. Several of the non-Mormon packers with the Flake-Rich party also joined Smith. The Flake-Rich company then headed south following Pahranagat Wash. They then followed down Moapa Valley, arrived at the springs that fed the Muddy River (also known to them as the Far Muddy). A short distance later, they intersected the Old Spanish Trail near the present community of Glendale, Nevada, and there found Jefferson Hunt and his small group.

Smith continued on for another two days and found that the conditions were even worse than they had experienced to date. Thoroughly disillusioned with his cutoff, Smith and most of his party decided to backtrack over the same route they had followed from the Old Spanish Trail near Enterprise, Utah. A few followed the route taken by the Mormon packers. Smith apparently intended to return to Salt Lake City. However, on the Old Spanish Trail, he encountered another southbound wagon train led by Howard Egan and joined with them to finally travel on to Southern California. Smith eventually arrived in California about a month after Hunt.

William Lorton, with a group of packers, left Mount Misery on November 10th and followed those packers who had gone ahead. His group caught up with O.K. Smith on November 18th past Division Springs. There, Lorton learned that Rich and the Mormon packers had gone south to intercept the Old Spanish Trail several days before. Smith had lost half of his animals and the situation was desperate. Smith decided to return to Salt Lake City. Everyone realized they were lost and facing a "life or death" situation (Lorton, November 18, 1849). Even these loose groups of packers were breaking up.

On November 19th, Lorton recorded the departure of the group that became known to Death Valley historians as the Pinney-Savage party. They decided to continue west and not backtrack or try to reach the Old Spanish Trail like the others. He names ten of the eleven men who began the journey. Only two, Pinney and Savage, are known to have survived, and some (or all) of the rest are believed to have died in Death Valley or in nearby deserts. The full details of this group have never been discovered and recorded definitively. On November 20th, Lorton started to backtrack and by November 25th was back on Beaver Dam Creek where they had camped on November 13th. In almost two weeks of travel across desert, they had not gained any ground, but had decimated their animals and provisions.

On November 26th, they headed south along Beaver Dam Wash and reached the Virgin River at present-day Littlefield, Arizona. For three weeks, they had wandered around lost in the desert in search of the cutoff. Their supplies had dwindled and the difficult conditions took their toll on both people and animals.

On that day, Jefferson Hunt and his small group were descending into Pahrump Valley, well over 125 miles to the west.

Knowing that those who had taken the shortcut were in for great difficulties, Jefferson Hunt continued along the Old Spanish Trail that he had traversed before. On November 10th, his party descended the plains along the route of Beaver Dam Wash and arrived near the Virgin River, after having first passed the location of the beaver dam that had given the wash its name. Addison Pratt noted that a flood had washed away the dam. His journal is the first to record the existence of Joshua trees that covered the flats. He also noted the abundant cottontail rabbits.

They descended to the Virgin River on the 11th and continued along the river, passing the present site of Mesquite, Nevada, fording it six times on the 12th. On November 13th, they traveled eight miles and ran across several men from the Independent Pioneer Company who were searching for lost cattle. They came across an Indian driving one cow from that company that had an arrow sticking in it, which they removed. A common practice of many of the Indians in the Great Basin was to kill or wound livestock and then hide, knowing that the emigrants would leave the animal and continue their trip. When the emigrants had gone, the animal or carcass would be recovered. Abandoned or incapacitated livestock were similarly used for food by nearby Indians.

On the morning of November 14th, Hunt's party came to the point where the pack trail left the Virgin River and ascended Virgin Hill, the most difficult single point on the entire trail. The only known wagons to ascend or descend this obstacle before were the those of Captain Davis in 1848, and the Independent Pioneer Company a week or so before them. Before noon, they arrived at Halfway Wash, about seven and one-half miles below the present site of Riverside, Nevada. There they were hit with a rain and windstorm. Addison Pratt and James Brown, who were guarding the cattle while they rested and fed before the climb, sought shelter in one of the small caves near the river (Hafen and Hafen 1954, 86).

At this point, Hunt's knowledge of the route and his experiences from his 1847-48 trip became very important for the small wagon company. He knew the route, distances and difficulties of the trail, but more importantly, he knew where there was likely to be water and grass. He knew where it was necessary to prepare for a long drive across the desert and where it was suitable to rest and feed the animals. This knowledge and his natural aura of authority gave him the ability to lead the others. Hunt would be much more successful than the Independent Pioneer Company that had preceded him.

After a brief rest, they commenced up the very sandy wash toward the point where the trail went up to the lip of Virgin Hill. On the trail they met Charles Dallas, William Lewis Manly's former employer, from the Independent Pioneer Company who was searching for some lost cattle. From Dallas, they learned that he had seven wagons. He had left them at the bottom of the hill, taken his ox teams to the top, and then dropped chains down to the wagons. Using the oxen on the top where they had good footing, they pulled up the wagons. Another wagon in the company broke loose while being pulled up and careened down the hill where it was smashed to pieces. Dallas recounted that it had taken two days to take the wagons up the hill. His wagons had gone on to the Muddy River while he looked for the lost cattle (Hafen and Hafen 1954, 86).

That evening, the Hunt party reached the trail up the hill and drove their wagons as far as they could up the steep slope. There they blocked the wheels and attached "ten or twelve yoke of oxen" on the wagon and pulled it up. Pratt noted that "it was so steep near the top that an ox could barely stand without pulling at all" (Hafen and Hafen 1954, 86). By using a large rope and all of the chains they could find, they pulled the wagons up the hill, finishing the difficult task by three in the morning. It was a moonless night and much of the work was done in the dark with very little natural light. The need to reach the Muddy River was so great that they had to struggle in the dark to complete the task.

Once on top of the hill, they traveled a little farther over what is now known as Mormon Mesa and camped about nine miles from the Virgin River. At daylight on November 15th, they continued on and after three miles found some wet bunch grass and stopped for an hour to let the cattle feed (Hafen and Hafen 1954, 87). At this point, they were not far from what is now a truck parking area on Interstate 15, east of Moapa/Glendale, Nevada. From there, they continued on the trail and went off the western side of Mormon Mesa at a point just north of today's Interstate 15 near a current Nevada Department of Transportation facility. They went west and then south in what is now known as Weiser Wash. They arrived at the Muddy River, about two miles downstream from present-day Glendale, Nevada, shortly after noon.

They found Dallas' wagons and "about a dozen others" from the Independent Pioneer Company camped there. Vincent Hoover and his group had arrived at the Muddy ten days before (November 5th) and left on November 9th for the springs at Las Vegas. The Independent Pioneer Company had also broken into groups, with some going ahead and others falling behind. Among the wagons was a yoke of oxen that had been taken from Chauncy West, a Mormon in Salt Lake City (Hafen and Hafen 1954, 87).

Hunt and his party camped there for the remainder of that day and the next. The Muddy River has a year 'round water flow that begins from a series of warm springs located about ten miles upstream from Glendale and flows through part of the present Moapa Indian Reservation. In 1849, the small stream flowed down to the Virgin River and then into the Colorado River. With the construction of Hoover Dam and the formation of Lake Mead, the Muddy now flows into the Overton Arm of the lake. Throughout historical times, and well before, there has been a significant group of Indians living along the Muddy River.

The Moapa band of Southern Paiutes was the largest group of Indians living on the Old Spanish Trail from central Utah to Southern California. Numbering 500 or more, they prospered along the Muddy River, raising crops and hunting game. The original packers and later wagon trains did much to disrupt their pastoral life, however. Livestock often got into the crops accidentally or were intentionally sent into the crops to feed. As travel increased along the trail, relations between these Indians and the travelers worsened and often led to conflicts and attempts by the Indians to extract a toll for using their resources by taking cattle. The Mormons, who had an effective program for maintaining good relations with Indian tribes, usually did not have the same difficulties as did the non-Mormons who passed through the area. There

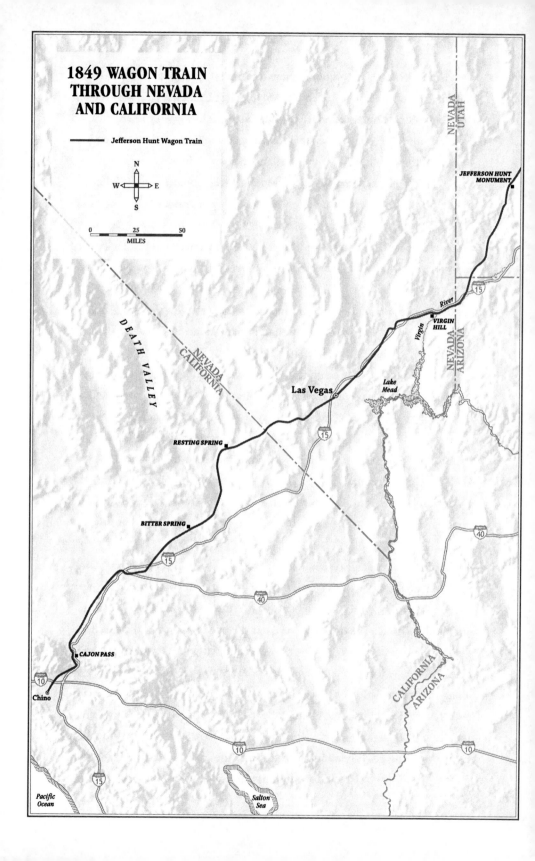

1849 WAGON TRAIN THROUGH NEVADA AND CALIFORNIA

—————— Jefferson Hunt Wagon Train

N
W ← ■ → E
S

0   25   50
MILES

NEVADA
UTAH

JEFFERSON HUNT
MONUMENT

15

River

Virgin

VIRGIN
HILL

DEATH VALLEY

NEVADA
CALIFORNIA

Las Vegas

Lake
Mead

NEVADA
ARIZONA

15

RESTING SPRING

BITTER SPRING

15

40

40

40

CAJON PASS

CALIFORNIA
ARIZONA

10

Chino

10

10

15

Pacific
Ocean

Salton
Sea

seems to have been no conflicts between the Hunt and Flake-Rich parties with the Moapa Paiutes.

After camping there for a day and a half, on November 17th Hunt moved his small party upstream about three miles to a point that offered the best ford of the Muddy. This site is located about one mile west of the Glendale interchange on Interstate 15. It provided a small, flat valley with significant grass to replenish the livestock. At this point, the trail left the Muddy, entered or followed California Wash and began the fifty mile dry segment to the verdant meadow at Las Vegas. Since they would have to make the entire journey without stopping, they again camped and allowed the livestock to rest, graze and drink water.

Where the Old Spanish Trail left the Muddy, the stream has cut a deeper channel than existed in 1849. Then, as well as now, there was a pond of water that provided a welcome desert stopping place for water fowl. On the following day, November 18th, Addison Pratt decided to hunt for ducks on the pond, and as he was crawling through the grass to get a better shot, he spotted Charles C. Rich on the other side. Rich called out to him and Pratt replied; at the same time, the ducks rose from the pond and Pratt fired, dropping two of them. Thus, the Mormon packers of the Flake/Rich party again joined their brethren in the Hunt party (Hafen and Hafen 1954, 88).

The Flake/Rich Company began descending Pahranagat Valley Wash after Rich made the decision to follow on to the Old Spanish Trail as he and Jefferson Hunt had discussed. Following that Wash, they entered the Moapa Valley on November 16th, arrived at the warm springs that fed the Muddy River on November 17th, and met Hunt's party at the Muddy crossing on November 18th. Although not planned, the timing of the two groups was impeccable. The Mormon packers had disproved the viability of the shortcut to Walker Pass and had quickly returned to the known route. Their information would benefit several decades of Mormon travelers along the trail.

There was jubilation on both sides following the reunion; however, the Flake-Rich company had lost animals and used up valuable supplies on the shortcut attempt. Chauncy West's cattle with the Independent Pioneer Company provided a partial solution to the packers' problems of supply. Addison Pratt explained that Jefferson Hunt and Charles Rich had been authorized by the Church in Salt Lake City to:

> "transact all business for the church, and the people of Salt Lake valley, that come within their reach, and they laid their authority before those men that had the cattle, at first they were quite unwilling to give them up afterwards consented to do so, and they sold the cattle to Dallas for provisions to fit out Bro. Rich's company to cross the deserts into California" (Hafen and Hafen 1954, 88-89).

The stolen cattle were seized and used to buy supplies to re-supply the packers.

After five days on this short section of the Muddy River, it was time for Jefferson Hunt and his party and the packers to move on. The next section of the trail was the dreaded fifty mile stretch to the great meadow at Las Vegas. Hunt's previous experience told him that it would be best to travel at night to avoid the direct sunlight and heat of the day. About noon on November 20th, the group left the Muddy and began the trek along California Wash. After sunset they traveled with very little moonlight. Fourteen hours and twenty-two miles later, they found some grass and pools of water from the previous rain and camped. The fresh grass and water was a welcome respite.

At ten in the morning of November 21st, they again moved and reached the meadow in the valley of Las Vegas Creek twelve hours later. As was often the case, Jefferson Hunt and some of the others rode ahead on horseback scouting the road. This time, Addison Pratt joined him and the others, probably the packers, and arrived about sunset. Vegas—Spanish for meadow—was an unpopulated but popular stopping point on the trail. Springs several miles west of the meadow provided ample water into the creek. It then flowed down a streambed into a "large valley, covered with immense quantities of good grass" (Hafen and Hafen 1954, 90). The valley was so attractive that the Mormons constructed a fort as an outpost there in 1855.

On November 22nd, they traveled several miles up the stream to the springs. There they found large quantities of water bubbling out of the ground, and they also found piles of clothing, bedding and other things abandoned by the Independent Pioneer Company ahead of them. The next day, they continued on over the desert to the west to Cottonwood Spring at the present community of Blue Diamond, Nevada. There, near Red Rock Canyon west of Las Vegas, they marveled at the colorful rock formations before them. On November 24th, they traveled about three miles over a ridge behind Cottonwood Spring and part way through a valley toward the pass through the Spring Mountains. One of the Mormons had a forge and they stopped in a grassy area and shod the oxen.

November 25th took them ten miles to Mountain Springs at the top of the pass that separated Las Vegas Valley from Pahrump Valley. At the summit they noted evidence of Indian occupation. The following day, the wagons descended into Pahrump Valley and continued on to Stump Springs, which was a well dug into the ground that offered a small amount of water. Pratt and some of the others explored the valley to the north and caught up with the wagons on the 27th, just after they left Stump Springs. A mile or so past Stump Springs, they crossed what is now the border of Nevada and California; the remainder of the Jefferson Hunt Wagon train entered the future State of California a short time later.

Still on horseback, Pratt and some of the others went ahead of the wagons to what is now known as Emigrant Pass on the Old Spanish Trail Highway between Pahrump, Nevada, and Tecopa, California. There, they moved stones out of the road and improved it to enable the wagons to climb up and over the steep and difficult grade of the old pack trail more easily (Hafen and Hafen 1954, 94). From there, they traveled to Resting Spring, just east of present-day Tecopa.

Resting Spring was the most famed spot on the Old Spanish Trail. With abundant water and grass, it was located about midway through the Mojave Desert. To the west was very little grass and very poor water over a long drive of about eighty miles to the Mojave River. Old Spanish Trail travelers, going either direction, usually stopped there to either prepare their animals for the trail ahead or to let them recover from the long and difficult drive. Its fame was increased by an account of an incident recorded by John C. Fremont during his 1843-44 trip. At the spring—then known by its Spanish name of Archilette—a small group of Mexican traders driving horses eastward were attacked by Indians. Only one man and a boy escaped. The others were killed or captured and many of the horses stolen. The pair traveled back on the trail toward Los Angeles where they encountered the Fremont party. Kit Carson and Alex Godey went to the site, tracked down those responsible, killed several of them and recovered a few horses. They made a round trip of about 100 miles in thirty hours to exact this revenge. Fremont's account of the retribution helped establish the legendary status of Kit Carson.

The Hunt party and the Mormon packers had traveled twenty-two miles from Stump Springs to Resting Spring. There they found more piles of discarded clothing and wagons that had been abandoned by those of the Independent Pioneer Company ahead. There was even a note left by the forward part of the Independent Pioneer Company to Charles Dallas telling him that they were "short of provisions and were in great distress [and] were living on the cattle that gave out" (Hafen and Hafen 1954, 94). They were hoping that Dallas, who had extra wagons and provisions, would be able to help them.

The wagons spent November 28th and 29th at Resting Spring preparing for the long push across the desert ahead. The Independent Pioneer Company wagons that had been on the Muddy caught up with Hunt's party on the 29th. The Flake-Rich packers were, however, able to travel much faster than the wagons; they left on November 29th, the day before the Hunt wagons. Once again, the wagons and the Mormon packers had separated, though this time it was to expedite the transit of the faster packers across the desert to Bitter Spring and the Mojave River.

From Resting Spring, the trail led to the canyon of the Amargosa River, then southward to Dumont Dunes and on to the Salt Spring Hills. The Hunt party began this portion of the trail on November 30th. Historians have generally believed that the trail led southwesterly from Resting Spring to near the Post Office at the present community of Tecopa, California, where it then followed the Amargosa River into its canyon, which begins immediately past Tecopa.

This route very likely existed during both the time of the Old Spanish Trail and the later Southern Route between Utah and Southern California. However, it appears that the routes taken by Fremont in 1844 and by the packers, the Independent Pioneer Company, and the Hunt wagons in 1849 followed variations that did not go into the Amargosa Canyon at Tecopa. Rather, other trails entered the Amargosa Canon via China Ranch and Willow Creek and via another canyon that met the Amargosa three miles upstream from the Willow Creek confluence.

The evidence indicates that several variations in the trail between Resting Spring and the Amargosa co-existed in the late 1840s. One, probably followed by Fremont, was a pack trail unsuitable for wagons because of a dry waterfall nearly twenty feet high that required travel on a very steep slope that wagons could not have negotiated without extensive cutting and preparation. The trail was seven miles long from Willow Spring in China Ranch to Resting Spring, just as described by Fremont. An alternate, discussed below, that departed to the west into Cowboy Canyon, went seven miles to a small spring in the Amargosa Canyon, just as described by those traveling with Hunt or in close proximity to him. A third trail was an old Indian trail that went southeast from Resting Spring to the eastern portion of China Ranch Wash, where it descended into that canyon and followed it to Willow Spring at China Ranch. Since this route was 8.5 miles from Resting Spring to China Ranch, it does not conform to the mileages in various accounts and was not used by those travelers in this discussion.

Noted Death Valley historians and writers LeRoy and Jean Johnson first told the author of the Fremont/China Ranch and Cowboy Canyon trail variations. The author has carefully reviewed the written evidence in journals from the 1840s, has traversed and inspected the various routes in the area, and believes they are correct in their analysis.

The first detailed journal of the trail was written by John C. Fremont in 1844 and described his northward journey from Southern California back to the United States. His mileage record of his route from Salt Spring to Resting Spring conforms almost exactly (within one-half mile) with the distances expected if the route went up Willow Creek and through China Ranch. More significantly, his description of "passing on the way a fork from the right" indicates he traveled up Willow Creek and not the Amargosa River. Fremont was following standard Army protocol of referring to "right" and "left" by facing downstream. This means that his "fork from the right" refers to facing downstream, or south, and the stream he followed was Willow Creek into China Ranch. He left the Amargosa at this point and followed Willow Creek into China Ranch (Johnson and Sutak 2011, 21). Additionally, his description of the "springs of excellent water" and the "best camping ground" seen thus far on the Old Spanish Trail best fit Willow Spring at China Ranch, and not the nearby Amargosa River or Canyon (Fremont 1970, 683). It is probable that Fremont, who had only riding and pack animals and no wagons, ascended the ridge directly north from China Ranch to Resting Spring. The wagons of the 1849 parties could not negotiate this route and followed a different variation.

George Q. Cannon, who left Resting Spring the day before Hunt, said that they had "some very steep descending to get in the bottom" (Landon 1999, November 29, 1849). William Lorton packing and following Hunt by about three weeks was even more explicit saying that the "road ascends a table [land] at 3 miles and then through rough rugged bluffs along a narrow ridge and steep pitches, and awful pitch into the valley of the springs" (Lorton, December 20, 1849). Lorton's account fits only a route that enters either China Ranch or enters the Amargosa Canyon via Cowboy Canyon. That route ascends a tableland and then steeply descends to the Amargosa River: the route from Resting Spring to Tecopa and into the Amargosa Canyon is completely downhill with no climb involved at all, and there is no bad descent into the canyon.

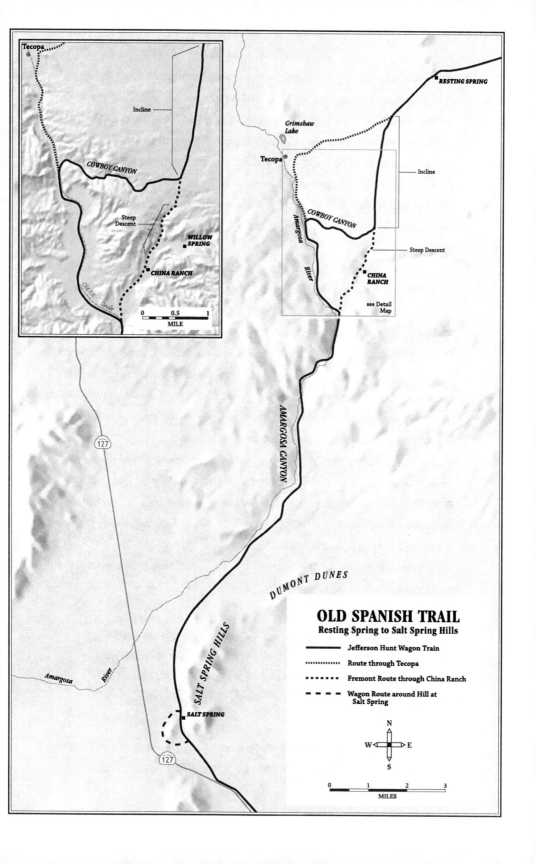

Tecopa

Incline

COWBOY CANYON

Steep
Descent

WILLOW
SPRING

CHINA RANCH

Old R.R. Grade

0   0.5   1
MILE

Grimshaw
Lake

Tecopa

Incline

COWBOY CANYON

Amargosa

River

Steep Descent

CHINA
RANCH

see Detail
Map

RESTING SPRING

AMARGOSA CANYON

127

DUMONT DUNES

SALT SPRING HILLS

Amargosa   River

SALT SPRING

127

OLD SPANISH TRAIL
Resting Spring to Salt Spring Hills

——————— Jefferson Hunt Wagon Train

················ Route through Tecopa

• • • • • • Fremont Route through China Ranch

– – – – Wagon Route around Hill at
          Salt Spring

N
W ← → E
S

0   1   2   3
MILES

The Amargosa River through its canyon drops approximately 650 feet in elevation over a distance of about twelve miles, or a one percent grade. By any standard, that is a fairly mild descent. In fact, the Tonopah and Tidewater Railroad chose the Amargosa Canyon as part of its route in the first decade of the Twentieth Century. On the other hand, a person first ascending to the ridge north of China Ranch and then descending into the Amargosa Canyon will descend about 550 feet in two miles or so, with one steep descent. This drop more closely conforms to the steep descent described by the journal writers.

Which route did Jefferson Hunt and his wagons take? It appears that he and his party, along with the Flake/Rich packers, the Independent Pioneer Company, and others all took a route that can be described as follows: From Resting Spring, the route went southerly toward the current intersection of Furnace Creek and China Ranch roads; then it paralleled China Ranch Road to nearly the summit before the descent into China Ranch. There the route turned right toward a canyon called by locals Cowboy Canyon, since it was later used by ranchers to access the bottomlands of the Amargosa Canyon. Before entering the steepest descent into the Amargosa Canyon, there is a segment of a more recent road that steeply descends into the bottom of the wash; from there the route followed the wash to the Amargosa River/Canyon. A small spring on the canyon wall just below where the wash enters the canyon is the springs described by the various authors. The distance from Resting Spring to this spring is seven miles.

Vincent Hoover of the Independent Pioneer Company described the route by saying:

> "You will descend down a very steep hill to Amargosa Creek or bitter water of the desert is the meaning of it. Here you will find a good place to camp & for some distance down the creek. Three miles farther down you will find a small stream running into this creek a good place to camp. Distance 7 ½" (Hoover Journal, November 27, 1849).

It is three miles from the spring where Cowboy Canyon reaches the Amargosa to the confluence of Willow Creek from China Ranch. Hoover's description and mileages are unambiguous and clearly describe where the route from Resting Spring reached the Amargosa.

Addison Pratt, traveling with Hunt, said that:

> "the head of the creek the bed of which is some 300 feet below the deserts around it and some 50 rods wide, we had to descend into it on a short and crooked ridge which was a divide between to [sic] rivers that discharged water into it in wet weather. The lower end was steep and it was with much difficulty we descended without upsetting our wagons. We traveled down the stream about five miles and camped on a fresh water stream that came into it. This stream is a grand curiosity. There is quite a stream about knee-deep and so strongly impregnated with alkali that it is about the colour of Madeira wine, and is said to kill cattle when they drink it" (Hafen and Hafen 1954, 95).

Pratt's description indicates they traveled seven miles to the Amargosa River from Resting Spring and then five miles from the start of the descent into Cowboy Canyon to the juncture of Willow Creek and the Amargosa, where they camped. Conversely, the Flake/Rich packers, traveling a day or so before, camped at the spring just inside the Amargosa Canyon near the mouth of Cowboy Canyon.

Why would the pack trail and early wagons use a route with an ascent followed by a steep descent? The answer may very well lie with the fact that the ground condition around today's Tecopa, and a logical entrance into the Amargosa Canyon, was very soft and often muddy. A number of springs— both hot and regular—surface at Tecopa and natural soil conditions can often be soft even with modern drainage systems installed. Animals and wagons could have easily become bogged down in the wet soil. Additionally, the trail down Cowboy Canyon avoided several miles of very rough and dangerous travel down the Amargosa Canyon.

The most difficult crossing of the Mojave Desert was about to begin. On December 1st, Hunt and his group continued down the Amargosa and left it at the mouth of the canyon near the location of Dumont Dunes. They then crossed the sandy tableland at the base of the dunes and headed south toward Salt Spring and the Salt Spring Hills. There, the pack trail went through a notch between the hills, but the wagons had to go west around one of the small hills, an extra half mile of travel.

The day before, the Flake-Rich packers had gone through this area on the pack trail and Henry Bigler wrote that "here I saw signs for gold" (Hafen and Hafen 1954, 168). When the Hunt wagon train got to the hills the next day, Hunt, Addison Pratt and two other men rode on horseback through the notch while the wagons went around the hill. Pratt, who like Henry Bigler had been in the California gold fields, noticed that the rock formation was similar to gold-bearing rocks he had seen before and commented to his three companions that if they could find quartz in the rock, they might find gold. The four men began to search. According to Pratt: "we had not gone far before Mr. Rowan says 'Here is gold,' on looking I saw that he had found some in a stratum of quartz about four inches wide running through a ledge of granite. It was a collection of small particles the largest about the size of a pea" (Hafen and Hafen 1954, 96). Rowan's identity is not clear, but he may have been a free Black who later settled in San Bernardino with the Mormons.

Pratt and others may have told Isaac Williams when they arrived at Chino. Williams' Register Book indicates that on February 23, 1850, about two months after Hunt's arrival, that the "Salt Springs or Marigosa [sic] Mining Co." left with equipment to operate the mine (Williams, February 23, 1850). Within a year, the Amargosa Mine, as it was called, was developed, probably by Mormons, and a steam engine was hauled in from Southern California to provide power for it (Lyman 1996, 205). The first building ever constructed by non-Indians in the Mojave Desert was built out of stone to house the miners. The Amargosa Mine was operated on and off for the next several decades.

Amargosa Spring was very salty and not drinkable; a second spring just to the south was salty and barely potable, but the Hunt party found some pools of rainwater that had also been used by the packers the day before. They likely missed a very small spring of potable water in the notch that could be dug out. In the Salt Spring Hills, Jefferson Hunt's experience on the trail became invaluable. The trail from Salt Spring Hills to the next water at Bitter Spring was across more than thirty-five miles of barren desert with no water other than that which might have accumulated in pools left by rain storms.

They camped there and left for the next leg of the journey about noon on December 2nd. That night, a nearly full moon was out and they chose to take advantage of the light by traveling at night when the temperature would be cooler and the searing sun would not be a problem. Twenty-four hours later, they reached Red Pass Lake, about thirty miles from Salt Spring Hills and about five miles short of Bitter Spring. There they found some dry grass and rain water in pools. They stopped until the next day, December 4th. They saw more and more dead cattle and horses along the trail, but Pratt noted that their cattle from the Salt Lake Valley seemed to be in better shape and survived better (Hafen and Hafen 1954, 96).

On December 4th, they continued on to Bitter Spring, now within the boundaries of Fort Irwin and the National Training Center. There they found the water tolerable, but little or no grass. Accordingly, they did not camp or stay long at Bitter Spring. About sundown, they again set out. The trail ahead took them over a ridge and then down to the Mojave River, about thirty miles from Bitter Spring. The drive was without any springs or grass, and time was of the essence. Hunt decided once more to take advantage of the moonlight and travel at night as fast as possible.

This particular night drive was to be one of the most discouraging and uncomfortable of the entire trip. It began to rain, and as they ascended to a ridge that had to be crossed, it started to snow. The animals began to fail; one of Pratt's oxen lay down and refused to move and had to be shot. Blackwell became distraught and believed that they would never make it. The rain and snow did provide both men and animals with fresh water, and when they began their descent to the Mojave, the oxen picked up the pace. As they descended, the snow began to melt as soon as it fell and things began to look more favorable.

As the wagons struggled to move ahead, Hunt stayed with those who had the most problems, but he gave Pratt, who had the strongest teams, instructions to continue ahead until they reached "a place of safety" and then return to help the others. Pratt did exactly that, proceeding downhill until he got to a sheltered place in a canyon with little wind, no snow and rainwater for his animals. He then returned to help the others. At daybreak on the morning of December 5th, Pratt recorded that: "Capt. Hunt came up nearly chilled. We turned out made fire and him some hot coffee and he revived again, said the snow had fallen 18 inches deep on the wagons and they were in a bad fix" (Hafen and Hafen 1954, 98).

Hunt, Pratt and those with them continued on for another six miles and camped. About three p.m. the remainder of the wagons was seen behind them and they arrived shortly thereafter, but had lost some of their cattle. On December 6th, they continued on to the Mojave River which they reached about four p.m. When they arrived at the Mojave, they were probably about eight miles east of the present town of Daggett, California, which, in turn, is about eight miles east of Barstow.

Once at the streambed of the Mojave, the driest and most difficult portion of the trip was behind them. But not everyone was safe. At the Mojave they found, according to Pratt, "about a dozen wagons camped there. They were in distress some of them had been out of bredstuff [sic] for 6 weeks" (Hafen and Hafen 1954, 100). Among those were the Gruwell families, which had gone ahead with the Independent Pioneer Company after the Gruwell brothers took the northern route to avoid contact with the Mormons. In one of the ironies of the trail, Pratt found that Charles Rich had given the anti-Mormon Gruwells flour to help them when he found them at the Mojave on December 3rd. Hunt's party also gave them some bread, since they had been eating only meat from their cattle for the last six weeks.

The Mojave River, then as now, was an intermittent stream most of the year. In some places, the water flowed on the surface; elsewhere the water flowed below the surface and could only be found in pools or in wells dug into the sand. Hunt's party camped there and stayed over for an extra day to rest the animals following the previous day's hard travel. On December 8th, they continued on for eleven miles and camped at a location that had running water in the river. On December 9th, they went another five miles and camped near present-day Barstow, because the trail they were following left the river for fifteen miles as the watercourse made a large bend to the west.

On December 9th, they were overtaken by a group of about twenty men on foot and with horses that had also tried the cutoff, but were now back on the Old Spanish Trail. On December 10th, they left the river and went across the desert to shortcut the bend, and they again reached the river after traveling fifteen miles. On December 11th, they encountered a group that had been sent by Isaac Williams from his Chino Rancho to sell provisions to those in short supply on the desert.

Peter Derr, J.D. Gruwell and others had left the Independent Pioneer Company at Las Vegas to ride ahead and get provisions for the straggling company. Other packers who had been lost on the desert or who had nearly run out of provisions had also gone ahead and Isaac Williams was made aware of the desperate circumstances of those in need in the desert. Accordingly, Williams sent a small crew forward with provisions including flour and live animals to give or sell to the emigrants as circumstances required. This relief camp was along the Mojave between present-day Victorville and Barstow, California.

At Williams' camp, Hunts' party had some fresh meat for the first time in weeks. Pratt tried hunting deer, but found that previous travelers, including the Flake-Rich company who shot five, had chased the deer away from the river.

On December 12th, they set out and traveled eight miles. Pratt again went hunting and was successful in getting one deer. The weather had been cold and often they found ice on whatever water was in the river in the mornings. They also found that the water in the Mojave would rapidly fluctuate with rain and snowstorms in the mountains to the south. They traveled eight miles and camped near the present community of Helendale, California. On December 13th, they traveled nine miles and crossed to the west side of the Mojave River and camped near what is now Oro Grande.

Here they left the Mojave River, which ran southward through present-day Victorville and on to its headwaters in the San Bernardino Mountains. They traveled a little to the southwest toward the low spot between the San Bernardino and San Gabriel Mountains, called Cajon Pass. Since it was a fairly long ascent with little grass or water, they laid over on December 14th. On December 15th they began the ascent toward Cajon Pass and camped about three miles from the pass in a hollow with some grass.

That night Pratt wrote that:

> "In the night there came up about twenty men more from those that had taken the cut off. The first that came from them did not like to tell much about their proceedings but there was an Irishman among these that was overjoyed to see Captain Hunt and told him that they were in great trouble and said that when they found so many mountains that they could get no farther they began blaming one another for leading them that way and saying if they had have followed Capt. Hunt they would have been safe, he said they would have sooner that he had have been there to have shown them the way to go than to have seen the face of God. And by such expressions as he made use of we found that Captain Hunt would have been looked upon as their Savior not withstanding some of them were so bitter against him when we were among them, I could pity them much as I knew their hatred was unfounded" (Hafen and Hafen 1954, 105).

Those that had taken the shortcut realized the folly of their decision and recognized that they should have never left the Hunt train.

The Jefferson Hunt Wagon Train, or what was left of it, was now very close to the end of their journey. On December 16th, in a heavy snow storm, they crossed over Cajon Pass and began the descent into the great inland valley below them. It would eventually would be called the Inland Empire and become the location of the cities of San Bernardino, Ontario, Riverside, Chino, Redlands, Rancho Cucamonga, and many others. According to historian Leo Lyman, they followed Coyote-Crowder Canyon, a little to the east of the present Interstate 15. This is a much narrower and steeper route than the present route of either the railroad or the highway. Pratt noted that they had to build the road and that they were forced to stop for two days because of heavy stream flow due to the storm. The Gruwells and other wagons caught up with them and everyone was camped together. The descent was so rough that Pratt called it the "roughest place we found between Salt Lake and California" (Lyman 2001, 93; Hafen and Hafen 1954, 106-107).

They resumed their travel on December 19th and went thirteen miles, probably to the place now known as Sycamore Flat, just beyond the present Glen Helen Park and the city of Devore. They were now out of the mountains, on the great alluvial fan that extends out from Lytle Creek. On December 20th, they continued to the valley floor and headed to the southwest. They traveled a total of ten miles that day. On December 21st, they continued to Rancho Cucamonga where they stayed overnight and bought "fresh beef, corn, wheat, and a little wine made on the ranch." Pratt was impressed with the "Immense herds of cattle and horses" and the abundance of fruits grown there. The steward at the ranch was a black man who Jefferson Hunt had known from his service in the Mormon Battalion where he was a servant to one of the officers (Hafen and Hafen 1954, 108).

On December 22nd, they continued the ten miles to Isaac Williams' Rancho del Chino where they found Charles C. Rich and his Mormon packers waiting for them. Rich and his group had arrived about ten days before. Hunt had successfully completed the journey from Salt Lake City to California, arriving three days before Christmas 1849.

Most of those in the Independent Pioneer Company were still spread out just behind them on the trail. Rynierson and the others who followed after Hunt were also still along the trail, as were many of those who tried the cutoff and returned. Just about everyone was desperately short of food. Those who had money bought supplies from Williams' men at the relief camps; those who had no money were given the food. For several months, and again the following year, Isaac Williams was the rescuer of dozens, if not hundreds, of ill-prepared emigrants along the southern trail to California. In 1850, he petitioned the California legislature for financial relief for his efforts, but was denied. Only in 1950 did the state government honor his efforts with a proclamation.

Jefferson Hunt and the Mormon packers spent Christmas Day in the comfort and abundance of Rancho del Chino. About 200 miles to the northeast, the situation was quite different for the Jay Hawkers and the several other small groups who were left of those that had taken O.K. Smith's shortcut to California. William Lewis Manly described how, late on Christmas Day, he came across the camp of Reverend Brier and his family in the lower end of what is now Furnace Creek Wash in Death Valley National Park. Brier, who was with his wife and three sons, was "very coolly delivering a lecture to his boys on education" (Manly 2001, 84). Manly couldn't help but note that because of starvation and their desperate circumstances, education seemed then to be of little importance at that point. Almost twenty miles to the northwest were the Jay Hawkers who were burning their wagons to dry beef from their slaughtered oxen in preparation of packing on. The Bennett, Arcan, and Wade families, along with others were beginning their descent down Furnace Creek Wash into Death Valley.

All of these emigrants were completely lost and fast running out of provisions. For over a month, they had followed the snow-capped beacon of Telescope Peak in Death Valley hoping that it was the crest of the Sierra Nevada Mountains. They were about to learn that the actual crest was more than seventy miles to the west, and that the nearest relief was about 200 miles to the south. For some, the ordeal would last almost two more months. At least four of those in Death Valley would die before reaching safety. Manly and John Rogers walked 225 miles to the present city of Santa Clarita, north of San Fernando, and then returned to lead the Bennett and Arcan families out. The Jay Hawkers struggled on to San Fernando also. The Brier family, which had been shunned for a time by the Jay Hawkers who did not want to be encumbered by a woman and children, survived largely because of the efforts of Juliet Brier, who soon became a heroine in the eyes of the Jay Hawkers.

Unknown to them, the Old Spanish Trail at the Salt Spring Hills was less than seventy miles to the south from where the Death Valley '49ers entered the floor of Death Valley, and only about fifty miles from where the Bennett and Arcan families waited for Manly and Rogers to return. They could have still tried to follow in the footsteps of Jefferson Hunt had they known that. Historians believe that the Harry Wade family escaped from Death Valley by going south and intercepting the Old Spanish Trail by that route, although some recent evidence raises the possibility that the Wades may have left by following Wingate Wash, the later route of the famed Borax wagons.

Thomas Morris, a Mormon Battalion veteran who traveled from Winter Quarters to Salt Lake City with Porter Rockwell in 1848, signed on with the Pomeroy brothers as a teamster and was traveling with them to Southern California in early 1850 when he met the Wades. His diary is unclear about the date or exact location, but most likely it was in mid-February 1850, and the location was on the Mojave River at Oro Grande, just downstream from present-day Victorville. Clearly his reference is about the Wade family.

Morris wrote that:

> "One poor wretched family, who had lost the track and wandered many weeks in the mountains, left a company of six wagons to perish in the mountains. He had packed his small children on his cattle and when an ox could go no farther, they ate the meat, having nothing else to subsist on for 6 weeks. The family were natives of London. One Frenchman was with them. The woman was sunburned and looked like a perfect skeleton. We relieved them from all want and were glad of the opportunity" (Thomas Morris Journal, 7-8).

Morris' account of meeting the Wades does not mention which route they may have taken to escape Death Valley, and the description of using oxen to carry out the small children does not preclude the existence of a wagon. In the absence of more compelling evidence, the author still accepts the traditional history that the Wade family escaped with their wagon and found the Old Spanish Trail as passed down through their family history.

The question naturally arises whether or not Jefferson Hunt was responsible for the disasters that befell the Death Valley '49ers and other groups who took O. K. Smith's shortcut. The short answer is that he was not at fault.

Hunt was never the leader of the wagon train; he was the guide hired to pilot them to California. The emigrants elected officers to be in overall charge and then divided themselves up into seven divisions, each headed by a cap-tain. The officers and captains acted as a council and governed the train as needed. However, within a month, this governing structure had broken down: Baxter, the chief elected officer had resigned, and individual captains were taking their divisions out on their own. This was not an unusual for a wagon train. The history of the Westward migration is filled with similar situations in which wagon trains would form, reform, disintegrate and then reform again as travel times and personal likes and dislikes and animosities came into play. Since Hunt was never the leader, elected or otherwise, of the wagon train, he cannot be held responsible for the collapse of its leadership.

However some, but not all, of the general dissatisfaction that prevailed in the wagon train can be laid on Hunt. He was far more successful in guid-ing the train to water and feed in a timely manner than was his counterpart, Antonio, with the Independent Pioneer Company. But his ill-fated attempt to find a more favorable route to avoid the Black Mountains south of the Beaver consumed a lot of time and energy and led to hostility and dissention within the train. That event, which coincided with the arrival of O.K. Smith and his map, led many in the train to believe that the shortcut alternative was viable. Clearly, there would have been less dissention within the train had Hunt not presented the possibility of a shortcut into the Escalante Desert to the wagon train's officers and council.

If Hunt had not tried the cutoff around the Black Mountains, would O.K. Smith, carrying Barney Ward's map, have caught up with the wagon train? The answer is yes. The day that the wagon train reached the Beaver River, October 18th, the packers were only about fifty-five miles behind the wagon train, and they were traveling about twice as fast as the train. Had the wagon train not turned west along the Beaver River but continued south over the Black Mountains, the packers would have caught up with them in the Little Salt Lake Valley, well before the beginning of Smith's cutoff. It was inevitable that Smith and his map would have influenced those in the wagon train looking for a faster route to California.

Hunt has been criticized by some for unnecessarily laying over and not traveling on Sundays and some other days early in the trip. However, the con-temporary documents written by Welch and Pratt indicate that the decisions to layover were made by Colonel Baxter and the other officers, and not Hunt. Others in the wagon train had strong religious beliefs also, and the decisions to stop on the Sabbath were not his.

A valid criticism is that Hunt did not divide the wagon train into smaller traveling units; that a train of 107 wagons was too large and unmanageable for the amount of water and feed available and took too long to form up and camp down each day. This is true, but again, how much of the responsibility is Hunt's? He could have—but apparently did not—advise the officers of the wagon train that the best way to travel was to break up into smaller units each comprising one-quarter or one-third of the total and have them travel a day apart. While his was not the final decision in this matter, he very possibly could have influenced the officers to arrange travel in such a fashion. However, during his Mormon Battalion experience, this was not done, and since he had not crossed from Winter Quarters to Salt Lake City with the other Saints, he probably had little exposure to such spaced divisions as an effective way to travel.

It has also been suggested that Hunt prompted the Flake-Rich packers to take the shortcut to lead the others away from him and remnants of the wagon train. However, other explanations seem more likely. First of all, most of the Mormon packers were sponsored or approved by elders in Salt Lake City to go to the gold fields. Mormon gold miners in California were primarily centered at the Southern Mines near Mariposa such as Mormon Bar, or within a twenty-five mile radius of Coloma at places such as Mormon Island. A cutoff over Walker Pass that would take them more directly toward Mariposa would save hundreds of miles and weeks of travel.

Even more important were the instructions given them in Salt Lake City to explore the route as much as possible. If, in fact, there did exist a better and shorter road to California, it was their duty to find and explore it. They could not pass up the chance to investigate Barney Ward's shortcut. Hunt, Rich and the others were most likely very skeptical of the existence of such a road since it had never before been mentioned to them. A number of men who had been over the Southern Route before had not mentioned it. Wakara never mentioned it to the Battalion members in Los Angeles at the time of their discharge. Miles Goodyear did not discuss it with Jefferson Hunt before his trip in 1847. Fremont did not mention it his book discussing the travel through the Great Basin even though he had been at both the western and eastern ends. Barney Ward had not mentioned it before to his Mormon friends in Salt Lake City. But if the road did exist, it was too good an opportunity to ignore. Hunt, Rich, Flake and others were skeptical enough to draw up an alternative plan just in case—and used it when they found that the road did not exist.

Additionally, when the time came for those who were going to follow Smith's cutoff to leave Hunt and his small remaining group of wagons, he clearly and carefully explained to them that he did not believe in the veracity of the map and that major trouble lay ahead for them. He stated that in his experience on the trail, the safest way to proceed was along the known route of the Old Spanish Trail and that he believed those who took the cutoff were going "into the jaws of hell." Reflecting back in later years, many of those who took the cutoff remembered his words and spoke favorably of him for warning them, even though they ignored his experience and sound advice. In retrospect, they wished they had followed his counsel.

Finally, Brigham Young's admonishment to them to "go in union" was not followed and his prediction that if they didn't they would be in "imminent danger" was prophetic. It is clear that the both Brigham Young and Jefferson Hunt had the best intentions and tried their best to safely conduct the emigrants to California. It was the emigrants themselves who marched into disaster.

Chapter 19

California and Return

Jefferson Hunt did not immediately return to Utah following his arrival in Southern California. Instead, he remained nearly a year before heading back. His travels and meetings around California are somewhat obscure for this period, but it appears that he may have been meeting with other Mormons and some of those persons he befriended during his Mormon Battalion days.

Addison Pratt indicated that those with him, including Hunt, remained at Isaac Williams' for a period of time because of the wet weather. He said they were ready to leave when William Lorton finally arrived at Chino on January 12, 1850. During the three weeks that Rich and Hunt were at Williams' Rancho, they had adequate time to discuss the particulars of his earlier offer to sell his ranch to the Mormons. There is no record of these discussions, but with a member of the senior leadership of the LDS Church present, we can be sure that they took place.

Brigham Young clearly was interested in extending the Mormon influence to the California Coast. A direct route from San Diego or Los Angeles to Salt Lake City would shorten the trip across the Continent by land for those Saints immigrating to the Valley of the Great Salt Lake. Emigrants could take ship passage to Panama, cross the Isthmus, and then take another ship to the California ports. Similarly, commerce conducted via California would be faster and less expensive than the overland route from the Missouri River.

Central to this effort would be the establishment of a Mormon outpost in California. In 1847, Isaac Williams had indicated to Jefferson Hunt his interest in selling his ranch at Chino to the Mormons. Its location near the southern end of Cajon Pass made it an ideal location for the Mormon's California headquarters. It commanded the southern end of the trail from Salt Lake City, and it was far enough away from the northern gold fields and cities of San Francisco and Sacramento to avoid unwanted outside influence from the non-Mormons in California. In the intervening two years, Young and his counselors, including Rich, had the opportunity to consider, discuss the offer and to prepare a favorable response.

As subsequent events show, it is very likely that Jefferson Hunt and Charles C. Rich specifically talked to Williams about his willingness to sell and his desired terms. As a member of the Quorum of the Twelve, Rich was most likely empowered to enter into such discussions. Hunt, for his part, was well known to Williams and other Southern Californians, and would have been in a position to lend credibility to any negotiations. Some portion of the three weeks spent at Chino was devoted to discussing a possible future Mormon colony in California at the Chino Rancho.

But Brigham Young wasn't just interested in extending Mormon influence to California; he was also interested in developing other portions along the Salt Lake–Los Angeles trail. In July 1849, after most of his crops failed in the Salt Lake Valley, Parley P. Pratt—another of the Quorum of the Twelve—began work on developing a road in what the Mormons then called Big Canyon, and what we now call Parley's Canyon. Today, Interstate 80 leaves Salt Lake City and goes eastward into the Wasatch Range through this canyon. In the 1840s, the lower end of the canyon was much narrower and filled with brush and trees. Wagon passage was so difficult through Parley's and nearby canyons that the ill-fated Donner/Reed Party spent too much time (ten days) trying to cut a road, left it near the present Mountain Dell, crossing over the northern ridge into what is now known as Emigration Canyon. This delay contributed significantly to the circumstances that led to the Donner tragedy. The Mormon Pioneers led by Brigham Young entered the Valley of the Great Salt Lake via the same route in 1847.

A road through Parley's Canyon would greatly simplify the effort needed to reach Salt Lake City from the East. Pratt recognized this need, explored the canyon for a road in 1848, and began work on it in 1849. Work continued until the weather worsened in November 1849, when he closed his camp and returned to the valley below. But his rest was short lived. Almost immediately, Brigham Young and the Deseret legislature called him to lead an exploring party of fifty men to the southern part of Utah.

Parley Pratt and his large group of explorers left Salt Lake on November 24, 1849. They traveled south and explored the headwaters of the Sevier River and then, in heavy snow, crossed westward over the mountains to Cedar Valley. Some went with Pratt as far south as the confluence of the Santa Clara and Virgin rivers. Generally, they recognized the potential for developing the Cedar Valley (present-day Cedar City) and other locations along the route. With their supplies dwindling, Pratt and about half the party pressed northward toward Salt Lake in bad weather, while the rest remained near Cedar Valley until the weather improved.

Upon his return to Salt Lake, Pratt reported favorably to the legislature and to Brigham Young. As a result, it was decided at the General Conference in April 1850, to send a permanent party to settle the Cedar Valley the following Fall. The steps were in place to form the Iron County Mission.

On January 6th, Howard Egan, who was leading another group of '49ers and Mormons from Salt Lake City, arrived at Chino. His group was known as the Salt Lake Trading Company and was enroute to the gold fields to establish a trading operation. Egan's party of wagons intended to keep going on toward San Gabriel and Los Angeles. It was decided to combine the two groups, and Jefferson Hunt was elected captain. The trip north began on January 12th, when Hunt, Rich, Addison Pratt and the others, all of whom were packing, started out and caught up with Egan and his wagons. By January 14th they were at San Gabriel. The next day, they arrived at the Pueblo of Los Angeles and stocked up on provisions for the journey north.

They left Los Angeles on the 17th and followed the El Camino Real, which is essentially today's Highway 101. On January 21st, they arrived at the mission at today's City of Ventura on the California coast. Two days later, they were at Santa Barbara, and two days after that, they were in the Santa Ynez Valley, having left the wagon road and crossed over the coastal mountains on a pack trail, probably over San Marcos Pass. Continuing past today's city of Santa Maria, they arrived at the ranch of William G. Dana on January 28th.

Captain William G. Dana was a cousin of Richard Henry Dana, author of *Two Years before the Mast*, and was himself a noted seafarer. In 1837, Dana was granted nearly 38,000 acres at the location of present-day Nipomo. He was a noted early pioneer of California and had strongly supported statehood. His rancho was a welcome stopping place for those persons traveling the El Camino Real. Jefferson Hunt had stopped and visited him on his 1847 trip north after the discharge of the Mormon Battalion. Hunt had the wagon train stop and enjoy Dana's hospitality.

Addison Pratt had another reason to visit with Dana. The Captain had acquired a significant portion of the Island of Tubuai in the Society Islands some years before. Pratt hoped to be able to buy the land since he was going to the South Pacific on a mission. He told Hunt and Rich of his desires and they agreed to pray for assistance in making the purchase. Hunt introduced Pratt to Dana, and after some discussion, Dana agreed to issue Pratt a quit claim deed for the island property if Pratt would only pay to have the papers drawn up. It was agreed to, and before they left Rancho Nipomo, Pratt had his ownership of a considerable portion of the Island of Tubuai. Hunt, Rich and Freeman S. McKinney witnessed the signing of the document on January 29, 1850 (Ellsworth and Pratt 1990, 558).

That same day, they returned to their journey, crossing the rain-swollen river of Arroyo Grande, and camped near the present-day City of San Luis Obispo. On January 31st, they crossed over Cuesta Grade, north of San Luis Obispo, and went on to the mission at Santa Margarita. By February 5th, they were at the Mission San Antonio, and by the 8th, they were on the Salinas River at the present-day site of Soledad. On the 10th, they were at San Juan Bautista, and the next day they arrived at the present location of the City of Gilroy. Here a road left for the east and went over Pacheco Pass. This was the route to the southernmost mines at Mariposa, and was the intended route of those who were going straight to the gold mines. However, they were out of provisions and it was decided that all should go on to San Jose where they could obtain supplies.

On January 12th, they arrived at San Jose. There Addison Pratt began to renew some of his acquaintances from his earlier trip, including that of William Eddy, one of the survivors of the Donner party. On the 14th, Howard Egan arrived and reported that his wagon train was at San Juan Batista and that they, too, were out of provisions; he had traveled on ahead to obtain relief. At this point, Hunt and Rich set out to obtain the needed supplies since they were responsible for the entire group of Mormons.

At that time, San Jose was the seat of government for California. A constitutional convention had been held, a constitution sent to Washington for statehood approval, and a slate of officers had been elected. When Hunt and the Mormons arrived in San Jose, the legislature was meeting, even though statehood would not be granted until September 9, 1850. The Governor was Peter Burnett, a lawyer from Missouri, who had represented the Mormons in their difficulties there and was likely known to many of the Mormons. He succeeded General Bennett Riley, who had replaced Colonel Mason as military governor. Riley called for the constitutional convention and suggested the election of a new governor. Upon election, Burnett effectively became the first governor of California.

Hunt and Rich attempted to obtain financial support for supplies from William Stout, one of the *Brooklyn* Mormons, but he claimed other obligations. Through William Eddy, they were introduced to Governor Burnett. Eddy agreed to exchange thirty-five dollars with Pratt for some seashells and a cached store of goods along the Humboldt trail. Through Eddy's intervention, Rich and Hunt were able to obtain the needed supplies from local merchants (Ellsworth and Pratt 1990, 428).

On February 15th, the party split up, with the miners heading for Mariposa and the others including Hunt, Rich, Pratt, Francis Pomeroy and James Rollins trekking to San Francisco. The following day, the party reached Mission Delores at San Francisco, where they met several more of the *Brooklyn* Saints. There they also learned that a small group under Apostle Amasa Lyman, and including Jesse Hunter, Robert Clift, and Charles Crisman had left by ship on February 8th to go to the southern part of the state to obtain a place for Mormon settlement. Lyman and his group arrived at San Pedro on February 20th and returned to San Francisco on March 13th. They did not achieve their goal of finding a location.

On February 17th, Rich, Hunt and Pratt went the three miles from the Mission Delores to the main City of San Francisco to meet with Sam Brannan, the man who had been the nominal leader of the California Saints—but they found that he had gone to Sacramento or the gold fields. During the several days they were in San Francisco, they met with the other Mormons who lived in the area. On the 22nd, Rich and his party, probably including Jefferson Hunt, left San Francisco for Mariposa.

Addison Pratt remained in San Francisco until he sailed for Tahiti on April 21, 1850. But before he left, he wrote Brigham Young on April 15th and complimented Jefferson Hunt saying: "Br Hunt's patients [sic], with the numerous perplexities of the emigrants, his skill as a mountaineer, his correct judgement [sic] of distances & his cheerful company renders him in my estimation, a skillful pilot among the deserts" (Ellsworth and Pratt 1990, 432).

On March 1st, the Rich/Hunt party crossed Pacheco Pass on the way to Mariposa. On March 7th, they arrived at Burns' Diggings, which was not far from the Merced River, about three miles from the present community of Hornitos and about fifteen miles from Mariposa. There they expected to find Howard Egan, but he had gone to Stockton. They did find other Mormons and remained there. Jefferson Hunt dropped out of Rich's journal for several months, so it appears that Hunt remained in the area of Mariposa or the southern mines. According to the historian J. Kenneth Davis, Egan established a trading post known as the Salt Lake Trading Company several miles east of the current location of Merced Falls, not far from Hornitos (Davies 1984, 207).

It is likely that Hunt remained at Egan's trading post or in the nearby mining areas around Mariposa. This ends a detailed account of the travels of Jefferson Hunt in California in 1850. Only small snippets on his activities were recorded by others during the remainder of the year.

Since the arrival in California of the ship *Brooklyn* in 1846 and the Mormon Battalion in 1847, there had been Mormons in Northern California. While some left for Salt Lake City during 1848 and 1849, many stayed in California. Quite a few of those remained in or near the gold fields east of Sacramento. It was the recently discharged members of the Mormon Battalion working for Sutter and Marshall that became the first gold miners and prospectors of the Gold Rush, and a strong Mormon presence remained in the gold fields after January 1848. Many of those present when James Marshall discovered gold at Coloma spent their infrequent days off searching for gold in nearby portions of the American River and adjacent streams.

One of their most productive discoveries was on the American River, about fifteen miles downstream from Coloma. The area known as Mormon Island is now under the waters of Folsom Lake, but during 1848-50 it was known as the most fruitful of all the placer gold fields found. Consequently, a number of Mormons mined that area and settled nearby. Some others settled in Sacramento and still others went to other mining areas near Coloma, such as Salmon Falls (close to Mormon Island), Greenwood Valley, Murderers' Bar, Georgetown and others.

A quick and imprecise survey of the locations of Mormon miners in 1850 seems to indicate that the majority of them were within a fifteen mile radius of the original discovery site of Coloma. While most of the Mormon miners didn't travel far, a few were in Calaveras and some were at Mormon Bar or other locations near Mariposa at the far southern end of the Mother Lode.

A similar survey of the travels of Charles Rich and Amasa Lyman shows that they spent much of their time in California in 1850 visiting those miners in the areas around Mormon Island and Coloma, with a few other

trips to San Francisco, Sacramento, and Mariposa. Rich and Lyman were administering to the Saints in much of California and were collecting tithing for
Salt Lake City. For the most part, Jefferson Hunt was not with them, but may
well have been performing a similar function in the area of Mariposa and the
Southern Mines. It appears that he resided for some time at Bear Valley, about
ten miles north of Mariposa (Smith 1958, 160).

On April 8, 1850, both Rich and Lyman went to San Francisco and
there met with Charles Crisman and Captain Jessie D. Hunter. According
to Rich they "held a council pertaining to making a settlement in the lower
country which we concluded to do if this worked to our mind" (Rich Journal,
April 8, 1850). Lyman's account was similar: "Today meet Brs. Crisman and
Hunter & settled an arrangement for purchase of the Ranch of Chino" (Lyman
Journal, April 8, 1850). Clearly, the plan first proposed by Jefferson Hunt several years before was now being seriously pursued.

After several weeks in San Francisco, Rich and Lyman went to Mission
San Jose in present-day Fremont, where they met with several other Mormons, then headed for the Merced River and Mariposa. On April 27th, they
arrived at Howard Egan's trading post on the Merced, but he was not there
and no mention is made of Jefferson Hunt being present when they arrived.
Egan returned on the following day. The day after, he, Rich and Lyman went
the short distance to Mariposa. When they returned to the trading post on
May 2nd, Hunt was there.

On May 3rd, Rich, Lyman, Hunt, Egan and several other Mormons began to travel north toward Sacramento, but the next day their animals stam-
peded near the Tuolumne River. Hunt recovered them and returned with
them the next day. On May 6th, they stopped at Mormon Gulch, near present-day Tuttletown, a small community four miles west of Sonora. They then
traveled to visit another Mormon near Calaveras. By May 10th, they were at
Mormon Tavern near Lathrop's, which was another Mormon-occupied area
just south of Mormon Island

Then they apparently broke up into several smaller groups that variously traveled to Sacramento, Greenwood Valley, Salmon Falls and other
nearby locations. During this time, James Flake was killed when he fell from
his horse near Georgetown. By June 3rd and 4th, Rich, Lyman and Hunt were

again together at Mormon Tavern where they met and presumably discussed their activities. On June 5th, Hunt and a Brother Clark left for an unknown destination, but Hunt returned to Mormon Tavern by June 20th when he again met with Rich, Lyman, and Egan. This is the last time that either Rich or Lyman mention meeting with Hunt in California in 1850.

In mid-August, Rich and Lyman traveled to the Carson Valley in the present state of Nevada, and Lyman began his return trip to Salt Lake City over the Humboldt Route on August 29th. Rich returned to Mormon Tavern, Sacramento and San Francisco. He left California for Salt Lake City on October 5th and arrived there on November 12th. Rich noted in his diary that when he arrived he found that the "Church had appointed Br. A. Lyman and myself to make a settlement in the lower part of California the coming spring" (Rich, Special Collections).

Where exactly Jefferson Hunt was and what he was doing in California during much of 1850 cannot be determined, but his past and future actions do give us some hint. Quite probably, he renewed some of the relationships he had developed during his Mormon Battalion sojourn in the Golden State. As someone who had been in California twice before the start of the Gold Rush, he held a degree of standing reserved to only a few hundred others. That fact was important to the political and territorial ambitions of Brigham Young and the LDS Church. It is very probable that he met with some of those federal and state officials. It is likely that Hunt also met with some of the Army officers from the Mexican War days who were still in California. It is certain that he met with many of his former comrades with the Mormon Battalion who were living and mining in the gold country.

It is also very likely that Hunt tried his hand at mining. Since many of the Mormons lived and mined together in groups, he could have joined with them easily. Since Hunt had a record of transporting cargo, it is possible that he also took on the role of a freighter or even a wholesaler for a while.

But what is known for sure is that Hunt stayed in California longer than both Rich and Lyman—and unlike them—he returned to Utah via the

Southern Route rather than the Humboldt Route. By taking the Southern Route, Hunt would have had sufficient time and reason to again meet with Isaac Williams and to discuss the possible sale of his ranch to the Mormons.

Hunt's discovery at Iron Springs in 1847 led to Parley Pratt's exploration of the ore deposits in the Winter of 1849-50. Brigham Young wanted to make the Mormons in the Great Basin as self-supporting as possible, and a source of iron only 200 miles from Salt Lake City was too enticing to pass up. If the Mormons could develop an iron industry, they would substantially benefit. Accordingly, at the Church's General Conference in April 1850, a decision was approved to settle the area of the Little Salt Lake Valley and to mine and mill the iron deposits. The move established what would become known as the Iron Mission and was the first step in creating Iron County, Utah. At that conference, the Apostle George A. Smith was elected to head the Iron Mission. Since it was too late in the year to effectively settle a new area and develop the required agricultural support, the actual establishment of the new community, farms and industry would have to wait until 1851.

Later in 1850 a call went out for settlers and experienced tradesmen for the Iron Mission. One of those who became part of the Iron Mission was John D. Lee, who was appointed clerk. Finally, on December 15th, the same day Hunt and his party left Williams' ranch at Chino for Utah, George A. Smith organized his settlers at Fort Utah. The *Journal History of the Church* recorded that the initial party consisted of 163 people, including 119 males over the age of fourteen. Smith's wagon train began its journey south the following day.

Smith's settlers followed the route taken previously by Hunt and relied on other information supplied by Parley Pratt—including the relatively mild climate of the southern Utah valleys. On January 13, 1851, the Iron Mission settlers arrived at Center Creek at the location of present-day Parowan. They immediately set about creating a camp that could be used as a base of operation while they scouted the remainder of the Little Salt Lake and Cedar valleys. Smith wasted no time in organizing an exploration of the area. That night, he arranged for some to scout the canyon to the east and some adjacent canyons; he prepared to lead a larger party south the next day.

John D. Lee's personal diaries, if any, for this period do not exist. The *Journal of the Iron County Mission* he prepared does exist, as do the journals of George A. Smith. As usual, Lee was complete and detailed in his entries—and did everything possible to ingratiate himself with his superiors in the Church while denigrating his equals and those below him.

On Tuesday morning, January 14, 1851, George A. Smith's party of twenty men began its exploration of the area south of Center Creek (Parowan). They expected to be gone about three days and took supplies with them as they headed south toward Summit Creek. Unknown to them, Jefferson Hunt and his party had spent the previous night in the Cedar Valley and were heading north, also toward Summit Creek. Both groups were heading up opposite sides of the alluvial fan that emanates from the mouth of the canyon. In one of those rare but significant encounters that sometimes occur on the trail, the two groups met, according to Lee at "11 minutes to 12 noon," at Summit Creek and near the site of the present-day community of Summit, Utah (Larson and Lee 1952, Vol. 20, 272). His account of the meeting gave the names of the eight people in Hunt's party and noted that Hunt had forty-two animals with him (Larson and Lee 1952, Vol. 20, 272).

Many of the men in the two groups were acquainted with each other and there must have been a general celebration. From Smith, Hunt learned that his earlier report to Brigham Young about the nearby iron ore had been taken seriously and had resulted in an expansion of the Mormon frontier in the Great Basin. From Hunt, Smith learned of the fate of Isaac Brown who had presumably been murdered along the trail days before, and he heard the downbeat reports of the miners in California. Most notably, he was the first in Utah to hear the news of the creation of Utah Territory and the appointment of Brigham Young as governor. Hunt had with him a copy of the October 11, 1850, *New York Tribune* which reported the creation of the Territory of Utah and the appointment of Brigham Young as territorial governor. This was the first news in Utah that Congress had created Utah Territory. The newspaper had traveled by sea from New York to the Isthmus of Panama, overland across the Isthmus, and then up the coast to California where Jefferson Hunt or another in his party obtained a copy. Because it was major news in Utah, the Hunt party brought the paper with them.

After a short discussion, Smith asked Hunt to join him on the brief exploration to the south, while the remainder of Hunt's party continued on to Parowan where they could rest. Hunt had made several trips through the Cedar Valley and knew the location of the iron ore deposits, and since Smith was a very senior Church official, he readily agreed. Smith, Hunt and the other nineteen men continued on about fifteen miles where they camped alongside of Coal Creek near the present location of Cedar City, Utah.

The following day, January 15th, Smith sent one group of men to explore the mouth of the canyon where Coal Creek entered the valley and another small group of men to inspect the downstream part of the valley. The remaining men under Smith were led by Hunt about eight miles west to Iron Springs and the mountains containing iron ore immediately nearby. There they climbed about and noted the obvious indications of iron ore. Samples were collected for further testing and analysis. They were visited by the Indian chief Peteetneet and a small band, who informed them that Chief Wakara was about twenty-five miles to the south.

After inspecting the iron ore and assessing its availability for processing, the group returned to their camp of the night before along the "Muddy" or Coal Creek. George A. Smith was anxious to capitalize on the information about the new territory, and accordingly, called a meeting that evening to begin the formal process of organizing Iron County. A committee, including Smith and Lee among others, was set up to nominate officers for the new county. In about an hour, a slate of candidates was selected, an election was called for at Parowan in two days, and the whole matter was unanimously approved. Hunt took the results of the Iron County organization effort to Salt Lake when he resumed his journey.

On January 16th, the morning after the organizational meeting, Smith again sent a group of nine men to explore higher up Coal Creek Canyon, and the rest of the party, eleven men total, including Smith, Hunt and Lee, began the return trip to the main camp at present-day Parowan. Many in the group felt that the barren appearance of Cedar Valley meant that it was not a good location for a future settlement of any size, and that the Parowan area presented the best location for their permanent home. On their return trip, they shortened the route from the mouth of Coal Creek to Summit Creek by about five miles by heading directly north instead of following the Old Spanish Trail which was further west.

John D. Lee recorded that:

> "At 20 minets [sic] to 12 noon the explorers arrived at Sumit [sic] Creek, day cool and cloudy—here Capt. Hunt showed the Pres. [Smith] a cash [cache] which he had made the season before, containing waggon wheels hand saw, planes chisels augers spades chains etc which he said Pres G. A. Smith might have & welcome & all he would ask was, if he (Capt Hunt) should remove to this county, & should need a spade or chain to give him" (Larson and Lee 1952, Vol. 20, 276).

Hunt had shown Smith the location of the tools and other supplies that he had accumulated and cached during his trip to California in the Fall of 1849.

The exploration party returned to Parowan, arriving just before four p.m. At six, George A. Smith called a meeting of all present and the Iron Mission organized itself into a caucus for the purpose of nominating officers for the new county. After the appropriate formalities, the slate of officers decided by the nominating committee the night before was accepted and an election was scheduled for the next day. John D. Lee, who had been nominated for recorder, withdrew his nomination since he intended to be gone from the county for a period of time to gather and move his families to their new homes.

His withdrawal was accepted and other offices were offered to him when he returned.

On Friday, January 17th, the election was held and all of the nominated officers were elected without opposition. According to Smith, 117 votes were cast and the vote was unanimous (George A. Smith Papers, Special Collections). Thus, Jefferson Hunt became the first officially elected representative to the Utah Territorial Legislature. This was Hunt's first effort at elected public office, but it would not be his last. We don't know for sure exactly what Hunt's intentions were; did he plan on relocating soon to Iron County or did he intend to carry out his new duties from his home in the north? His comments the following day indicate that he was seriously considering a move, and he always seemed to prefer to live away from the urbanized or more heavily populated communities and Provo/Ft. Utah was becoming more crowded.

At three p.m. that afternoon, a large celebration honoring both the creation of the new county and the visitors from California was held. According to Lee:

> "At 3 the whole citizens of Iron Co. sat down at once upon the ground around a public dinner which was spread upon Buffalo Robes next to the ground & table cloths clean & white up on which was spread a variety of refreshments of life" (Larson and Lee 1952, Vol. 20, 279).

Following dinner, Hunt delivered a speech.

At seven p.m. the settlement gathered for an open air dance and singing in honor of Hunt and those returning from California. That evening George A. Smith wrote petitions to the new legislature, reports, and letters to Brigham Young and other Church leaders. Many in the settlement wrote to friends and family in Salt Lake City.

At ten a.m. on Saturday, January 18th, Jefferson Hunt and the California party left Parowan, hoping to arrive in Salt Lake in ten days. In addition to the petitions and official reports, they carried with them about 100 letters.

What about the cache of tools and supplies left by Hunt at Summit Creek? George A. Smith gives us the answer in his journal entry for February 7th: "Br. Wheeler and myself went to Summit Creek to open a casch [cache] made by Capt. Hunt its supposed contents was missing" (George A. Smith, February 7, 1851). There is no indication in the report of January 16th that the cache had been disturbed. Hunt would have clearly seen any effort to dig up the contents. So it appears that the most likely suspect for the removal of the cache was one of the settlers who were present when Hunt showed Smith the location. We can immediately remove both Hunt and Smith as suspects since they "owned" the contents of the cache and would have had no reason to clandestinely dig it up. That leaves the other ten men present. The suspect in the removal must have been one of them.

An investigator today might look at those ten and determine which, if any, had a record of criminal convictions or had allegedly appropriated the property of others for personal use. The investigator would immediately note that there was one man among them who had a reputation of taking the property of others for personal use and was eventually convicted of murder and executed. That man was John D. Lee, who had been accused of misappropriation of Mormon Battalion pay funds in 1846, was accused of removing clothes, cattle and other property belonging to the victims of the Mountain Meadow Massacre, and was executed in 1876 for his participation in that slaughter.

Was John D. Lee responsible for digging up the cache? We cannot say for certain and there certainly is not sufficient information to convict him nearly 160 years later. But we can look at his movements during the days between January 16th when the cache was disclosed and February 6th when it was found missing. Lee gave an account of his activities during that time period. On February 9th, he wrote the following in the *Journal of the Iron County Mission*:

> "A minute account of passing events connected with the mission during the interval between date 3 & 9 [of February] is not here in recorded. The most prominent features of the times above are noticed from the fact, the general clerk or historian of the Mission [John D. Lee] having been absent during the week in the kanyon [sic] preparing logs for house to shelter his family" (Larson and Lee 1952, Vol. 20, 374).

In other words, Lee had absented himself to go into the mountains for about a week to cut and prepare logs. He would have had ample time to clandestinely travel from there to Summit Creek, remove the cache and hide it for his own future use. Whether or not he did this, we cannot be certain. However, we can say that he had the opportunity to do it, and a record of behaviors that indicates that he was capable of doing it.

The *Journal History of the LDS Church* on January 27 and February 1, 1851, along with the *Deseret News* of Saturday February 8th, gives us some information regarding Jefferson Hunt's return. Thomas Bullock recorded the arrival in Salt Lake City of Henry E. Gibson, a member of Hunt's return party on January 27th. The significant thing about this arrival was that Gibson was carrying the mail from Southern California and the newly-created settlement of Iron County in the Valley of the Little Salt Lake. Most importantly, he carried that copy of the *New York Tribune* reporting the creation of the Territory of Utah and the appointment of Brigham Young as territorial governor.

Very shortly after congressional action creating the territory, a courier was sent West with the documents. That courier traveled partly by rail, partly by riverboat and the remainder of the way overland by horse or mule. The newspaper beat the courier by quite some time. Meanwhile, since the family lived at Fort Utah, it seems that Hunt had stopped to reunite with his family in Fort Utah, and allowed Gibson to carry the paper and mail north.

Brigham Young had been visiting Ogden in the days before January 27th and was not present when the news of his appointment as governor arrived. A runner was sent out to find Young, and he probably returned to Salt Lake City on January 29th to celebrate the good news. The need for the State of Deseret was gone—Utah Territory was now the official governing body of the area, and Brigham Young was officially in charge.

Jefferson Hunt did not stay long with his family at Fort Utah. By February 1st, he traveled to Salt Lake City and was prepared to report to Brigham Young and the other Church officials. The *Deseret News* article of February 8th, reports that Hunt's party consisted of eight people and was accompanied by his son, Marshall, Henry E. Gibson, Levi Fifield and his son [Byron], James Brooks, John W. Berry and John Macky. This is one of two indications that Marshall accompanied Hunt on the trip. It is possible that Marshall joined his father after traveling in a later company, but it is more probable that he was one of the young men who traveled all the way with and stayed with Hunt during his yearlong travels.

The same article stated that the party left Sacramento on November 25, 1850, arrived in Stockton on November 30th, and arrived at Isaac Williams' ranch on December 15th. From there they were on the trail for twenty-seven days and stopped for several days. The *Journal History of the Church* under the date of February 1, 1851, adds that the party of packers stopped for two days at Cajon Pass, six days at the Muddy River and three days with Apostle George A. Smith and his Iron Mission settlers, who they found on January 14th. They were on the trail for thirty-one days. Both the *Deseret News* and the *Journal History of the Church* reported that Isaac Brown, who had left alone on the route before the Hunt party, was murdered by Indians at the Muddy River.

The *Deseret News* article of February 8th, also included excerpts from a letter dated October 24th from George Q. Cannon (who was now on a mission to Hawaii) to his aunt, Mrs. John Taylor, in which he reported that a cholera outbreak was devastating Sacramento. He wrote that forty-eight people had died, eighteen of them on October 23rd.

A *Journal History of the LDS Church* entry on February 2nd noted that Hunt was in Salt Lake City and met with

> "President Young and other leading brethren in Willard Richards room and gave a report of his journey to California and the route over which he traveled, the gold mines, etc. He reported the brethren employed around the gold mines in California were anxious to return home" (Journal History, February 2, 1851).

It is very likely that the conversation extended beyond this report; it also covered his meeting with Isaac Williams and the plans for the creation of a Mormon settlement in Southern California. Hunt was probably also informed that he would be part of that settlement.

By early February 1851, Jefferson Hunt had been to California three times and had spent nearly two years there. He was thoroughly familiar with both Southern and Northern California and had personally met many of the important figures in the new state. He had met with Isaac Williams on at least five occasions and specifically discussed with him the possible Mormon acquisition of the Chino Rancho. Hunt had also been over the Salt Lake to Los Angeles trail four times and pioneered the use of that route for a number of other parties of Mormon travelers. Finally, Hunt had advocated the purchase of the Chino Rancho for use as a Mormon settlement in the strategically important role as the western terminus of Mormon trade and migration.

Hunt's stay at his home in Utah Valley would be short. Within less than two months of his return from the 1849-50 trip to California, he was again on his way back, this time with his family, as a permanent settler. Hunt would not get to fulfill his role as member of the legislature of the Territory of Utah from Iron County.

PART III

Settler and Politician

Jefferson Hunt's involvement with Death Valley and Southern California history was not finished with his return to Fort Utah and Salt Lake City. He was destined to spend another seven years in California. He would again contribute to the history of the state as a settler, politician and military officer.

Chapter 20

San Bernardino

As early as 1847 some Mormon leaders, including Jefferson Hunt, saw the advantage of establishing a Mormon outpost in Southern California. Hunt and others determined that Isaac Williams was willing to sell his Chino Rancho at terms that would include his cattle—which would make the purchase more financially viable. Williams' interest was confirmed by Hunt in 1848, by Rich and Hunt and others in 1849, and again by Hunt in late 1850.

The two apostles assigned to California, Charles C. Rich and Amasa Lyman, both expressed their feelings to Brigham Young about the need for a Southern California settlement. Such a community would serve as a regional headquarters for the numerous Saints in California and provide a link between the Salt Lake City Church headquarters and the ports on the California coast. Most importantly, a strategically placed settlement near Cajon Pass would enable the Mormons to control, to a large extent, the important route to California. This latter consideration could be critical to the Mormons' hope of one day extending their Territory of Utah throughout the Great Basin and to the Southern California coast.

The area around Williams' Ranch at present-day Chino was nearly ideal for the proposed settlement. It was close to Cajon Pass, which was the main entry point from the Mojave Desert into the basin that extends about ninety miles from east of present-day San Bernardino to the Pacific Ocean at Los Angeles.

Cajon Pass had been the entry point for Old Spanish Trail traffic for thirty years, and the Salt Lake City/Southern California traffic naturally crossed over this pass. Amasa Lyman realized that Chino was fine for raising livestock, but that growing crops was a more difficult problem due to a lack of water. However, there were other locations that were closer to Cajon Pass and more favorable for establishing a settlement.

On April 11, 1850, Lyman penned a letter to James H. Flanigan in England in which he mentioned that he had met with Jesse Hunter and Charles Rich and that "we concluded to make a settlement, an effort was made to purchase a large tract of land" (Journal History of the Church, April 11, 1850). Clearly, the creation of a Southern California settlement was high on Lyman's and Rich's agendas.

While no mention of the Southern California settlement was made in the public records of the Annual Conference of the LDS Church in April 1850, or at the Semi-Annual Conference held in September 1850, it was clearly an issue for the top leaders. On September 27th, the First Presidency of the LDS Church (Brigham Young, Heber Kimball and Willard Richards) issued a General Epistle to all Saints in which they said: "Charles C. Rich is expected to continue his labors in California and commence a settlement with such of the brethren as wish to tarry there, in the Southern part of the Territory" (Journal History of the Church, September 27, 1850). By the Fall of 1850, plans were well on the way for creating a Southern California settlement.

On December 17, 1850, Robert Clift, a former member of the Mormon Battalion, wrote a letter to Brigham Young at the request of Jefferson Hunt, encouraging the purchase of Williams' Rancho. Two days later, Isaac Williams wrote to Charles Rich regarding the sale of his ranch to the Mormons. On February 2, 1851, Hunt, who had just returned from a year in California, met with Brigham Young, Parley Pratt, Rich, Lyman, William Crosby and Willard Richards to report on his trip and locations such as Beaver Creek, Las Vegas Creek and the gold mine at Salt Spring (Church Historian's Office Journal, February 2, 1851). Presumably one of the main topics of conversation was also the organization of the new settlement and the purchase of Williams' Rancho.

Of note is that of the seven men present, five (Young, Richards, Pratt, Lyman and Rich) were in the top leadership of the LDS Church and the other two, Hunt and Crosby were to play significant roles in the management and administration of the new settlement. William Crosby, one of the Mississippi Saints who met the Battalion along the Santa Fe Trail, would soon be elected as presiding Bishop in Southern California. While no complete record of that meeting can be found, subsequent events indicate that the senior members of the Church and Hunt probably discussed his involvement with the new colony and role as the best-known Mormon in Southern California.

On February 23rd, a meeting was held in Brigham Young's office at which Amasa Lyman and Charles Rich were "set apart" to "take a company . . . to Southern California" and "to preside over the affairs of the Church in that land and to establish a strong hold for the gathering of the Saints" (Journal History of the Church, February 23, 1851). At the same time, Parley Pratt was "set apart" on a mission to the Pacific Islands, Lower California and South America. Thus, a formal commitment was made for the organization of the Southern California settlement.

The call went out to the Saints in Salt Lake City for recruits to go to California. It is hard to tell how many volunteered to go without persuasion and how many were directly recruited by Lyman, Rich, Young and others. But as the historian Leo Lyman, a descendant of Amasa, points out, most of the 437 people who left for California were closely affiliated with the Southern Saints, or Lyman or Rich, or were former members of the Mormon Battalion. Leo Lyman says that one-half of the settlers were from the Southern United States, eighty others were closely associated with Amasa Lyman, over fifty were former Battalion members or members of their families; less than 100 were not affiliated with the others except by their religion (Lyman 1996, 35-36).

During the first two weeks of March 1851, those going to California began to gather near the southern end of Utah Lake. They formed a fairly cohesive group that was bound together by friendships, family, allegiances and most significantly, religion. In addition, three of those traveling were members of the Quorum of Twelve: Lyman, Rich and Parley Pratt. There would be none of the dissention that plagued the 1849 Jefferson Hunt Wagon Train within this group.

It has been mentioned by Leo Lyman and others that the large number of settlers who prepared to go to California far exceeded the number desired by Brigham Young and the leadership. They preferred to see a smaller group of about twenty families, but when over 400 people prepared to leave, they were taken aback at the number of Saints that wished to leave the Salt Lake Valley.

Brigham Young, Heber Kimball—a member of the First Presidency of the Church and second only to Brigham Young—and others left for Utah Lake on March 17th. Young and his party caught up with Rich and his camp on March 19th near Fort Utah. After several days there spent organizing and addressing the Utah Valley Saints, Young and the others moved on south to Payson, where the main camp was located, arriving on March 21st. James Pace was the community leader there. Two days later, March 23rd, Rich, Lyman and Kimball addressed those preparing to travel to California. Leo Lyman says that Young did not address the group because he was so distressed to find so many Saints willing to leave Utah for California. Kimball attempted to discourage many from going (Lyman 1996, 39-40). But no one pulled out. They had already sold their properties, sold or given away excess possessions, said their goodbyes to family and friends, and had packed and prepared for travel. Those who showed up at Payson had little alternative other than to continue to California, and they were determined to do so.

There were now 150 wagons with 437 people and 588 oxen, 336 cattle, 21 calves, 107 horses and 52 mules gathered and ready to go (Rich Journal, April 14, 1851). This assemblage was even larger than the Jefferson Hunt Wagon Train of 1849, and was the largest single wagon train to attempt the Southern Route to date. Hunt, Rich and others had firsthand knowledge of the problems associated with such a large group traveling together along the trail. Not only would they be forced to travel slower, they would find water sources and livestock feed dangerously overtaxed if they all tried to go together at once. A decision had been made—most likely at the suggestion of Hunt and Rich—to organize the company in such a way as to lessen the impact of its size.

The solution to their organizational difficulties came directly from Section 136 of the divinely inspired Doctrine and Covenants of the LDS Church. Set forth by Brigham Young at Winter Quarters on January 14, 1847, the first portion of the section deals with how the Westward Migration was to be organized. This structure was used by the Mormons throughout the Westward Migration and most of them were familiar with it and with the obligations that fell to the members of the various units. So it comes as no surprise that at the meeting on March 23rd, the company was organized into hundreds, fifties and tens. Andrew Lytle, who had served with the Mormon Battalion, was elected to be in overall command and to command a fifty. Joseph Mathews, who had been with the Parley Pratt Exploring Party, and David Seeley were made other captains of fifties. Captains of tens included Lyman, Rich, Parley Pratt, William Crosby, and Jefferson Hunt.

Once organized, they determined to travel in smaller groups rather than one large train. On that first day of travel, March 23rd, the wagon train was split into two divisions for the trip to the southern part of Utah. Once they encountered the deserts beyond, it would be split even further and the distance between groups would be spread out to lessen the impact on feed and water.

On their first day, the migration traveled eight miles. By March 28th, they reached the Sevier River where they stopped for several days to ford the stream and let the animals rest and feed.

Jefferson Hunt had not started with the group on March 23rd. Since he had been back in Utah for less than two months, he did not have the advantage of more time to get his affairs in order and to prepare his families for travel. He probably first learned of his new assignment in early February and had to work quickly to prepare for a major life change to move his home to California. It is not surprising that he jumped at the chance to move to California, given his taste for settling outside population centers. And once again, he was instrumental in creating the new settlement.

Charles Rich recorded in his journal that Hunt arrived at the main camp along the Sevier River on March 30, 1851. Hunt took his place as the head of his ten. His party consisted of twenty people, including eleven adults and nine children under the age of eighteen. In addition to Hunt and his wives, Celia and Matilda, the group included Gilbert and his wife, Lydia, and baby daughter, Marshall and his fiancée, Sarah Ann Runyon, Hunt's recently-married daughter Jane, her husband, Sheldon Stoddard, his daughter, Nancy, her husband, Edward Daly, two infant children, eighteen-year-old John, and nine younger children. In addition, Matilda's siblings, Peter and Ellen Nease, were likely also part of the family group. The entourage must have included at least six wagons and probably more. The Hunt family contingent was almost certainly the largest in the entire wagon train.

The following day, the camp began to move with Lyman, Rich and Parley Pratt taking their tens in the lead and moving faster than the others, again with the idea of keeping some spread in the large wagon train. Rich and others met the ever-present Wakara on April 1st, somewhere near his home area of Meadow/Kanosh. By April 8th, they had reached Beaver Creek and prepared to cross over the difficult Black Mountains. On April 10th, the vanguard of the wagon train was met near Parowan by the Apostle George A. Smith and a delegation of Saints from the Iron Mission. They arrived at Parowan the next day. The last element of the wagon train did not arrive until April 19th. It appears that Lyman and Rich had spread the various subunits out so that only about twenty or so wagons were traveling and camping together. This process would continue for the whole of the trek.

Most of the California-bound settlers remained at Parowan or nearby Summit Creek for a week or more. On Sunday, April 13th, the Apostles Rich, Parley Pratt and George A. Smith all addressed the assembled camp. Smith attempted to convince some of the emigrants to remain with his Iron Mission but, just as with the earlier attempt at Payson, he was unsuccessful. Everyone was still committed to continuing to California, even though Smith feared some were ill-prepared for the journey. One man from the Iron Mission joined Parley Pratt as a missionary and four others joined the wagon train without authorization from Smith, simply to go to California.

From April 14th to the 21st, most camped at Summit Creek. On April 21st, tens under Parley Pratt, William Seeley and David Seeley left on their long trek ahead. Other tens followed on subsequent days. The last finally left on April 28th, by which time the vanguard was already at Mountain Meadow (Journal History of the Church, April 29, 1851; Rich Journal, April 27, 1851). Thus, the 150 wagons were spread out over a distance of nearly sixty miles; seven days separated the lead wagons from those at the end. Lyman and Hunt left on April 23rd in the middle of the groups, and Andrew Lytle's group came at the rear.

By May 6th, Rich and his group had reached the point where the trail left the Virgin River and began the climb up Virgin Hill. A week later, May 13th, Hunt and Lyman reached the same spot, but Hunt, in an effort to find a less steep route with more water, explored along the Virgin River toward the mouth of the Muddy. His preliminary belief was that the route was acceptable so the Hunt and Lyman groups continued along this way. Unfortunately, they were forced to cross the Virgin multiple times and found the riverbed heavy with what they called quicksand. When they got to the Muddy and began ascending it, they found that the road was "sandy & mountainous" and was much longer than they expected. Lyman recorded that the known road was twelve to fifteen miles from the confluence of the Muddy and Virgin Rivers, rather than the six they expected (Lyman Journal, May 16, 1851). The road was over twice as long and about as difficult as the old road. The "shortcut" was not adopted.

After two days on the Muddy, preparing for the fifty mile drive to Las Vegas, Hunt's ten and one other group left two hours before Lyman's group. They arrived the next day, May 19th, where they stopped for several days to rest and feed the animals. Andrew Lytle and Joseph Matthews were both behind the Lyman/Hunt group and arrived over the next several days. Amasa Lyman gave some indication of the preliminary plan when he recorded on May

23rd that Matthews arrived at Las Vegas to go with Lyman and Hunt to Chino, presumably to complete the purchase of the ranch. But according to Amasa Lyman, this early departure was postponed (Lyman Journal, May 23, 1851).

By May 23rd, Rich was at the Amargosa Mines at Salt Spring and was preparing to go to Bitter Spring. There was a rather substantial active mining operation there. The miners—who well may have been Mormons—had transported a boiler and steam engine from the coast to the location. Also at the mine was a rock building used as a residence for the miners. This building, built by Mormons, was the first permanent structure erected in the Mojave Desert and its walls remain standing today.

On May 26th when Jefferson Hunt left Las Vegas, Rich was at Bitter Spring. In spite of the poor water and feed, he remained there for several days and rescued several of his animals that had been left behind on the trail. On May 31st, Rich was resting on the Mojave River and Hunt was watering and feeding his animals at Resting Spring. But by June 7th, Rich, Lyman, Hunt, Matthews, Crosby and others were all together on the Mojave River, ten miles or so southwest of present-day Barstow, California. The next day, they traveled to the point near present-day Oro Grande where the trail left the Mojave River and ascended to Cajon Pass.

On June 9th, the group led by Amasa Lyman and Charles C. Rich and including Jefferson Hunt, crossed over Cajon Pass and stopped to camp at a place they called Sycamore Grove, which is at the site of the present Glen Helen Regional Park at the intersection of Interstates 15 and 215 in Devore, California. At this point, the leaders were well ahead of the rest of the wagon train. The plan called for them to continue on to see Isaac Williams and purchase the Chino Rancho, while the remainder of the settlers camped at Sycamore Grove until they got the word to continue on ahead to their new home.

The Lyman/Rich party met with Isaac Williams at his Rancho del Chino on June 12, 1851. Even though Williams had been talking about a sale of his ranch to the Mormons for over four years, and had talked to Jefferson Hunt only about six months before, he changed his mind. Most likely his change of attitude was a result of an increase in the price of beef cattle created by California's expanding population. A steer which had been valued at two dollars (the price of its hide) in 1847, was now worth fifty when sold in the north for meat. It made more sense for him to continue his ranching operation. It is also quite likely family issues (he was an in-law of the important Lugo family) caused him to reevaluate his offer to sell. In any case, he was resolute when Rich approached him in revoking his earlier offer to sell to the Mormons. The Lyman/Rich party only spent one day at the ranch and then returned to the gathering camp at Sycamore Grove.

According to the historian Leo Lyman, Amasa Lyman was not disappointed at the decision. Having seen the Chino property, Lyman was discouraged. The ranch was suitable for raising livestock, but lacked the water and wood resources needed for a full-scale settlement if it were to be successful. Lyman, contrary to being disappointed in the news, saw it as an opportunity to purchase an even more attractive location for the Mormon settlement.

But Lyman and Rich had an immediate problem. They had nearly 450 settlers gathering at the mouth of Cajon Pass and no permanent place to take them. Provisions were running short and there was little likelihood that they would be able to grow crops for the following Winter. If they were going to be successful in creating a Mormon settlement in California, they needed to find land, food and supplies, and to organize the Saints into a cohesive community even if they did not yet have land to settle.

Upon returning to Sycamore Grove, they told the arriving Saints that Chino was not to be their new home and that they should settle in camp for what might be an extended period. The next day, June 14th, the party again under Lyman and Rich and with Hopkins, Hunt and others, set out to explore possible new locations for settlement.

During the week that they were gone, they traveled first to the nearby ranch of the Lugo family at San Bernardino, then on to Isaac Slover's ranch on the Santa Ana River at the present-day City of Colton. Next, they went downriver to near Yorba Linda and the Yorba family ranch, and on to Jesse Devine Hunter's home at San Luis Rey. From there they pressed on to Temecula and back to Sycamore Grove. They traveled nearly 200 miles in one week. Hunter, the Indian Agent for the area, was unable to give them any help, and none of the ranches they visited indicated any willingness to sell. By June 20th, they were back in camp (Rich Journal, June 20, 1851; Lyman 1996, 48). While no one recorded the uncertain situation that was facing the settlement, we can be sure that it was a major topic of concern about the camp.

During the next several days, the leaders focused on their options and decided that they should go to Los Angeles to see if they could possibly obtain government land. Otherwise, the Lugos's San Bernardino Rancho offered them the best possible solution for their problem. It was close to the mouth of Cajon Pass; the land supported excellent crops; there was heavy timber in the mountains just to the north; and there was an abundant supply of water for crops, mills and livestock. In fact, the Lugo property was much more attractive than the Chino property they originally hoped to buy.

On June 22nd, Lyman and Rich left for Los Angeles to see if public land was available. They were unsuccessful, but did receive a warm welcome from the local residents who expressed favorable comments about their presence in Southern California and welcomed them to settle near Los Angeles. By June 27th, they were back at Sycamore Grove. The next day, they went again to the Lugos' San Bernardino Ranch to inspect it more closely and to talk to the family about selling. Again, they were not successful in closing a deal, but apparently made some progress in negotiations and returned to Sycamore Grove.

The first week of July 1851, was spent in organizing the settlers. Many had been in camp for over two weeks and local affairs had to be addressed. A conference which dealt with both religious and civic matters was held on the weekend of July 5-6. Religious leaders were selected and a high council was created to administer the civil affairs of the community. Included in the twelve man high council was Jefferson Hunt. On July 7th, Lyman, Rich and Hopkins left for San Francisco and the gold country to obtain provisions for the camp and financial support from the northern Saints to help buy their new home.

Rich returned to the Port of San Pedro on August 19th where he found forty teams ready to haul supplies back to their camp. He arrived back at Sycamore Grove late on August 21st. Lyman arrived on August 29th with more cash.

The purchase price of their new settlement would fully fall on the settlers; no financial support came from the Church, which was sorely strapped for cash. In order to create a new community, the leaders and individual members would have to assume the debt necessary for the purchase. Fortunately, a large portion of the financial support in the form of loans came from Saints in the Northern part of California.

At the end of August, serious negotiations for the purchase of the San Bernardino Ranch were begun with the Lugo family. This culminated in an agreement on September 22ⁿᵈ for a purchase price of $77,500 with $7,000 down (Lyman 1996, 58). Rich and Lyman had purchased the Rancho using money and credit obtained from other Saints in California and on credit terms from the Lugo family. Technically, the entire rancho was the property of the two apostles, but they had of course purchased it for the community.

After more than three months at Sycamore Grove, the settlers were anxious to begin their new lives at San Bernardino. With Winter approaching, there was a rush to build shelter and establish those fields, corrals, irrigation canals and other needed infrastructure to guarantee their success. Most of the building was done in the area near the present San Bernardino County Courthouse. Trees on the plains were cut for timber for the new homes, and water was channeled for domestic use. The months of relative inactivity led to many months of intense work to develop new homes and community buildings.

California in 1851 had changed significantly from what it had been during the Mexican War four years before. The discovery of gold had brought in several hundred thousand new residents, the great majority of whom lived and worked in the Northern portion of the State. In 1847, the majority of people lived in Southern California and the owners of the large ranchos were the social, political and civil elite of the West Coast. But by 1851, the leaders of the new state lived in the cities of San Francisco or Sacramento or in one of the myriad gold camps in the Sierra Foothills some 300 to 400 miles north of Los Angeles. The most heavily populated county in the state was El Dorado, east of Sacramento and the location of the gold discovery and first mining camps.

With statehood, the new California Constitution, and the first meetings of the California legislature came the need for money to support the government. Money was borrowed, bonds issued, a tax of twenty dollars per month was levied against foreign miners in the gold fields, and a five dollar poll tax was imposed on voters between the ages of twenty-one and fifty. But the main source of state funding was a property tax on real and personal property levied at the rate of fifty cents per $100 on taxable property, less certain exemptions. Most of the miners, workers and city dwellers of the north had very little or no taxable property.

Mining claims were regulated on a local basis using locally developed rules in the absence of any federal or state laws. Most importantly, the land was considered to be owned by the federal government and not the miners— who were only extracting the gold from federal land. Therefore, the miners did not own the land and only occupied it while engaged in mining. Consequently, a disproportionate share of the taxes fell on the large ranchers and grant holders in the southern half of the state.

For the fiscal year ending July 1851, California Governor John McDougall reported that twelve mining counties with a population of 119, 917 and forty-four legislators paid taxes of $21,253.66 while six Southern California counties with a population of 6,367 and twelve legislators paid $41,705.26. He also reported that the agricultural counties with a population of 79,778 paid $246,247.71 (Assembly Journal 1852, 12-13). Almost sixty percent of the population was paying only seven percent of the taxes; the average Southern Californian was paying $6.55 per person, while the average miner was paying only eighteen cents. Clearly, this was an example of the most numerous group imposing their will on the minority. Southern California assessors responded to this, in part, by lowering land valuations and assessments (Cleland, 1941, 160-161.)

A related issue was the value of money in the two areas. The northern economy was more vibrant, with many more dollars in circulation. The southern economy was seen more as a subsistence economy. To those in Southern California, any method of taxation that was the same for both ends of the state was seen as being discriminatory simply on the basis of the discrepancy in the value of the dollar between the two areas. Those in the lower counties believed that the northern majority was financially persecuting the Southern California minority for their own benefit. Additionally, the large land owners in the south feared that the northern interests would soon use their power to dissolve or divide the southern ranchos.

Another issue of great political importance was the country's escalating feeling over the slavery issue. Whether California should be a free or slave state had been seriously discussed during the Constitutional Convention in Monterey, and was a contentious item during the congressional discussions about admitting California to the Union. Eventually, California was admitted as a free state, and many of the pro-slavery proponents saw the balance between slave and free states being eroded. In fact, the United States was on a course that would culminate in the Civil War in only a decade. Southern sympathizers in California continued to believe they could do something to strengthen their cause if only the agrarian southern part of the state could become independent and then seek admission to the Union as a slave state.

These two issues led many to hope for a division of the State of California. If so divided, Southern California would become a territory within the United States and later be able to apply for statehood on its own terms. The Southern California landowners saw this as a solution of their taxation problem, and the pro-slavery forces saw it as a possible first step in creating a new slave state which might help their cause.

The state division issue was increasing in momentum in the summer of 1851, just as the Mormon settlers were camped at Sycamore Grove. The *Los Angeles Star* newspaper on August 23, 1851, stated: "Sooner or later the division must take place," and "Under the present condition of affairs, we are more like a conquered province than a free and in dependent [sic] state." They pointed out that California was so large that "a trip to the capital [of California] is an undertaking almost as great as a trip to the capital of the Union" (Los Angeles Star, August 23, 1851). A week later on August 30th, a meeting of residents was held in San Diego, and they issued a statement that called for a convention to be held by delegates from each of the affected counties to discuss the division of the state issue. They suggested that the convention be held in Santa Barbara on the third Monday of October (Alta California, September 12, 1851).

The affected counties began the process of selecting delegates for the convention. And the sentiment for state division was so geographically widespread that a meeting was held in Santa Cruz on September 24th to select delegates (Alta California, September 28, 1851). A meeting of citizens of Los Angeles County was held on September 12th and they offered to host the meeting there in November. However, the San Diego committee replied that Santa Barbara was more centrally located and the October date made more sense because the results of the convention could be presented to the legislature when it began its session in January 1852 (Alta California, October 6, 1851). On October 8th, a meeting was held in Monterey and the attendees supported the call for a convention (Alta California, October 13, 1851).

The *Alta California,* in the same issue, took the stand that such a meeting was not needed and that the supporters of the division movement simply did not have the correct statistics and little chance for success. The same issue also had a favorable report on the acquisition of the ranch at San Bernardino by the Mormons and their plans to use the nearby ports as entry points for converted Saints coming to America.

Thirty-one delegates met in Santa Barbara on October 20th for four days. One of the eleven delegates from Los Angeles County was "J. Hunt, (Mormon from San Bernardino)" (Alta California, October 26, 1851). Jefferson Hunt had entered public life in California.

The delegates unanimously agreed to resolutions that called for a division of the state and the creation of a new territory consisting of the Southern California counties that would be placed under the jurisdiction of the federal government. They stated that the issues were so diverse that a single government could not fairly administer the civil, criminal and revenue laws for the entire area then incorporated into the State of California. Their resolutions would be presented to the governor and to all of the senators and representatives in the California legislature for further action. Two resolutions dealt with a proposed dividing line that would have begun at the northern point of Monterey County, continued east to the coast range, then south to a point a little to the southwest of present-day Fresno, and then northeast to a point near Mono Lake at today's Nevada border. All of the area below that line would be withdrawn from California and become part of the new territory.

Some of the delegates objected to this boundary line, believing that the legislature should fix it. As with any meeting of representatives with diverse opinions, there was some dissention and lack of unanimity, although all agreed with the general principle of division. After some discussion, a vote was taken and the delegates voted sixteen to fifteen to remove the proposed dividing line. Jefferson Hunt was one of those who voted to place a definitive line in the resolutions (Alta California, October 27 & 28, 1851),

Hunt's attendance at the meeting bears some consideration. Clearly, the Mormons wanted a West Coast port to be part of their Territory of Utah, in hopes of simplifying the transport of goods and people to Salt Lake City. They wanted to control the overland route from the port to Utah. To do so would protect their interests and make them less vulnerable to interference from others. It was in their best interests to try to get Southern California back into territorial status in hopes that someday at least the critical areas would become part of a larger Territory or State of Utah.

Hunt was in an ideal position to push for the division on behalf of the Mormons. He was well known and trusted in Southern California because of his role in the Mormon Battalion and other visits. Furthermore, he had firsthand knowledge of the geography of most of the state and especially of Southern California and the desert areas. While he was the only person pushing for his point of view, it was fully consistent with the overall objectives of the convention. State division might benefit the Mormons regardless of the reasons why it occurred.

It must be noted that the San Bernardino Ranch had been purchased on September 22nd, less than a month before the Santa Barbara meeting. Every one of the Mormon colonists was involved in settling in. They were busy building permanent homes, obtaining timber for construction, preparing irrigation ditches and fields for farming, fencing in pastures to protect livestock, and doing all those other things that had to be done to create a new settlement for nearly 450 people. With his extended family, Jefferson Hunt would have been busier than most, although he would have had the assistance of his older sons and sons-in-law. But to take two weeks or more off his labor to attend a meeting in Santa Barbara during this important time would have been a hardship. Hunt possibly also attended the September 12th meeting in Los Angeles to consider the issue and select delegates, which would have meant even more time away from his new home.

Santa Barbara is about 150 miles from San Bernardino, and Hunt had to spend at least five or six days traveling in each direction to attend the meeting. That time, combined with the four days spent in session, meant that Hunt was away from home for at least two weeks, and probably longer, right at the time when the settlers were creating their community. In essence, he sacrificed his personal needs and comfort for the larger interest of the Mormons community. This was probably not something he decided on unilaterally.

While there is no direct evidence that he attended the Santa Barbara meeting at the request of Lyman, Rich or any other Mormon official, it stands to reason that he went at their request, or as part of his role in a larger assignment to participate in the political affairs of California to benefit the Mormons and their overall goal of controlling a corridor to California.

This event and subsequent political activities by Hunt strongly indicate that he had been assigned to be the Mormon political front man in California. He was the ideal choice because of his reputation and experience in California. Whether the assignment came from Brigham Young and other Church leaders in Utah before he left, or whether it was given by the leaders in California, it certainly appears that Jefferson Hunt was chosen to become the political voice of the California Mormons.

Chapter 21

Assemblyman Hunt

San Bernardino's location at the eastern edge of the fertile basin extending east from Los Angeles made it potentially vulnerable to attack. For years, Indian raiders from the Mojave Desert and beyond—such as Wakara—used the nearby Cajon Pass as the main entry point into settled California. Similarly, other Indians directly to the east, the southeast and south were in a position to threaten the security of the new colony. Most of the threats came in the form of isolated raids on livestock or threats against travelers along the desert trails. But within two months of the purchase of the San Bernardino Rancho, the threat became much more serious.

Antonio Garra, the chief of the Cupeños tribe, which was based about seventy-five miles southeast of San Bernardino very near Warner's Ranch, called on other tribes in California and Mexico to join him in a revolt against the increasing presence of the Americans and the damage that was being done to his people. Garra had gone to school at the Mission of San Luis Rey and had firsthand experience with the Indians' loss of life and land that occurred with increased settlement in Southern California. His plans for revolt never reached fruition because he was betrayed by Juan Antonio, a chief of the Cahuillas. He was executed after only a few raids on outlying ranches and settlements before he could rally other tribes to join in a full revolt.

However, the threat from Garra and possibly other Indian tribes caused the Mormons in San Bernardino to review their settlement plans. They gathered information and determined the threat was real and that they should take precautions. Their first step was to organize a local militia or military unit to provide protection. Jefferson Hunt was selected as the commander of this unit, with former Mormon Battalion officers Jesse D. Hunter and Andrew Lytle as subordinate officers (Lyman 1996, 60). Hunt would have military command responsibilities for most of the remainder of his stay in California.

It was decided on November 25, 1851, to build a fort for their protection. Almost immediately, they began the construction of Fort San Bernardino. It was 300 feet wide and 700 feet long and enclosed an area of about five acres, or about the size of four football fields. The fort was built with a northeast/southwest trend line. The northwest corner was located in the middle of what later became Fourth Street in downtown San Bernardino. The southeast corner was located in the middle of the present Arrowhead Avenue, about halfway between Second and Third Streets. The eastern wall was located where the present-day San Bernardino County Courthouse is located.

Much of the western wall of the fort was comprised of the backs of log houses that had been constructed before the threat arose and then hauled into their new positions. Elsewhere, the walls were a palisade of poles and logs about twelve feet long, buried three feet into the ground. They used mostly cottonwood, willow and other trees that grew in the valley. The bigger pines were close by, but were in the high mountains to the north and still largely inaccessible to the colonists because of the steep slopes. Log and adobe homes were then built along the inside walls. Gates were located on the west, north and east walls. Jefferson Hunt occupied a house immediately next to the gate on the west wall. Next door to him was Jesse D. Hunter, his fellow officer from the Mormon Battalion. It is quite likely that Hunt's location next to a gate was not random; there, he was in a position to assume command and control in the event of an attack or intrusion.

Within just a few months of the construction of the fort, the threat diminished and conditions returned to normal. But the fort had been built and became the home of the colony as they had other tasks to perform. So the enclosed fortification and its crowded condition remained the home of the San Bernardino Mormons until the tenants began relocating to homes outside of the fort in 1854.

When the California Constitution was adopted, all lawmaking was vested with the state senate and assembly since only the state government had that authority. The ability for local governments at the city and county level to enact laws depended on the state legislature granting that right. As the new state government settled in, such authority was granted to more and more local jurisdictions. Such was the case with Los Angeles County, one of the original twenty-seven counties created when the state constitution was approved.

The original county boundaries were often arbitrary and for many of the sparsely settled counties included substantial land area, especially when compared to the population. The boundary issue was considered to be a work in process by the constitutional convention and subsequent legislatures. When an area became settled and conditions changed, the legislature was prepared to move boundaries as needed. Originally, Los Angeles County covered only a small area near the coast and a much larger San Diego County contained most of desert area to the east of Los Angeles. But by 1852, Los Angeles County extended from the Pacific Ocean to the Colorado River, and included the Mormon colony of San Bernardino. By the summer of 1852, San Bernardino was the second largest community in the county and rivaled Los Angeles in size and importance.

Initially, the citizens of Los Angeles County elected a three member Court of Sessions to serve as the local governing body. But as the legislature began to authorize local governments, they abolished the Court of Sessions and created a five member County Board of Supervisors in 1852. On June 14, the election was held for the new Board of Supervisors. The citizens of San Bernardino elected Jefferson Hunt as their representative on the first Los Angeles County Board of Supervisors.

Meetings were held in Los Angeles, about fifty-five miles from San Bernardino. Generally, a mounted traveler took two days to travel each direction between the two cities. That travel time, coupled with the actual meeting days and additional days conducting other business meant that a simple Board of Supervisors meeting would involve five to seven days away from home for

Hunt. Between July and October, there were seven sessions, involving eleven meeting days. Hunt was present for four of those sessions, covering seven days of meetings. For his services, he collected ten dollars per day, or seventy dollars total. He was gone from his home for nearly thirty days over a period of three months.

Hunt did not attend the first meeting held on July 5th, which was essentially an organizational meeting. He was present for the next meeting on July 19th, when the primary topics dealt with finance issues and the need for the construction of a jail, for which the Board called for sealed bids.

The next session met for three days, beginning on August 4th. The focus of the meetings was the financial matters facing the Board. They authorized the payment of some bills, arranged for compensation for the jailor and arranged for assessments and the collection of taxes. One of their decisions was to order former minister Lewis Granger, of Hunt Wagon Train fame and who had become an attorney, to refund $375 to the county for overpayment for his services as District Attorney. On August 6th, the last day of the three day session, the Board approved Jesse D. Hunter's $3,000 construction bond for the new jail. The contract was not awarded, but it was the first step.

Hunter, of course, was the next door neighbor of Jefferson Hunt at the fort at San Bernardino and probably learned of the contract from him. In his own right, Hunter was very well known in Los Angeles because of his service as a captain in the Mormon Battalion and as Indian Agent after the Battalion's discharge. He was awarded the contract at the meeting of August 30th, which Hunt did not attend. Hunter was given an advance of $3,000 with an additional $4,000 to be paid upon completion. However, he was never able to complete the construction of the jail. The next Board of Supervisors, on January 5, 1853, cancelled the contract, but allowed Hunter to keep the $3,000 advance. Hunter reported that "an act of providence" prevented him from completing the jail and the Board determined that the location was unsuitable and did not meet legal requirements (Los Angeles Board of Supervisors Minutes, January 5, 1853).

Hunt was not present at the meetings of August 14th or 30th, when again the main items of discussion were financial conditions and tax collection. The Board ordered the Sheriff to travel to San Bernardino to collect taxes during the last week of September. His base of operation was designated to be the Hunt home in the fort.

At the September 15th meeting, with Hunt present, the main item of discussion was the election of a new Board and County officials that Fall. On September 16th, Hunt proposed the creation of two towns, San Salvador and Agua Mansa, near San Bernardino. This was approved.

The next meeting of the Board was October 12. Hunt was present and requested some modifications of the charter for the town of San Salvador. There was some discussion of the accounts presented by Sheriff Barton but the four members present were split two to two and deferred the matter to the next Board. Records show the San Bernardino Rancho at that time was valued at fifty cents per acre for an estimated 40,000 acres, or a total valuation of $20,000.

The final meeting of the Board was held on November 8th; Hunt was not present. The new Board met for the first time on November 15th. But Jefferson Hunt was no longer on the Board; he had been elected to the State Assembly from Los Angeles County.

One of Amasa Lyman's first projects in 1851 was the building of a grist mill to grind their wheat crop into flour. The next biggest need was for a sawmill. Wood for building had been obtained from the lower elevations around San Bernardino and the hills to the east. A substantial amount of timber was located at the top of the San Bernardino Mountains to the north of the colony, but the grade from the settlement to the top was steep—it climbed 3,400 feet in elevation in about 4.5 miles of lateral travel. To get access to the timber it was necessary to construct a road up the steep slope and build sawmills.

In the Spring of 1852, Lyman and a group of other leaders, including Robert Clift, Jesse D. Hunter, Charles Crisman and William Crosby, surveyed a location for a road from San Bernardino to the summit via the route now known as Waterman Canyon. Lyman called for volunteers from the Mormon community and about 100 men responded with animals and equipment. Over a ten day period at the end of April and the first of May, a new road was built up the precipitous slope through the canyon. The effort took the equivalent of 1,000 man days of work, but was successfully completed. As the historian Leo Lyman points out, this difficult task was an outstanding example of the Mormons' ability to muster their forces for the community's benefit (Lyman 1996, 75).

Jefferson Hunt is often credited with supervising the building of the logging road. While it is clear that Amasa Lyman was responsible for the idea and location of the road and was in overall charge of the effort, Hunt served as construction manager and contributed his knowledge of road building gained during his Mormon Battalion experiences.

Charles Crisman, who was experienced in building and operating sawmills, soon purchased and hauled the now-abandoned steam engine from the Amargosa Mine at Salt Spring to a location in the lower part of Waterman Canyon. The boiler for the steam engine was left at the mine because of the effects of the mineralization in the water. In late July, he opened the first Mormon sawmill in the San Bernardino colony. Additional sawmill operations would soon be opened in the mountains above. Timber cut at these mills provided the lumber that built San Bernardino and generated much-needed cash for the community. Hunt would soon join with Crisman in the ownership of this mill.

Jefferson Hunt was a lifelong Jacksonian Democrat. John Hunt, Jefferson's father, was a strong supporter of Thomas Jefferson, naming two of his sons after the president. When Jefferson Hunt was a young adult, Andrew Jackson was elected president (1828-1832.) He was very popular both for his military accomplishments and his political beliefs. Chief among Jackson's platforms was the expansion of the nation from the Atlantic to Pacific oceans—what became known as the concept of Manifest Destiny. Jackson was also the favorite of agrarian Americans and the common man. He espoused the views of frontier farmers and Westward expansionists like Hunt. It is easy to see why Hunt thought so highly of him.

The two most active political parties in 1852 were the Democrats and the Whigs. The Whig party had been formed in 1832 mostly to oppose Jackson and his policies. The Mexican War seriously divided the Whig Party and, to a lesser extent, the Democratic Party. Both parties were also deeply divided over the issue of slavery and whether new territories should be admitted as free states; however, the leaders of both parties tried to avoid confrontation over the issue. As the election of 1852 drew close, the division within the Whigs grew even more serious. Millard Fillmore, the Whig president, was not nominated for re-election and the party's candidate was General Winfield Scott, a Mexican War hero. This division proved fatal and 1852 was the last year that the Whigs mounted a serious campaign for president. In the election of 1856, the Whigs were gone and the new Republican Party arose to oppose the Democrats with John C. Fremont as their presidential candidate.

Even though it was badly divided, the majority of Americans voted for the Democratic Party in the elections of 1852. This was especially true in the West where Manifest Destiny and expansion were the center of everyone's lives. Most Mormons and many of the population of California were Democrats, and Jefferson Hunt was no exception.

It should be noted here that the Democratic Party of the mid-1800s bore little resemblance to the Democratic Party of today. The party had changed significantly from the time of Thomas Jefferson and it would go through several more changes before modern times. For example, their expansionist policy of the 1840s, their widely held attitudes towards slavery, and their policies toward Indians stands in sharp contrast with their policies today.

When the Fall elections approached in 1852, Hunt decided to run for the California Assembly as one of the two members from Los Angeles County. He must have realized that if he was successful, he would be spending months away from his families 500 miles to the north in Vallejo, then the location of the State Capital. And this would have come at a time when his family most needed his presence to help establish them in the new colony. What was Hunt's motivation to run for election to the Assembly?

As before, no direct evidence has been found to show that Hunt ran at the direction of Lyman or Rich, the local leaders, or at the direction of Brigham Young in Salt Lake City. But there is evidence that Hunt consulted with them and sought their approval, and that Lyman and Rich strongly supported his candidacy. Lewis Granger, who had been a minister and an organizer of Hunt's 1849 wagon train and became a prominent attorney and Democratic Party leader in Los Angeles, wrote Hunt on September 18, 1852, asking him to accept the party's nomination. Hunt gave the letter to Lyman and Rich. They responded to Granger on September 22nd, advising him that they were not going to endorse "either political party," but that if Hunt was nominated they would "cordially give him our undevided [sic] support" (Granger 1959, 32-33).

As a result, Jefferson Hunt ran as a Democrat for election to the California Assembly in the fall of 1852. Los Angeles County was assigned two Assemblymen and the top two vote-getters would be elected. While the San Bernardino settlement was the second largest community in the county behind only the City of Los Angeles, the number of votes in San Bernardino was not sufficient to elect him outright. This is where Hunt's reputation, prior experiences in the region and contacts in Southern California came to his aid. When the election was held on November 2, 1852, Hunt received 474 votes, the second highest number. J.P. McFarland, an incumbent from Los Angeles, received 595 votes, and three other candidates got 454, 414 and eight votes respectively.

Furthermore, his actions during his first year in the Assembly certainly make it appear that he was there to fulfill an important mission for the Mormon Church and the San Bernardino settlement. His only accomplishment that year—and a very important one—was to create a new San Bernardino County. It appears that was his agenda at the time of his arrival at the Capital.

On the surface, it appears to some that Hunt's inspiration for the introducing the legislation for San Bernardino County came from a petition to create a new county that was circulated after he arrived in the Capital. However, the evidence indicates that the legislation was part of a well-calculated plan that was put into effect before Hunt arrived at the Capitol, and that the petition he presented was part of the legislative process for forming a new county. This suggests that Hunt was acting at the direction of Lyman and Rich, or even Brigham Young, or at least his actions were approved by them in advance. Any decision of that importance and complexity would be left for the highest level of authority within the Church, and was probably part of the larger plan to secure a Mormon corridor.

Jefferson Hunt was about to leave his home and family for almost five months. His two oldest sons with Celia, Gilbert and Marshall, were both married, as were his daughters, Nancy Daley and Jane Stoddard. His son, John, was nearly twenty years old, and his son, Joseph, was fifteen. Harriet and Hyrum were adolescents, and his daughter Mary, whose twin brother Parley had died in El Pueblo, was seven. His two children with his plural wife, Matilda, were Sophronia, who was four, and Julia, who was only seven months old. With three adult sons and two sons-in-law, his family would be well taken care of. As usual, Gilbert would take the primary role of watching over family affairs in his father's absence.

His departure would be a hardship on the rest of the family, but he would be relatively well compensated for his work as a legislator. Hunt probably left home for Northern California and the State Capital in Vallejo shortly before Christmas Day in 1852.

Chapter 22

The Creation of
San Bernardino County

California began as a state without a political infrastructure. All of the lawmaking authority was granted to the legislature. Cities and counties could assume local lawmaking authority only if granted by the legislature. Consequently, at the beginning of the state, nearly every law governing local activities came from the capitol. The legislature was confronted with a wide range of bills that tried to resolve everything from questionable tidal land sales in San Francisco, to costly printing expenses, to individual requests for compensation by citizens.

As a consequence, legislators had a wide range of legislation to ponder and become involved with. Those with personal financial interests in San Francisco land might pay particular attention to the tidal land sales issue and attempt to get on committees that dealt with those issues. Others might try to position themselves where they could best deal with some other matter they were particularly interested in. So much was going on in the legislature that it was an exciting time to be an elected official.

Jefferson Hunt was about to arrive into this dynamic hive of activity at a good time to influence legislation for the benefit of the Mormons.

Hunt left his home in San Bernardino a few days before Christmas 1852. Hosea Stout, who had just arrived from Utah on his way to his China mission, recorded in his diary that on December 16, he went to Gilbert Hunt's home for a party "made expressly for his father's enjoyment" before he left for the 1853 legislative session. Stout says that they "kept the fiddle & bow in operation till 5 a.m" (Stout and Brooks 1964, 465). There is no record of exactly when Hunt left, but it was very soon after the party.

From the earliest days of the American presence in California, the major Southern California port was at San Diego. The port of San Pedro, located about twenty-five miles south of the Pueblo of Los Angeles, was of secondary importance, but was gaining in use by 1852. From San Bernardino, it was seventy-five miles to San Pedro and about 100 miles to San Diego. Travelers from San Bernardino could use either port, although it appears that more ships still called at San Diego than at San Pedro, and thus it would be easier to obtain passage from San Diego to San Francisco than it would be from San Pedro. Much of the cargo headed from San Francisco to San Bernardino was shipped by sea to San Pedro since it was closer and offered a shorter travel time and cargo shipments from north to south could be more easily coordinated.

In any case, whether Jefferson Hunt left from either San Pedro or San Diego, he would have had to spend about three days in overland travel to the port and there wait for the next available ship to take him north. While there were some attempts to publish shipping schedules, weather and mechanical problems frequently disrupted those schedules. By 1852, demand for passenger and cargo shipping along the West Coast from Panama to San Francisco was heavy enough that steamships were used, rather than sailing vessels, and a number plied the coastal trade. Others worked San Francisco Bay and the rivers in the Delta that extended to Benicia and Sacramento.

But sea travel by either sail or steamship was still uncertain, especially in Winter. Weather conditions changed as ships traveled along the coast, and fog presented difficulties for navigation, especially when very near the coast. Ships were crowded and uncomfortable and illness remained a problem. Safe arrival in San Francisco by sea was not certain. In April 1853, banker, former Mexican War Army officer and future Civil War hero, William Tecumseh Sherman, was shipwrecked twice on the same day within sight of the Golden

Gate (Clarke 1969, 17). A safe and secure trip up the coast was not something someone could expect with a high degree of certainty.

Jefferson Hunt arrived in San Francisco aboard the steamer *Sea Bird* from San Diego on December 30. It had spent four days in transit from San Diego and he had probably boarded it there, although he may have boarded the ship if it also stopped in San Pedro (Rasmussen 1970, Vol. IV, 226). Other steamers that year had made the San Diego-San Francisco run in a little over two days, but the *Sea Bird* was delayed during its next trip, according to Stout who took it to connect in San Francisco with a ship to China. By contrast, a coastal sailing ship took thirteen days to make the passage in the same year. Two other assemblymen, including J.P. McFarland of Los Angeles, were on the same ship as Hunt.

The 1849 Constitutional Convention to create the new state of California was held in the former Mexican and Spanish capital of Monterey. The first two sessions of the California Legislature (1850 and 1851) were held in San Jose in a former hotel building. The building and the accommodations were considered inadequate and an effort was made to obtain a new location for the capital. Several proposals were made, but the legislature finally decided to accept the offer of General Mariano Vallejo to construct a capitol building at the new community of Vallejo, at the north end of San Francisco Bay. The matter was submitted to the voters in October 1850, and was approved.

The third session of the legislature began at the new Vallejo location in January 1852. The capitol building was inadequate and housed a bar in the basement. There were so few rooms available for legislators and others that a steamer was brought in to house 250 people. Furniture, supplies, printing material and even basic personal items were unavailable, and the legislators clamored for better accommodations. After less than two weeks, the legislature moved to Sacramento to complete the session with the understanding that Vallejo would remain as the capital and the 1853 session would be held there.

On January 3, 1853, the fourth session of the California Legislature began in the Vallejo capitol building. Jefferson Hunt, however, was not present for the first day, nor was he present on the second. There is no indication why Hunt was not there, but we can assume that he was probably meeting with other Mormons either in San Francisco, Mission San Jose, Sacramento or the Gold Country. However, by January 5th, Hunt was present and was qualified to take his seat as a representative of Los Angeles County (Assembly Journal 1853, 7). Subsequently, the Committee on Mileage reported that Hunt had traveled 1,200 miles (round trip) and received travel expenses of $480. He was tied with Assemblyman Tilghman of San Diego for the most mileage to the capital.

Upon his arrival in Vallejo, Hunt was quickly exposed to the realities of California politics. While the Democratic Party was the dominant party, it was seriously divided between those who supported slavery—and hence the Southern states—and those who supported the abolitionists—and hence the Northern states. The dominant politician of the former group, called the Chivalry Faction of the Democratic Party, was U.S. Senator William M. Gwin from San Francisco. The dominant abolitionist was David Broderick, a former state senator and challenger for the other U.S. Senate seat. During his years in the Assembly, Hunt and all other assemblymen and senators were to be drawn into this internal party conflict.

The first order of business of the new Assembly was to elect a speaker, and Hunt was present to vote. He voted for the successful candidate, Isaac B. Wall, whose first task as speaker was to appoint committees for the session. Then, as now, some committees were considered more important and politically significant; such as finance, land claims and printing. The latter two were significant because of ongoing scandals involving tidal land sales by the City of San Francisco and excessive printing charges incurred by prior legislatures. A number of Assemblymen clamored for these committee assignments. Jefferson Hunt was not among them.

Assemblymen could be assigned to more than one committee depending on their preferences, the whims of the speaker, and the need for members on some of the less desirable committees. The speaker undoubtedly exercised considerable power and discretion in making assignments. Members of the more popular committees were decided by political influence. Membership of the lesser committees probably fell to those who were willing to participate or who were not in favor with the speaker. One of the committees with little to do, and therefore not considered significant, was the Committee on Counties and County Boundaries. And this was the only committee to which Jefferson Hunt was assigned.

We can assume that the assignment of Hunt to this committee was not an arbitrary and capricious act of the speaker or that it reflected any political motivation toward Hunt. Most likely, Hunt specifically requested that he be placed on the committee however limited its power might be and however infrequently it met. Placement on the Committee on Counties and County Boundaries put Hunt exactly where he needed to be to influence Mormon control over the California portion of the road to Salt Lake City.

The original California constitution created twenty-seven counties. Some boundaries conformed with the location of the population in 1849; others were largely arbitrary since they enclosed mostly unoccupied territory and even unexplored areas. The legislators recognized that California was a work in progress.

In some instances, such as the well-populated Gold Country, the county boundaries conformed with both local interests and natural features. Some counties such as Tulare, Mariposa and San Diego encompassed large areas of land that had not been settled. Elsewhere, where there was little population or interest in the area, the counties were haphazardly drawn with the expectation that new counties would be created or boundaries changed as the population in that area grew, conditions changed, and local wishes became known.

For example, the original boundary for Mariposa County included a huge chunk of the central part of the state that extended from the Coastal Range to the eastern state boundary. The original San Diego County extended from the coast to the eastern boundary and from Mexico north to beyond the latitude of the San Gabriel Mountains, while Los Angeles County occupied a relatively narrow strip along the ocean. But by 1852, San Diego County had been reduced in size and Los Angeles County greatly increased to become the second largest county after Mariposa.

The first legislatures also realized that they needed to establish a procedure for creating new counties. By the time Jefferson Hunt arrived at the capital in 1853, this procedure was in place and well established. In the Assembly, the process called for a large group of the citizens of the area wishing to become a new county to sign a petition, which was then given to their assemblyman and introduced into the Assembly. The speaker then referred the matter to the Committee on Counties and County Boundaries and/or a subcommittee composed of the assemblymen of the county or counties from which the new county would be created. These, in turn, discussed issues such as boundary lines and how the new county would be divided from the existing county or counties and how financial obligations would be divided.

Then the committee and subcommittee reviewed and modified or approved the final bill, which was then reported to the full Assembly. The Assembly then acted on the bill. During the years Hunt was in the Assembly (1853-1857), several new counties were proposed and all were approved using the same procedure.

If Hunt arrived for his term in the Assembly with the idea of creating a new county that could control California's portion of the Mormon road to Salt Lake City, then his first task was to determine the procedure to be followed. Hunt learned about the proper way to go about it and was told that the first step required getting the citizens to sign a petition to create a new county. Now that Hunt was on the appropriate committee and understood the process, he was ready to proceed to organize a new county.

On February 24, 1853, Jefferson Hunt presented a petition for the creation of San Bernardino County. The entry in the Assembly Journal for that day reads: "Mr. Hunt presented the petition of citizens of Los Angeles, praying for the erection of a new county out of certain territory now belonging to that County, which was read, and referred to the Committee on Counties and County Boundaries" (Assembly Journal 1853, 179). Thus, the legislation was introduced that would shortly culminate in the creation of a new Mormon-controlled county.

It is of note that the petition was presented on February 24th, about seven weeks after Hunt's appearance in the Assembly. Clearly, he had not arrived in Vallejo with the petition or he would have presented it sooner. Most likely, Hunt first determined how the process worked and then communicated with Lyman, Rich and others in San Bernardino so that they could gather the required signatures and send them on to him at the capital. Unfortunately, that petition cannot now be found in the California State Archives and no reference to any communication with Lyman or Rich on the matter has come to light. However, the seven weeks delay in presenting the petition and starting the process is consistent with sending a written or verbal message from the Bay Area to San Bernardino, gathering the signatures, and then awaiting the arrival of the petition back at the capital.

One month later on March 24th, Chairman Ewing of the Committee on Counties and County Boundaries reported on the bill to the full Assembly.

It was then read the first and second times, part of the standard procedure for any bill that moved through the Assembly. Then it was referred by the Speaker to the members from that county, Hunt and McFarland. Four days later, March 28th, the bill was taken up again and passed. The Assembly Journal states: "Assembly Bill for an Act dividing the County of Los Angeles, and making a new county therefrom, was taken up, read a third time and passed" (Assembly Journal 1853, 343). Having been passed by the Assembly, the bill moved on to the Senate.

On April 21st, the bill was heard in the Senate and passed with an amendment that changed the title to read: "An Act for dividing the County of Los Angeles and making a new county therefrom, to be called San Bernardino County" (Senate Journal 1853, 380). The following day, the bill was returned to the Assembly, the amendment was approved and the bill was sent to the Governor. On April 26th, the Governor returned the signed bill to the Assembly, and it was properly enrolled as a law. Thus, San Bernardino County was created and named.

The bill contained rather ill-defined boundary lines that refer to mountain ranges and peaks as well as homes and ranches as reference points. However, at that time, the lines were no doubt understandable to those familiar with the area. The bill also specified the county officers and provided for an election for them during "the fourth week of June next" (Laws of the State of California, Fourth Session 1853, 119-123). The new law also created a Board of Commissioners to establish precincts and conduct the election. That board consisted of: Isaac Williams of the Chino Rancho; John Brown, a mountain man who had met the Mormons in El Pueblo in 1846-47 and had settled in the area; David Seeley, who had been one of the leaders on the journey to California; and Henry G. Sherwood, who was a surveyor and friend of Amasa Lyman. Two of the commissioners were Mormons with stature within their community; the other two were non-Mormon residents of the new county who had close ties with the Mormons extending back to 1846-47. Each was in a position to give credibility to the election whether viewed by Mormons or non-Mormons. Their selection was carefully crafted, and may well have reflected the views of Lyman and Rich.

The bill also called for both San Bernardino and Los Angeles counties to each have one assemblyman and share one senator in the Legislature. A court was created and provision was made for both counties to create a commission to fairly divide the debt of Los Angeles County so that San Bernardino would be responsible for its share. Other similar administrative functions were also addressed.

Today, San Bernardino County is the largest county in the lower forty-eight states, covering over 20,000 square miles. It is thirteen times the size of Rhode Island, almost three and a half times the size of Connecticut, and larger than the states of Massachusetts and Vermont combined. It is twice as large as Israel, and larger than several European countries including Switzerland, the Netherlands, Belgium, Denmark and Slovakia. In 1853, it was even larger. The size was reduced later in the Nineteenth Century when the counties of Inyo, Kern, Riverside and Orange were created out of parts of San Bernardino County. The size was also reduced in the 1870s when the boundary with Los Angeles County was moved eastward and the definition of the county boundaries was refined and defined more precisely.

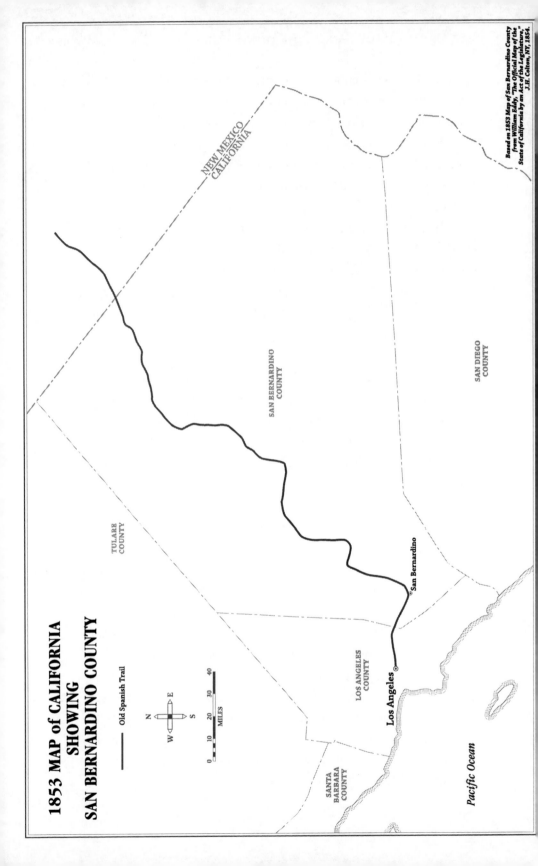

1853 MAP of CALIFORNIA
SHOWING
SAN BERNARDINO COUNTY

—— Old Spanish Trail

N
W E
S

0 10 20 30 40
MILES

TULARE
COUNTY

NEW MEXICO
CALIFORNIA

SAN BERNARDINO
COUNTY

SANTA
BARBARA
COUNTY

LOS ANGELES
COUNTY

Los Angeles

San Bernardino

SAN DIEGO
COUNTY

Pacific Ocean

Based on 1853 Map of San Bernardino County
from William Eddy, "The Official Map of the
State of California by an Act of the Legislature,"
J.H. Colton, NY, 1854.

The City of San Bernardino was in the southwest corner of the new county. The southern-most boundary of the county extended nearly 200 miles eastward to the California boundary at the Colorado River. The northern boundary extended in a northeasterly direction nearly 200 miles to what is now the California/Nevada border northeast of Furnace Creek in Death Valley. Inside this boundary was the entire route of the Old Spanish Trail within California and the lower third of Death Valley. Much of the Mojave Desert in California was within the county, as was the entire California portion of the future Mojave Road trail from the Colorado River and the eastern approaches to Walker Pass. The county covered both the known route and possible future roads from Salt Lake to Southern California.

In 1853, the bulk of the non-Hispanic and non-Indian population of the county was Mormon. A few non-Mormons, including several former mountain men, also lived in San Bernardino and nearby, but the Mormon populace clearly was in the political majority and in control of the county, and by extension, the access roads from Salt Lake City.

During the session, Jefferson Hunt did not attend twenty-one days of meetings, and on twelve of those days he was granted a leave of absence. Many of the missed days were Mondays or Mondays and Tuesdays, and once he was absent for an entire week, April 11th through April 15th, which may have coincided with local Church conferences. We have no indication where he was on those days, but he would have not have had time to go home and return. The implication is that he was possibly visiting other Mormons in San Francisco, Mission San Jose, Sacramento or the Gold Country.

But Hunt was not alone in missing meetings. Others missed many more. On six days the Assembly couldn't meet because of a lack of a quorum and several times the Assembly adjourned early because of a lack of members present. Most weeks, the Assembly met on Saturday. The members were anxious to get their work done and get back home. As they had in 1852, the legislators found the conditions in Vallejo deplorable. The accommodations were sparse, there was no entertainment, and it was difficult to obtain supplies and goods. Something had to be done.

The City of Benicia, about eight miles away, had recently built a City Hall at a cost of $25,000 and they offered it to the legislature as a Capitol Building if the legislature would move there. The Assembly and Senate considered the arguments against the Vallejo location and decided to move. Benicia was located where Suisun Bay meets the Carquinez Straits that lead to San Francisco Bay. Benicia, named after a daughter of General Vallejo, was more centrally located and was on the main water route to Sacramento, Stockton and the Gold County. Consequently, it was considered to be a major Northern California city. Many of the legislators or their families went there from Vallejo to shop for clothes, shoes and other necessities.

On February 4 1853, the Assembly and Senate began meeting in Benicia; they remained there for the rest of the session and for the beginning of the next. The Benicia Capitol Building still exists, has been restored and, as part of the State Parks system, is open to visitors as a museum. This is the only one of the original State Capitol buildings still remaining. The only other public building from the earliest days of the State of California history that exists is Colton Hall in Monterey where the State Constitution was drafted in 1849.

Looking over Hunt's voting record in his first year in the Assembly, it is clear that he tried to avoid appearing to favor one side or the other on contentious matters such as the San Francisco tidal land sale issue, or the movement of the capital, or the excessive printing cost issue. Perhaps he felt that it was best to avoid upsetting either side as long as he had a major piece of legislation pending. He seemed to be conservative in fiscal matters, often voting to avoid more spending unless it was for infrastructure such as road building. Hunt represented a number of Hispanic constituents and, accordingly, he declined to vote on a bill which sought to impose a punitive tax on foreign miners which was aimed primarily at miners from Mexico and Chile. But he did join with all other Assemblymen in a unanimous vote to reject an act allowing "colored people to testify in courts of this state" (Assembly Journal

1853, 259-261). In a similar action, he voted in favor of a bill to return a fugitive from labor (either a slave or apprentice) that had arrived in California prior to statehood.

One bill that was introduced during the session undoubtedly caught Hunt's close attention. That bill would have set the punishment for adultery and polygamy, which had been outlawed by the state constitution. Even though polygamy had been found in the Mormon Church for nearly twenty years, only a select few were involved and the practice was not publicly acknowledged until 1852. Many of the strongly religious Americans of the time found this one more reason to distrust and disdain the Mormons. Jefferson Hunt, of course, was a polygamist, and that fact was known to his Mormon community, and most likely, to others in Southern California. There is no indication, however, that his polygamy was ever an issue, or even mentioned, by his fellow legislators during his five years in the Assembly. The bill was discussed on the floor only once and then tabled. Several days later, it was referred to a special committee of three members and no further action was taken on it.

Hunt introduced several other bills during the session. On February 18th, he introduced a petition from "Powell Wever" asking for payment for feeding and caring for the Indians from Juan Antonio's tribe following the capture of Antonio Garra (Assembly Journal 1853, 159). According to the petition, he fed about 150 men for several weeks and not only depleted his supplies but had to buy three head of cattle from a neighbor. Since Garra was taken into custody by General Bean of the Militia and the capture of Garra was a great service to the people of Southern California, he believed he was entitled for reimbursement for his expenses. "Powell Wever" was Pauline Weaver (who also called himself Powell Weaver), a former mountain man who was a guide for Cooke and the Mormon Battalion. When the Mormons arrived in San Bernardino, Weaver owned a ranch at San Gorgonio, about twenty miles east of San Bernardino.

The next day, Hunt introduced a similar bill providing relief for Samuel Whiting, presumably for similar actions at the same time. Both bills were read once and then referred to the Committee on Indian Affairs. Neither was acted upon again, and both were withdrawn by Hunt on April 2nd. The Committee was not prepared to report favorably on either bill.

Since Hunt's district included a number of Hispanic residents, and he was looking out for their interests, on March 16th he proposed legislation to translate the laws of the state in to Spanish. Two other bills introduced by him dealt with regulating appeals from local courts. Both were referred to the Judiciary Committee.

In summary, Hunt's freshman year in the Assembly was marked by one significant piece of legislation; that of the creation of San Bernardino County. He also showed that he represented the interests of his constituents. His voting record was relatively non-controversial and did not offend the special interests of some of his colleagues. He showed a good deal of political savvy and conducted himself with the same respectful and ethical attitudes that he demonstrated during his tour in California with the Mormon Battalion.

The Assembly met until May 19, 1853, when it adjourned for the year. Jefferson Hunt was away from his home in San Bernardino for five full months.

Following the end of the legislative session, Hunt returned home to San Bernardino. In his absence, his oldest son Gilbert had directed family affairs as he usually did while his father was away. Now back home, Hunt could again resume a relatively normal life for the remainder of the year.

On August 12th, tragedy struck the Hunt family. Hunt's son Marshall, now twenty-four years old and married with a one-year-old daughter, got his left leg caught in a threshing machine and had to have it amputated below the knee. It must be remembered that the use of anesthetics was not yet a common practice, especially on the frontier, and that the mid-Nineteenth Century physicians had few, if any, resources to combat infection following major injury and surgery. Amasa Lyman witnessed the surgery and described it as "painful and severe." Three days later, Lyman visited Marshall and described him as being "more than usually free from pain," but also records that "Dr. Burrus expressed to me some doubts as to his recovery" (Lyman Journal, August 12 & 15, 1853). However, Marshall did survive and lived another sixty-two years with an artificial leg.

Jefferson Hunt was not content to remain a farmer and legislator. He was always on the lookout for additional ways to support his large and growing family and to exploit his entrepreneurial spirit. Soon after his return to San Bernardino, Hunt bought out Charles Crisman's two partners in his sawmill, which was probably located just west of the present location of Lake Gregory in an area where the timber was very favorable. The Crisman mill had the steam engine from the Amargosa Mine at Salt Spring and was not dependant on flowing water for power as were the other mills in the area. Hunt augmented this engine by purchasing another from a wrecked ship at San Pedro (Lyman 1996, 114). Gilbert watched over the family interests as a manager at the mill as indicated by a surviving document from the mill located in the LDS History Department Archives.

Overall, the sawmill operations were very lucrative for the Mormons at San Bernardino. Not only did the lumber provide necessary building material for their use, it provided an important source of income. Much of the lumber supply for Southern California was met by the mills in the mountains north of San Bernardino. Shingles were often nicknamed "Mormon dollars" by those who bought the products of the Mormon's work.

In the 1850s, the term of an Assemblyman was only one year. Accordingly, it was necessary for an incumbent to run for office every Fall if he wished to remain in the legislature. The 1853 election for the 1854 legislative year was held in early September, and Hunt ran unopposed for reelection to his Assembly seat; he received 224 votes. Anti-Mormon political opposition had not yet surfaced. Once again, he would be leaving San Bernardino in mid- to late-December for the capital.

One other matter of official business remained, and that was the settlement of the finances between the new county of San Bernardino and the older county of Los Angeles. Hunt's legislation provided for an equitable division of the debts of Los Angeles County. To achieve this it was necessary for a special commission with representatives from each county to meet to reach an agreement on what portion of the debt was to be the responsibility of San Bernardino County. Since he was the author of the bill and was very well known in Los Angeles, Jefferson Hunt was one of the San Bernardino commissioners. In November, the commissioners met in Los Angeles and resolved the debt issue. Hunt returned to his home in San Bernardino on November 16th (Lyman Journal, November 16, 1853).

The California State Agricultural and Horticultural Society was organized in San Francisco late in 1853. Jefferson Hunt, who was probably not present, was elected as one of twenty-four vice presidents of the new society, joining such prominent Californians as John Bidwell, C.M. Weber, P.B. Reading, Mariano Vallejo, John Sutter and Abel Stearns (Alta California, December 16, 1853). As 1853 drew to a close, he again turned family affairs over to Gilbert and headed north for the next legislative session.

Chapter 23

Back to the Assembly

Once again, Jefferson Hunt left home just before Christmas to travel north to Benicia for the 1854 session of the California Legislature. He arrived in San Francisco on December 27, 1853, aboard the steamer *Southerner*. The Assembly began meeting on January 2nd, and finally adjourned its last meeting of the year on May 15th. During that time, Hunt missed sixteen days of the session, including one full week in February and most of one week in mid-April. Again, it's possible that this time was spent visiting other Mormons in Northern California.

With a year's experience and his major goal of creating the new county behind him, Hunt was now prepared to assume the role of a more seasoned legislator. His goal of creating a new county for the Mormon Corridor had been accomplished during the previous session and his presence on the County Committee no longer benefited his constituency, so he did not seek reappointment. This session, he was assigned to two other committees: the Agriculture Committee and the Military Affairs Committee. These assignments didn't stray far from his interests and skills. As a lifelong farmer and the representative of one of Southern California's major new farming centers, he was a natural selection for the Agriculture Committee. But it was his assignment as the chair of the Military Affairs Committee that recognized his military leadership during the Mexican War. He was one of the very few legislators who were present in California during the Mexican War, and he was the most senior officer from that period in the Assembly. This assignment reflected, more than any other, his stature among those that knew him.

Once again, Hunt tended to vote with the majority of his colleagues and maintained a non-adversarial position, even though he would occasionally vote his conscience on issues of moral or practical importance to him. At the start of the session, Hunt voted to certify the election of Governor John Bigler, who had received 253 of the 255 votes cast in San Bernardino. Bigler had won the popular vote by less than two percent and his election was challenged.

The political conflict between Senator Gwin and David Broderick surfaced in the legislature during this session. Broderick forces attempted to pass an election bill that would set a specific day for the legislature to select a successor to Senator Gwin, whose forces then fought to delay the bill. Both sides resorted to threats and intimidation. In one bizarre incident, Jacob Gruwell—the Missouri mobber and '49er whose family was part of the Independent Company ahead of Hunt's and now a state senator from Santa Clara—was kidnapped and held against his will until he changed his vote (Bancroft 1970, Vol. 23, 684-685). The battle between Gwin and Broderick was not resolved this year and continued into the following.

Early in the session, the permanent location for the state capital again became an issue. Lack of accommodations in the small community of Benicia, coupled with a strong offer from Sacramento caused many of the legislators to consider moving the capital. This issue was discussed a number of times throughout January and February. To gain the favor of the legislators, Sacramento promised to pay for the removal of the government, offered fireproof vaults for record storage and a site for a permanent capitol building. This, coupled with the fact that Sacramento was a larger city and was closer to the mining areas of the state, won the day. Finally, on February 24th, the legislature decided to move the seat of government to Sacramento. Hunt voted against the move, but the decision was made and the next day was the final day that Benicia served as the California capital. The Assembly met in the County Courthouse in Sacramento on March 1st.

Hunt introduced several bills during the session. The first, on January 25th, was "an Act for the government and Protection of Indians" (Assembly Journal 1854, 118). This bill reflected both the Mormons' concern about Indians and Hunt's interest and care for the many bands that lived near San Bernardino. He felt a moral obligation to try to protect them, and felt that well-governed and protected Indians would present much less threat to the citizens of Southern California. His bill was referred to the Committee on Indian Affairs and was eventually reported back with a no support recommendation, based on the committee's belief that current law was adequate; the bill was not passed.

On March 28th, Hunt introduced legislation to incorporate the City of San Bernardino, which was passed the following day.

Not all legislation he proposed was that significant. At that time, few bureaucratic agencies had been established and even matters dealing with individuals were handled in the legislature. For example, a bill was introduced in the Senate to change the name of "William Alexander Smith" to "Amor de Cosmos." No matter was too trivial for the legislature.

The Military Affairs Committee was actively considering how best to organize the state's military arm. By 1854, there had been several incidents of rebellion involving Indians, and some of the criminal gangs in both Northern and Southern California had been very active. The need for an organized militia was clear to most Californians. On March 21st, the Committee reported its findings and Hunt introduced a bill to establish the militia.

Three days later, the legislature voted to appoint W. C. Kibbe as the quartermaster general of the California militia. In this capacity, Kibbe would be responsible for supplying and organizing the various militia units in the state. Because of the difficulty of communications and long distances involved, it was not realistic to appoint a commanding general who would be able to assume field command duties in a timely manner. Command of units would be left to local officers of the units, who would be able to respond to problems more effectively.

One other action Hunt took was to introduce a petition from the residents of Yolo and Sacramento counties to protect salmon runs in the Sacramento River. The legislature also adopted the first regulations providing for hunting seasons for elk and antelope. Even at this early stage in California history, there was interest in protecting California's wildlife. Also during this session, Pauline Weaver's petition for relief for his expenses dealing with the capture of Antonio Garra was again introduced, and then approved.

One issue that concerned many Californians, and especially the Mormons in San Bernardino—including Lyman and Rich—was the title to land that had previously been part of grants during the Spanish and Mexican periods. The final resolution depended on the actions of the federal government, not the state. As the San Bernardino representative, Hunt was very interested in this issue, and on January 20th, he was appointed to a select committee to reconsider a resolution with the federal Land Commissioners.

Following the adjournment of the Assembly on May 15th, Jefferson Hunt returned home, first taking a boat to San Francisco, then a steamer down the coast, where he then headed inland. When he arrived home, he saw his daughter, Olive Isabelle Hunt, who was born to his wife, Matilda, on March 12th, for the first time. That same summer, Gilbert and his family returned to Utah, leaving Hunt to make other arrangements for managing the family business and necessities during his absences. But the family farming operations and lumbering operations were progressing well, and the Hunt family continued to thrive within the community.

During this year, Hunt bought a lot and built a new home in San Bernardino. It was located on the south side of 5th Street, between Arrowhead and Mountain View streets, where now is located a parking lot for the county government complex. Back then it was just beyond the old fort that had been the site of the family home for several years.

The San Bernardino Saints held a conference which coincided with the Semi-Annual Conference in Salt Lake City. They met on September 29th, 30th, October 1st, and again on October 8th. On the first day, Hunt was sustained as a member of the High Council of the Branch. On October 1st, he gave the day's opening prayer. During the afternoon session "Elder Jefferson Hunt followed with a retrospection of the instruction given during conference; and bearing testimony of this being the work of God; and the necessity of opening the way to gather the Saints from abroad and assist in forwarding them to Zion" (Journal History of the Church, October 8, 1854). The *Journal History of the LDS Church* further stated that there were 960 members in the San Bernardino Branch.

The 1855 Appendix to the Assembly Journal gives us some idea of the productivity of the San Bernardino Ranch for the year 1854. The Report of the Surveyor General states that the ranch had 4,000 acres under cultivation and that it produced 50,000 bushels of wheat, 25,000 bushels of barley and oats, 1,000 bushels of corn, 2,000 bushels of potatoes, 2,000 bushels of beans, and 200 pounds of grapes, but that 50,000 vines had been planted. It further reported that five sawmills were operating in the mountains (Appendix to the Assembly Journal 1855, Document 5, 67-68).

On September 6, 1854, the election was held and Hunt ran for his Assembly seat. Again, he was unopposed and was elected with 262 votes. As the year came to a close, Hunt left Southern California for the capital at Sacramento.

A new year brought the California Legislature back to work on January 2, 1855. Jefferson Hunt was in his third term and was even more experienced. Where he played a sideline role in his earlier terms, Hunt now took a more active role in the affairs of the Assembly. An illustration of his new prominence occurred on January 3rd, the second day of the session, when the Assembly elected a new speaker. On the first two votes, Hunt and three others voted for E. Gould Buffum of San Francisco. No candidate got the requisite number of votes to be elected. On the third vote, Hunt and his three colleagues then changed their votes to William W. Stow of Santa Cruz, who was then elected as speaker. Hunt had begun to use his status as a seasoned veteran to influence major decisions of the legislative body and to exert greater influence in Sacramento.

Hunt was placed on two committees, the Military Affairs Committee and the Printing Committee. The former was his usual assignment, but the latter a new and important appointment. While the Committee on Printing might sound somewhat dull today, in 1855 it was very important. Printing costs during the 1854 legislative year were outrageously high and created a major scandal in California. The 1854 legislature spent about $202,000 printing bills and laws, which was more than the per diem and expenses of both the Assembly and the Senate, and was more than the combined costs of the Executive and Judicial branches of the state government. The excessive printing expenses undoubtedly lined the pockets of some of the legislators and their friends. The committee, including Hunt, was assigned to rectify this problem.

The year 1855 also brought with it a new twist in politics; the rise of the "Know-Nothing" party in California. This unique political movement began in the Eastern cities as a reaction to what many urbanites of the 1850s saw as a rising influence of foreign-born immigrants. It was primarily an anti-Catholic and anti-Irish movement that reached its peak in 1854-1855. Formally called the American Party, its common name derives from its mostly secret meetings and the tendency of its members to simply state "I know nothing" when questioned about its philosophy and its meetings. The anti-foreign miner sentiment throughout most of Northern California led to the election of a number of "Know-Nothings" in 1855. This led to a defeat of Governor Bigler and the election of J. Neely Johnson as the new governor in 1856.

The Broderick-Gwin battle now rose to the center stage of California politics. Three major candidates surfaced for Gwin's senate seat. On the first ballot held by the Senate and Assembly meeting as a convention in joint session, Gwin, who was pro-slavery, had forty-two votes; P.L Edwards, the Whig Party candidate had thirty-six; Broderick had twelve. Six other candidates had the rest of the votes. Fifty-four votes were necessary to elect a new senator. One of the twelve voting for Broderick was Jefferson Hunt, who held abolitionist sentiments and was a confirmed Democrat. The convention met a number of days, and on the fiftieth ballot, the vote was still the same with no winner and with Hunt and his associates holding out their votes against Gwin. Consequently, no candidate was elected to fill the seat, which remained vacant for a year. Hunt had become a committed politician willing to take a strong public stand for what he believed in. He was no longer content to take a non-adversarial stance in his public service.

During this legislative session, Hunt focused his efforts on three issues. The first was road construction. In most parts of the state, roads were often nothing more than the trails created by the first wagons following older pack routes or even older Indian trails. The users of these roads sometimes improved them for their own use as they passed through, but no one was willing to spend the time and effort necessary to make a good road for future users. Road building was sometimes done by local communities or entrepreneurs looking to operate toll roads. But most often the building of good long-distance roads fell to the military or to the federal or state government.

A good road system was certainly in the best interests of the San Bernardino community and Southern California in general. Hunt's first effort was a proposal presented to the Assembly in the second week of the session to "construct a Military Road, to connect with the Government Road, at the Eastern Boundary of the State" (Assembly Journal 1855, 98). Two weeks later, he gave notice of another bill to construct a road from San Bernardino to the Southern Mines at Mariposa. His third bill, presented on March 3rd, was to construct a wagon road from Santa Barbara to Stockton via Los Angeles and Tejon Pass, the part north of Los Angeles essentially following the route of today's US 99. The fourth and final bill was introduced late in session on April 4th. This bill was "An Act appropriating Money for the Improvement of the Immigrant Road from the Eastern Boundary of this State, through the Cajon Pass, to San Pedro" (Assembly Journal 1855, 608).

Of these four bills, clearly the last was the most important for Hunt. It would have improved the California portion of the road that followed the Old Spanish Trail from San Bernardino toward Utah and Salt Lake City. This route was now of great importance to the Mormons, their internal communications and for moving converts from the Coast to the Mormon heartland. Travel along the route was frequent and included mail carriers and freighters, in addition to families and individuals.

Hunt was not alone in his proposed legislation for roads. A number of other roads were proposed, mostly extending from the northern mining camps to the eastern state boundary. The citizens and towns sponsoring these routes hoped that new roads would bring better travel and increased business to their communities. Hunt believed that he was responsible for the rash of road construction bills. In a letter to Rich written on March 7th, Hunt said in part: "I have presented a Bill to get in a proposition to open the Rode [sic] from Salt Lake and since I have did that it has got the hole hose [sic] a fire and they are now trying to get three or four across the mountain and what we shal [sic] do I can't tell" (Smith 1958, 272).

The many road proposals were referred to the Committee on Internal Improvements. In a March 12[th,] report presented after Hunt's first three bills, C.T. Ryland, the committee chairman, reported that each of the road proposals presented various benefits and difficulties and that cost was a major concern for each route. The report concluded by recommending only one possible central route, at an undetermined cost, from Placerville to the Carson Valley that approximately coincided with today's Highway 50.

In the end, Jefferson Hunt's efforts to obtain funding for new roads met opposition and were defeated—not because the roads were considered unimportant, but because the cost for new roads was beyond the financial means of the young state, and because the political power was centered in the northern districts of the gold fields. An additional factor was the general California economy in 1855. In his letter to Rich, Hunt stated that:

> ". . . State Script is only worth sixty sense [sic] an the members cant get money to pay our board . . . . All the banks grate [sic] and small broke in one day—but two or three little ones that was not notice taken of them" (Smith 1958, 272).

The second issue addressed by Hunt had little chance for passage but was one that could substantially benefit the Mormons—the division of the State of California. On February 27, 1855, Hunt introduced legislation to "create a new state out of a potion of the territory of California" (Assembly Journal 1855, 259). Again, this legislation was contrary to the interests of those who controlled the legislature and did not move forward. Hunt's bill created a firestorm of action as he stated in the March 7th letter to Rich:

"All so you will see be the with in a Bill to divide the State Well that has set every thing in an uproar and now from thee [sic] look of every thing I can see it appearse [sic] to me that before we break up we shall divide it in to three parts and make three States of it" (Smith 1958, 272).

Another Assemblyman, David F. Douglass of San Joaquin County, introduced the bill to create three states out of California on March 14th. This bill was different from Hunt's and was referred to a special Select Committee for consideration. Hunt was immediately placed on that committee, which eventually reached thirteen members. The committee report, which is basically unknown today, is worth noting. First, the bill would have extended the eastern Boundary of California well into the modern State of Nevada by annexing a significant portion of what was then in the Territory of Utah and a small portion of the Territory of New Mexico (that portion of present day Nevada south of 36° 30'). The new boundary would have begun at a point where 119° W longitude intersected 42° N latitude and would then have extended southeastward to the point where 35° N latitude intersected the Colorado River (the current southernmost point in Nevada. This line would have included today's Reno (Truckee Meadows), Carson City, Virginia City, Tonopah, Goldfield, and the westernmost areas of the Las Vegas Valley (Appendix to Assembly Journal, Report, 1855, 3-4).

The proposal then called for the creation of three states out of the expanded territory. The northernmost state would be named "Shasta" and would include all of the area north of a line that roughly went along the borders of Yuba, Butte, Sierra, and Plumas counties, then east to the new eastern boundary. The southernmost state would be named "Colorado" and would encompass the area south of a line that began where the Parajo River enters Monterey Bay, then went to the Merced River and followed it to the Sierra summit and then to the eastern boundary. Unknown to the legislators involved, this dividing line would have split Yosemite Valley into two different states. The area between the two new states would have continued to be named California (Appendix to Assembly Journal, Report, 1855, 4).

The report is an interesting document. It begins with a review of California's growth during the preceding six years and then discusses the current economy and the prospects for future economic growth. The report also discussed the dissimilar nature between the different regions of the state and the need for better local judiciary and legislative control. Then it pointed out that this proposed enlarged area was more than 23,000 square miles greater in size than the ten Northeast states including Delaware, and that those states had twenty United State senators compared to California's two.

The report then noted that the addition of two more states would upset the balance of slave verses abolitionist states in Congress, since neither of the new states of Shasta or Colorado would benefit from slavery, nor was it likely that the remaining portion of California would adopt slavery either. The select committee recognized that this issue alone would prevent Congress from taking any action on the request. Although the committee reported favorably on the bill, no action was ever taken to submit it to Washington. A similar bill in the California Senate the following year suffered the same fate.

Hunt's third effort was his role as chair of the Military Affairs Committee. California in the 1850s was a long distance from the rest of the United States and there were few military units stationed in the state. If needed, it would take months for troops to be summoned and transported to California. There were real and perceived threats from a few of the Indian tribes; concern about possible incursions across the Mexican border; and a number of the bandit groups that freely operated in the less populated regions and often brought terror and chaos to ranches, farms and smaller communities. In the political and governmental policies of the time, responsibility for responding to these threats lay with militias organized by communities within the state.

There already existed militia units within California, but as the population grew it became necessary to better organize the state and federal support for militias. Hence, the Military Affairs Committee took up the issue with the idea of more formally organizing California's military units. They introduced a bill which passed both houses and was approved by the governor on April 23, 1855. The legislation stated that:

> "All free, able-bodied white citizens, between the ages of eighteen and forty-five years, residing in this State, and not exempt by law, shall be subject to military duty, and shall be enrolled as hereinafter directed" (Statutes of California 1855, 136).

The law created six divisions; each composed of two brigades, and specified the method of appointment of the general officers in charge of them. Brigade One of Division One was comprised of the counties of San Diego, San Bernardino and Los Angeles. The statute further provided for a Quartermaster General who would also serve as Adjutant General. He would be responsible for supplying arms and supplies to the units as needed and would perform the other administrative duties necessary for the functioning of the militia.

For Jefferson Hunt, this legislation was more than a successful military plan; he was appointed by Governor John Bigler as the brigadier general in charge of Brigade One, Division One—his home area. Thus, Hunt who had served as a major in Nauvoo Legion and as an Army captain during the Mexican War now became a general officer in the California Militia. With the appointment, he became the first Mormon ever to be appointed by a non-Mormon as a general officer of a non-Mormon military unit. While it was not a compensated position, it carried considerable responsibility and conferred great status on Hunt. His responsibilities were more administrative than command because of the volunteer nature of the militia, and because any deployment was rapid and under the field command of local unit officers. Nonetheless, it was an important position and one that he took seriously. He remained in this position until he prepared to leave San Bernardino late in 1857.

Throughout most of the 1800s, a man's military rank was considered socially important; the higher the rank, the greater the respect given to the bearer. High military rank was considered so important that many men affected a title they had never held. It was also commonplace to address a former officer by his military rank. Jefferson Hunt was no exception. For the remainder of his life, he was often addressed as General Hunt by both Mormons and non-Mormons alike. Today, Hunt is most often referred to as "Captain

Jefferson Hunt," a reference to his rank within the Mormon Battalion, but which was the lowest rank he ever held. Today, as in the past, it is correct protocol, when referring to someone by their military rank, to call them by the highest rank they held. Unless someone is specifically referring to his service in the Mormon Battalion, Hunt should properly be called "General Jefferson Hunt," if someone is referring to him by his military title. Furthermore, as an elected member of the California Assembly, he was eligible to be referred to using the style "The Honorable"; it was proper to use this following his departure from the Assembly.

When the legislature adjourned on May 7, 1855, Hunt again returned to San Bernardino and his various business ventures. In 1855, the Mormon Church established a small settlement at Las Vegas to serve as a way station for travelers between Salt Lake City and San Bernardino. About thirty men arrived there in June 1855 and built a small adobe fort, about four miles east of the springs next to the creek where it began a steep decline that could be used to power a mill. This site, just east of downtown Las Vegas, is now part of the Nevada State Parks system and is well worth a visit. While the Mormon settlement at Las Vegas lasted only a few years and the city did not begin to grow until the arrival of the railroad fifty years later, this outpost provided an important respite for those traveling the Mormon Corridor.

From the beginning, communications between San Bernardino and Salt Lake City were haphazard. Letters between Church officials and family and friends went with those other Mormons traveling the route. Initially, mail service was not scheduled and was subject to interruption by Indian conflicts and weather conditions. The original mail route established by the United States Post Office for California was awarded to a firm headed by Absalom Woodward and George Chorpenning, who used the Humboldt route between Salt Lake City and Northern California. However, because of snow, this was not usable during the Winter months. Accordingly, they began using the Mormon Corridor route through San Bernardino. Jefferson Hunt was quick to capitalize on this and obtained a subcontract with Woodward and

Chorpenning for the route between San Bernardino and Salt Lake City. After Woodward was killed by Indians near the Malad River, Chorpenning took over and continued to renew Hunt's contract.

Hunt's mail carriers included some of his sons and sons-in-law. John Hunt was one of those who made the frequent trips. The Mormon carriers did not abuse the Indians along the route and treated them with respect, with the result that Hunt's carriers did not suffer many of the problems faced by others on the trail. Usually, two carriers traveled the route together and were often accompanied by other travelers between the two cities (Lyman 1996, 246).

Also by 1855, the Mormons had developed an alternate road that by-passed that older portion of the Old Spanish Trail that went through Salt Spring, up the Amargosa River Canyon to Resting Spring, and on over Emigrant Pass. This route, the Kingston Springs Cutoff, went northeast at Silurian Dry Lake and through the Kingston Range with springs at Kingston Springs and Coyote Holes. It was about the same length as the older one, but was much less rigorous and could be traveled faster by pack animals. Consequently, the mail and other packers often used this route as did some of the wagons on the trail. However, the older route was still heavily used by many wagon trains because of the greater availability of feed.

The Journal History of the LDS Church reported Hunt was home on July 4th. Subsequently, George Q. Cannon wrote from San Francisco on July 21st that a number of Saints had come north from San Bernardino to "labor" and that Amasa Lyman and Jefferson Hunt were staying with him. J.L. Heywood, also in San Francisco, wrote to George A. Smith in Salt Lake City that he had met with Lyman and Hunt (Journal History of the Church, July 21 & 25, 1855). Clearly, Hunt's responsibilities in the Church required him to do much more than care for his own affairs.

However, all was not well within San Bernardino County. There were serious problems with the crops, and the fabric of the community was also showing stress. There was a nearly continuous arrival of families and small groups of Mormons fleeing the stricter control in Utah, and this flight of the disaffected seriously influenced Brigham Young's attitude toward the colony. According to historian Leo Lyman, San Bernardino gained a "reputation as a refuge for the unfaithful" (Lyman 1996, 51). For a thorough discussion of the dissention within San Bernardino County, the reader is encouraged to read Leo Lyman's book. At the same time that the religious foundation of the community was being challenged, many of the apostates and non-Mormons began to question the political power of the Church leaders in the county as well.

In April of 1855, while Hunt was still away in Sacramento, elections were scheduled for the newly-created county board of supervisors. Some of the non-Mormons, including a small group of former mountain men, decided to challenge the Church leaders' practice of picking candidates to run unopposed. One of those mountain men, Louis Rubidoux, was elected. About the same time, Valentine "Rube" Herring, a former mountain man who was in El Pueblo at the same time as the Mormon Battalion's sick detachment, and who was briefly the superintendent of schools in San Bernardino and joined LDS Church for a short period, announced that he would oppose Jefferson Hunt for the Assembly seat in that Fall's election (Lyman 1996, 152). After running unopposed for three years, Hunt now faced an adversary for elected office.

As the election approached, the importance of the Mormon vote was not lost on the Know-Nothings who were attempting to win the state senate seat for Los Angeles and San Bernardino counties held by Lewis Granger, a member of the Hunt Wagon Train, a Democrat, and a lawyer who had assisted Lyman and Rich. Apparently, there were two attempts made by the Know-Nothings to influence the Mormons; one involved an offer to Lyman of $7,000—a very significant amount of money at the time (Lyman 1996, 179-180). Lyman and the other Mormons firmly rejected the overtures and remained loyal to the Democratic Party. In the election held on September 5, 1855, the Mormons of San Bernardino voted for Granger, incumbent governor John Bigler, and of course, Jefferson Hunt. Granger was defeated by Benjamin Wilson, Bigler was defeated by J. Neely Johnson, but Hunt was reelected by a vote of 257 to eighty-seven for Rube Herring.

Hunt continued to manage his affairs while home. The lumber mill and mail route were functioning quite well and the family was prospering.

But all was not well for the family. Just before the election, Marshall Hunt and another man were accused of helping a man named Frank Dixon stab John Carroll, who nearly died from his wounds. Only Dixon was convicted and sentenced to prison for the attack. But Marshall was excommunicated the following year (Lyman 1996, 176).

About Christmas time, Jefferson Hunt left his San Bernardino home for the Assembly in Sacramento. When he arrived, he found that only four other assemblymen had the same or more seniority as him. He was now one of the most experienced members of the lower house. The first day of the seventh session of the legislature began on January 7, 1856, with Hunt present. On the second day, Hunt introduced a resolution to honor Andrew Jackson, his idol and the acknowledged founder of the Democratic Party as Hunt knew it. Very possibly his motives were not only to honor Jackson, but also to place the Know-Nothings—or at least the former Democrats who defected—in an embarrassing position.

In the 1855 election, the Know Nothings, or American Party, swept the ticket for statewide offices and gained significant strength in the legislature. Most of this support came from people who had previously voted with the Democrats. The most upsetting of the results was the defeat of four-term governor John Bigler by J. Neely Johnson. Loyal Democrats, including Jefferson Hunt, regarded this defection by Democratic Party supporters as grave misconduct by those who should have been faithful. But in San Bernardino party loyalty was supreme; the county voted for Bigler by a margin of 332 to fourteen—the highest ratio of any county in California. It is no surprise that Hunt would want to remind his colleagues of the foundation of the party. Thus, on January 8, 1856, Hunt began the session with the following:

> "Mr. Hunt offered the following resolution: Resolved, that in honor of the ever glorious battle of New Orleans, fought on the eighth of January, and in honor of the ever-memorable name of Andrew Jackson, the hero of that day, this House do now

adjourn until 10 o'clock, A.M., tomorrow" (Assembly Journal 1856, 6).

Richard Hopkins, the branch and stake clerk in San Bernardino, had a different take on the effort. In a January 30th letter to Lyman, then in Utah, he wrote:

> "Capt Hunts patriotism got the better of his discretion and induced him to make a motion on the 8th of January that the assembly adjourn and thereby show their respect for the gallent [sic] Old Hickory. The motion to the opposite party had the appearance of extravagance, the KN [Know Nothings] having the majority compelled the old man to smother his patriotism and return to long speaches [sic] on financial reform. I judge the Capts influence is not felt as it used to was [sic]" (Lyman Papers).

With Rich, Hunt's longtime friend and confidant, also in Utah, Hopkins and others were more outspoken in writing their impressions of Hunt to the absent apostles. Hunt was often solemn and brusque to those around him, and Hopkins' comments reflect their feelings. But in this case, Hunt's gruff demeanor seems to have been directed at the party defectors who joined the Know Nothings, and was not random.

Hunt's resolution was defeated by a vote of twenty-four to fifty-one, and the Assembly moved on to the next item of business, the election of a Speaker for the year. In that vote, James T. Farley was elected over T.W. Taliaferro by more than a two-to-one vote. Hunt voted for Taliaferro, but in an apparent show of thanks for his party support, Taliaferro himself, cast the only vote for Hunt as speaker. At the end of that day, another member offered a resolution recognizing Andrew Jackson, which was supported by the full Assembly.

The following day, outgoing Governor Bigler gave his annual speech before the confirmation and swearing in of incoming Governor Johnson. His talk took the high road and he pointed to the continued success of gold mining, the rising importance of agriculture, the need for improved roads and a railroad to connect California with the rest of the nation.

Beneath his speech lay the fact that conditions had deteriorated in California and in state politics. Heretofore loyal Democrats wanted things to change, and they were willing to move to another party to make that point. The people were not satisfied with the ruffians and rising crime that would lead to the rebirth of the San Francisco Committee of Vigilance in just a few months. Nor were they satisfied with what they perceived as corruption in many state services, such as the prison system. They wanted to send a message that politics as usual was no longer acceptable. The American or Know Nothing Party gave them that opportunity.

In the context of the political situation in California and within the Democratic Party, we can easily see why Jefferson Hunt, a party loyalist and firm Jacksonian, wanted to remind his colleagues of their foundation and heritage. Thus, he used the timing of the situation to introduce his resolution recognizing Andrew Jackson.

Hunt's next action came on the fourth day of the session when he introduced a resolution to "procure for each member of this House, during the Session, six daily newspapers, or their equivalent in weeklies" (Assembly Journal 1856, 90). The resolution was postponed for one day but no action was ever taken on it. On January 14th, the speaker appointed committees and Hunt was again made chair of the Military Affairs Committee, his only committee assignment. In making this appointment, the speaker was recognizing Hunt's military experience, his standing within the Southern California community and his ability to handle the responsibility.

On January 18th, a petition was introduced from residents in the Carson Valley area of what is today's western Nevada to annex a broad area to California. The area involved was part of Utah Territory and included Pyramid Lake, the Truckee River, the Humboldt Sink, the Carson Valley and the Walker River areas, and thus by extension, an area extending from north of today's Reno, east to near Lovelock, and south to Hawthorne. The first settlers in the area were Mormon pioneers who established the community of Genoa after hearing of the Carson Valley from returning Mormon Battalion members. But by 1856, others, including miners, were moving into the area. The discovery of the Comstock Lode silver deposit in the mountains on the eastern side of the Carson Valley in 1858 would lead to the creation of the State of Nevada. But for the 1856 legislature, all they could do was refer the matter to Congress, who controlled state boundaries. The federal legislators took no action to annex the territory to California.

Hunt introduced no further bills or resolutions until the second half of March, but he was granted a three day leave of absence on February 8th. On March 17th, Hunt introduced a resolution calling for weekly mail service between San Diego and San Pedro via Los Angeles and San Bernardino. This was an overland route that would have connected the four cities and greatly enhanced regional mail service, and Hunt might have benefited from his subcontract with the primary contractor had the U.S. Post Office instituted such a service. However, no further action was taken on the resolution.

On March 18th, the Military Affairs Committee under Hunt reported back to the Assembly that a bill to prohibit the carrying of concealed weapons in California was "inoperative" in the rural and more desolate parts of the state and that it should be postponed indefinitely (Assembly Journal 1856, 498). California was still considered to be too hostile and unsettled of a place to expect that citizens would not carry weapons for self-defense.

In February 1851, the Oatman family, heading to California along the Southern Trail from New Mexico, was attacked by either the Apache or Yavapai Indians along the Gila River in Arizona. The father, mother (who was pregnant) and three children were killed. One son, Lorenzo, age fourteen, was left for dead, and two girls, Olive, age sixteen, and Mary Ann, age ten, were taken captive. The girls were eventually traded as slaves to the Mojave Indians along the Colorado River near present-day Needles, California. Later in the 1850s, Lorenzo searched for his sisters and aroused significant public interest in their plight. After several years, Mary Ann died in captivity, but in early 1856, Olive was rescued when she was "traded" to the Army at Fort Yuma. Her story of captivity and survival quickly captured the interest of the public.

On March 20th, Jefferson Hunt gave notice to the Assembly that he was going to introduce bills for relief (compensation) for Olive Oatman, to extend the time for collection of taxes in San Bernardino and Los Angeles Counties and for relief for the San Bernardino Rangers, a militia unit under his command. These bills were introduced during the next several days and each passed the Assembly before the end of the session, although the Oatman bill never became law. About the same time, Hunt's Military Affairs Committee recommended passage of a bill regarding the militia, although one member of the committee gave a minority view recommending against it. On April 10th, the same situation occurred with another bill from the committee.

As the session drew to a close, Hunt made one more attempt to honor Andrew Jackson. On April 12th, he introduced a bill to commission the painting of a portrait of Jackson to be hung in the capitol. The bill was read a first and second time, and then referred to a committee of the whole, effectively halting it. Hunt then called for a rule change which failed to reach the two-thirds majority needed for passage. Thus, the bill was stopped.

Official records of the Assembly do not give accounts of oral arguments and speeches made by members. Accordingly, we have very little record of what Hunt or others said in support or opposition to bills. There is, however, one account of Hunt's comments regarding Governor Johnson's veto of an Orphan Asylum Bill on April 21, 1856. The *San Francisco Daily Evening Bulletin* reported on April 26th that Hunt was the second speaker to speak against the veto:

> "The next speaker was the Hon. Jefferson Hunt, of San Bernardino, the Mormon member. His remarks were made with a natural pathos and in Good sound sense. He said that if he were Governor, and had constitutional doubts as to the propriety of any subject, that against individuals he would have no hesitation to decide; but that when he had to pass upon a measure in which two hundred fatherless children were dependant for bread and shelter, that he believed that he would be obeying the wishes of the Great Father of all by giving those doubts in favor of the orphans" (Daily Evening Bulletin, April 26, 1856).

Hunt's final act of the session occurred on April 19th, two days before the Assembly adjourned, when he introduced a resolution calling on the federal government to give California 3,000 rifles or muskets worth $60,000. This resolution was passed by the Assembly and by the Senate on the final day of the session, April 21st.

At San Bernardino, Hunt's wife, Matilda, had given birth to a son named Thomas Jefferson Hunt on April 6, 1856. When he arrived home after his fourth session of the legislature, he saw his new son for the first time.

His son, John, had been busy with the mail route between San Bernardino and Salt Lake City. According to the minutes of the Las Vegas Mission—the Mormon outpost at Las Vegas that had been established in June 1855—John Hunt, with others, passed through with the mail at least six times during the year. It appears that these probably represented four round trips (Jenson, History of the Las Vegas Mission, Nevada State Historical Papers, Vol. 5, 1925-26). From Las Vegas to Salt Lake City and back—a distance of about 850 miles—usually took thirty-five or -six days, an average of about twenty-five miles per day. Since some time was undoubtedly spent resting the animals, we can project that he was actually traveling at a faster rate than that. The 460 mile round trip from Las Vegas to San Bernardino and back took twenty-nine days. Most likely, the full trip of 660 miles from San Bernardino to Salt Lake City took about thirty days of travel, and the round trip of more than 1,300 miles took about two months.

Jefferson Hunt was involved that Summer with his normal business affairs. He also took time to speak at the Fourth of July celebration and at Sunday services. Army Captain Edward Ord, touring the Southern California cities, recorded in his diary on Sunday, July 27[th], that "Genl. Hunt" was one of the "preachers," and that "Rich helped on [e]xcitement by saying keep cool & that we'd defy the world. Hunt d[itt]o, d[itt]o" (Ord 1978, 20-21). It seems that Hunt's fiery rhetoric at Church services had not changed much from what was seen in 1849 in the Bowery. Ord found the dissention amongst the Mormons obvious during his short visit. In his official report, he states that they "have discontent and dissention at home . . ." but then observes that they were "under excellent control of shrewd Elders, the Elders will preserve peace without and good order within, as well as possible, because their community is surrounded with unscrupulous squatters and dissenters, anxious for an excuse to drive them from the country. . . ." (Ord 1978, 35).

The dissention in San Bernardino involving both disaffected Mormons and the non-Mormon populace of the county was affecting Hunt's family. On Pioneer Day, July 24th, it was revealed that "someone was circulating 'notorious lies' about. . . Harriet Hunt and Matilda Lyman" (Lyman 1996, 329). Soon after, a local merchant fled the community following the disclosure that he may have been responsible for the comments.

In the local and national election of 1856 held on November 4th, there were three candidates for president. The Republican Party had just surfaced drawing most of its members from the now defunct Whig Party, and John C. Fremont—still a great American hero—was their first candidate for president. Nationally, the Republicans ran on a platform that opposed what they referred to as the "twin relics of barbarism" or polygamy and slavery. This opposition to polygamy was not aimed at destroying the Mormon religion; it was designed to rally the populace around Victorian sensibilities and attract voters to the new party. Unfortunately for the Mormons in Salt Lake City and elsewhere, making polygamy a political issue drew attention to them and created more hostility.

In San Francisco, George Q. Cannon, once a young packer who caught up with the Jefferson Hunt Wagon Train on Beaver Creek, published a newspaper; the *Western Standard* was first printed on February 23, 1856. Much of its content was aimed at defending Mormonism from its critics, especially those in other West Coast newspapers. For nearly two years, Cannon was the voice of support for the California Mormons. We can assume that Hunt periodically met with Cannon in San Francisco or Sacramento and kept him apprised of activities in the California government and in San Bernardino.

Former president Millard Fillmore was the candidate of the Know-Nothing Party, and James Buchanan was the Democratic Party candidate. Buchanan had previously been elected to both the House and the Senate and had served as Secretary of State during the Mexican War, and was elected president. Although Buchanan was from Pennsylvania, he supported the Southern view on slavery. He was never able to resolve any issues regarding slavery and the split between the North and the South, and is regarded today as one of the least effective presidents in American history. Ever loyal to the Democratic Party, the Mormons of San Bernardino voted for Buchanan, a decision they would soon regret. In California, Buchanan won the overall vote over Fillmore, with John C. Fremont coming in last. The population of California had changed and national concerns took precedence over Fremont's status as a hero of the West.

In the November 4th election, Jefferson Hunt ran for Assembly for the fifth and final time. In this election, he had two opponents. One was Duff Weaver, brother of Pauline (Powell) Weaver and the other was A. Boren, a sometime-Mormon. Prior to the election, an Independent Party was formed and it could not decide between Weaver and Boren to run against Hunt. A compromise broke down, and both ran in the election, thereby splitting the dissenters' vote (Lyman 1996, 331). Once again, Hunt won with 240 votes while Weaver got eighty-five and Boren got seventy votes. The total count reveals that Hunt captured the Mormon vote in San Bernardino, but that the dissidents and non-Mormons were gaining in numbers.

By 1856, gold production in California was decreasing as the easily-removed placer ore was depleted. The individual miner working a simple claim was becoming a thing of the past. Gold mining was changing toward larger organizations that could finance underground operations.

California's agricultural potential was widely recognized and more and more farms and ranches were created. But reaching the state's full potential depended on improved transportation systems and more settlers willing to farm and settle the valleys and coastal areas.

The San Francisco banker and future Army general, William Tecumseh Sherman, observed that California had a large disparity between legislative representation and taxation. Santa Clara County had one state senator and $9 million in assessed valuation while El Dorado County had four senators and $3 million in valuation (Clarke 1969, 304). The disparity that previously caused a discussion of the separation of the state could still be found.

Lawlessness, political corruption, bribery, rigged elections, and the lack of a competent justice system reached new heights in San Francisco in late 1855 and early 1856. The Vigilance Committee that had first been created in the City in 1851, and that was partly headed by Sam Brannan, was reinvigorated following the May 14, 1856 murder of newspaperman James King of William (according to historian Theodore Hittell, King had added the "of William" to his name to distinguish himself from others with the same name (Hittell 1897, Vol. 3, 463)) by James P. Casey, a member of the San Francisco Board of Supervisors and a former convict at Sing Sing Prison in New York. Following the attack, Casey was aided by several men, including Edward McGowan, who had known in advance of the plan. It was widely believed by the law-abiding citizens of San Francisco that Casey and a man named Charles Cora who had killed a U.S. Marshall the previous November, would escape justice because of the rampant corruption.

The Vigilance Committee was reorganized with William Tell Coleman, a prominent San Francisco businessman, at the head. Soon after the murder, Cora and Casey were tried by the Committee and executed. Edward McGowan fled to Santa Barbara and successfully evaded capture for some time. Order was eventually restored to San Francisco. William T. Coleman went on to play an important role in Death Valley history when he acquired the borax deposits on the valley floor from Aaron Winters in 1881. It was Coleman who first developed the Harmony Borax Works at Furnace Creek to process borax, and who used the famous Twenty Mule Teams to haul the borax from the Valley to the rail head.

Meanwhile, in Salt Lake City, all was not well. In November, two large companies of Mormon immigrants, mostly from Great Britain, pulling small, light carts by hand, got caught in the heavy snows in Wyoming. Having run out of supplies, they could do little but wait for relief parties from Salt Lake City. Nearly 200—or twenty percent—of those immigrants lost their lives to exposure, exhaustion and starvation. This was the largest single loss of life during the entire Western Migration.

The political climate in Utah was not well. Most of the federal officials appointed to territorial offices had fled and tensions were growing between Brigham Young, the Church hierarchy, and the federal government.

But the year 1856 was a good one for Jefferson Hunt. His family was enjoying their new home in San Bernardino and his various business affairs were flourishing. He had been elected to his fifth term in the Assembly and was now one of the senior politicians in Sacramento. But this would be his last full year in California. Everything was about to change.

Chapter 24

Back to Utah

As he returned to Sacramento for the 1857 legislative session, Hunt could not have foreseen the changes that were about to take place that Summer. One of the new members of the Assembly was Orson K. Smith, the leader of the packers who had intercepted Hunt's wagon train on Beaver Creek and owned the misleading map. Smith represented Fresno and Tulare counties and was one of the few American or Know-Nothing Party members elected that year; their popularity had been very brief.

Now in his fifth session as an Assemblyman, Jefferson Hunt was the second-most senior member of that body and one of the more influential members of the Democratic Party. Only José María Covarrubias of Santa Barbara County, who also was a Brigadier General in the militia, was more senior. Accordingly—and probably on behalf of his controlling party's leaders—Hunt's first effort of the session, on January 6th, was to nominate Elwood T. Beatty of Calaveras County as Speaker of the Assembly. Beatty was elected over two other candidates.

Later that day, Hunt and two others were selected by the full Assembly to report to the Governor that they had organized and were ready to conduct business. During his address to the legislators on January 7th, Governor Johnson complained that the tax for the support of the militia was being largely ignored. He called for reform and revision of the state's constitution. He also spoke of the need for a railroad connecting the States to California, and the more immediate need for a quality wagon road to the Mississippi River. Both the issues of the militia support and the need for better transportation were important to Hunt.

Once again on January 8th, the anniversary of the Battle of New Orleans, Hunt introduced his resolution to adjourn in honor of Andrew Jackson. It was tabled temporarily while some other business was conducted and then approved; the Assembly adjourned until the following day. Two days later, Speaker Beatty made committee assignments; Hunt was made chair of the Military Affairs Committee and placed on the committees for Indian Affairs and Agriculture.

That same day, the legislature finally resolved the United States Senator issue that had been pending for two years. The agreement David Broderick brokered called for his election to replace outgoing Senator John Weller; Gwin was to be reelected. Once again California had two senators in Washington. Broderick's plan had been to make himself the power broker for patronage jobs in California, and he believed that had been part of the deal with Gwin. However, Gwin was close to the newly-elected President James Buchanan—who was sworn in on March 4, 1857—and kept that power for himself.

On January 28th, Hunt introduced a joint resolution calling for a constitutional convention. While a revised constitution was needed, the issue was contentious and, as a result, was tabled. On February 3rd, he introduced a bill to create a Board of Water Commissioners for San Bernardino County. This bill, which was approved and became law on March 2nd, provided a process for allocating, controlling and protecting water rights and the construction and maintenance of ditches within the county. This was an important matter for agricultural and domestic water use in a semi-arid climate such as that of San Bernardino. Part of the problem of water for San Bernardino occurred when Rich failed to use the colony's water rights in the wet year of 1855, thereby relinquishing water rights to upstream users (Lyman, 2009, 236).

Two weeks later on February 17th, Hunt introduced legislation to redefine the boundary line between Los Angeles and San Bernardino counties. This bill clarified the line and moved a small portion of area back into Los Angeles County. But the description of the exact boundary still lacked the precision that we are accustomed to today, or that would even have satisfied the surveyors of the time. A competing bill backed by a petition from some of the San Bernardino dissidents was introduced by Hunter from Los Angeles. After discussion between Hunt and the Los Angeles delegation, an agreement was reached and a final bill was approved and signed. The same day he introduced the county boundary bill, Hunt also again introduced a bill to commission a portrait of Andrew Jackson to hang at the Capitol. But with California's finances in chaos, no further action was taken on this expensive gesture of party loyalty.

On March 3rd, Hunt introduced a highly controversial bill to bring to trial Edward McGowan for his role in the murder of James King of William in San Francisco. McGowan supporters immediately attempted to sideline the bill, but it was modified to change the venue. A trial was eventually held in Napa County, where McGowan was acquitted because of insufficient evidence that he participated in the actual planning of the murder. Since Hunt rarely, if ever, introduced legislation that didn't directly involve his specific interests in Southern California or the military, it can be assumed that he was selected by the law-and-order faction of his party to present this controversial issue because of his seniority and stature in the Assembly.

The criminal activities plaguing Southern California were a concern of Hunt's. On March 6th, he introduced legislation to build a jail in San Bernardino; a week later he introduced a bill to provide funds to Los Angeles and San Bernardino counties "for the arrest and suppression of bands of armed banditti" (Assembly Journal 1857, 530). The jail bill authorized the county to levy a tax, specified how the contract would be let and the funds administered. The California constitution and laws still did not enable local governments to make such tax decisions. The "banditti" bill authorized the state to give Los Angeles County $3,000 and San Bernardino County $2,000 for the specific purpose of stopping the outlaw gangs. Both bills passed and became law.

His final piece of legislation of the year, presented on March 28th, enabled David Seeley, his friend and fellow lumberman, to collect tolls on the road into the mountains from San Bernardino. The legislature adjourned for the year on April 30th.

From his arrival in the Valley of the Great Salt Lake, Brigham Young set out to form a tightly-controlled theocracy which would govern not only the population but hundreds of thousands of square miles of land. From his creation of the Council of Fifty to the State of Deseret, his objective was to establish political control. With the establishment of the Territory of Utah and his appointment as governor in 1850, Young had the political control he desired. The territorial legislature and the local appointees were composed of Church members and followed the desires of the Church leadership. But not all territorial officials were locally elected or appointed. Some were federal appointees.

When the first non-Mormon appointees arrived in Salt Lake City in 1851 to assume their offices, they found open hostility to their presence. They were often ignored or their efforts were simply bypassed. Judges and others immediately grew disheartened, and even fearful, by the reception they received in the territory. The first federal appointees to flee Utah did so shortly after their arrival. Historian David Bigler relates that "at least sixteen federal officers . . . would abandon their posts in Utah out of frustration, fright, or both, over the next dozen years" (Bigler 1998, 59).

As early as 1851, reports began to flow to the President about the opposition to federal authority and non-Mormons in Utah. When James Buchanan was sworn in as President on March 4, 1857, the Utah problem was well-known. In addition, the public acknowledgement of the doctrine of plural marriages in 1852 had fanned the anger many Americans held toward the Mormons in Utah. Buchanan had little choice but to relieve Brigham Young as governor and appoint federal officers who could regain control over the territory. Things had deteriorated so much that Buchanan realized that doing so meant dispatching military troops to enforce federal law and resist any violent opposition. Sending federal troops to Utah would at least make it appear that Buchanan was taking decisive action in some matter; he found that he was unable to do anything to resolve the slavery issue that was dividing the country.

The President appointed Alfred Cumming, a former mayor of Augusta, Georgia, as the new governor of Utah Territory. It was difficult for Buchanan to find someone who would accept the appointment, but getting him there and installing him in office proved to be even more difficult. On May 28, 1857, General Winfield Scott, the commanding officer of the United States Army, ordered Brigadier General William Harney to take 2,500 men (about one-sixth of the Army) to Utah (Bigler 1998, 141). This began the federal government's Utah Expedition and what has come to be called the Utah War. Over the next two months, various military units began the march toward Utah.

Brigham Young probably found out about the coming Army sometime in late June or early July, but the news was disseminated to the general populace in a carefully staged and very dramatic event during the Pioneer Day celebration on July 24th. It was the tenth anniversary of the arrival of the first Saints in the Valley, and the celebration was held in Big Cottonwood Canyon. Midway through the day's events, Orrin Porter Rockwell and two others arrived with great fanfare and announced to everyone gathered that the Army was on its way to Utah. This news, especially when combined with the Mormons' history of persecution, stirred the emotions of all those in Utah.

Captain Stewart Van Vliet, an emissary of the Army, arrived in Salt Lake City in mid-September to arrange for the arrival and accommodations of the military units. Brigham Young told him that the Army was not welcome and would be resisted. After the Army units crossed the Green River in present-day western Wyoming, Mormon raiders under the command of Lot Smith began a series of raids on the supply wagons and livestock. Other Nauvoo Legion units under the command of General Daniel Wells fortified Echo Canyon, the main entry point into Utah, just west of the present Wyoming border. The effect of these actions was to stall the westward movement of the Army. General Harney was replaced by a new commander, Colonel Albert Sidney Johnston, who was soon promoted to Brigadier General.

By mid-November, Johnston's Army, as it has come to be called, arrived at Fort Bridger, 130 miles east of Salt Lake City. The Mormons, who had purchased the old trading post and fort from Jim Bridger, burned it to the ground. Johnston's army was forced to camp on the plains during a very cold and windy Wyoming Winter. Just after Johnston arrived at Fort Bridger,

Governor Cumming arrived with a military escort led by Colonel Philip St. George Cooke, the Mormon Battalion's former commander after Santa Fe. The Mormon raiders and forces placed in Echo Canyon and elsewhere forced the Army to stop well short of their goal. It appears that Johnston did not want an armed confrontation with the Mormon civilians if it could be avoided. He had the authority to use force if necessary, but quite likely realized that exercising military might against civilians, even if they were clothed in the colors of the Nauvoo Legion, would likely damage his career. In 1857, most federal officials and senior military officers realized that the country was headed toward a major confrontation over the issue of slavery, and that is where major career moves could be made, if not damaged beforehand.

For those in Utah in during the Winter of 1857-58, Johnston and his Army represented the latest and most serious threat to the survival of the LDS Church. And, the beliefs, attitudes, and actions of the Mormons reflected that fear.

Three other events further stirred up emotions among the Saints of Utah. The first has become known as the Reformation. Led by Brigham Young and Apostle Jedediah Grant, the Reformation was what historian Will Bagley has called "an orgy of religious extremism" (Bagley 2002, 49). Sermons became harsher; the focus moved toward reaffirming people's faith and the cleansing of sins. As a result of the Reformation, religious excitement significantly increased in Utah beginning in 1856 and lasted through 1857.

As the Reformation developed, Brigham Young became aware of a revival of threats and animosity toward the Mormons. He warned his people to prepare for possible hostilities from yet unknown adversaries. On January 8, 1857, Peter Conover, a neighbor of the Hunts at Fort Utah and an officer in the Nauvoo Legion, wrote the following to Hunt in California:

> "[The Reformation] makes those who are ill disposed towards us
> make some pretty threats about destroying the authorizes of this
> church and the Gentile merchants that are here, have refused to

let the Mormons have any ammunition to defend themselves
with. So I thought . . . I would just say to you to bring or send as
much powder in as you can get hold of, for we shall need it by
the time we can get it here. I want you to bring me 1000 lbs for
my Brigade. It will bring the money before anything else you can
bring here at present, if you could send a Keg by the mail every
time they come it would be a good plan by that means we could
be supplied at Uncle Sams [sic] expense. Now Brother Hunt if
you feel like helping any you can do it in this way more than any
other, we are expecting some U.S. troops next summer, but we
do not anticipate as much trouble from them as we do from the
apostates that are here in our midst but from all appearances we
will need powder and caps before long and if you cannot sent
it before you come be sure to bring it with you." (MacKinnon
2008, 269).

There is no record of Hunt's response or information regarding his
compliance with this request. He had the subcontract for mail service and
was a Brigadier General in the militia. Accordingly, he was well placed to
respond favorably to Conover. But there are no documents to be found in the
California militia archives that show any unusual activity and no accounts of
any arms shipments via either Hunt or the mail. None of the San Bernardino
militia units received any arms or ammunition during 1857. If Hunt did obtain any arms or ammunition that year, he or others did so in the regular
market and left no indication of their purchases. Since other travelers often
accompanied the mail carriers, it would have been little problem for them to
add supplies going to Salt Lake. But if any such shipments were made, those
involved would have likely kept the matter very confidential.

The connection between the Hunts and Conovers strengthened when
Hunt's son, Joseph, married Peter Conover's daughter, Catherine, on August
8, 1857. Of particular note in this correspondence is the belief held within the
hierarchy of the Church of possible military action against the Mormons by
the federal government before Buchanan was inaugurated, and more than six
months before the first word of the advancing troops reached Salt Lake.

The second event associated with the Reformation was what was called
blood atonement. Briefly summarized, this essentially said that some sins—

and consequently some sinners—were so terrible that only the spilling of the persons' blood could atone for their sins. While not an actual doctrine of the Church, exhortations of the influential were so strong that the concept came to be accepted by some of the Utah Saints. One of the hot spots for the Reformation was the Southern Utah area.

The third event was the murder of Apostle Parley Pratt in Arkansas by Hector McLean. Pratt had taken Eleanor McLean, Hector's former wife, as a plural wife. Pratt was arrested at Hector's instigation and put on trial. Shortly after the judge in the case released Pratt, Hector and several others tracked him down near Van Buren, Arkansas, not far from Fort Smith, and murdered him. News of Pratt's death on May 13, 1857, reached Salt Lake City by July 1st, and caused a great uproar among the Saints. They saw the death of one of their most important leaders as one more incident of persecution.

These three events, combined with the march of Johnston's Army, caused considerable uproar in Utah. Emotions and uncertainty ran high and everyone was uneasy about the future. By the Fall of 1857, Utah was in a state of turmoil.

A wagon train formed near Harrison, Arkansas, about ninety miles from Van Buren. It was headed toward California and led by Alexander Fancher and John Baker. Fancher had been to California several times and was returning with his family and others. The party consisted of about 135 persons in family units and about a thousand cattle. With their livestock, wagons, family possessions and money, some considered this train to be one of the wealthiest to cross the American West. Their route took them to Salt Lake City and south along the Southern Trail toward California.

As they moved through Utah, the Mormons refused to trade with the train and the travelers experienced some animosity. On Sunday, September 6th, the wagon train camped near a spring at the southern end of Mountain Meadow. At dawn the next morning, a small force comprised of some Indians and a number of local Mormons dressed like Indians under the leadership of John D. Lee—who held the title of Farmer to the Indians (or Indian Agent) in Southern Utah—began firing at the camp. A number of the emigrants, including a child, were wounded—some fatally. The camp quickly returned fire, killing one Indian and wounding several others. From their open position, they were easy targets for the better-concealed aggressors, and were unable to access a spring a short distance away (see Will Bagley, *Blood of the Prophets*, for an excellent and detailed treatment of this incident).

The siege lasted for the next five days. Finally, on Friday, September 11, John D. Lee and others approached the camp under a white flag of truce. They entered and explained that they could save the emigrants from the "savage Indians" by escorting them back to Cedar City, provided they surrendered all of their weapons and marched out in an orderly file. Given no other choice, the emigrants agreed. The emigrants were divided into groups: the wounded, children, women, and able-bodied men. They were led out of the area on foot, each man being escorted by a local Mormon resident; the wounded and some of the women and children were in wagons. As the groups stretched out, Lee, who was leading the forward group, gave a signal. Each escort turned, shot, and killed his assigned emigrant. The women and many of the children were killed by gunfire, knives or simply physical force. When all was done, about 120 men, women and children were dead. Some of the children under the age of eight—seventeen in all—were spared and taken into captivity. Eventually they were taken back to Arkansas and reunited with relatives. The Indians and Mormons collected and kept all of the valuables, including clothes off of the victims, housewares and anything else of use, and as much of the cattle and horses as they could round up.

By September 28th or 29th, Lee traveled to Salt Lake City to report to Brigham Young. Various accounts exist as to what he might have said. But in any case, it is likely that Young was already apprised of the massacre, possibly by mail carriers, one of which was possibly John Hunt, and was prepared to deal with the consequences in light of the approach of the Army. A cover-up began almost immediately. Young and the other Church officials placed the entire blame on the Indians. Those in Southern Utah who knew better were told to hold the matter in the utmost secrecy. At the same time, stories were created that justified the attack, at least as far as many of the ardent Mormons were concerned.

Lee was exiled by Brigham Young to a remote crossing of the Colorado River in Northern Arizona. The point where the Paria River enters the Colorado is the only place in 600 miles between Moab, Utah to below Las Vegas, Nevada where a ferry service could easily transport people across the mighty Colorado. Located where the Colorado River begins its descent into the Grand Canyon, Lee's Ferry served as a crossing until the Navajo Bridge was completed several miles away in 1929. Today, Lee's Ferry is a fly fisherman's mecca, and the starting point for thousands of rafters who annually descend the Grand Canyon.

There has been much discussion about who was responsible for the Mountain Meadows Massacre. Clearly, the tensions caused by approach of Johnston's Army, the religious fervor of the Reformation, the murder of Parley Pratt in Arkansas, the uncertainty of what was to come, and the previous persecutions of the Mormons all played a role. Most likely, the pronouncements of Brigham Young did much to inflame the passions in all of Utah, and especially the south. Did Young want the entire wagon train slaughtered? Most likely not; he was only using the rhetorical techniques that he had been using for his entire career as leader of the Church. But many, and especially John D. Lee, were quite possibly confused about what he wanted. In light of what we know about the events that took place, and what we know about Lee's temperament and prior behavior, he was very likely the person most responsible for arousing his fellow Mormons to murder. This author believes that had Lee not been there, the Mountain Meadows Massacre would have never taken place.

As it was, the Massacre took more lives than any other emigrant attack in the history of the Westward Migration. Its repercussions still reverberate in Utah today.

As historian Leo Lyman points out, the recall or departure of Mormons from San Bernardino was more a result of Brigham Young's displeasure with the settlement and what it represented than it was of the threat from Johnston's Army to Utah or from the internal dissent within the colony. From the beginning, Young was not happy with the popularity of California and saw it as more of a drawback than a positive influence on his power and the strength of the LDS Church. It was inevitable that the official position of the Church would be to disavow support for the San Bernardino settlement. From the very beginning, Young had expressed displeasure with the idea of San Bernardino, and his opposition grew over the years (Lyman 1996, Chapter Eight, 371-431).

As 1857 approached and the Reformation peaked, the feelings about the viability of the remote settlements began to spread beyond just the Church hierarchy. Following a meeting of the territorial legislature in Salt Lake City in December 1856, the bishop of Nephi, Jacob Bigler, reported back to his fellow Mormons that "The Saints in Carson [Genoa, Nevada] and Sanbernidino [sic] are called to Come Home. . ." (Bigler 1998, 129-130). Whether this was his own interpretation of the events of the Reformation or an expression of the feelings of higher Church authorities is not clear, but in this case, it foretold the future for the Mormon Settlements in and near California.

By early 1857, the apostles Amasa Lyman and Charles C. Rich had been in California for nearly six years, a long time for the two Church leaders to be occupied on such a singular mission. The community was established and flourishing, the local infrastructure and government was in place and effective even though there was some local dissent from non-Mormons and apostates. The ranch debt had not been paid off, in spite of the significant buy-in of Ebenezer Hanks, who invested more than $25,000 to become a full partner. Hanks had lived at Salmon Falls, very near Mormon Island, and divested his property in the northern part of the state to move to San Bernardino. In spite of the remaining financial, spiritual and administrative needs of the settlement, Brigham Young recalled both Lyman and Rich to Utah in early 1857 to attend to other Church matters and prepare for European missions. William J. Cox, the stake president, became the ranking Mormon in the community, and Hanks was in charge of the ranch.

The approach of Johnston's Army to Utah and the possibility of armed conflict probably became known to the more senior Mormon officials, including Jefferson Hunt, by August 1st. Certainly, by September 1st, the information had come to all San Bernardino residents, and there was probably general anxiety and confusion about what might happen. Some, especially those most committed to the Church, expected to be recalled to Utah, or wished to go there to assist their friends, family and faith. Others may have viewed the pending events with fear and trepidation. Most considered a recall to Utah to be in effect and prepared to leave California.

Brigham Young and Church officials made it known that those returning to Utah should remain in the southern part of the territory, since Salt Lake City and other locations in the north were going to be evacuated. They also put out a call for arms and ammunition to be sent from California, and a number of the California brethren responded with money and supplies to bolster Utah should armed confrontation be unavoidable. Many wagonloads of arms and supplies were shipped north along the trail.

In spite of the possible recall or departure of many of the Saints, the Church officials and residents still felt obliged to settle the debts incurred in buying the ranch and founding the colony. Historian Leo Lyman says that:

> "During an August meeting Cox requested that fifty settlers make good on a previous promise that if necessary they would 'pay for the whole of the ranch.' Assemblyman Jefferson Hunt, perhaps in a sincere effort to bolster their resolve, made a speech that insulted Brother Gale and number of others, creating a situation serious enough that Cox intervened, saying he had convened the meeting and presumed he could 'get through it' without abusing anyone. Hunt thereupon removed his name from the list of those committed to assist as promised, which in turn elicited comment that a half dozen others had made greater pledges than he. The incident clearly alienated a number of participating brethren from the longtime assemblyman, and stake president Cox soon requested that Hunt be reassigned to a Utah location for his own benefit" (Lyman, 1996, 380).

Lyman believes that this incident led many to support those who wished to replace Hunt in the Assembly.

In addition, the dissident apostates and non-Mormons called for a meeting with the Mormon leaders to agree on a ticket for county officers that both sides could support. It was held on August 15th and a slate of candidates was agreed to (Beattie & Beattie, 1939, 276). It is possible that this conference agreed to replace Hunt in the Assembly. In any case, Hunt did not run in the September 1st election. The newly-elected Assemblyman for the district was Dr. Isaac Smith, who had previously purchased Pauline Weaver's ranch and claimed to be a cousin of Joseph Smith, but was not a member of the LDS Church (Lyman 1996, 381).

On September 9th, Richard Hopkins wrote to Rich in Utah about the election and Dr. Smith. He included the following comments about Hunt:

"The old Captain or I should have said General was considerable discontented and in his way used his influence against us. Though his influence has greatly declined since your departure. But when he found the work did not stop if he was not sent to the legislature he turned around and voted the ticket. Though the old man thinks our influence in the north is gone. (I presume departed with his greatness)" (Rich Papers).

While possible, it is not likely that Hunt was forced out of office by those who opposed him. It was more likely that he chose not to run for re-election. He was probably aware of the pending recall and had already been summoned to return to Utah, or had already decided to return on his own. Horace Rolfe recorded that:

"It was thought by many that the reason General Hunt did not run for the assembly at the last preceding election was because he had a foreknowledge of the general breakup that was soon to take place, but which did not seem to be generally known among the church members previous to the actual 'counsel' which came from their headquarters to that effect" (Beattie and Beattie, 1939, 288).

Hunt's long-time friend, Charles Rich, along with Amasa Lyman, had already left for Utah, and true to his strong faith and his religion, Hunt probably felt that he would be more useful and comfortable in Utah. If he continued in San Bernardino, he knew he would be accepted, but he also knew that he would soon be living in an area mostly populated by non-Mormons. His history at Far West and Nauvoo, with the Mormon Battalion, and at Fort Utah and San Bernardino indicates that he probably felt that a return to Utah was the most appropriate thing to do. Unfortunately, his return would separate him from some of his children.

Hunt's political legacy in California was a success. If we are to presume, as the evidence indicates, that he was assigned by Brigham Young or Rich and Lyman to represent the Mormon community in politics, then he did very well. His initial attendance at the division of the state convention followed by his brief term on the first Los Angeles County Board of Supervisors established his, and consequently Mormon, credibility among the non-Mormon residents of Southern California. In his freshman year in the legislature, he succeeded in forming the expansive San Bernardino County which gave local Mormon leaders control over their settlement and the northeastern approaches to it from the eastern boundary of the state. And his subsequent reelections and seniority status in the Assembly reinforced his influence during a time of instability in California politics his appointment as a brigadier general in the militia responsible for the southernmost and most threatened and lawless section of the state was a further result of his political activities. In all, these activities caused him to be away from his family and business affairs for a total of almost two and a half years, but his personal sacrifice greatly enhanced the cause of the Southern California Mormons and contributed to the family's financial stability.

Although no longer in the Legislature, Jefferson Hunt still played a role in Democratic Party politics. The *Los Angeles Star* newspaper reported on August 1, 1857, the proceedings of the party convention to select a candidate for State Senator for District 1 which was composed of San Bernardino, Los Angeles and San Diego counties (Los Angeles Star, August 1, 1857). Hunt held a proxy and was a member of the San Bernardino delegation. It was challenged by a group of independents, and there followed a two hour discussion during which delegates from both sides were asked about their voting in the prior presidential election. Eventually, a compromise was reached, and six members of the Hunt delegation, including Hunt himself, and two of the independents were seated.

Cameron Thom of Los Angeles was nominated for the state senate seat and after a considerable break for discussion, Hunt also nominated Cave Coutts of San Diego. A vote was taken and Thom was selected as the candidate; the vote split along county lines with the independents voting with Los Angeles County delegates. Hunt was one of four men appointed to the District Central Committee.

Also that summer, the *Los Angeles Star* reported that Hunt delivered an oration at the Fourth of July celebration held in the newly-completed bowery that could hold 1,000 people. On that same day, John Hunt married Lois Pratt, the daughter of Hunt family friends, Addison and Louisa Pratt. The *Star* also reported on August 8th that a forest fire had been burning for two weeks in the mountains above San Bernardino. The fire had "consumed about 3,000 acres of timber, and reaching the vicinity of Capt. Hunt's mill destroyed saw logs and lumber to the value of about $3,000" (Los Angeles Star, August 8, 1857). In the 1850s, little could be done to fight large forest fires; effective firefighting equipment did not exist. We don't know the extent of this fire or how long it burned, but Hunt's mill was not destroyed.

The *Los Angeles Star* seems to have taken a deferential approach to reporting and editorializing about events in Utah and San Bernardino. For example, the August 29th issue mentioned the troubles in Utah and anticipated the arrival of federal troops. The same issue also commented about Cannon's recent defense of polygamy in the *Standard*, and then stated that Utah would not be admitted to the Union as long as polygamy existed. On the other hand, the *Star* simply did not discuss similar issues that were undoubtedly known to exist in San Bernardino. Several of the more prominent Saints in San Bernardino, including Hunt, were polygamists, and that fact was probably known both inside and outside the community. The San Bernardino Saints were good neighbors who provided economic, agricultural and military support to all of

Southern California and were, therefore, exempt from the same criticism that was levied against the Utah Saints.

By early October, word of the Mountain Meadows Massacre had reached Los Angeles from other travelers who had followed the Baker/Fancher party on the trail. The *Los Angeles Star* published a full report in its October 17th edition, quoting two travelers who had surprisingly accurate information about Mormon involvement, especially considering the cover-up that was being carefully crafted in Utah. The *Star* also reported on a mass meeting that was held in Los Angeles on October 12th and 13th to discuss the massacre and its consequences. A resolution was passed which called on the President to take "prompt measures. . . for the punishment of the authors of the recent appalling and wholesale butchery of innocent men, women and children." It also noted that San Bernardino was largely populated by Mormons "many of whom are living in open violation of one of the most important and sacred laws [polygamy] of our State," and called on the governor "to enforce its laws upon the people." Finally, the attendees offered "to respond to the call of the proper authorities, to assist, if necessary, in enforcing obedience to the laws" (Los Angeles Star, October 17, 1857).

The *Daily Alta California* in San Francisco, on October 27, 1857, printed a letter from a correspondent in Los Angeles who used the pseudonym of "Yo Mismo" (myself). The article described the reports about the Mountain Meadows Massacre coming in from Utah by those who followed the Baker/Fancher wagon train. One of those quoted extensively was George Powers from Little Rock, Arkansas. He said:

> "Whilst in San Bernardino, I heard many persons express gratification at the massacre. At the church services, on Sunday, Capt. Hunt occupied the pulpit, and, among other things he said that the hand of the Lord was in it: whether it was done by the white or red skins, it was right! The prophecies concerning Missouri were being fulfilled, and they would all be accomplished" (Daily Alta California, October 27, 1857).

At the end of the same article, the correspondent also said:

"I nearly omitted to tell you that I am informed by a person who saw the document, that Capt. Hunt, of San Bernardino, has written by this steamer to the Governor, for rifles and ammunition to *suppress insurrection* [emphasis as printed] in that county, and also to fight Indians! This is all pretence. All the rifles and ammunition they receive are instantly forwarded to Salt Lake, where the majority of these people are expected soon to depart" (Daily Alta California, October 27, 1857).

Even with the angry attitude shown against the Utah Saints, the reaction of the Southern Californians to their San Bernardino neighbors was relatively mild. The *Star* continued to report San Bernardino news and there was no further mention of disobedience by the Saints in San Bernardino. The November 7, *Star* reported that the mail had arrived in San Bernardino from Salt Lake City, carried by John Hunt and John Mayfield (who married Hunt's daughter, Harriet, in 1859), who had left Salt Lake City on October 5th and arrived on October 30th after twenty-four days on the trail.

But as 1857 drew to a close, many of the loyal Mormon residents of San Bernardino heeded Brigham Young's call to return, and many others were making the final preparations to join them in Utah.

While Hunt was no longer in the legislature, he was still a Brigadier General in the California Militia and had duties to do before departure. San Bernardino had militia units from the very start, but in 1855, pursuant to a decision of the state attorney general, they reorganized and the San Bernardino Mounted Rangers under the command of Andrew Lytle and the San Bernardino Rough and Ready was organized. That same year, both units deployed men in response to incidents. Indian problems sent men from the Rough and Ready to Warner's Ranch; the Rangers to the San Gorgonio Pass area. While it does not appear that Hunt ever took command of a field unit, he was responsible for the overall command and administration of these units and all others in the three most southern counties.

Late in 1857 and in early 1858, there was much interest in California in the formation of additional units to support federal troops in Utah or to avenge the deaths at Mountain Meadow. In his 1857 report, General Kibbe, the Quartermaster General and Adjutant General of the California Militia, stressed the need for more funding, weapons and supplies and cited the seriousness of the Utah situation. However, "although he was undoubtedly seriously concerned about providing aid in the Utah situation, he was perhaps more interested in bolstering the position of the California militia" (Dayton 1951, 131).

As one of his final acts as a general officer, Hunt sent Kibbe a memo on August 1, 1857, which reads in part: "Enclosed you will please find a bill for services rendered in this county by the San Bernardino Rangers. This bill is made out at a low figure. . ." (State Archives, 1857). At some point after this, Hunt resigned his commission, but having been duly appointed and served as a general officer, he retained the honor of being addressed as "General Hunt" for the remainder of his life.

Those who were leaving San Bernardino disposed of the property they had worked so hard to purchase, build and develop. But because of the flood of property on the market and the realization by purchasers that the sellers had little recourse, the prices plummeted and most were forced to sell at a steep discount from actual worth. *Alta California* estimated that homes and property were sold for about a quarter of their actual value. Hanks sold the San Bernardino ranch for $18,000 even though it was worth closer to $100,000. The irony of these moves was that Amasa Lyman had written a letter to the San Bernardino Saints advising them not to "sacrifice their property" and that the Utah troubles would likely be resolved (Alta California, January 12, 1858).

Hunt sold his property and his interest in the saw mill. He received $2,500 for the sawmill, which was worth $25,000 (Smith 1958, 176). According to the *Alta California*, Hunt and his family were among the last to leave San Bernardino. They reported that:

"He was strongly opposed to the breaking up of the settlement, wishing earnestly to remain and enjoy the pleasant homes which their industry had built up. But the order was regarded as peremptory, and he preferred to sacrifice his property and his enjoyments to illustrate his faith in his prophets" (Alta California, January 12, 1858).

For the third time since he joined the LDS Church, Hunt fled his home and suffered severe financial losses. However, as he had in the past, he would again find stability and prosperity.

Not all of Hunt's family left San Bernardino. His married daughters, Nancy Daley and Jane Stoddard, and their families remained behind, as did his unmarried daughter, Harriet, now twenty (Smith 1958, 176). These daughters would provide a California base for the Hunt family for the rest of the century.

Throughout November and December 1857, hundreds of returning Mormons gathered at Sycamore Grove where they had first camped on the initial colonizing trip six years before. Wagon trains were then formed and the Saints aided one another on the journey to Utah. Among those joining them was a "Dr. Osborne," who, in reality, was Colonel Thomas Kane. He had assisted the Mormons eleven years before when they had appealed to President Polk for assistance in moving West. Kane was on a mission from President Buchanan, also a friend of his, to try to resolve the troubles in Utah.

The Hunts left San Bernardino on January 1, 1858. By January 8th, they were at the Mojave River, which they followed until January 14th. By January 20, they were in "camp at the headwaters of saleratus creek. Called Amagasia [sic]" (Crosby Journal, January 20, 1858). Here, according to diarist Caroline Barnes Crosby who was traveling in the same party as the Hunts, Jefferson Hunt repaired a badly broken wagon wheel that had been damaged in the Amargosa Canyon. The next day, three of Hunt's sons traveled twelve miles to retrieve some cached goods. When they returned on January 22nd, they reported that most of the goods had been dug up and taken by someone else. The cache was likely along the Kingston Cutoff, which was frequently used by the Hunts while carrying the mail. The party remained in camp, probably along Willow Creek in China Ranch, for three days resting their stock following the difficult drive to fresh water. Crosby reported they had a difficult ascent out of the Amargosa Canyon and then a very muddy descent to Resting Spring. Hunt had to rescue several of the wagons that got stuck.

After several more days feeding their stock at Resting Spring, the party moved on and reached the springs at Las Vegas on January 31st, and again rested before heading across the long desert to the Muddy. They arrived at their destination of Parowan, Utah Territory, sometime late in February. The family remained in Parowan for some months, where Hunt's wife, Matilda, gave birth to James Franklin Hunt on May 7th. Hunt appears to have returned to Southern California on a trading and/or mail trip during the Spring.

Jefferson Hunt's six and one-half years in San Bernardino and California were both rewarding and productive. His family grew and matured; he prospered financially; and he achieved political leadership, becoming the second most senior member of the lower house of the legislature. He was respected by both Mormons and non-Mormons, and served his Church and his regional community well. He gained general officer status in the state military and was recognized by many Californians as one of the original pioneers who helped develop California and bring it into the Union.

Ironically, in California today, he is remembered most for guiding the wagon train from which the Death Valley '49ers, in spite of his warnings of looming disaster, left several months before entering Death Valley. His other contributions, such as the successful presence of the Mormon Battalion during the Mexican War or the creation of San Bernardino County are remembered only by a few. Hunt's contributions to California's pioneer history are much greater than commonly recognized.

Epilogue

The Hunt family stayed in Parowan for a period of time following their arrival in Utah. This was a result of the major evacuation of Salt Lake City following the approach of Johnston's Army. Many of the residents left their homes and traveled to the southern settlements. Thus, Parowan was seen as a safe and secure stopping place for many leaving San Bernardino.

By May 30, 1858, Hunt was again in northern Utah. According to the *Journal History of the Church*:

> "Messrs. Clarkson and Booky, of San Francisco, in company with Jefferson Hunt and Robt. Cliff [Clift] called upon the President [Young]. Mr. Clarkson said the proposition to sell Mosquito Coast was known to Pres. Buchanan, and all operations of the army were suspended, until the result of Mr. Cooper's mission was ascertained, as it was expected we would accede to the proposition; he believed that government would give us 12 to 12 [sic] million dollars and pay our transportation, as they had spent eight million dollars now, to no purpose, in the war against us" (Journal History, May 30, 1858).

At that time, an American named William Walker was filibustering—or attempting to control—Nicaragua. Walker had previously been unsuccessful in trying to gain control over Baja California, and had made several unsuccessful attempts in Nicaragua. Very likely, "Clarkson and Booky" were associates of Walker and were trying to get federal support for their efforts by having the Mormons move en mass to the Mosquito Coast of Nicaragua. They had probably enlisted the aid of Hunt and his friend from the Battalion and San Bernardino, Robert Clift, to gain access to Brigham Young—who wisely rejected the overture.

Johnston's Army had been forced to spend the Winter of 1857-58 at the burned-out Fort Bridger. Alfred Cumming, President Buchanan's choice to replace Brigham Young as governor of Utah Territory, arrived there under the escort of Colonel Philip St. George Cooke. After some negotiations between the Army and the Mormons, which were in part facilitated by Thomas Kane, Cumming was allowed to enter Salt Lake City and assume his office in April 1858. The main part of the Army, however, remained at Fort Bridger until a full agreement between the Mormons and the government was reached.

Buchanan created a two-man commission to go to Utah and negotiate with the Mormons in hopes of settling the crisis. Brigham Young created his own commission to assist him in negotiations. On this team were ten or so of the most prominent men in Salt Lake City, including Amasa Lyman, Charles Rich and Jefferson Hunt. As the highest ranking Mormon in the Mormon Battalion, a veteran California politician and a Brigadier General in the California militia, Hunt was a logical choice since he was known to some of the federal officials and Army offices.

On the evening of June 10th, Young and his delegation briefly met with the federal commissioners and invited them to a meeting the following day. On June 11th, the groups met formally and discussed how the situation could be resolved. A number of speakers, including Hunt, addressed the issues on both sides (Journal History of the Church, June 11, 1858). The following day, another meeting was held, and an agreement was reached wherein the government issued a pardon to the Mormons. The troops would be permitted to encamp in a non-populated area. The Utah War had been peaceably resolved.

On June 26th, Johnston's Army rode through Salt Lake City en route to Camp Floyd in Cedar Valley (not the same Cedar Valley at Cedar City), west of Utah Lake. As they moved through a nearly deserted city, the *Journal History of the LDS Church* states that Philip St. George Cooke "passed through the City with his head uncovered as a token of his respect for the Mormon Battalion" (Journal History, June 27, 1858).

Cooke was promoted to Brigadier General during the Civil War and wrote the first Army manual for the cavalry. His son-in-law was the noted Confederate General Jeb Stuart. Albert Sidney Johnston resigned from the Army at the start of the Civil War and became a high-ranking general in the

Confederate Army. At the Battle of Shiloh, Johnston faced the troops of Union General Andrew Jackson Smith, the Lieutenant who had commanded the Mormon Battalion. During the battle, Johnston was fatally wounded.

Since Hunt had suffered a substantial financial loss when he fled San Bernardino, it appears that he continued carrying the mail and also went into the freighting business to earn money. Settling at a new farm was not yet an option because of the uncertainty of the Utah War and the displacement of the residents of Salt Lake Valley. In September 1858, Hunt was reported to have been exploring a new freight or stage route to Nevada and California that would be 150 miles shorter than the common one. He explored the Goose Creek area of present-day Nevada, very near where the current states of Utah, Nevada and Idaho meet (Thompson and West 1881, 104). The Oregon Trail went through that area, and it is likely that he was trying to find a shorter way to that trail from the Salt Lake Valley.

In late September or early October, Hunt and Dr. Forney, the recently appointed federal Indian Agent for Utah, were camped with the Shoshones at Gravelly Ford, about forty miles west of present-day Elko, Nevada. The report from a mail carrier said that Forney and Hunt had successfully negotiated an agreement with the Indians and that the mail and travelers would be safer (Thompson and West 1881, 104-105).

On October 30th, General Daniel Wells of the Nauvoo Legion in Salt Lake City met with Dr. Forney and was told that he had met with 1,500 Indians, had given them presents and was told that they would stop killing whites (Journal History, October 30, 1848). The next day, Jefferson Hunt met with Brigham Young and had a different take on Forney's meetings with the Indians. He told Young that Forney "had made the Indians on the Humboldt many promises that he would never fulfill" (Journal History of the Church, October 31, 1858). From these conversations, it appears that Hunt and Forney traveled together both to explore a new route and to settle the Indian issue along the Northern Route to California.

Enlistments were ending in Johnston's Army. Generally, the Mormons regarded the soldiers as rough and undisciplined and wanted no part of them in the area. For their part, the discharged soldiers wanted to go to California. Some soldiers had already been discharged and traveled West over the Northern Route, but more were scheduled for discharge soon. A group of quartermaster troops, which would have included teamsters and freighters, was scheduled to be discharged on November 1st. They were considered to be even worse that the regular soldiers. Governor Cumming was trying to find someone to guide them to California, and a man named Dodson—probably Peter Dotson, the United States Marshall assigned to Salt Lake City—offered to do that for fifty dollars for each man who walked, or seventy-five if they had to be provided with a ride (Journal History of the Church, October 28, 1858). The Army could not accept such a prohibitively expensive proposition.

Brigham Young met with General Johnston the following day and this was apparently one of the topics they discussed. Young brought the subject up to Jefferson Hunt during their meeting. Hunt discussed a rumor that Judge Eckels and others wanted the Army to remain in Cedar Valley so that they could contain the Mormons to the valley and then attack them when Winter snows came (Journal History of the Church, October 31, 1858). While not true, it does show the fears that the Mormons had of the large number of troops in their midst. And with Winter fast approaching, it was imperative for the Mormons to get the discharged troops out of the area as fast as possible, and that would have to be along the Southern Route.

Hunt told Young that he had met 500 troops on his recent trip along the Humboldt and that they were "in a state of starvation." According to the *Journal History of the LDS Church*, Young gave Hunt specific orders: "The President [Brigham Young] told Capt. Hunt to get up trains and carry the discharged soldiers to California" (Journal History, October 31, 1858).

Just as in 1849, Young called on Hunt to rid the Valley of the Great Salt Lake of unwanted visitors. As before, this called for Hunt to guide them along the safer Winter route on the trail to Southern California. The Hunt family apparently then drew up and implemented a plan to carry out Young's instructions. As the troops, teamsters and freighters were discharged, many of them began the exodus from Utah. A few went to Salt Lake City and caused some turmoil there, about 100 were seen heading East toward the States through Provo Canyon and about 200 were noted passing through Cedar City on their way to California (Journal History of the Church, November 10 & 12, 1858).

Gilbert Hunt, now thirty-three years old, went to Camp Floyd and made arrangements to conduct 100 wagons to California for ten dollars each, the same arrangement made by his father with the '49ers nearly a decade earlier. Hunt's biographer, Pauline Udall Smith, writes that on November 13th, Gilbert was at Camp Floyd, collected the money and made final arrangements for the departure. On his way home that night or early the next morning he was ambushed and murdered; the money, presumably about $1,000, was stolen (Smith 1958, 187).

The *Deseret News*, however, reported Gilbert's death differently. The November 17th edition reported:

> "Sudden Death by Accident.— On Saturday last Gilbert Hunt, son of the Hon. Jefferson Hunt, left this city with passengers to California by the southern route. He had not driven far out of the city, when by some accident he fell from the wagon, and his head struck the ground, bending his neck shortly and severely towards his breast. He was raised from the ground and drove on to Cottonwood, where his family resides, but was unable to proceed any further. He suffered much pain from the fall. The greatest care and attention were shown to him by his friends, but in the course of a few hours he expired. He is reported as being a young man well respected" (Deseret News, November 17, 1858).

Whether his death was by accident or murder, the impact on the Hunt family was tremendous. He left his wife, Lydia, and five children.

Gilbert had been more than Hunt's eldest and first-born son; he was his business partner, confidant and friend. He had been the adult male responsible for the family at El Pueblo, accompanied his father and brothers on the supply expedition to California during the Winter of 1847-48, and had run the family businesses in San Bernardino when his father began his political efforts While two other of Jefferson's children preceded Gilbert in death, it was his death that hit Hunt the hardest.

There is no indication of when or how the veterans Gilbert was to guide to California left, but throughout 1858-1859 large numbers of veterans and military contractors departed for California and Eastern states from the Valley of the Great Salt Lake.

Sometime during that Winter, Hunt traveled to Washington D.C. and met with President Buchanan. The details of the trip are sparse, and there is no apparent record in the Buchanan papers indicating a meeting. But on June 26, 1859, the *Journal History of the LDS Church* recorded that: "A letter was read from Gen. Jeff Hunt, dated Philadelphia to C.C. Rich; he had visited Prest. Buchanan and had a long conversation with him. The President insulted him and he in turn insulted the President, but come to amicable terms and parted with the President's blessing" (Journal History, June 26, 1859).

Later that year, the *Journal History of the LDS Church* recorded a clipping from the *Deseret News* that read:

> "Arrived. – On Thursday last, Daniel Davis with a small train of merchandise; on Friday, [October 7, 1859] M.J. Snedeker and Gen. J. Hunt with four or five wagons each, and on yesterday, A.R. Wright with a train of eight wagons arrived from the States, all well and in good condition" (Journal History, October 11, 1859).

For his letter from Philadelphia to have arrived in Salt Lake City by June 26th, it would have been written during the first weeks or May, or even earlier since the mail would have taken forty-five days or longer to travel that distance by river and overland. For Hunt to have traveled to the Capital, he probably left early in the year, and since Winter conditions prevailed across the mountains and plains, he may well have traveled to California and then by ship to Panama, where he crossed the Isthmus and then traveled by ship to the Gulf or East Coast. In any case, it was a major trip for him to take.

The reason for the journey is uncertain. Some have maintained it was to discuss the Indian conditions and hostilities along the trail. Or the trip may have been to secure federal mail or freight contracts. But a more likely reason was to discuss the state of affairs that resulted in his son's death—what Hunt probably believed was further unwarranted persecution of the Mormons by undisciplined troops serving under governmental authority and as ordered by President Buchanan.

But true to his work as a freighter, he capitalized on the journey to return with four or five wagons of badly-need merchandise to be sold in Salt Lake City. Once again, his entrepreneurial spirit was used to capitalize on an otherwise difficult situation.

Jefferson Hunt continued as a freighter following his return from the East. Late in December 1859, Hunt again went to California on a freighting trip, taking his son, John, along. He returned to Provo by May 2, 1860, with about five wagons of merchandise (Journal History of the Church, May 2, 1860). That summer, the Hunt families relocated to Ogden. From there, Hunt went east into the Wasatch Mountains about fifteen miles and settled in a valley along the Ogden River. There he founded the community of Huntsville, Utah—today the home of the Snowbasin Resort, a 2002 Olympic venue. Hunt also maintained a home in nearby Ogden, where his wife, Celia, lived and their daughter, Mary, attended school (Smith 1958, 190).

On Pioneer Day, July 24, 1860, which celebrated the arrival of the pioneers in Salt Lake City in 1847, Hunt was the "orator of the day" at the celebration in Ogden (Journal History of the Church, July 24, 1860). During his absence and on that same day, his wife, Matilda, gave birth to her sixth child, in Huntsville. This newest member of the Hunt family was aptly named Liberty Independence Hunt in honor of the day and month of his birth (Smith 1958, 256).

Hunt spoke at the General Conference on April 7, 1861. He was the final speaker before the concluding blessing, benediction and adjournment.

According to the minutes of the Conference: "Elder Jefferson Hunt made a few enlivening and interesting remarks" (Journal History of the Church, April 7, 1861). In 1861, and again in 1863, Hunt attended reunions of the Mormon Battalion and gave talks at each. By then, the general attitude toward the Battalion had changed and the members were honored and their accomplishments recognized. An experienced politician, Hunt also served in the Territorial legislature representing Weber County.

In September 1861, Mary Hunt, the last born of Celia's children, married and set up her own home. For thirty-six years, Celia had been raising her children—much of the time under very difficult circumstances. In the Fall of 1864, she accompanied Hunt on a freighting trip to San Bernardino where she could visit her three daughters and their families, including fifteen grandchildren (Smith 1958, 196-7). For much of the rest of her life, she spent time visiting her children and grandchildren in Utah, Arizona and California.

In 1865, Hunt decided to relocate, this time to an area in the upper part of the Cache Valley near Oxford in present-day Idaho. Matilda was almost due to give birth and was left with Joseph Hunt and his family in Millville, Utah, just south of present-day Logan. On October 22, she delivered twin girls. But the birth did not go well and Matilda died shortly after. One of the twins died very shortly after that (Smith 1958, 201). Sophronia, now seventeen, assumed much of the responsibility for raising her seven siblings.

The extended Hunt families soon numbered five married children plus the younger children and grandchildren. The Hunts needed more land to farm and ranch, and moved to a point about nine miles north, called Red Rock Pass, while still maintaining their home in Oxford (Smith 1958, 203). Hunt probably didn't understand the full geological significance of the land at his new home. Later geologists determined that this point exactly on the northern rim of the Great Basin was where ancient Lake Bonneville overflowed and discharged a massive amount of water into the Snake/Columbia River Basins about 15,000 years ago. For a brief period of time, this was probably the largest river in the world.

In 1875, further troubles befell the Hunt family. Joseph Hunt had divorced his wife and moved to Beaver, where his brother, John, was sheriff. Joseph and two other men were arrested for murder following a barroom brawl during which a man was shot when Joseph's revolver discharged as he was trying to hit the man with the weapon. Although Joseph was eventually acquitted of the charge of murder, he was held in the territorial prison in Salt Lake City while awaiting trial in the Spring of 1876.

Also in the prison at that time was John D. Lee, who had been arrested in 1874 for his role in the Mountain Meadows Massacre. At his first trial in 1875, he went before a Territorial judge and a jury composed of eight Mormons, one apostate, and three non-Mormons. Brigham Young provided the financial support for Lee's defense. The Mormons on the jury understood that Young was in full support of Lee. As a result, the jury deadlocked nine to three for acquittal.

Lee was returned to the territorial prison to await his second trial. It was during this period that Lee saw Joseph Hunt, who was being held in prison pending his upcoming trial. In his diary, Lee refers to Joseph on several occasions and once asked for Joseph to be placed on a work crew headed by Lee that planted fifteen bushels of seed potatoes at the prison farm.

Soon, a new United States Attorney was assigned to Utah Territory, and the following year he reached an unwritten agreement with Young which provided that only Lee would be prosecuted for the massacre and the Church would cooperate. The second trial began on September 11, 1876, nineteen years to the day of the start of the massacre.

During the trial, several prominent Mormons testified about Lee's involvement, and the all-Mormon jury understood that Lee no longer had Brigham Young's protection. Lee was convicted on September 20, 1876, after less than four hours of jury deliberation, and sentenced to die. He chose to be shot. The execution was carried out at the scene of the massacre on March 23, 1877; he was shot by a firing squad as he sat on the edge of his own coffin.

Whether Lee was *the* principle organizer of the massacre or whether he was "only" a major participant has been clouded with time. Lee maintained that his actions at Mountain Meadows simply followed the directions given by Young and the Church leaders in Southern Utah. What is certain is that Lee's role was significant in that he led both the Indians and many of the Mormons in the attack. Scapegoat or not, Lee was to a large extent responsible for the emigrants' murder.

Those interested should read historian Will Bagley's definitive book on the Mountain Meadows Massacre entitled *Blood of the Prophets*. Bagley writes:

> "Blustering and dictatorial, John D. Lee could be a hard man to like. When the 1848 emigration had assembled on the Elkhorn River, Lee had 'hard work to raise his 50,' Hosea Stout noted. 'The people do not like to go with him.' Lee was an aggressive, relentless personality and a mass of contradictions. His generosity was legendary, but he could be a ruthless businessman. 'He was kind to his wives, a generous father, full of high spirits, and very fond of his numerous family,' John Steele said. But Lee's reputation as a braggart and sexual predator dogged him. An apostate who knew him well characterized Lee as 'a man who would divide his last biscuit with the traveler upon the desert, and cut that traveler's throat the next hour if Brigham Young said so'" (Bagley 2002, 53).

Six months later, on August 29, Brigham Young died at his home in Salt Lake City. He was succeeded by John Taylor as President of the LDS Church. At this time, George Q. Cannon, Taylor's nephew, was the territorial representative to Congress. He was a member of the Quorum of the Twelve Apostles for eighteen years and served twenty-three years as a member of the First

Presidency of the LDS Church. At the time of his death, he was next in line to
become President of the Church.

Jefferson Hunt died from cancer at his home on his ranch on May 11,
1879. He was buried at a site he had selected next to Red Rock Knoll. Today,
Hunt's grave is well-marked, and other family members are buried in the same
plot. The family placed a monument to Hunt atop Red Rock; another sign
near the road explains the geological importance of the area. Other monuments and signs pertaining to Hunt are located in Huntsville and along Interstate 15, south of Beaver. Another commemorating the Hunt Wagon Train of
1849 and the split of the Death Valley '49ers is located along the Old Spanish
Trail, about six miles northeast of Enterprise, Utah, and just a few miles north
of the Southern Rim of the Great Basin.

Celia spent her remaining years with John in Snowflake, Arizona, and
with her daughters in San Bernardino. She died in San Bernardino on December 28, 1896, at the age of ninety-one. She is buried in the pioneer cemetery
there, not far from her original San Bernardino home.

Some insight into Jefferson Hunt can be gained from excerpts from a
letter from Samantha Brimhall Foley to Lois Hunt West, John's daughter and
Hunt's granddaughter, describing her memories of him in Idaho (Smith 1958,
206-207):

> ". . . Captain was not an old man then. He was tall, stately, with
> sharp features, a forceful character. The very air and even the
> earth seemed to move as he went on his way about his work.
> Stern, kindly hearted, all the elements of a warrior and of a
> home man, a kindly husband and father were blended in his
> nature . . . ."

". . . He was noble but not proud. He was a natural orator, con-
vincing, with an overflow of well spoken language. As to Church
history, he seemed to know every step of Church history from
the beginning. He voice was often heard at celebrations of the
Fourth and Twenty-fourth of July. He was a high Priest and
magnified his office with great dignity . . . ."

Bibliography

Abbreviations

Bancroft Library *The Bancroft Library, University of California, Berkeley*

LDS Archives *Church History Department, The Church of Jesus Christ of Latter-day Saints, Salt Lake City, Utah*

The Huntington Library *Henry E. Huntington Library, San Marino, California*

Alta California. San Francisco: 1851-1857

Appendix to Assembly Journal, 6th Session 1855. Sacramento: State Printing Office, 1855.

Arrington, Leonard J. *Brigham Young: American Moses.* New York: Alfred A. Knopf, 1985.

Arrington, Leonard J. "Mississippi Mormons." *Ensign*, June, 1977.

Babcock, Leonard. Leonard Babcock Reminiscences, with Letter to the History Co. BANC MSS C-D 789, The Bancroft Library.

Bagley, Will. *The Pioneer Camp of the Saints.* Spokane: The Arthur H. Clark Company, 1997.

Bagley, Will. *Scoundrel's Tale: The Samuel Brannan Papers.* Spokane: The Arthur H. Clark Company, 1999.

Bagley, Will. *Blood of the Prophets.* Norman: University of Oklahoma Press, 2002.

Bagley, Will. *So Rugged and Mountainous: Blazing the Trails to Oregon and California 1812-1848.* Norman: University of Oklahoma Press, 2010.

Bancroft, Hubert Howe. *History of California Vol. VI, 1848-1859.* Santa Barbara: Wallace Hebberd, 1970.

Barton, John. *Buckskin Entrepreneur: Antoine Robidoux and the Fur Trade of the Uintah Basin, 1824-1844.* Vernal: Oakfield Publishing Company, 1996.

Battalion Correspondence: Various Letters. LDS Archives.

Bauer, K. Jack. *The Mexican War 1846-1848.* Lincoln: University of Nebraska Press, 1992.

Baugh, Alexander L. *A Call to Arms: The 1838 Mormon Defense of Northern Missouri.* Dissertation. Brigham Young University. 1996.

Bauman, Robert & Gabriele G. Carey. *Guide to the Historical Records of Los Angeles County.* Los Angeles: Los Angeles County, 1991.

Bean, James. *George Teancum Bean: Lawyer in the Old West.* Las Gatos: Jim Bean Associates, 1994.

Bean, James A. *Poorets: George Washington Bean, Mormon Pioneer of 184, Indian interpreter, explorer, judge.* Los Gatos: Jim Bean Associates, 1992.

Beattie, George William and Helen Pruitt Beattie. *Heritage of the Valley.* Pasadena: San Pasqual Press, 1939.

Bennett, Richard E., Susan Easton Black, Donald Q. Cannon. *The Nauvoo Legion in Illinois.* Norman: The Arthur H. Clark Company, 2010.

Bieber, Ralph P., Editor, in collaboration with Averam B. Bender. *Exploring Southwestern Trails 1846-1854 by Philip St. George Cooke, William Henry Chase Whiting, Francois Xavier Aubry.* Glendale: The Arthur H. Clark Company, 1938.

Biggs, Donald C. *Conquer and Colonize: Stevenson's Regiment and California,* San Rafael: Presidio Press, 1977.

Bigler, David L. *Forgotten Kingdom: The Mormon Theocracy in the American West 1847-1869.* Spokane: The Arthur H. Clark Company, 1998.

Bigler, David L. and Will Bagley. *Army of Israel: Mormon Battalion Narratives.* Spokane: The Arthur H. Clark Company, 2000.

Bigler, David L. and Azariah Smith. *The Gold Rush Journal of Azariah Smith.* Salt Lake City: University of Utah Press, 1990.

Bigler, Henry W. Journal 1849-1850. HM57022, The Huntington Library.

"Biographical Sketch of Jefferson Hunt." MSS SC 410, Harold B. Lee Library. Brigham Young University.

Blackburn, Abner, and Will Bagley, Editor. *Frontiersman: Abner Blackburn's Narrative.* Salt Lake City: University of Utah Press, 1992.

Broadhead, Edward. *Fort Pueblo.* Pueblo: Pueblo Historical Society, 1995.

Brooks, Juanita. *John Doyle Lee.* Glendale: The Arthur H. Clark Company, 1973.

Brooks, Juanita, Editor. *On the Mormon Frontier The Diary of Hosea Stout 1844-1861.* 2 Vols. Salt Lake City: University of Utah Press, 1964.

Brooks, Juanita Editor. "Diary of the Mormon Battalion Mission." *New Mexico Historical Review* July, 1967 & October 1967. Albuquerque: University of New Mexico.

Brown, James S. *Life of a Pioneer.* Salt Lake City: Geo. Q. Cannon & Sons, 1900.

Brown, Jr., John for San Bernardino and James Boyd for Riverside. *History of San Bernardino and Riverside Counties.* Chicago: The Lewis Publishing Company, 1922.

Browning, John and Curt Gentry. *John M. Browning: American Gunmaker.* Garden City, N.Y: Doubleday & Company, Inc., 1964.

Bryant, Edwin. *What I Saw in California.* Lincoln and London: University of Nebraska Press, 1985.

Buckles, William G. *The Search for El Pueblo.* Denver: Colorado Historical Society, 2006.

Burnett, Peter H. *An Old California Pioneer.* Oakland: Biobooks, 1946.

California Voting Records. Roll 3, MF2:7 (11). California State Archives, Sacramento.

Campbell, Eugene A. "Authority Conflicts in the Mormon Battalion" from *Studies*, Vol. 8, Winter 1968, Brigham Young University.

Cannon, Donald W., and Lyndon W. Cook, eds. *Far West Record: Minutes of the Church of Jesus Christ of Latter-day Saints, 1830-1844*. Salt Lake City: Deseret Book Company,1983.

Carter, D. Robert. *Founding Fort Utah*. Provo: Provo City Corporation, 2003.

Carter, Kate B. *Heart Throbs of the West*. Salt Lake City: Daughters of Utah Pioneers, 1951.

Carter, Kate B. *The Mormon Battalion*. Salt Lake City: Daughters of Utah Pioneers, 1956.

Carvalho, Solomon N. *Incidents of Travel and Adventure in the Far West*. New York: Arno Press, 1973.

Caughey, John Walton. *Southwest from Salt Lake in 1849 and the Jacob Y. Stover Narrative*. Glendale: Reprint from Pacific Historical Review June, 1937.

Chalfant, William Y. *Dangerous Passage: The Santa Fe Trail and the Mexican War*. Norman: University of Oklahoma Press, 1994.

Christiansen, Larry D. "The Struggle for Power in the Mormon Battalion." *Dialogue: A Journal of Mormon Thought*, Vol. 26, No.4, Winter 1993.

Church Historian's Office. Journal, 1844-1879. (CR 100 1). Selected Collections, Brigham Young University, Vol. 1, DVD 17.

Clarke, Dwight L. *William Tecumseh Sherman: Gold Rush Banker*. San Francisco: California Historical Society, 1969.

Clarke, Dwight L. *Stephen Watts Kearny: Soldier of the West*. Norman: University of Oklahoma Press, 1961.

Cleland, Robert Glass. *The Cattle on a Thousand Hills*. San Marino: The Huntington Library, 1941.

Cooke, Philip St. George. *The Conquest of New Mexico and California*. Oakland: Biobooks, 1952.

Coy, Owen Cochran. *The Great Trek*. San Francisco: Powell Publishing Company, 1931.

Crosby, Caroline Barnes. Journal. In the Jonathan Crosby Papers, MSS B89, Box 3, Folder 18. Utah State History, Research Center and Collections. Salt Lake City.

Cumming, John, Editor. *Long Road to California*. Mount Pleasant: The Private Press of John Cumming, 1985.

Daily Alta California. San Francisco. 1851-1857.

Daily Evening Bulletin. San Francisco. 1856.

Daughters of Utah Pioneers. *Pioneer Women of Faith & Fortitude*. Salt Lake City: Publication Press, 1998.

Davies, J. Kenneth. *Mormon Gold*. Salt Lake City: Olympus Publishing Company, 1984.

Dawson, Joseph G. *Doniphan's Epic March*. Lawrence: University of Kansas Press, 1999.

Daynes, Kathryn M. *More Wives than One: Transformation of the Mormon Marriage System 1840-1910*. Urbana and Chicago: University of Illinois Press, 2001.

Dayton, Dello Grimmett. *The California Militia, 1850-1866*. Dissertation, University of California, Berkeley, 1951.

Dees, Harry C. "The Journal of George W. Bean." *Nevada State Historical Society Papers*, Vol. XV, Fall, 1972.

Deseret Evening News. Salt Lake City. October 7, 1905.

DeVoto, Bernard. *The Year of Decision 1846*. Boston: Houghton Mifflin Company, 1942.

Dillon, Richard. *Great Expectations: The Story of Benicia, California*. Fresno: Thomas Lithograph & Printing Co., 1980.

Donovan, Frank. *River Boats of America*. New York: Thomas Y. Crowell Company, 1966.

LeRoy R. Hafen and Ann W. Hafen. Editors. *Central Route to the Pacific*. Glendale: The Arthur H. Clark Company, 1857.

Edwards, Eddie I., Editor. *The Westerners Brand Book, Book Ten*. Los Angeles: The Westerners, Los Angeles Corral, 1963.

Egan, Howard. *Pioneering the West 1846-1878*. Richmond, Utah: 1917.

Ekins, Roger Robin. *Defending Zion: George Q. Cannon and the California Mormon Newspaper Wars of 1856-1857*. Spokane: The Arthur H. Clark Company, 2002.

Ellsworth, S. George. *The Journals of Addison Pratt*. Salt Lake City: University of Utah Press, 1990.

Ellsworth, S. George, Editor. *The History of Louisa Barnes Pratt*. Logan: Utah State University Press, 1998.

Emigrant Rosters. LDS Archives.

Emory, Lieutenant W. H., Introduction and notes by Ross Calvin, Ph.D., *Lieutenant Emory Reports*. Albuquerque: University of New Mexico Press, 1951.

Etter, Patricia A. *To California on the Southern Route 1849*, Spokane: The Arthur H. Clark Company, 1998.

Evans, John Henry. *Charles Coulson Rich: Pioneer Builder of the West*. New York: The MacMillan Co., 1936.

Faulk, Odie B. and Joseph A. Stout Jr. *The Mexican War: Changing Interpretations*. Chicago: The Swallow Press, Inc., 1973.

Fleek, Sherman L. *History May Be Searched in Vain*. Spokane: The Arthur H. Clark Company, 2006.

Franzwa, Gregory M. *Maps of the Santa Fe Trail*. St. Louis: The Patrice Press, 1989.

Franzwa, Gregory M. *The Santa Fe Trail Revisited*. St. Louis: The Patrice Press, 1989.

Fremont, John Charles, Edited by Donald Jackson and Marly Lee Spence *The Expeditions of John Charles Fremont*. Urbana, Chicago, and London: University of Illinois Press, 1970.

Blackburn, Abner, Edited by Will Bagley. *Frontiersman: Abner Blackburn's Narrative*. Salt Lake City: University of Utah Press, 1992.

General Church Minutes 1844-1879. Selected Collections, Brigham Young University, Vol. 1, DVD 18.

Gilbert, Bil. *Westering Man: The Life of Joseph Walker.* Norman: University of Oklahoma Press, 1983.

Golder, Frank Alfred *The March of the Mormon Battalion.* New York The Century Co. 1928

Granger, Lewis, LeRoy Hafen, Introduction and Notes. *Letters of Lewis Granger.* Los Angeles: Glen Dawson, 1959.

Gregg, Josiah. *Commerce of the Prairies.* Norman: University of Oklahoma Press, 1954.

Hafen, LeRoy R. and Ann W. Hafen. *Old Spanish Trail: Santa Fe to Los Angeles with Extracts from Contemporary Records and Including the Diaries of Antonio Armijo and Orville Pratt.* Glendale: The Arthur H. Clark Company, 1954.

Hafen, LeRoy R., Editor. *The Mountain Men and the Fur Trade of the Far West.* Glendale: The Arthur H. Clark Company, 10 Vols., 2000-2004.

Hafen, LeRoy R. and Ann W. Hafen. *Journals of Forty-Niners, Salt Lake to Los Angeles.* Glendale: The Arthur H. Clark Company, 1954.

Hafen, LeRoy R. and Ann W. Hafen. *The Utah Expedition 1857-1858.* Glendale: The Arthur H. Clark Company, 1958.

Hafen, LeRoy R. and Ann W. Hafen. *General Analytical Index and Supplement to the Journals of Forty-Niners Salt Lake to Los Angeles.* Glendale: The Arthur H, Clark Company, 1961.

Hammond, George P. *The Larkin Papers.* Berkeley: University of California Press, 1960.

Hancock, Charles B. "Journal of Charles B. Hancock." MS 1569. LDS Archives.

Hancock, Charles B. "Autobiography of Charles Brent Hancock." MS 5285. LDS Archives.

Hancock, Herbert A. *The saving sacrifice of the Mormon Battalion from the journals of Levi Ward Hancock.* Bystander at Large Productions, 2000.

Hansen, Klaus J. *Quest for Empire.* East Lansing: Michigan State University Press, 1967.

Hansen, Lorin K. and Lila J. Bringhust. *Let this be Zion: Mormon pioneers and modern Saints in Southern Alameda, California: from a colony of refugees in gold-rush California, to "Stakes of Zion" in a world-wide church*. Fremont: Fremont and Fremont South Stakes, 1996.

Hardesty, Donald L. *The Archaeology of the Donner Party*. Reno: University of Nevada Press, 1997.

Harlow, Neal. *California Conquered: The Annexation of a Mexican Province, 1846-1850*. Berkeley: University of California Press, 1982.

Hayes, Benjamin. *Pioneer Notes from the Diaries of Judge Benjamin Hayes 1849-1875*. Los Angeles: Privately printed, 1929 (reprint).

Hayes, Benjamin. *An Historical Sketch of Los Angeles County California*. Los Angeles: O.W. Smith, 1936 (reprint).

Heath, Dr. Steven H. "Jefferson Hunt, Bad Judgement, the 49'ers, and the Mormon Battalion." *Pioneer*, Summer, 1995. National Society of the Sons of Utah Pioneers.

Hess, John W. "With the Mormon Battalion." *Utah Historical Quarterly*, Vol. 4, No2, April, 1931.

Hill, Donna. *Joseph Smith, The First Mormon*. Garden City, N.Y.: Doubleday & Company, Inc., 1977.

History of the LDS Church. Selected Collections, Brigham Young University, Vol. 1, DVD 2 1833-1852.

Hittell, Theodore H. *History of California*, Vol. IV. San Francisco: N.J. Stone Co., 1897.

Holland, S. Dennis. *A Brief History of the Mormons in Western El Dorado County 1847-1997*. Placerville: S.D. Holland Publishing, 1997.

Hoover, Vincent A. "Gold and the Arduous Road: The Journal of Vincent A. Hoover and Other Personal Narratives of the Pioneering of the Salt Lake-Los Angeles Road in 1849." Unpublished BANC MSS 71/161 c, reel 56. The Bancroft Library. University of California, Berkeley.

Hoover, Vincent A. "Notes for a Overland Guide." Typescript. Dale Lowell Morgan papers. BANC MSS 71/161 c, reel 56. The Bancroft Library. University of California, Berkeley.

Hunt, John Addison. "Autobiography" (copy of holograph.), FAC 1435 The Huntington Library.

Hunter, J.D. "Letter to his wife Keziah." MS 2070, Folder 17. LDS Archives.

Ingersoll, Luther A. *Ingersoll's Century Annals of San Bernardino County, 1769 to 1904*. Los Angeles: L. A. Ingersoll, 1904.

Jenson, Andrew. "History of the Las Vegas Mission." *Nevada State Historical Society Papers*, Vol. 5, 1925-6.

Johnson, LeRoy and Tom Sutak. Jargon: Historians' Nemesis." *Spanish Traces: Journal of the Old Spanish Trail Association*, Autumn, 2011

Journal History of the Church. LDS Archives.

Journal of the Eighth Session of the Assembly of the State of California. Sacramento: James Allen, State Printer, 1857.

Journal of the Fifth Session of the Legislature of the State of California. Sacramento: B.B. Redding, State Printer, 1854.

Journal of the Fourth Session of the Legislature of the State of California. San Francisco: George Kerr, State Printer, 1853.

Journal of the Seventh Session of the Legislature of the State of California. Sacramento: James Allen, State Printer, 1856.

Journal of the Sixth Session of the Legislature of the State of California. Sacramento: B.B. Redding, State Printer, 1855.

Kane, Michael David. "William Lewis Manly." Dissertation, University of Utah, May, 2008.

Kelly, Charles. "On Manly's Trail to Death Valley." *Desert Magazine*, February, 1939.

Kelly, Charles. Papers. J. Willard Marriott Library, Special Collections, University of Utah.

Kelly, Charles. Papers. Utah State History, Research Center and Collections, Salt Lake City.

Kelly, Charles, Editor. *Journals of John D. Lee, 1846-47, 1859*. Salt Lake City: University of Utah Press, 1984.

King, Joseph A. *Winter of Entrapment*. Lafayette, CA: K&K Publications, 1992.

Korns, J. Roderic, and Dale L. Morgan; Revised and Updated by Will Bagley & Harold Schindler. *West from Fort Bridger.* Logan: Utah State University Press, 1994.

LaFuze, Pauliena B. *Saga of the San Bernardinos.* San Bernardino: San Bernardino Museum Association, 1971.

Landon, Michael N., Editor. *The Journals of George Q. Cannon: To California in '49.* Salt Lake City: Deseret Book Company, 1999.

Larson, Gustave O., Editor. "Journal of the Iron County Mission: John D. Lee, Clerk, December 10, 1850 – March 1, 1851." *Utah Historical Society Quarterly,* 1952, Vol. 20.

Lee, John Doyle. *Mormonism Unveiled: The Life and Confessions of John D. Lee.* Albuquerque: University of New Mexico Press, 2001 (copy of 1877).

Long, Dr. Margaret. *The Shadow of the Arrow.* Caldwell: The Caxton Printers, 1950.

Lorton, William B. William B. Lorton Diary. BANC MSS C-F 190. The Bancroft Library.

Los Angeles County Board of Supervisors – Minutes. Los Angeles: 1853.

Los Angeles Star. Los Angeles: 1851-1857.

Lyford, Jeremiah Hall. "The First Upper End Physician & Surgeon." Biography. Augustana College, Sioux Falls. Online Interview, n.d.

Amasa Lyman Collection 1832-1877. Selected Collections, Brigham Young University, Vol. 1, DVD 37.

Lyman, Edward Leo. *San Bernardino, the Rise and Fall of a California Community.* Salt Lake City: Signature Books, 1996.

Lyman, Edward Leo. *The Overland Journey from Utah to California.* Reno & Las Vegas: University of Nevada Press, 2004.

Lyman, Edward Leo. *Amasa Mason Lyman, Mormon Apostle and Apostate: A Study in Dedication.* Salt Lake City: The University of Utah Press, 2009.

Lyman, Edward Leo; Payne, Susan Ward; George S. Ellsworth, Editors. *No

Place to Call Home, The 1807-1857 Writings of Caroline Barnes Crosby. Logan: Utah State University Press, 2005.

Lyman, Leo and Larry Reese. *The Arduous Road: Salt Lake to Los Angeles, the Most Difficult Wagon Road in American History*. Victorville: Lyman Historical Research and Publishing Company, 2001.

MacKinnon, William P. *At Sword's Point Part I*. Norman: The Arthur H. Clark Company, 2008.

Madsen, Brigham D. *A Forty-niner in Utah : With the Stansbury Expedition of Great Salt Lake: Letters and Journal of John Hudson*. Salt Lake City: University of Utah, 1981.

Madsen, Brigham D. *Gold Rush Sojourners in Great Salt Lake City*. Salt Lake City: University of Utah Press, 1983.

Madsen, Carol Cornwall. *Journey to Zion*. Salt Lake City: Deseret Book Company, 1997.

Manly, William Lewis; Jean and LeRoy Johnson, Editors. *Death Valley in '49*. Berkeley/Santa Clara: Heyday Books, 2001.

Mazariegos, Darla Greb. *The Plow and the Temple*. Oakland: Alameda County Historical Society, 2001.

McGlashan, C.F. *History of the Donner Party*. Stanford: Stanford University Press, 1993.

Morgan, Dale L. *The Humboldt: Highroad of the West*. New York: Farrar & Reinehart Incorporated, 1943,

Morgan, Dale L., Editor. *Overland in 1846*. Lincoln: University of Nebraska Press, 1963.

Morgan, Dale Lowell. Papers. BANC MSS 71/161 c. The Bancroft Library. University of California, Berkeley.

Morris, Thomas. Journal (Typed manuscript). LDS Archives.

Nunis, Doyce B. Jr. *From Mexican Days to the Gold Rush*. Chicago: R.R. Donnelley & Sons Company, 1993.

Oatman, Olive and Lorenzo D. Oatman. *The Captivity of the Oatman*

Girls among the Apache & Mohave Indians. Mineola, NY: Dover Publications, 1994.

Ord, Edward O.C. *The City of the Angels and the City of the Saints.* San Marino: The Huntington Library, 1978.

Owens. Kenneth N. *Gold Rush Saints.* Spokane: The Arthur H. Clark Company, 2004.

Parkman, Francis. *The Oregon Trail.* Boston: Little, Brown, and Company, 1872.

Patton, Annaleone D. *California Mormons by Sea and Trail.* Salt Lake City: Deseret Book Company, 1961.

Peck, David J. *Or Perish in the Attempt.* Helena: Farcountry Press, 2002.

Preston, R.N. *Early California Atlas - Southern Edition.* Portland: Binford & Mort Publishing, 1988.

Preuss, Charles. *Exploring with Fremont.* Norman: University of Oklahoma Press, 1958.

Quinn, D. Michael. *The Mormon Hierarchy.* Salt Lake City: Signature Books, 1994.

Rank Role of the Nauvoo Legion. M277.73, R198. LDS Archives.

Rasmussen, Louis J. *San Francisco Ship Passenger Lists*, Vol. IV, June 17, 1852 - Jan 6, 1853. Colma: San Francisco Historic Records, 1970.

Raymond M. Smith. *Nevada's Northwest Corner.* Ware, MA: Progressive Graphics, 1996.

Record of Jefferson Hunts Wagon Train to California. MSS P-F 332. The Bancroft Library.

Reid, John Phillip. *Law for the Elephant.* San Marino: The Huntington Library, 1980.

Rencher, Nettie Hunt. *John Hunt: Frontiersman.* Salt Lake City: Publishers Press, 1966.

"Report of the Select Committee with Reference to the Division of the State" in *Reports of the Legislature on Counties, Boundaries, etc. 1850-1874.* California Assembly.

Ressler, Theo. C. *Trails Divided A dissertation on the Overland Journey of Iowa "Forty-Niners" of the Sacramento Mining Company.* Williamsburg, Iowa, 1964.

Reynolds, Robert E., Jennifer Reynolds, Editors. "Death Valley: The Amargosa Route." *San Bernardino County Museum Association Quarterly,* Vol. 44(2), Spring 1997.

Charles C. Rich Collection. Selected Collections, Brigham Young University, Vol. 1, DVD 36.

Richards, Elizabeth W. *Guideposts to History.* San Bernardino: Santa Fe Federal Savings and Loan Association, 1966.

Ricketts, Norma B. *Melissa's Journey with the Mormon Battalion: The Western Odyssey of Melissa Burton Coray: 1846-1848.* Salt Lake City: International Society Daughters of Utah Pioneers, 1994.

Ricketts, Norma Baldwin. *Mormons and the Discovery of Gold.* Placerville: Pioneer Press, 1966.

Ricketts, Norma Baldwin. *The Mormon Battalion.* Logan: Utah State University Press, 1996.

Robinson, John W. *Gateways to Southern California.* City of Industry: The Big Santa Anita Historical Society, 2005.

Rolfe, H.C. *The Early political History of San Bernardino County.* Feldheym Central Library, San Bernardino, 1910.

Ruxton, George Frederick, LeRoy R. Hafen, ed; Foreword by Mae Reed Porter. *Life in the Far West.* Norman: University of Oklahoma Press, 1951.

Salt Lake High Council Minute Book, Salt Lake High Council, 1847 October - 1848 July. MS 3426, LR604 109, LDS Archives.

Sanchez, Joseph P. *Explorers, Traders, and Slavers: Forging the Old Spanish Trail.* Salt Lake City: University of Utah Press, 1996.

Sanderson, George B. "Journal," (Typescript by W. M. Glasgow). Accession 2134, J. Willard Marriott Library, Special Collections, University of Utah, 1995.

Schindler, Harold. *Orrin Porter Rockwell Man of God/Son of Thunder.* Salt

Lake City: University of Utah Press, 1993 edition (2nd edition, 1st paperback edition).

Seegmiller, Janet Burton. *A History of Iron County*. Salt Lake City: Utah State Historical Society, 1998.

Sessions, Patty. "Journal." LDS Archives.

Shepard, M.L. "Colonizing of San Bernardino." MSS C-E 148. The Bancroft Library, 1884.

Shirts, Morris A., Kathryn H. Shirts. *A Trial Furnace*. Provo: Brigham Young University Press, n.d.

Smart, William B. & Donna T. Smart. *Over the Rim: The Parley Pratt Exploring Expedition to Southern Utah 1849-1850*. Logan: Utah State University Press, 1999.

George A. Smith Papers, 1834-1875. Selected Collections, Vol. 1, DVDs 34-35. Brigham Young University.

Smith, Pauline Udall. *Captain Jefferson Hunt of the Mormon Battalion*. Salt Lake City, Nicholas G. Morgan Sr. Foundation, 1958.

Smith, Pauline Udall. Papers, Utah State University.

Sonne, Conway B. *World of Wakara*. San Antonio: Naylor Publishing Co., 1962.

Standage, Tom. *The Victorian Internet*. New York: Walker and Company, 1998.

The Statutes of California: The Fourth Session of the Legislature. San Francisco: George Kerr, State Printer, 1853.

The Statutes of California: The Sixth Session of the Legislature. Sacramento: B.B Redding, State Printer, 1855.

Stegner, Wallace. *The Gathering of Zion*. Lincoln: University of Nebraska Press, 1992.

Steiner, Harold. *The Old Spanish Trail Across the Mojave Desert*. Las Vegas: The Haldor Company, 1999.

Stephens, L. Dow. *Life Sketches of a Jayhawker of '49*. San Jose: Notta Bros., 1916.

Stewart, George R. *Ordeal by Hunger*. Boston, New York: Houghton Mifflin Company, 1936.

Stout, Hosea; Reed A. Stout, Editor. "Autobiography of Hosea Stout 1810-1844." *Utah Historical Quarterly*, Vol. XXX, 1962.

Stout, Wayne. *Hosea Stout: Utah's Pioneer Statesman*. Salt Lake City: 1953.

Stover, John F. *American Railroads*. Chicago: University of Chicago Press, 1997.

Sunder, John E. *Matt Field on the Santa Fe Trail*. Norman: University of Oklahoma Press, 1960.

The Southern Trail to California in 1849. MSS P-F 331. The Bancroft Library.

Thompson, Thomas H. and Albert Augustus West, (known as Thompson & West). *History of Nevada*. Oakland: Thompson & West, 1881.

Thorndike, Rachel Sherman, Editor. *The Sherman Letters*. New York: Charles Scribner's Sons, 1894.

Tinkham, George H. *California Men and Events*. Stockton: Record Publishing Company, 1915.

Toxicological Profile for Mercury. U.S. Department of Health and Human Services, Public Health Services, Agency for Toxic Substances and Disease Registry. Atlanta, Georgia: ASTDR, March, 1999.

Turner, Frederick Jackson. *The United States 1830-1850*. New York: W.W. Norton & Company, 1965.

Tyler, Sergeant Daniel. *A Concise History of the Mormon Battalion in the Mexican War 1846-1847*. Grantsville, Utah: Archive Publisher, 2000 (copy of original 1881 edition).

Walker, Dale. *Eldorado: The California Gold Rush*. New York: Tom Doherty Associates, 2003.

Walker, Ronald W.; Richard E. Turley Jr.; Glen M. Leonard. *Massacre at Mountain Meadows*. New York: Oxford University Press, 2008.

Warren, Elizabeth von Till and Ralph J. Roske. Cultural *Resources of the California Desert 1726-1980; Historic Trails & Wagon Roads*. Bureau of Land Management, 1981.

Watson, Douglas S. and John Augustus Sutter. *The Diary of Johann August Sutter*. San Francisco: Grabhorn Press, 1932.

Welch, Adonijah Strong. Diary. Dale Lowell Morgan Papers. The Bancroft Library.

Werner, Emmy E. *Pioneer Children on the Journey West*. Boulder, San Francisco, Oxford: Westview Press, 1995.

Williams, Isaac. "Register Book: Rancho del Chino." The Huntington Library.

Works Projects Administration. *National Guard of California*. 1940.

Young, Otis E. *The West of Philip St. George Cooke 1809-1895*. Glendale: The Arthur H. Clark Company, 1955.

Yurtinus, John F. "The Mormon Volunteers: The Recruitment and Service of a Unique Military Company." *The Journal of San Diego History*. Summer, 1979.

Yurtinus, John Frank George. "A Ram in the Thicket: The Mormon Battalion in the Mexican War." Dissertation. Brigham Young University, 1975.

Zimmer, Carl. "Taming Pathogens: An Elegant Idea, But Does It Work."

Index